Understanding the Victorians

D0024029

Understanding the Victorians paints a vivid portrait of this era of dramatic change, combining broad survey with close analysis and introducing students to the critical debates taking place among historians today. Encompassing all of Great Britain and Ireland over the whole of the Victorian period, it gives prominence to social and cultural topics alongside politics and economics and emphasizes class, gender, and racial and imperial positioning as constitutive of human relations.

This second edition is fully updated throughout, containing a new chapter on leisure in the Victorian period, the most recent historiographical research in Victorian Studies, and enhanced coverage of imperialism and working-class life. Beginning with the Queen Caroline Affair in 1820 and coming up to the start of World War One in 1914, Susie L. Steinbach uses thematic chapters to discuss and evaluate politics, imperialism, the economy, class, gender, the monarchy, arts and entertainment, religion, sexuality, religion, and science. There are also three chapters on space, consumption, and the law, topics rarely covered at this introductory level.

With a clear introduction outlining the key themes of the period, a detailed timeline, and suggestions for further reading and relevant internet resources, this is the ideal companion for all students of the nineteenth century.

Susie L. Steinbach is Professor of History at Hamline University, Minnesota, USA. She is the author of *Women in England 1760–1914: A Social History* (2004) and the editor of *Millicent Garret Fawcett by her Contemporaries* (2008), and has written widely on Victorian history, with a particular emphasis on gender and the law.

Understanding the Victorians

Politics, culture and society in nineteenth-century Britain

Second edition

Susie L. Steinbach

Routledge
Taylor & Francis Group

LONDON AND NEW YORK

This edition published 2017
by Routledge
2 Park Square, Milton Park, Abingdon, Oxon OX14 4RN

and by Routledge
711 Third Avenue, New York, NY 10017

Routledge is an imprint of the Taylor & Francis Group, an informa business

© 2012, 2016 Susie L. Steinbach

The right of Susie L. Steinbach to be identified as author of this work has been asserted by her in accordance with sections 77 and 78 of the Copyright, Designs and Patents Act 1988.

First edition published 2012 by Routledge

British Library Cataloguing-in-Publication Data
A catalogue record for this book is available from the British Library

Library of Congress Cataloging-in-Publication Data
Names: Steinbach, Susie, author.
Title: Understanding the Victorians: politics, culture and society in nineteenth-century Britain / Susie L. Steinbach.
Description: Second edition. | Milton Park, Abingdon, Oxon; New York, NY: Routledge, 2016. | "First published 2012"—Title page verso. | Includes bibliographical references and index.
Identifiers: LCCN 2016002743| ISBN 9781138906082 (hardback: alkaline paper) | ISBN 9781138906105 (paperback: alkaline paper) | ISBN 9781315545301 (ebook)
Subjects: LCSH: Great Britain—History—Victoria, 1837–1901. | Great Britain—Politics and government—1837–1901. | Great Britain—Economic conditions—19th century. | Great Britain—Social conditions—19th century. | Politics and culture—Great Britain—History—19th century. | Social classes—Great Britain—History—19th century. | Sex role—Great Britain—History—19th century.
Classification: LCC DA550. S73 2016 | DDC 941.081—dc23
LC record available at https://lccn.loc.gov/2016002743

ISBN: 978-1-138-90608-2 (hbk)
ISBN: 978-1-138-90610-5 (pbk)
ISBN: 978-1-315-54530-1 (ebk)

Typeset in Baskerville
by Keystroke, Station Road, Codsall, Wolverhampton

For Sam, Sophie, and Benjamin

Contents

List of figures   ix
Preface to the second edition   xi
Acknowledgements for the second edition   xiii
Acknowledgements for the first edition   xv
Timeline   xvii

"Playing on the piano-forte": Introduction   1

1 A "green and pleasant land" of cities and slums: Space 12

2 "Discussions on the subject of reform": Politics   35

3 Ruling the world: Imperialism   65

4 Wealth and poverty, growth and slumps: The economy   84

5 "Bristling with shops": Consumption   106

6 "Born into the lower-upper-middle": Class   123

7 "Oh, I do like to be beside the seaside": Leisure   145

8 "A common cause with all the females in this kingdom":
   Gender   165

9 A "dignified part": Monarchy   182

10 "The court was crowded all day": The law and the police 195

11 "Good, murderous melodramas": Arts, entertainment,
    and print culture   211

12 Marriage, free love, and "unnatural crimes": Sexuality   240

13 "Begin and end with the Church whatever you do
    between-whiles": Religion   260

14 Vestiges and origins: Science and medicine   279

    Index   305

List of figures

0.1   Pianoforte advertisement circa 1870   8

1.1   A typical late Victorian slum   19

2.1   1886: A mob kicking British Prime Minister William Gladstone in the air   57

3.1   A British depiction of the 1857 "Massacre at Cawnpore"   77

4.1   Charing Cross Railway Station   98

5.1   A department store: Bunney's Establishments   115

6.1   This engraving from the *Illustrated London News* depicts class distinctions through the division of rail travel into first, second, and third class   127

7.1   "Punch and Judy on the beach at Llandudno"   161

8.1   Circa 1912: a horse-drawn campaign van driven by the suffragettes   172

9.1   The Royal Family of Queen Victoria   187

10.1   Judge Alexander Cockburn presiding over the trial of the Tichborne Claimant   206

11.1   "My Missis Thinks She's Trilby" comic song   216

11.2   *Stage and Screen*, Personalities   230

12.1   Ernest Boulton and Frederick William Park   255

13.1   The Salvation Army   268

14.1   Etching by Thomas Kearnan showing apparatus and visitors in the Adelaide Gallery   283

Preface to the second edition

Britain began and ended the Victorian period as the most powerful state on earth. But this statement tells us little about who the Victorians were or what they believed. This book is an introduction to Victorian Britain that explores what it meant to be the most powerful nation in the world, and who the Victorians were: how they lived, what they did, what they believed, what they valued. It is intended for any and all interested readers. Many of these will be undergraduate students taking courses on the history of Victorian Britain and its empire; others will be undergraduate and graduate students taking other history courses, or studying literature or other subjects. It tries not to assume any prior familiarity either with British history or British usages of language, and so to be welcoming to all readers.

As historian John Tosh notes, "[t]he word *history* … refers both to what actually happened in the past and to the representation of that past in the work of historians."[1] *Understanding the Victorians* aims to introduce its readers to both of these: what happened in Victorian Britain (which does not change) and how historians currently explore Victorian Britain (which does). The book is organized into an introduction and 14 chapters, which address a wide variety of topics. It begins with a chapter on space, an only-recently studied aspect of the past, and includes one on the law, which though it was pervasive is rarely discussed at any length in textbooks. The order in which the topics are presented is not mere happenstance—for example, the chapter on space comes first in part to signal its new importance in historical practice—but they can be read (or assigned) in any order.

Although the last 50 years have witnessed the rise of social and cultural history, most overviews and textbooks have chosen to focus on the more traditional areas of political and economic history. In contrast, *Understanding the Victorians* focuses on the social and cultural realms. While high politics, foreign policy, and macro-economic developments have their place here, the focus is on lived experience, dominant representations, and shared (and conflicting) assumptions and beliefs. It explores not just the production but the consumption of goods; treats sexuality as deserving of extended historical analysis; takes music halls and popular literature as seriously as it does Parliament; considers Victoria *Regina et Imperatrix* (Queen and Empress) a meaningful aspect of Victorianism; and looks at both religion and science without positioning them as reflexive enemies of one another.

The wonderful thing about a second edition is the opportunity it provides for improvement, and many changes have been made in this edition. The timeline is now shorter and clearer. Chapters have been updated to reflect new scholarship and reorganized to provide a better sense of change over time. There is a new chapter on leisure, and new or expanded sections on music halls, print culture, policing, and medicine. Finally, the chapters now conclude not only with lists of relevant fiction that students might enjoy, but also with lists of further reading and of internet resources. The speed of online developments means that the latter is inevitably contingent, but nonetheless useful.

Of course, *Understanding the Victorians* cannot and does not cover all aspects of Victorian life or of historical practice. It says little or nothing about some topics and some approaches: music, architecture, military history, and the minutiae of the processes by which bills became laws via Parliamentary debate all might get more attention in another book. I can only hope that this presentation of what seems to me most important about Victorian Britain resonates with readers and their engagement with both the past and the present.

Note

1 John Tosh, *The Pursuit of History: Aims, methods and new directions in the study of history* (Routledge, 2015, 6th edition), p. x.

Acknowledgements for the second edition

First and foremost I am grateful to readers, including instructors and students, who liked the first edition of this book well enough to warrant a second edition; to Eve Setch for noticing and making it possible, to Amy Welmers, for her editorial assistance, and to my exemplary copy editor Jonathan Merrett.

Several people were generous enough to write reports that helped me to improve the book. I am grateful to Gary Moses, Dane Kennedy, Carol Engelhardt Herringer, and two anonymous readers who wrote reports for Routledge, and to Naomi Lloyd, John Griffiths, and Philippa Levine, who were kind enough to write reports just because I asked for their help. All of these people did work that will almost certainly never 'count' for anything; they are evidence of how much generosity and fellowship exists in the academy. In addition, readers have contacted me pointing out errors and opportunities for improvement in the first edition. I am grateful to all of these people, and I hope they will see that I took their comments to heart and that they will regard the book as improved as a result of their always gently-worded comments. Of course, errors remain, and these are my responsibility.

I thank again all the institutions and scholars noted in the acknowledgement to the first edition, and the local friends who proved that the Victorians were right about friendship networks and philanthropy by supporting me and my family over the past four years: Kris Deffenbacher, Mike Reynolds, Sara Mack, and Stephen Kellert. Special thanks go to Jo Glass, a former student whose determination to read Emily Eden's entire corpus led me to use the piano the way I have in this book; I should have thanked her in the first edition. For love and support I remain grateful to my extended family, which now includes Simon Cane. Most of all I am grateful to, and dedicate this book to, Sophie, Samantha, and Benjamin Elwood.

Acknowledgements
for the first edition

I am grateful to the many people and institutions who made the completion of the book possible. These include Hamline University's College of Liberal Arts, Department of History, and Bush Library; the Department of History at the University of York; and the online community of H-Albion.

Since she first approached me about this project, Eve Setch has been an exemplary editor; Laura Mothersole has been all an author could wish for in an editorial assistant. Peter Mandler, Miles Taylor, and two anonymous readers offered helpful suggestions on the original proposal. Chris Renwick was generous with his expertise on Victorian science. A third anonymous reader gave insightful criticisms of the completed manuscript. Kelly Boyd and Rohan McWilliam have both inspired and supported me and this book in many ways, first by publishing their invaluable *Victorian Studies Reader*, later by reading an early version of the entire manuscript, and throughout by offering friendship the likes of which few people are privileged to experience. The breadth a textbook offers to students is made possible by the work of dozens if not hundreds of historians which has, I trust, been sufficiently acknowledged in the notes and lists of further reading. Those whose published work has been especially influential or helpful include Andrew August, Peter Bailey, Michael R. Booth, Peter J. Bowler, Callum G. Brown, Harry Cocks, Hera Cook, Martin Daunton, Margot C. Finn, Judith Flanders, Roderick Floud, Ginger S. Frost, Catherine Hall, Lesley A. Hall, Margaret Homans, Philippa Levine, Bernard Lightman, Angus McLaren, Hugh McLeod, Rohan McWilliam, Iwan Rhys Morus, Dave Russell, James A. Secord, Andrew Thompson, John Tosh, Charles Upchurch, Martha Vicinus, and John Wolffe.

For love and support I am grateful to my extended family, Carole Steinbach and Pete Rose, Stacey, Jeff, Jacob, Abby, and Sadie Herman, Jennifer, Jon, Maddie, and Julia Klonsky, Rachel Cane and Tony Keefe, Jonathan Cane and Nicole Sin Quee, and Josh Elwood. The memories of Sam Steinbach, Phil and Audrey Elwood, and Sy and Helene Cane are with me every day.

As discussed in Chapter 1, the Victorians were keen to separate the home from all other spaces and to construct it as a haven. I am privileged to come home every day to Sophie, Samantha, and Benjamin Elwood. This book is for them.

Timeline

Date	Event
1820	Queen Caroline Affair
1820	Pianos are found only in elite homes
1820	Working-class people have little time or money for leisure
1820	Beer and gin are both widely consumed
1820	George III dies; George IV (who has ruled as regent since 1810) becomes king
1820	London's Regent Street built for shopping
1820	Decline in births begins
1820	Couples decorate their homes once, usually upon marriage
1820	Malicious Trespass Act
1820	There are no science examinations or degrees at Oxford or Cambridge (though there are at Scottish universities)
1821	Population of England and Wales is 11.5 million, Scotland 2 million, Ireland almost 7 million
1821	Cities are growing: population of London is 1.5 million. Liverpool, Manchester, and Birmingham together are home to over 400,000, and 15 towns have populations of more than 25,000
1821	Banking system is headed by the Bank of England, which is beginning to function as a central bank
1821	Liverpool shopping bazaar opens
1823	Catholic Association founded
1823	*The Lancet* founded by Thomas Wakley
1823–1826	First Anglo-Burmese War
1824	Vagrancy Act
1825	First passenger railways open
1825	Combination Act
1827	Larceny Act
1827 and 1828	Laws pass that made it easier to prosecute men for attempted sodomy and easier to prove sodomy in court
1828	Repeal of the Test and Corporation Acts grants Nonconformists the vote

1828	George Combe's *The Constitution of Man Considered in Relation To External Objects* promotes phrenology and scientific naturalism
1829	Catholic Emancipation grants Catholics the vote
1829	Professional police forces established in England and Wales (they are already in place in many Scottish burghs)
1829	Felicia Hemans' popular poem "Casabianca" published
1829	Metropolitan Police Act
1830s	Sports become an important part of the culture of elite boys' public boarding schools
1830	William IV becomes king
1830	The British now use 30 million tons of coal per year
1830	There are 286,000 British Methodists
1830	Charles Babbage criticizes the Royal Society in *Reflections on the Decline of Science in England*
1830	Beer Act
1831	Major slave rebellion in Jamaica during Christmas
1831	Population of England and Wales is almost 14 million, Scotland 2.3 million, Ireland over 7 million
1831	Cities are growing: Manchester and Birmingham have populations of about 145,000 each
1831	Cotton comprises over one-fifth of British industry
1831	Cholera outbreak
1831	British Association for the Advancement of Science (BAAS) founded
1832–36	Voyage of the HMS *Beagle*
1832	Great Reform Act gives middle-class men the vote
1832	Chartist movement begins
1832	Sadler Committee Report on child workers in factories
1832	Adelaide Gallery opens
1832	Provincial Medical and Surgical Association (PMSA), a forerunner of the British Medical Association, is founded
1833	Factory Act limits hours of children's work
1833	Parks movement begins (with Select Committee on Public Walks)
1833	Oxford Movement begins
1833	Irish Church Temporalities Act reduces the power and wealth of the Church of Ireland
1833–1836	*Bridgewater Treatises*
1834	New Poor Law
1834	Slavery ended in the British empire
1834–1836	Xhosa War
1835	Newcastle's bazaar, Grainger Market, opens
1835	Church of England forms its Ecclesiastical Commission
1835	Temperance movement formally begins with the founding of the British Association for the Promotion of Temperance
1836	Prisoners' Counsel Acts

1836	Marriage Act allows non-Anglican clergy to perform legal marriages
1836	Births and Deaths Registration Act establishes a civil procedure for recording births, marriages, and deaths
1836	Royal Polytechnic Institution opens
1837	Caroline Norton's *Observations on the Natural Claim of a Mother to the Custody of her Children as Affected by the Common Law Right of the Father* published
1837	Victoria becomes queen
1838	Anti-Corn Law League (ACLL) founded
1838	Charles Dickens' *Oliver Twist* published
1838	Isambard Kingdom Brunel's SS *Great Western* goes from England to New York in 14 days with fuel to spare
1839–1842	First Anglo-Afghan War
1839–1842	First Opium War
1839–1843	Rebecca Riots in Wales
1839	Custody of Children Act
1839	Bedchamber Crisis
1839	William Harrison Ainsworth's Newgate novel *Jack Sheppard* published
1839	Charles Darwin's *Voyage of the Beagle* published
1839	Rural Police Act empowers Justices of the Peace to establish county police forces
1840	Victoria and Albert marry
1840	Francois Benjamin Courvoisier claims he was inspired by Newgate novel *Jack Sheppard* to murder his employer
1840	There are over 3,000 textile factories in Britain, and large factories are common
1840	The parlor is now the center of the middle-class home; some can afford a piano in it
1840	Steam printing makes books cheaper
1840	Vaccination Act makes smallpox vaccinations free to the poor
1841	Population of England and Wales is almost 16 million, Scotland 2.6 million, Ireland 8 million
1841	1.7 million people work as servants
1841	Public hangings now only for murder
1842	Income tax reinstituted by Prime Minister Robert Peel (the first ever during peacetime)
1842	ACLL bazaar in Manchester raises £10,000
1842	Edwin Chadwick publishes his *Report on the Sanitary Condition of the Labouring Population of Great Britain*
1842	Lord Ashley's Mines Commission Report
1842	Pentonville Prison in London built
1842	Churchill and Stringer Case
1843	Theatre Regulation Act
1843	Thomas Carlyle's *Past and Present* published

1843	Disruption of Scottish Kirk results in establishment of Free Church of Scotland
1844	Factory Act
1844	Bank Charter Act strengthens role of Bank of England as a central bank
1844	Coal miners' strike, one of the largest early strikes
1844	Rochdale Pioneers, one of the first co-operative stores
1844	Friedrich Engels' *The Condition of the Working Class in England* published
1844	Railway Regulation Act mandates cheap tickets on all lines
1844	*Vestiges of the Natural History of Creation* published
1845	First commercial telegraph service in UK
1845–46	First Sikh War
1845–1872	Maori Wars
1845	Great Famine in Ireland
1845	Prime Minister Peel embraces free trade, splitting the Tory Party
1845	ACLL bazaar in Covent Garden raises £25,000
1845	Disraeli's *Sybil, or the Two Nations* published
1845	Bastardy Clause of the 1834 Poor Law repealed
1845	John Henry Newman converts to Catholicism
1846–1847	Xhosa War
1846	Manchester opens three new parks
1846	Anti-Corn Law League succeeds in repealing protective grain tariffs
1846	County Courts established
1847	Factory Act reduces workday to 10 hours
1847	Charlotte Brontë's *Jane Eyre* and Emily Brontë's *Wuthering Heights* published
1847	Introduction of antiseptic measures during childbirth
1847–48	William Makepeace Thackeray's *Vanity Fair* published
1848–49	Second Sikh War
1848	Chartist movement declines
1848	Public Health Act
1848	Mrs Gaskell's *Mary Barton* published
1848	Pre-Raphaelite movement founded
1848–1849	Cholera outbreak
1849	Charlotte Brontë's *Shirley* published
1849–1850	Charles Dickens' *David Copperfield* published
1849–50	Henry Mayhew's "London Labour and the London Poor" articles appear in the *Morning Chronicle*
1850s	First large purpose-built music-halls open in London
1850s	The British now use 70 million tons of coal per year
1850s	Telegraph cables laid across the English Channel and the Irish Sea
1850s	Feminists found first academic secondary schools for girls
1850–1853	Xhosa War

1850s–1860s	Railways become pervasive
1850	Britain now has many pubs
1850	20% of MPs are middle-class
1850	Middle class is about 25% of the population
1850	23% of British cotton exports go to India
1850	Overseas investments are £225 million per year
1850	Factory Act
1850	68 million railway passenger journeys made annually; average journey is 16 miles
1850	90% of cases are tried before juries
1850	Wales has two and a half times as many nonconformist chapels as Anglican churches
1850	The British government allows the Roman Catholic hierarchy to be reinstated in England and Wales
1851	Great Exhibition of the Works of Industry of all Nations
1851	Britain is the richest nation on earth
1851	Average people's lives are beginning to improve; real wages are 28% higher than they had been in the 1760s
1851	Textiles, railways, shipbuilding, iron, and steel employ 40% of the workforce
1851	There are 161,000 commercial horse-drawn vehicles on the road, most linked to railway travel
1851	Population of England and Wales is almost 18 million, Scotland 2.8 million, Ireland 6.5 million. 54% of the population lives in cities
1851	Census sparks 'redundant women' panic
1851	Religious census
1851	England and Wales have 750,000 Catholics; Scotland has 172,000
1851	Mrs Gaskell's *Cranford* published
1851	William Thomson (later Lord Kelvin's) *On the Dynamical Theory of Heat* published
1851	Museum of Practical Geology opens
1852	Economic slump
1852–53	Second Anglo-Burmese War
1852–53	Charles Dickens' *Bleak House* published
1853	Economic boom
1853	Transportation to Australia ends
1853	Explorer David Livingstone crosses the entire African continent
1853	Factory Act
1853	Betting Houses Act
1853	Vaccination Act makes smallpox vaccinations compulsory
1853–54	Cholera outbreak
1854	Caroline Norton's *English Laws for Women in the Nineteenth Century* and Barbara Leigh Smith's *Brief Summary . . . Concerning Women* published

1854	Factory Act
1854	Dr. John Snow maps the East End cholera outbreak
1854	The unconsummated marriage between John Ruskin and Effie Gray is annulled
1854	Oxford University Act means that Oxford now admits nonconformists
1855	Mrs Gaskell's *North and South* published
1855	Charles Kingsley's *Westward Ho!* published
1855	Demonstration in Hyde Park over Sunday shopping
1855	British Medical Association founded
1855	Anthony Trollope's *The Warden* (the first of his *Chronicles of Barsetshire* novels) published
1856–1860	Second Opium War
1856	County and Borough Police Act establishes police forces all over England and Wales
1856	Garroting panic
1857	Indian Rebellion
1857	Divorce Court created
1857	Economic slump
1857	Doctor William Acton writes in *The Functions and Disorders of the Reproductive Orders* that "the majority of women … are not very much troubled with sexual feeling of any kind"
1858	Government of India Act
1858	General Medical Council founded to maintain a central registry of doctors
1858	Irish Republican Brotherhood (IRB) founded
1858	The Great Stink
1858	Jewish Emancipation allows Jews to serve in Parliament; Lionel Rothschild becomes first Jewish MP
1858	The SS *Great Eastern*, the largest ship ever built, is launched
1859	Wilkie Collins' *The Woman in White* published
1859	George Eliot's *Adam Bede* published
1859	New houses of Parliament built
1859	Charles Darwin's *Origin of Species* published
1860s	Pianos are now affordable for middle-class and some lower middle-class families
1860s	Power binding makes book cheaper
1860s	Germ theory slowly begins to replace miasma theory
1860s	For the first time, upper-class men are not the majority in the House of Commons
1860	Dion Boucicault's play, *The Colleen Bawn*, is a big hit
1860	31% of British cotton exports go to India
1860	Britain is prosperous: per capita income is £32 in Britain but only £13 in Germany and £21 in France
1860	The number of people working in agriculture declines
1860	First British mosque built in Cardiff

1860	Nightingale Training School for nurses founded
1860–61	First Taranaki War
1860–61	Charles Dickens' *Great Expectations* published
1861	Population of England and Wales is 20 million, Scotland 3 million, Ireland 5.7 million
1861	Prince Albert dies
1861	Mrs. Henry Wood's *East Lynne* published
1861	*Hymns Ancient and Modern* published
1861–1865	United States Civil War causes cotton famine in textile industry
1862	Economic slump
1862	Mary Elizabeth Braddon's *Lady Audley's Secret* published
1862	Garroting panic (dramatized in Anthony Trollope's *Phineas Finn*)
1862	Thomas Huxley popularizes Darwin's work with his lectures "On Our Knowledge of the Causes of the Phenomena of Organic Nature"
1863–66	Second Taranaki War
1863	Tom Taylor's *The Ticket of Leave Man* first performed
1863	"Pepper's Ghost" display
1863	Football Association (FA) founded; adopts the "Cambridge rules" of play
1864	Contagious Diseases Acts
1864	Anthony Trollope's *Can You Forgive Her?* (the first of his Palliser novels) published
1864	Mrs Eliza Warren's *How I Managed My House on Two Hundred Pounds a Year* published
1864	Economic boom
1864	Factory Act
1865	Morant Bay Rebellion in Jamaica
1865	House of Commons remains elite: 220 members (of 658) are sons of peers, grandsons of peers, or baronets
1865	Salvation Army founded
1865	Elizabeth Garrett Anderson becomes the first woman doctor
1865–1868	Governor Eyre controversy
1866	Cholera outbreak
1866	Permanent telegraph cable laid across the Atlantic
1866	Sanitary Act requires local authorities to provide sewers and water
1866	Victoria opens Parliament, but without robes or crown
1866	Women's suffrage amendment fails to be added to the bill that will become the Second Reform Act
1866	George Leybourne becomes a music hall star as "Champagne Charlie"
1866	Mrs Oliphant's *Miss Marjoribanks* published
1866	Demonstration in Hyde Park over electoral reform
1867	Economic slump

1867	Factory Act
1867	Canada granted Dominion status
1867	Married Women's Property Committee founded
1867	Second Reform Act gives the vote to many urban working-class men
1867	IRB uprising
1868	Disraeli, brief ministry
1868	First Trades Union Congress (TUC) meeting held
1868–1874	Gladstone's first ministry
1869	Anglican Church disestablished in Ireland
Early 1870s	Britain produces over 500,000 tons per year of steel and dominates international trade in iron and steel
1870s	Alcohol consumption in Britain peaks
1870s	Tichborne cases
1870	Irish Land Act
1870	Education Act
1870	Britain is a steam-powered nation: it uses two million horsepower of steam every year, half of it in the textile industry
1870	Charles Dickens dies
1870	There are now over 30 large music halls in London, and almost 400 large music halls in Britain
1870	The average worker's work week is down to only 60 hours
1870	First Married Women's Property Act
1870	Fanny and Stella scandal
1870	First university laboratory (the Cavendish Laboratory at Cambridge University) built
1870–71	Smallpox epidemic
1871	Population of England and Wales is 22.7 million, Scotland 3.3 million, Ireland 5.4 million; Manchester has a population of over 400,000; 65% of the population lives in cities
1871	First Bank Holidays Act creates four unpaid days off of work per year
1871	George Eliot's *Middlemarch* published
1871	322 million railway passenger journeys made annually
1871	One third of working-class women work as servants
1871	Church of Ireland disestablished
1871	Jews admitted to Oxbridge
1871	Rugby Football Union founded
1872	Victoria returns to public life and becomes a symbol of Britain and its empire
1872	Secret Ballot Act
1872	Public Health Act requires the appointment of a medical officer in each area of the country
1873	Scottish Football Association (Scottish FA) founded
1873	Germany and the United States surpass Britain in iron and steel production

1873–1875	Judicature Acts
1874	45% of MPs are middle-class
1874	Factory Act
1874	James Maxwell named Cambridge's first Cavendish Professor of Experimental Physics
1874	London School of Medicine for Women (LSMW) founded
1874	J.G. Wood's *Man and Beast* published
1875	Overseas investments are now £1 billion per year, mostly in railway construction
1875	Public Health Act
1876	Royal Titles Act makes Victoria Empress of India
1877–1879	Xhosa War
1877	Afghan war
1877	Lewis department store opens in Manchester
1877	Telephone service arrives in Britain
1877	Secularists Charles Bradlaugh and Annie Besant publish birth control pamphlet *The Fruits of Philosophy* and are prosecuted for obscenity
1877	Sophia Jex-Blake becomes the second woman doctor
1878	Congress of Berlin
1878	Marital separations can now be granted by local magistrates
1878–1880	Second Anglo-Afghan War
1879	Zulu War
1880s	120,000 Jewish immigrants arrive in London, fleeing anti-Semitic persecution in Russia
1880s	Football, rugby, and cricket become large, commercial, spectator sports
1880s	Agents that cause cholera, diphtheria, and consumption are identified
1880	65% of MPs are middle-class
1880	Charles Bradlaugh is elected to Parliament, but cannot serve because he is an atheist
1881	Population of England and Wales is almost 26 million, Scotland 3.7 million, Ireland 5.1 million
1882	Second Married Women's Property Act
1882	Charles Darwin dies
1883	Corrupt and Illegal Practices Act
1883	John Addington Symonds' *A Problem with Greek Ethics* published
1884	Fabian Society founded
1884	Third Reform Act gives the vote to many rural working-class men
1884	Marks & Spencer opens, as a stall in Kirkgate, Leeds, indoor market
1884	First university settlement house, Toynbee Hall, founded in London's East End
1885	Redistribution Act
1885	Criminal Law Amendment Act

1885	W.T. Stead's *The Maiden Tribute of Modern Babylon* published
1885–1886	Third Anglo-Burmese War
1885–1914	Football becomes a central part of male leisure and culture
1886	Contagious Diseases Acts repealed
1886	Liberal Party splits over the issue of Home Rule
1886	Colonial and Indian Exhibition
1886	A demonstration in Trafalgar Square protesting unemployment turns violent
1886	Salvation Army has 1,749 congregations and over 4,000 officers in Great Britain
1886	Medical Act Amendment Act—all registered medical practitioners have to have qualifications
1887	Queen Victoria's Golden Jubilee
1887	Edward Lyttelton's anti-masturbation pamphlet *The Causes and Prevention of Immorality in Schools* published
1888	Trade Union membership 750,000
1888	Jack the Ripper murders
1888	Secular affirmation made available for MPs
1888	Edward Clodd's *Story of Creation* published
1888	British Nurses Association founded
1889	London Dockers' Strike
1889	Arthur Pinero's *The Profligate* first performed
1889	Charles Booth's *Life and Labour of the People in London* published
1889	Cleveland Street Scandal
1889	Aspirin replaces opiate-based painkillers
1890	Irish Home Rule leader Charles Parnell's political career ends when he is named in the O'Shea divorce case
1890s	Germ theory becomes widely accepted
1890	Oscar Wilde's only novel, *The Picture of Dorian Gray*, published
1890	Average rail journey is now 9 miles
1891	Population of England and Wales is 29 million, Scotland 4 million, Ireland 4.7 million
1891	11.2% of the population of England and Wales is living in overcrowded quarters
1891	George Gissing's *New Grub Street* published
1893	Second Irish Home Rule Bill defeated
1893	Arthur Pinero's *The Second Mrs. Tanqueray* first performed
1893	Sarah Grand's New Woman novel *The Heavenly Twins* published
1894	Local Government Act
1894	Cure for diphtheria developed
1895	Actor Henry Irving knighted
1895	Two Oscar Wilde plays, *The Importance of Being Earnest* and *An Ideal Husband*, are both playing in London
1895	Oscar Wilde's trials
1895	Edward Carpenter's *Homogenic Love, and its Place in a Free Society* published

1895	Thomas Hardy's *Jude the Obscure* published
1895	Rugby splits into working-class and middle- and upper-class styles of play
1897	Queen Victoria's Diamond Jubilee
1897	Oscar Wilde writes *De Profundis* in prison
1898	Fenwick's department store opens
1899	Seebohm Rowntree's *Poverty, A Study of Town Life* published
1899–1902	Second South African War
1900	Every city has a range of shops, with the most expensive and most spectacular stores in city centers
1900	Seaside holidays replace days in the countryside
1900	State schools adopt football for their male students
1900	88% of non-violent larcenies are tried without juries
1900	Trade Union membership is 2 million
1900	Oscar Wilde dies
1900	The average worker's week is only 55 hours
1900	Britain produces only a third of the steel that Germany and the United States together do
1900	The average middle-class and upper-class family spends one third of its income on services; the average working-class family spends one tenth of its income on services
1900	10,000 spouses per year—mostly wives—request separation orders
1900	Maternal and infant mortality rates peak
1900	Almost 9,000 men in England and Wales have been indicted for sodomy, gross indecency, or other "unnatural misdemeanors" since 1827
1900	First Sikh temple built in London
1901	Victoria dies; Edward VII becomes king
1901	Population of England and Wales is 32.5 million, Scotland 4.4 million, Ireland 4.4 million; the population of London is over 6 million
1901	Seebohm Rowntree's *Poverty: A Study of Town Life* published
1901	J. Cuming Walters' "Scenes in Slumland" series published in the *Birmingham Daily Gazette*
1901	There are 412,000 British Methodists
1902	Education Act adds state-provided secondary education
1902	Midwives Act establishes the Central Midwives Board
1903	Liberal Unionists split over tariff reform
1903	Women's Social and Political Union (WSPU) founded
1905	The agent that causes syphilis is identified
1905	Tory party splits over tariff reform; Liberal governments come to dominate
1905	Irish nationalist party Sinn Fein founded
1906	Labour Party founded
1906	First cinema (movie theatre) opens in London

1907	Triple Entente
1907	Steam power has replaced water power
1907	Imperial College London, Britain's first university of technical education, founded
1907	Electricity powers only 10% of British industry
1907	*Lusitania* launched
1907–1913	Agitations for women's suffrage
1908	Old Age Pensions instituted
1908	Children's Act
1908	Prevention of Crime Act
1908	Edward Carpenter's *The Intermediate Sex* published
1909	Trade Union membership is 2.3 million
1909	People's Budget proposed
1909	Selfridge's department store founded
1909	Salvarsan, first effective treatment for syphilis
1910	Pianos are now common even in working-class homes; there are 2–4 million pianos in Britain, one for every 10–20 people
1910	People's Budget passed
1910	Edward VII dies; George V becomes king
1910	Only one in six couples uses a mechanical form of birth control
1910–1911	Strikes of coal miners in Wales, and of cotton and jute workers, transport workers, dock workers across Britain
1911	Population of England and Wales is 36 million, Scotland 4.7 million, Ireland 4.4 million
1911	7.8% of the population of England and Wales is living in overcrowded quarters
1911	55% of Britons now live in large cities with populations of over 100,000
1911	6.2 million people work as servants
1911	Only 8% of Britons are now employed in agriculture or fishery
1911	Cotton textiles still employ 1.5 million people, 16% of the industrial labor force
1911	Parliament Act
1911	There are about 5,000 scientists in Britain (by 1951 there will be 49,000)
1912	Conservative Party absorbs Liberal Unionist Party
1912	Third Irish Home Rule Bill passed but suspended because of World War One
1912	National miners' strike
1912	Suffragettes break the plate glass windows of London stores
1912	*Titanic* launched
1913	Emily Wilding Davison rushes the King's horse at the Derby and dies
1913	Prisoners' Temporary Discharge for Ill Health ("Cat and Mouse") Act
1913	Trade Union membership is 4.1 million

1913	Railways are central: 1.5 billion passengers travel every year on 20,000 miles of track, as do almost three quarters of the goods that circulate in the economy, and over 832,000 commercial horse-drawn vehicles make journeys to and from railway stations
1913	11% of urban working-class households live in poverty
1914	70% of British babies receive Anglican baptism
1914	Coal miners' strike in Yorkshire
1914	Britain makes only half as much steel as Germany, and a quarter as much as the United States; it is now one of the world's biggest importers of iron and steel
1914	Britain relies on imports for over half of its food—the only country to do so at this time—and agriculture is no longer an important part of the national economy
1914	In addition to the Catholic majority in Ireland, there are 2 million Catholics in England and Wales and 244,000 Catholics in Scotland
1914	World War One starts

"Playing on the piano-forte"

Introduction

Historians have been attempting to provide overviews of Victorian Britain for a long time. One of the first and most influential of these works, published in 1936, was G.M. Young's *Victorian England: Portrait of an Age*. Born in 1882, Young was himself a Victorian. He was what we would today call a "cultural historian," most interested in Victorians' mindset and beliefs. He argued that the Victorians shared certain key assumptions, beliefs, and habits of mind. These included curiosity, a willingness to question assumptions, and a vigorous but "disinterested intelligence." Young's *Portrait* was in many ways a retort to the early twentieth-century Bloomsbury group's snide criticisms of the Victorians. Perhaps the most important of these critiques was Lytton Strachey's *Eminent Victorians* (1918), an attack on Victorian values and hypocrisy that in some ways announced the definitive end of the Victorian era. But while Young celebrated the age Strachey savaged, and his early and mid-Victorian periods saw England (not Britain) grow into a "rounded and solid culture," his later Victorian period was one of decline from basic decency into faddish vulgarity.

[margin note: Disproves Young's 1st statement?]

A generation later, historian Asa Briggs, in the words of one admirer, became "the man who put the history of the Victorian era on the academic map," in part through the publication of his influential work of political, economic, and social history entitled *The Age of Improvement, 1783–1867* (1959). (Briggs, an astonishingly prolific writer who died in 2016 at the age of 94, also wrote many other works on the Victorians, including a trilogy on *Victorian People* (1954), *Victorian Cities* (1963), and *Victorian Things* (1988).) As its title indicates, *The Age of Improvement* stressed the origins of many Victorian institutions and traditions in the eighteenth century, and overall judged the Victorian period—at least up to 1867—as a period of "improvement" in which government modernized, the electorate enlarged, manufacture industrialized, and trade expanded. Optimism and self-confidence reigned through the book, but with the implication that the end date of 1867 ushered in not only a major Reform Act but skepticism and doubt. For both Young and Briggs, then, the Victorian period was one of a glorious rise and an inglorious descent.

Since the 1960s, there have been many more attempts to summarize or provide an overview of nineteenth century or Victorian Britain, England, or the United Kingdom. Coverage varies, with start dates ranging from the mid-eighteenth

[margin note: ...rd to ...scern ...at ...kes ...mething ...ictorian]

century to somewhere in the nineteenth century and end dates similarly varied. G.M. Young looked only at England; others include Wales, Scotland, and Ireland. Curiously, although the last fifty years have witnessed the rise of social and cultural history, most overviews and textbooks have chosen to focus on political and economic history. *Understanding the Victorians* is a new introduction to the period. While it includes political and economic history, it foregrounds social and cultural history, including attention to gender, race, and class. It focuses on lived experience: what life was like for the diverse people living in Victorian Britain.

Since every summative work on Victorian Britain takes on a slightly different geographical sweep and time period, it is important to define ours. Victorian Britain was a nation that, confusingly, encompassed four smaller nations. The United Kingdom of Great Britain was made up of two parts: Britain—which was in turn made up of England, Scotland, and Wales—and Ireland, which had a more separate history and a troubled relationship with Britain. England, Scotland, and Wales are on a single geographical island but have separate political (and other) histories. Wales had been united to England since the sixteenth century and shared with it a legal system and an educational system. In Victorian Wales, English and Welsh were both spoken, and although there was a Church of England in Wales, the majority of the population attended other churches. Wales was, by the nineteenth century, only tenuously distinct from England; its "national" language, Welsh, was no longer spoken by middle- or upper-class people, and it had no political institutions of its own. The 13 counties that made up Wales shared characteristics—they were rural, remote, and poor—but little sense of national identity. To most Britons, "Wales" was a romanticized wilderness, a slice of the past in the present. Scotland had been linked to England by virtue of a shared monarch from 1603 and had sent representatives to the Westminster Parliament since 1707. (But note that late twentieth-century calls for more Scottish self-governance led to the reestablishment of a Scottish parliament in 1998 and to a referendum on Scottish independence in September 2014; the latter did not pass, despite strong support in some areas. Author J.K. Rowling famously donated £1 million to the "Better Together" campaign opposing independence.) Scotland maintained its own separate legal and educational systems. Several languages were spoken there—not only English but Scottish Gaelic in the highlands and Scots in the lowlands. Its most-practiced religion was Presbyterianism. In general, Scotland maintained an identity more distinct from England's than did Wales.

Until 1922, the United Kingdom of Great Britain also included Ireland, a separate island across the Irish Sea. Like Scotland, Ireland had a long and separate history from England, but was politically merged with it. From 1801 it sent 100 representatives to the British House of Commons. It had an established Anglican church, in spite of the fact that the majority of the population practiced Roman Catholicism. However, these political and ecclesiastical facts were of more recent vintage, and were more deeply resented, in Ireland than elsewhere. This is one reason that the "Irish Question" was for decades the most important problem in British politics. Today, the island is divided, and the Republic of Ireland is an independent country, while the six counties that constitute Northern Ireland remain part of the United Kingdom.

To speak of Victorian Britain, then, is to speak of England, Wales, Scotland, and Ireland. However, lived prejudice and inequalities of wealth and political power, along with historical practice, tended to privilege England as first among these equals. Furthermore, separate national historical traditions have developed that sometimes act as a bar to a thoroughly integrated British history. Insofar as is possible, this book seeks to address the history of all of Britain. ← can you though?

The question of when to begin and end the Victorian period is, similarly, more complicated than it seems at first glance. The most obvious limits of the "Victorian" period would be the regnal dates, that is, the dates of the reign of Queen Victoria, from 1837 until 1901. However, strictly regnal periodizations of history have fallen out of favor, largely because they privilege the lives of a very few individuals to characterize human history. (Recently, however, historian Martin Hewitt has argued in favor of analyzing a regnal Victorian period.) Other common start dates for histories of nineteenth-century Britain include 1815, the year the British decisively defeated Napoleon; 1800, in the interests of century-oriented clarity; and the mid- to late-eighteenth century, in the interests of addressing industrialization from its beginnings.

using this would 'homogenize' the entire era

Because this book declines to privilege politics and economics over social and cultural concerns, it eschews a start date that emerges from high politics, diplomacy, or economics. It begins in 1820 because that was a liminal year. In 1820, Britain was certainly industrializing and urbanizing, and just as certainly neither an industrial nor an urban society. Politically, the nation was riveted by the Queen Caroline Affair (see Chapter 2), in which we see the persistence of a culture of deference and hierarchy, and the importance of traditional ideas of government, but also the harbingers of a more representative, perhaps even democratic, system, and a middle class that is emerging but not yet emerged. We see women positioned as both outside and invested in politics. All in all, we see a Britain poised for change, which it was to experience in large doses: attempting to characterize his era, liberal philosopher John Stuart Mill (1806–1873) called change "the first of the leading peculiarities of the present age."[2] The book continues past the death of the queen because although the nation mourned the loss, it saw little change otherwise, and continued on its previous paths until the start of World War One, when this book ends.

Victorian Britain had a rapidly growing population. There were 24 million people in Britain and Ireland in 1831, twice as many as in 1761. The population was 30.5 million in 1871, 37.7 million in 1891, 41.5 million in 1901, and 45.3 million in 1911. This is an astonishing amount of growth, especially when we consider that the birthrate was declining, millions of people emigrated, and infant and child mortality were high. The term "infant mortality" refers to the death of babies before the age of one year, "child mortality" to the deaths of children younger than five years. Until the 1890s, about one-third of children died before their fifth birthdays. But for those who survived to their fifth birthday,

life expectancy was about 74 years, comparable to our own. This growing population was also a very young population: in 1851 half the population was under
age 21, and only 7% were over the age of 60. However, the early twentieth century
population had proportionately fewer children, and more adults over 60, than
had been the case in 1851, or even 1871. Until the 1870s population growth was
maintained largely though a high birth rate of about 32–35 births per thousand
people. The woman who married in the 1820s would bear an average of over
seven children. But a woman who married in the 1860s would bear only six
children, and the woman who married in the first decade of the twentieth century
would have only three.

While we cannot speak of a single Victorian worldview any more than we
can of an early twenty-first century worldview, we can explore the range of
worldviews that were available. The Victorian age was, among other things, a
period of reform. Liberalism dominated the political and philosophical temper,
and debates of the day, and encouraged an atmosphere of gradual and moderate
but deliberate and persistent reforms. These led to restrictions on work hours,
improvements in public health, the growth of civil service bureaucracies, and
enlargements of the electorate towards a more representative system. Victorians
pursued reform as a way of improving their state and their society, and as a way
of helping others. One tool, statistics, became almost an obsession, as Parliament
and other bodies commissioned endless studies that attempted to precisely
measure and quantify all aspects of human experience.

A related pursuit was the Victorian commitment to philanthropy. Philanthropy,
the practice of charitable giving and other forms of assistance to the needy,
was so highly developed in its particular Victorian form as to qualify as a worldview. Victorians believed strongly in helping the poor, and equally strongly that
such help should come with conditions. To receive help, the poor had to agree to
attend church, to live austerely, to give up drink, to change their sexual habits,
to improve their housekeeping—Victorians had a fear of dirt and a commitment
to cleanliness that preceded the acceptance of germ theory. Philanthropists tried
persistently, even obsessively, to distinguish between real and "feigned distress,"
and between the "deserving" and "undeserving" poor. They spent hours inter-
viewing candidates and visiting homes and institutions to judge the relative
worthiness of potential recipients. Yet we should also acknowledge that they
gave thousands of pounds to the poor and otherwise needy, and that these were
desperately needed in a society that had almost no state-provided safety nets.

Much philanthropy was organized around churches, and the Victorians were
a religious people. They went to church, if not on Sundays, then for events like
weddings and baptisms and holidays like Easter. When they joined a club, it was
more likely than not to have some religious cast (this was especially true for women,
who felt more justified leaving their homes and families for an evening if there was
some religious or moral aspect to the event they attended). Many of their leisure
activities were church-sponsored. They had bibles and Christian images on
display in their homes, their workplaces, and their civic buildings. While Darwinian

evolution sparked a crisis of faith for some, Victorians—whether they were elderly in 1820, or young in 1914—lived in a Christian country.

While they are caricatured as straight-laced to the point of absurdity, Victorians were also hot in pursuit of distraction, sensation, and pleasure. Victorians drank to excess, in part because beer was often cleaner and safer than water, especially in cities. Beer was also considered a form of sustenance; many manual workers believed that they needed a pint in the morning before work, and several more throughout the day. Consumption of alcohol—chiefly in the form of beer—rose from 1820 until the mid-1870s (it then declined until 1900, and thereafter remained at a stable level). The pub was a critical social center, especially for working-class men. Contemporary social researchers Charles Booth and Seebohm Rowntree, who studied the urban poor in London and York respectively, estimated that the average working-class family spent between one-sixth and one-third of its weekly wages on alcohol. Tobacco was also popular, especially late in the century; Britons spent £3.5 million on smoking in 1870, but by 1914 this figure had multiplied several-fold to £42 million. Gambling, especially on sports, was another form of leisure. So were exhibitions, from a Crystal Palace made entirely of iron and glass to exhibitions of exotic imperial goods and peoples to scientific displays, as well as plays, concerts, and performances of all sorts. Middle-class reformers worried constantly about the amusements of the working-class, though they had very little success in attracting them to more "improving" forms of leisure.

Yet Victorians were also obsessed with personal discipline. Most believed in the power of the individual to improve his or her circumstances, and indeed self-help was a gospel. The leading preacher was Scottish author Samuel Smiles (1812–1904). As a young man Smiles was a political radical, but he came to believe in individual effort over collective action. In his 1859 book *Self-Help*, he emphasized the importance of character to improved fortunes in life, and supported his argument with biographical examples of successful businessmen who had rescued themselves from poverty through thrift, self-sacrifice, and hard work. The book sold 20,000 copies in its first year of publication—an incredibly high figure for the period—and over a quarter of a million copies by 1905. Temperance was a large, if never widely successful, movement. Thrift was admired, as was sexual restraint. Self-improvement was also widely promoted, by the middle class, who tried to interest the working class in rational recreation (rambles in the country rather than afternoons at the pub), and by working-class autodidacts bent on self-improvement.

Yet self-improvement took place in the context of a deep belief in racial, class, and other hierarchies. Most working-class people agreed that they owed their social superiors deference. Most Britons both at home and abroad believed that Christianity, white skin, and a constitution made them superior to those who lacked them. Xenophobia was rampant, racial hierarchies were real, and patriotism was strong (especially among the deferential majority of the working class).

***

This book focuses on the social and the cultural and on the interplay between received ideas and lived experience. Because of this, we will begin by looking at change over time in Victorian Britain not by charting changes in Parliamentary politics, or by demonstrating the growth of manufacturing, but by looking at the changing meanings of a single object, the piano, in both print culture and lived experience. This focus will, it is hoped, demonstrate cultural history's ability to illuminate and connect us to the past.

In 1820, the different classes of Britons—aristocracy and gentry, middle class, and working class—lived extremely different lives. The classes were highly stratified and easily distinguished by their material possessions and their forms of domesticity and leisure. Industrialization had been underway for over half a century in certain areas, but had yet to improve most people's lives. The working-class majority worked long hours, often in dangerous conditions, for low pay, and had little time, money, or space for leisure, home decoration, or discretionary purchases.

In this world, a piano was for the elite. We see this in Jane Austen's novel *Emma* (1815). In it, Frank Churchill, heir to a fortune, buys a piano for the genteel Jane Fairfax, to whom he is secretly betrothed. As a wealthy man, Mr Churchill can afford a piano; having been fashionably raised in London, he is knowledgeable enough to purchase the right sort, one made by the preeminent British firm of Broadwood and Sons. Miss Fairfax's position demonstrates that gentility was not always synonymous with wealth, especially for unmarried women; she is from a good family and is an excellent pianist, but she cannot afford a piano and until her betrothal was in danger of becoming a governess. Two other minor characters, Mr and Mrs Cole, make clear that even as early as 1820, wealth was not synonymous with social status; the Coles are *nouveau riche* and while they have a "new grand pianoforte in the drawing-room," Mrs Cole admits that she does "not know one note from another."[3]

Austen's depiction of the piano as an elite object—owned by elites or by those with money and social ambitions who wished to be perceived as elite—captures its social and material meanings at the start of the Victorian period. Pianos were new, strange, and rare. Jane Fairfax (and Jane Austen), Emma Woodhouse, and their circle entertained one another on the piano, but when typical Britons played music at home, they played the more common and more affordable fiddle or flute. The piano had been invented—originally as an improvement on older instruments such as the clavichord—during the early modern period, and established as a recognized instrument by the early eighteenth century, but in 1820 most Britons had probably never touched one. Each year fewer than 50,000 were made in the entire world (half of them in Britain) by skilled craftsmen. They were quite large, but this was no barrier to ownership as anyone who could afford one had a large drawing room. These extremely expensive luxury items graced the drawing rooms of the aristocracy, the gentry, and (as in the case of the Coles) the wealthy. And owning a piano was only a first step. Because printing was expensive, published music was almost unheard of, so players could obtain new pieces to play only through laborious hand-copying. And since there were very few professional musicians in Britain, finding a teacher was difficult and lessons were expensive.

By the 1850s, Britain had changed. It was now a more industrialized and urbanized society. The middle class was larger, richer, and more powerful than it had been in 1820, and sought to establish itself culturally. Mass production made many goods more affordable to the middle class, who forged and performed their identities in part through consumption and display. Literacy was much higher, and books and magazines were more plentiful and cheaper, thanks to the development of machine-made paper, the rotary steam press, and power-binding. Britain was now a middle-class nation.

We see aspects of all this in a mid-century novel, Emily Eden's *The Semi-Detached House* (1859). The genteel young heroine Blanche is horrified at the prospect of a temporary stay in a semi-detached villa whilst her husband Arthur is away because her middle-class neighbors are sure to have "daughters who will always be playing . . . on the piano-forte."[4] Blanche is certain that this middle-class family's musicality will be a sign of their pathetic social aspirations, and her condescending anxiety is typical of the elite belief that aspiring families cared about the piano only as a social and not as a musical object. However as the novel progresses, Lady Blanche discovers that the Hopkinson daughters are not only lovely young women but also accomplished musicians.

The piano in this novel is a middle-class object. Pianos were no longer restricted to the homes of the elites. By the 1850s and 1860s, many pianos were manufactured in Germany and in the United States as well as in Britain, and were made by machine; both changes made pianos less expensive. Changes in financing also helped. Middle-class buyers could now use the hire-purchase system (called an installment plan in the United States), in which they put down a large deposit but not the entire purchase cost, and then made monthly payments. Industrialization and mass production made not only pianos but their accoutrements—stools, metronomes, sheet music—more affordable; in fact, sheet music was now plentiful and inexpensive. The piano was now the center of music-making and leisure more generally in public arenas, and was especially popular in urban pubs.[5] Furthermore music enjoyed in the middle-class home was now likely to center on the piano. As the 1860s and 1870s progressed, piano ownership spread even farther down the social scale to the lower middle class, though it remained firmly out of the reach of the working class. While Blanche looks down on the comfortable middle-class Hopkinsons, most middle-class and working-class people would have envied them their piano and all that it implied.

In mid-Victorian Britain the piano was an object of social emulation, of domesticity, and of leisure, in a society in which all three were important. Blanche's prejudice against the Hopkinsons reflects the complex meanings of the piano. On one hand, the piano was a potent social symbol that many bought simply to broadcast what they hoped was their perceived social status. A piano in the parlor, and the ability to play at least a little, said worlds about a family's respectability. But on the other hand, many people were quite musically proficient (in part because one had to make music to hear it), and the home was a principal site of

Figure 0.1 Pianoforte advertisement circa 1870.

© Amoret Tanner/Alamy.

leisure, including music. Many who owned a piano were good players who enjoyed making music. The multiple meanings of, and the wider reach of, the piano were symptomatic of mid-Victorian society. As the Victorian period progressed, it became more difficult to distinguish between classes of people based on their clothes, their literacy, their leisure habits, and other previously stable signifiers.

The late nineteenth century and early twentieth centuries saw yet more changes. The Reform Acts of 1867 and 1884 had given the vote to millions of working-class men and fundamentally changed the nature of politics. Working-class people finally enjoyed sufficient hours outside of work, and sufficient discretionary income, to participate in consumer culture. Some had been able to join the lower middle-class: the dramatic expansion of education and literacy on the one hand, and bureaucracies on the other, had created a huge number of low-level white collar workers who, a generation before, would have done manual labor. In the public sector alone, there were 50,000 civil servants in 1881, but this number had more than doubled to 116,000 civil servants (predominantly postal workers and elementary school teachers) in 1901 and continued to rise until 1914. Furthermore consumer credit was now routinely extended to working-class customers.

All of this is evident in the piano in George and Weedon Grossmith's famous comic novel *The Diary of a Nobody* (1892). It features a first-person narrator, City clerk Charles Pooter, and is a gentle satire on lower middle-class and suburban life. Early in the novel, Mr Pooter extols the pleasures of spending evenings at home with his wife, who "is not above putting a button on a shirt, mending a pillow-case, or practicing the "Sylvia Gavotte" on our new cottage piano . . . from Collard and Collard."[6] That the lower middle-class Mrs Pooter plays the piano tells us that pianos are more common by now. Advances in manufacturing and production continued to make pianos less expensive; those made in Germany, and even more those made in the United States, where more than half the world's pianos were now produced, were especially cheap. Printed sheet music and accessories were also far less expensive.

Every region of the country had its own piano-making firm; every town had a piano dealer, and large cities had several. In the half-century before 1901, world production of pianos had increased tenfold, from 50,000 per annum in 1851 to 500,000 per annum in 1901. By the 1880s, piano dealers were willing to accept very small deposits on three-year hire-purchases, putting pianos into the reach of the lower middle-class and parts of the working-class (though not the poorest and least skilled); in *The Diary of a Nobody*, the Pooters have purchased their piano "on the three years' [hire-purchase] system."

As the twentieth century began, pianos came into the reach of the working class as well. A social investigator's report on Bradford, in northern England, noted that pianos, once a sign of affluence, "may now be found almost in house-rows," typical urban working-class dwellings.[7] By 1900, manufacturers had developed smaller pianos designed expressly to fit in smaller homes, and dealers offered pianos with no deposit at all, only regular monthly payments; these were two reasons that by 1910 pianos were common features in working-class homes. Teachers, who had been rare and expensive in 1820, were now neither. Britain had many more professional musicians than it had a century ago, and most did at least some teaching, including not only expensive private lessons but classes at working-class institutions (such as mechanics' institutes). In addition, many amateur musicians from the upper working-class and the lower middle-class— skilled workers, clerks, and the like—offered lessons for as little as 3d. per hour.

Pianos were no longer elite objects. Still desirable, they were (in certain forms) within the reach of many people, as were musical instruction, printed music, and other necessaries. While the quality of pianos and musical ability still varied widely, and was often marked by class, it was no longer a case of have and have-not, but rather of the qualities of having. Britain in 1914 was, in many ways, a different nation from the one it had been in 1820.

Notes

1 Miles Taylor, "Review of Briggs, Asa, *The Age of Improvement, 1783–1867*," H-Albion, H-Net Reviews. October, 2000. Available online at: www.h-net.org/reviews/showrev.php?id=4622
2 John Stuart Mill, "The Spirit of the Age," in G.L. Williams (ed.), *Mill on Politics and Society* (1976), p. 170.
3 Jane Austen, *Emma*, edited by Alistair M. Duckworth (New York: Palgrave Macmillan, 2002), p. 179.
4 Emily Eden, *The Semi-Detached House* (Boston: Ticknor and Fields, 1859), pp. 5, 8.
5 Dave Russell, *Popular Music in England 1840–1914: A Social History* (Manchester: Manchester University Press, 1987), pp. 135, 139, 142–144.
6 George and Weedon Grossmith, *The Diary of a Nobody* (1892), pp. 9–10.
7 William Cudworth, *Condition of the Industrial Classes of Bradford and District*, 1887, p. 58, quoted in Russell, p. 139.

Further reading

These works are relevant to many of the topics covered in this book:

Kelly Boyd and Rohan McWilliam (eds), *The Victorian Studies Reader* (Abingdon, UK: Routledge, 2007).
Martin Hewitt, ed., *The Victorian World* (Abingdon, UK: Routledge, 2012).
Sally Mitchell, *Daily Life in Victorian England* (Westport, CT: Greenwood, 1996). The Praeger *Victorian Life and Times* series.
F.M.L. Thompson (ed.), *The Cambridge Social History of Britain, 1750–1950*, Volume 3: Social Agencies and Institutions. Cambridge: Cambridge University Press. Online Publication, 2008.
Chris Williams, ed., *A Companion to Nineteenth-Century Britain* (Oxford: Blackwell, 2004).

Online resources

Many of these online resources are general or very comprehensive, and so are relevant to many of the topics covered in this book:

Victorian Web: www.victorianweb.org/
Oxford Dictionary of National Biography: www.oxforddnb.com/
History in Focus: The Victorian Era: www.history.ac.uk/ihr/Focus/Victorians/www.html
Spartacus Educational: http://spartacus-educational.com/
Victorian Research Web: http://victorianresearch.org/
The British Library—go to Help for Researchers (www.bl.uk/reshelp/findhelptime/index.html) and look around

The British Library—go to Victorian Britain: www.bl.uk/victorian-britain

BBC History: www.bbc.co.uk/history/—surprisingly good short intros www.bbc.co.uk/history/british/victorians/

Victorian History, an idiosyncratic selection of short bits about elements of Victorian history: http://vichist.blogspot.co.uk/

Two Nerdy History Girls: http://twonerdyhistorygirls.blogspot.com.au/

Reviews in History: www.history.ac.uk/reviews/

History Compass: http://history-compass.com/

BHO British History Online: www.british-history.ac.uk/

British History Sources, 1500–1900: www.connectedhistories.org/Default.aspx

Victorian links: www.sylviamilne.co.uk/vic.htm

The official websites of English, Scottish, and Irish Heritage and the National Trusts (organizations that preserve cultural heritage by caring for historic buildings, monuments and sites): www.english-heritage.org.uk/, www.historic-scotland.gov.uk/index/heritage.htm, www.heritageireland.ie/, https://www.nationaltrust.org.uk/, www.nts.org.uk/Home/, www.antaisce.org/

Internet Modern History Sourcebook: http://legacy.fordham.edu/halsall/mod/modsbook.asp

Irish History Online: www.irishhistoryonline.ie/

Scottish Bibliographies Online: www.nls.uk/catalogues/scottish-bibliographies-online

Institute of Historical Research: www.history.ac.uk/ British & Irish Bibliographies Online: www.history.ac.uk/projects/bbih Eurodocs: Online Sources for European History. Britain, 1816–1918: http://eudocs.lib.byu.edu/index.php/Britain_1816–1918

Scotland's written history: http://digital.nls.uk/scotlandspages/

Europeana collections: www.europeana.eu/portal/

EHPS—European History Primary Sources: http://primary-sources.eui.eu/

1 A "green and pleasant land" of cities and slums

Space

Introduction

Until recently, history has been about time, not space. Space was simply the places where history happened, and historians paid it little attention, preferring to cede its study to geographers and specialist historians of architecture, landscape, and design. But this has begun to change. In the mid-1980s, scholar Michel Foucault (1926–1984) suggested that while "[t]he great obsession of the nineteenth century was ... history ... [t]he present epoch will perhaps be above all the epoch of *space*."[1] Since then a number of historians have recognized that space is not simply a neutral background for events, and that we can deepen our analyses of political, social, and cultural developments over time by situating them in space, and by integrating our analyses of space into our histories of people. Town halls, city parks and commercial pleasure gardens, slums, urban tenements and suburban homes, parlors, sculleries, and bedrooms, railway stations and carriages—all of these spaces have meanings.

Awareness of spaces reshapes our interpretations of the human inter-actions that are so often structured by them: a pub conversation could never take place in a church or bedroom. Spaces can have unanticipated meanings; those we might assume are inherently domestic might also be places of violence, as in the case of rape; spaces we consider public might be quite intimate, as in the case of sex between men "cottaging" in public urinals. One space can have different meanings for its various occupants; an upper middle-class woman doing needle-work in her parlor is at home, but her servant cleaning it is at work. Spaces also have shifting meanings depending on the time of day. Many Victorian city centers that in daylight were bustling financial, political, and commercial districts were transformed at nightfall into spaces of drink, crime, and illicit sexuality.

In the Victorian period, spaces became separated, with city and country and public and private particularly distinct from one another. Cities became large and densely populated. Rural areas were dotted with small towns, each of which provided the county's residents with a single high street on which could be found—in novelist Anthony Trollope's description—nothing more than "two pumps, three hotels, ten shops, fifteen beer-houses, a beadle and a market-place."[2] In industrializing Georgian Britain, professional men's offices were rooms in their homes, and shopkeepers and their families lived above the shop; even wealthy manufacturers lived near their warehouses. But in the Victorian period domestic space became distinct from, and often far from, commercial and industrial space. Offices were, increasingly, placed in office districts in city centers; stores were on shopping high streets; factories were on major transportation routes outside of cities. Living in a city center became less common for everyone except the working poor. This dramatic change in the built environment was one of the biggest changes in the Victorian period.

The key spaces with which Victorians concerned themselves were the city, seen as the quintessentially public place, and the home, the very definition of the private. Neither, of course, was new to the Victorian period, but each took on a pressing new significance because to the Victorians urban and domestic space had tremendous moral power. The crowded rooms in slum tenements were not just physically unhealthy, but rendered their inhabitants immoral. The Birmingham *Daily Post* called the city's slums places of "disorder and sin" that were "physically, mentally, and morally degrading to many of those who lived in them."[3] The *Liverpool Argus* called for city parks because "[w]e want open spaces where our little ragamuffins"—the word denoted children who lived in slums— "can exercise their limbs and fashion themselves into healthy Englishmen."[4] Similarly, well laid-out streets created an orderly population; properly designed, decorated, and managed homes enabled their inhabitants to be good and to do good. In 1875, the fashionable periodical *Queen* stated confidently that "the owners of a pretty house are likely to be more estimable characters than others less happily situated." In the *Contemporary Review*, the Reverend Foster Barham Zincke (1817–1893) declared in 1880 that "every improvement in the house is an improvement in morality."[5] The first part of the period saw the growth of the British city and concerns about the British city, along with shifts in the layouts and meanings of homes. The later Victorian period saw the rise of well-developed city centers and suburbs, a determination to solve the problem of slums, and the persistence of multi-use spaces in working-class homes.

where you live defines who you are

1820–1870: City, countryside, and home

During the first half of the nineteenth century, Ireland remained largely rural, but England, Scotland, and Wales all urbanized. In 1700, Britain and Ireland had been home to about 14 million people, and three-quarters of them lived in rural areas; there were only a half a dozen towns with populations of 10,000 or more. But there was tremendous population growth during the eighteenth century. The population of England and Wales almost doubled, the population of Scotland increased by over a million, and the population in all three became highly concentrated in cities. As a result, in 1821, the population had reached almost 21 million (and this was almost 2 million more than it had been only ten years earlier in the 1811 census). London's had reached 1.5 million, and there were 15 towns that had populations of more than 25,000.

Population boom & massive urbanization

It is no surprise that Victorians thought a lot about cities: in their lifetimes Britain became an urban society. By 1851 England had 151 cities with populations of more than 20,000, and ten of these had populations greater than 200,000. That same year in Scotland, Glasgow had a population of 330,000 and Edinburgh had a population of 170,000. (We should note that these urban populations were not native—in 1851, of every 33 people who lived in a city, only 13 had been born there.) Industrial Northern and Midlands cities were of particular note: Liverpool, Manchester, and Birmingham, which in 1700 had had a combined population of fewer than 20,000, by 1820 were home to over 400,000 people. In the 1820s, 1830s and 1840s visitors from continental Europe, the United States, and elsewhere in the British Isles came to marvel at the new industrial metropolises of the Midlands. Smaller cities also grew quickly. Merthyr Tydfil in Wales went from an 1801 population of 7,700 to an 1851 population of 46,400.[6] By 1851, a majority of the population of England—54%—lived in cities. England was the first country to cross this threshold.

Cities varied widely: the ancient, enormous capital differed from the new industrial towns of the North and the Midlands, and both were different from smaller, older regional centers. But cities and ideas about cities were in many ways consistent across Britain. In discussions and depictions, cities were generally characterized by their public streets, impressive centers, distressing slums, and growing suburbs. There was a constant interplay and tension between freedom and order, public and private, surveillance and anonymity. The majority-urban figure should be treated with caution: even when the 1851 census revealed that the new urban majority of 54% living in cities, that still left fully 46% in the country. And the census considered every town with a population of more than 2,500 to be an urban area, which means that the image it presented of a truly urban Britain was somewhat illusory. Many parts of England, Scotland, Wales, and Ireland were still dominated by villages and very small towns that had a single small high street dominated by the Anglican church at one end and perhaps the town's only mill at the other. Large aristocratic estates and gentry houses, where they existed, dominated the landscape. Many people made their living farming for large- or medium-sized farmers. The largest farmhouses (of farms of more than 100 acres) would dominate the village or hamlet, standing out from the small cottages in which the farmer's workers lived. The smallest farms, of 25 acres or less, were usually farmed by the family, but were not sufficient to support them without other trades.

Even so, the rise of the cities changed the meaning of the countryside. One immediate response to urbanization was the growth of the notion of the "pastoral." The pastoral mode, in poetry, the arts, and culture more generally, was an idealization of rural space beautiful and unspoiled, of rural life as free from modern stresses and anxieties, of rural society as a quickly-disappearing one in which loyalty to family and community were more important than profit. Many Victorians sought to spend time in the pastoral countryside. This was new; as historian Peter Mandler points out, "a nation that lives in the country has no special reason to holiday there"; as Britain urbanized (with England leading the way), a visit to the country became an increasingly important form of leisure and a way to signal a connection to England's rural past. As early as the 1820s, and certainly by the 1850s, vacation escapes from the city were popular. The wealthy had country homes; the well-off had country cottages; the middle and lower middle classes took short jaunts. By the 1850s the week-long holiday, formerly the preserve of the self-employed middle classes, had become the norm for many lower middle-class and upper working-class families. Even more popular was the day-trip, first in horse-drawn wagons and later by railway. People took day trips to the countryside to get out of the city, see green spaces, and breathe fresh air. They frequently visited stately homes and their grounds, which were open to the public for tours and recreation. By the 1850s most big cities had at least one great estate open to public recreation within an easy rail journey. Londoners could go south to Knole, north to Hatfield, or west to Cliveden; for those in Manchester, Dunham Massey was "a perfect paradise"; those in the Midlands could visit Trentham Gardens, while for those in the Black Country Hagley was "the resort of excursionists." Countryside visits were popular until the end of the century, when they were replaced by seaside holidays.[7]

In rural Britain, the aristocracy owned most of the nation's land and derived much of their wealth from agricultural products, both grain and livestock, and from rents paid by their tenants, the rural working class who lived in small cottages on their land. Thousands of people lived on agricultural estates and farmed land owned by aristocrats. Aristocratic landlords might be a very visible and philanthropic presence, or they might be distant, relying on agents and stewards to look after their tenants and their land. Today the term "cottage" conjures up something idyllic, but in the Victorian period the term implied that the inhabitants were poor; the word's connotations were not unlike those of the word "hut" today. Rural workers might enjoy snug, well-built homes, especially as the spirit of social reform inspired some philanthropic landlords to provide well-built cottages. However, more often cottages were small, shabby, and insubstantial dwellings, made using "stud and mud" or "wattle and daub" techniques. Roofs were made of thatch, which deteriorated and dropped into the house. Early in the period the clay or "cob" cottages that were most common were damp and needed frequent repair. Fuel was expensive, so homes were cold. The abolition of a tax on bricks helped to make brick building more common after the mid-century, but even at the end of the period many lived in homes that were made of little more than mud. Scottish farm servants lived in "cottar houses" made of stone, lime mortar, and timber; they were supposed to be an improvement on older cottages made of turf and thatch, but were so damp and drafty that they were a major source of complaints. All over Britain and Ireland, women worked hard to keep cottages comfortable, warm, and clean, lighting fires when they could and sweeping constantly, but it was an uphill battle. Most Victorian rural dwellings were so insubstantial that no trace of them remains. And while the urban population increased faster, the rural population increased until the 1860s, so that insufficient housing was also a problem.

One response to rural poverty was migration. This might be abroad, to the United States or to one of the "settler" colonies in search of a better life—often, emigrants hoped to be able to afford a farm of their own, as they could not in England (see Chapter 3). It might also be to the nearest town in search of work—Victorian cities were largely peopled by immigrants, but ones who had not come very far. They swarmed into the cities, only to find new problems, including overcrowding and disease. Victorian responses to urban life included anxiety, debate, and reform, especially on the topics of civic pride and public health. Victorian cities had many places of enjoyment: municipal parks, pleasure gardens, museums and art galleries, libraries, fashionable shopping streets, arcades, bazaars, and department stores, large and brightly lit pubs and cafés, theatres, concert-halls, and music halls. These same spaces were also spaces of inconvenience and danger—dirt, mud, drunkenness, confrontation, property theft, harassment, physical or sexual violence.

Victorians used various strategies to understand their cities. One very impor-tant response to increasing urbanity was mapping, the attempt to comprehend and control urban space by creating various kinds of maps. Maps organized cities according to public health, housing, culture, or other priorities. They were both representations of reality and ways of disciplining that reality. The Ordnance Survey, the national agency that produces maps of all of Great Britain, was started in the mid-eighteenth century but came into its own in the nineteenth century: an official map of all the counties in Ireland was completed in 1846, and all the English counties were mapped by 1891. Maps made cities more accessible, but were also regulatory, limiting gestures. For example, in mid-century many sanitary and medical mapmakers created maps that charted the progress of diseases (particularly cholera) through cities in an attempt to understand their origins and ultimately to control them. In 1854, Dr John Snow (1813–1858) used careful mapping to identify a single well in the East End of London as the source of a cholera outbreak (many cities suffered from terrible epidemics of cholera and typhus; see Chapter 14).

One way of understanding cities was to compare them to people: Victorian depictions of the city as a human body were common. In these models, new sewage systems were intestines, allowing waste to be disposed of; parks were lungs, allowing fresh air in; streets were circulatory systems, which had to flow freely for optimal health. (The problem of breathing was not always metaphoric: during the Great Stink of 1858, the Thames became so choked with human feces that the city's air became unbearable to breathe.) Another oft-used metaphor was that of the city as theatre, in which the streets were a stage, and the people on them were both actors and audience. Many saw themselves as spectators who traversed the urban landscape whilst observing its actors. Such a spectator is referred to by scholars as a *flâneur*; the word comes from the French verb *flâner*, to stroll, and was used by the mid-century French novelist Charles Baudelaire (1821–1867) to describe the gentleman who rambled through nineteenth-century cities, keenly observing, and whom Baudelaire saw as critical to both urbanity and modernity. In 1858 the London *Daily Telegraph* described *flâneurs* as "the inveterate 'mooners' of the metropolis," "peripatetic philosophers . . . whose delight it is to wander about the streets of crowded cities at nightfall."[8] If the city was a theatrical production, the *flâneur* was simultaneously a character and an audience member who delighted in what he saw. Many novelists and journalists positioned their characters or themselves as *flâneurs*; Henry Mayhew's exhaustively descriptive *London Labour and the London Poor* (1851), which he began as the "metropolitan correspondent" for the *Morning Chronicle*, was in many ways the work of a *flâneur*.

Not everyone could take on the role of *flâneur*: the leisure to spend the day walking and observing, the courage to begin conversations with strangers, the discretionary income to spend in cafés, and the ability to enter into unfamiliar neighborhoods with impunity were all reserved for middle- and upper-class men. Working men had neither the time nor the cultural capital to enter elite neighborhoods and institutions; they stayed close to home, walking to work in the morning and back again at night. Women of all classes faced multiple barriers in any attempt to wander freely. Women were gazed upon, but could not themselves employ the gaze; they were objects of *flânerie*, not *flâneurs*—or, more properly, *flâneuses*. The *flâneuse* was, in many ways, an impossibility, because women did not enjoy men's freedom to enjoy public space, a problem exemplified by the fact that the term "public woman" was a euphemism for a prostitute.

Street space was defined as "public" in that the entire population had access to it; the perceived right of all citizens to walk freely in the streets was such an important tradition that one historian has only half-jokingly referred to the "Free-Born English pedestrian."[9] Victorian streets swarmed with pedestrians, commuters, delivery boys, and shoppers, all on their way somewhere, not to mention those whose work was in the streets—prostitutes, street sweepers, vendors, beggars, entertainers. (In 1844, French political journalist Leon Faucher noted the many prostitutes near the Manchester Exchange at dusk.) On the streets, hundreds or even thousands of strangers were brought together and expected to behave appropriately. As a result, Victorians—including the new professional police forces (see Chapter 10)—directed much energy towards maintaining public order. The maintenance of public order also relied on less obvious tools such as street lights (the streets of most cities and large towns in Britain were lit by gas from the mid-1820s) and new rules of conduct. Ordinary citizens did not leave the job of surveillance to the police; they were eager to engage in it as well. Working- and middle-class Britons alike came to expect order and became both objects and subjects of their fellow city-dwellers' judgmental gaze. Provincial newspapers were full of evidence of this constant mutual surveillance in the form of letters from readers and editorials. For example in 1849 a resident of Truro, Cornwall, wrote to his local paper to complain about some young gentlemen who, while in overly high spirits, had broken windows and door knockers.[10]

A key Victorian tension was between a city's center and its slums. On the one hand, these two spaces were geographically and conceptually distinct from one another: one was commercial, the other residential; one had broad boulevards, the other crooked alleyways; one was safe, the other dangerous; one was for the respectable and middle class, the other for the rough and working class. In his

1845 novel *Sybil* politician Benjamin Disraeli (1804–1881) famously said that England was divided into two nations, the rich and the poor, "between whom there is no intercourse . . . as if they were dwellers in different zones,"[11] and the stark division between city centers and city slums seemed to bear this out. But despite all this, centers and slums were also very near to one another. To consult a map, a census or local tax record of London, Birmingham, or Merthyr Tydfil is to see that "centers" and "slums" were often only a few steps from each other. Slums were such an intense topic of discussion and writing that one historian argues that they were at heart a narrative construct (though the poverty and misery that many urban residents suffered was not), in the sense that descriptions of slums made them seem more discrete than they actually were. Working-class and poor city dwellers lived in quarters that were extremely cramped and offered little in the way of fresh air or easy access to it. Toilet and washing facilities were shared by many families. Lack of adequate sewage systems meant that urban air and water were frequently unpleasant, when they were not actively unhealthy. In the early 1840s, a quarter of Liverpudlians lived in cramped courtyards in which multiple families shared a single faucet and outhouse. Those homes that did have indoor plumbing flushed their raw sewage into the nearest river. Overall Victorian Britain had profound, and largely negative, effects on the environment, only some of which were addressed in the later part of the period. In 1854, half of the families in Newcastle-upon-Tyne lived in a single room. These conditions meant that urban working-class families had little space and little comfort; families could not all sit down to eat together, were often cold, and rarely had clean clothes.

The dwellings of the poor were shockingly described in reformer Edwin Chadwick's (1803–1890) 1842 *Report on the Sanitary Conditions of the Labouring Population*, which used novelistic and melodramatic rhetoric to depict the terrible conditions in which the urban poor lived, and called for better drainage, sanitation, and water provisions. During the 1840s, 1850s, and 1860s, reformers were optimistic about the power of sanitary and housing reform, which they were certain would elevate the poor physically and morally. Homes that were infused with fresh air and middle-class ideals would be unlikely "to harbor either miasmic vapors or criminals"[12]—the phrase shows how physical and moral problems were associated with one another. Focusing on the cholera epidemic of 1834, Chadwick's report graphically described the physically dirty and morally degrading conditions in which many (if not most) working-class Britons lived, and blamed these on a lack of sewers, drainage, and clean water supplies. The report popularized the notion that the government was responsible for public health. It was the critical precursor to the 1866 Sanitary Act, which required local authorities to provide sewers and water, and the 1848 and 1875 Public Health Acts, which required local officials to deal with infectious diseases and with burials, among other things. Unfortunately none of these Acts provided funding for inspectors, leaving them in many cases little more than empty gestures.

One key response to urbanization and especially to urban poverty and slums was the promotion of city parks. The earliest municipal parks in Britain date from the early seventeenth century, but the nineteenth century was the heyday

Figure 1.1 A typical late Victorian slum: two women pose with their children, Eagle and Child Yard, Hunslet, Leeds, 13 May 1896 (b/w photo) by English photographer (nineteenth century).

© Leeds Library and Information Service, Leeds, UK/The Bridgeman Art Library.

of park development. The movement began in 1833, when the Select Committee on Public Walks (SCPW) presented to Parliament its report, which surveyed what accessible open space existed in towns and cities and recommended government actions for the future. The report stressed the importance of green space for health and as a solution to the "problem" of working-class leisure time. It was believed that green spaces were necessary correctives to urban living, and while parks were not literally a city's lungs, Victorian cities were often so dirty that the bodily metaphor seemed almost real. Working-class leisure was just as pressing. John Finch, an iron merchant from Liverpool, complained that "[it] is a very absurd thing that on Sunday . . . all the public houses are open and all the public walks, cemeteries, zoological gardens, and botanical gardens where people might amuse themselves innocently, are closed."[13] Manchester opened three new parks in 1846, including Peel Park; Leeds had Woodhouse Moor, and Birmingham had Aston Lower Grounds. London had nine public parks at mid-century, but only one, Victoria Park, was in the East End, so many poor London children had to walk a mile or more to get to a park.

Parks were characterized by walking paths, lodges, boathouses, pagodas, and bandstands. Some were sites of public debate—London's Victoria Park in the

East End and Hyde Park in the West End were both known for their speakers and debates—but many cities prohibited political or religious meetings in public parks. Parks were also popular places for sport. Sport areas were always segregated by gender, and were dominated by middle-class men. Archery, shuttlecock, and rope-skipping (by children and adults) were all popular, and cycling became something of a fashion in the later Victorian period. Football (which Americans call soccer) was the last sport allowed entrance to the parks.

Municipal parks were important arenas for the middle classes, who took a leading role in establishing and maintaining them, and used them as arenas in which they could perform and display their class status and their civic authority. Parks were seen as ideal spaces that would transmit middle-class values to the working classes. The opening of the parks in Manchester in 1846 was a festival of middle-class ceremonial. However, the middle class, having opened parks with such fanfare, discovered that they were often used in unintended ways. Female prostitutes regularly worked in city parks, and men often had sex with each other in parks, and in particular in the parks' public toilets—relabeled "cottages" for this new use. Attempts to exclude undesirable elements from parks became a growing preoccupation.

Because municipal parks had such restrictive rules, many working-class people who could afford the admission fees preferred commercial pleasure gardens. These included Vauxhall Gardens and Cremorne in London, and Belle Vue Gardens and Pomona Gardens in Manchester. The need to attract custom made these gardens more flexible about behavioral standards. They featured theatres, circuses, and other spectacles, and tended to come alive with music, drinking, and dancing—as well as prostitution and illicit sexual activity—at night. Their licentious atmosphere posed a striking contrast to that of the more sober municipal parks. When working-class people could afford them, they often preferred them to the censorious gaze they were under in public parks; when they could not, they tried to use the parks for activities they, and not the middle class, saw as fit, which usually included football and drinking.

Another key development in urban space was the rise of the suburbs. By the 1840s, suburbs such as Edgbaston, west of Birmingham, were becoming more popular and more affordable, but before 1880 suburban living was the preserve of those with some modicum of time, money, and steady employment. The most desirable suburbs were populated by the comfortable middle classes, who over the first half of the nineteenth century embodied their ideas about separate spheres in geographical separations between suburban homes and urban workplaces (though until the 1870s city centers remained fairly socially mixed). These included the London suburbs of Penge and Ealing for the middle class and Hampstead for the upper middle class, the Leeds suburbs of Headingley and Potternewton, and the Birmingham suburbs of Edgbaston and Moseley. Physical distance from the city made the city center and slums seem even more dangerous to suburban dwellers. It also meant that, for men, the railway commute became an urban public ritual; for women, entering the city center was an occasion, one that involved planning, dressing, and checking railway schedules. Once the

*Seems that with the creation of urban living, the higher and lower classes became separated even further.

middle class began leaving the center for the suburbs, the lower middle class and better paid artisans followed suit; for example in London they left Poplar and Bethnal Green to move to newer, modest suburbs such as Camberwell. From the 1850s, the gap between London and provincial rents grew, and working-class housing began to vary more by region. In many areas employers built "model villages," in which they provided better housing nearer to work than their workers would otherwise have been able to afford. Saltaire, built in 1853 by industrialist Titus Salt near Bradford, is a famous example.

While Victorians were passionately debating the meanings of that most public and performative of spaces, the city, they were also working out their ideas about the home, which they saw as private (though most people, even in the middle class, rented) and a refuge. A rhetoric of domesticity was well-articulated by the time Queen Victoria took the throne. Furthermore homes, once near or coeval with places of work, were by the Victorian period separate from work. Domestic ideology positioned home as a refuge from public life, with its anonymity and rejection of the spiritual and moral concerns. As such it facilitated a growing notion of privacy and of the home as a private space. Women were to make sure that it was a refuge from the hustle and bustle of public life, especially for their husbands, who returned there eagerly from work each evening.

For all classes, the Victorian ideal was of highly differentiated domestic spaces. In the eighteenth century, multifunction rooms were common; a general room in which most gathering, cooking, and eating took place—a sort of kitchen-living room—was called the "houseplace" and was the center of the house. But this eighteenth-century style was replaced by a Victorian preference for houses in which every room had a single and specific use even when this resulted in small rooms and inconvenient layouts. Servants did not sleep in their masters' bedrooms; bedrooms now separated servants and employers, parents and children. Public rooms were no longer for sleeping at night. This ideal was firmly in place by the 1850s: an 1838 book on suburban villas carefully explains that a nursery was a special room dedicated to children, but an 1864 book assumes that dedicated nurseries were common and had always existed. The journal *The Architect* explained that "every important function of life required a separate room," and that to proceed otherwise was "unwholesome [and] immoral."[14]

Both privacy and single use were ideals, not realities. Within the home, families below the upper middle-class level found themselves too strapped for space to differentiate as highly as standards dictated. Many kitchens remained resolutely multi-purpose, especially in smaller homes. Children of the same sex often shared bedrooms. And although servants were, ideally, far away and neither seen nor heard by the family and its guests, the reality was that the sounds and smells of cleaning and cooking preparation were often in evidence, and lower middle-class women often worked alongside their servants. They might also have their sitting room do double duty as the dining room or even as a secondary kitchen. But dining rooms and parlors were never used for sleeping or other private functions if it was at all possible.

Upper-class homes were quite public, the site of various formal and political displays and of weeks-long house parties with numerous guests. Even for the middle class, homes were never entirely private; guests would not typically see bedrooms, but they would certainly be in the dining room and parlor. And in both of these classes, the presence of servants, who could both see and hear as well be seen and heard, introduced strangers into the home. For the lower classes, homes remained places of work, especially women's outwork, throughout the era. For example, early in the period, working-class women might prepare cotton for weaving in the home; Samuel Crompton remembered that his mother would "bat the cotton wool on a wire riddle"; once it had been soaked and cleaned, "each separate dollop of wool [was] placed on the bread rack under the beams of the kitchen-loft to dry."[15] Home, then, was not private. Nor was it always a refuge: as the site from which working-class women struggled to feed and clothe their families, home was for them a site of unending labor.

Homes varied by social station. The richest aristocrats had a house in London and one or more large country houses at which they spend some part of the year. Provincial elites would not have second homes in London but would have large houses with many rooms. In either, there would be separate space for the many live-in servants needed to run such establishments. For the middle classes, there were two main types of house: the row or terrace house, and the detached or semidetached villa. Terrace houses were more common, more concentrated in cities, and until the later nineteenth century more popular; for much of the century they were the norm for the urban middle class. They had a hall that ran the length of the house, with doors on one side that led into the various rooms, and a stairway up the center. Villas were found mainly in the suburbs, and were likely to have many small rooms and clear boundaries between public and private spaces. An upper middle-class family might have 12 rooms on five floors; a lower middle-class family would have four to six rooms on three floors. In larger homes, reception rooms included a dining room and morning room on the ground floor and a drawing room on the first floor, plus perhaps a library, conservatory, or billiard room; upstairs there would be bedrooms for adults on the second floor, and for servants and children on the upper floor or floors. In smaller homes (where only one servant worked), the ground floor would have public gathering rooms, and the upper floor would have all the bedrooms. Whatever the size and location of the home, various rooms had specific connotations. Since visits to the doctor or hospital were rare, every bedroom was also a potential sick-room or lying-in room, and women were held responsible by doctors for the health of their families. The library, study, and dining room were all seen as masculine spaces, though the dining room was a gathering place in which some families spent much of the day. Morning rooms, where they existed, were female; better-off women used them to conduct their housekeeping and correspondence and to receive more intimate friends.

Home decoration was extremely important. For much of the Victorian period, design experts despaired over the tastes of the middle class; indeed the Great Exhibition of 1851 was intended in part to educate the public in such matters (though the public remained resolutely committed to whimsical items of which designers disapproved). The Victorian middle classes were deeply committed to home decoration; while today we think of this as a feminine pursuit, earlier in the period Victorian middle-class men were quite interested in and even dominated home interior decisions. The middle classes decorated to demonstrate their taste, to claim or cement their social status, and by the end of the century as a form of self-expression. However in the earlier Victorian period it remained fairly restrained; middle-class couples decorated their homes once, usually upon marriage, and rooms were fairly spare.

The physical and ideological center of the middle-class home was the parlor (also called the drawing room). By the 1840s it was for entertaining and relaxing only, never for working or sleeping; callers were received here, and the family might read, do fancy work, or hold family prayers. Simultaneously public and intimate, parlors combined domestic ideology with consumerism and proclaimed a family's values and taste to itself and to the world. In upper middle-class families used daily, in lower middle-class homes kept "for best" and rarely entered, the parlor was both intimate, the symbol and space of the family, and public, where they displayed their best selves to the world.

Working class homes were quite different—smaller and more likely to be in the city center. Before 1850, the best working-class housing was in "through terraced" houses. These had two stories with two rooms on each floor, and were attached to other homes only on the sides, allowing both light and access at front and back. Far more common were back-to-back houses. These housed the majority of the urban industrial working class, and were especially common in the Midlands, West Riding, and South Lancashire. Back-to-back houses were attached to other homes on the backs and sides, with light and their own wall on the front only, and shared central courts or alleys with many other families. Back-to-back houses could be one-up-one-down, with two rooms total on two floors, or two-up-two-down like through terraced houses. Families who could not afford even a one-up-one-down back-to-back house lived in one or two rooms carved out of a larger house, or in cellar dwellings, which were often damp or even wet. Unmarried workers often could not afford their own homes and boarded with others.

1870–1914: Centers, slums, solutions

Over the later Victorian period, Britain continued to urbanize, with cities becoming much larger. In 1871, Manchester was home to 400,000 people. Glasgow's population more than doubled from 330,000 to 785,000 in 1911, and Edinburgh's nearly tripled to 507,000. Coatbridge, an iron and coal mining town in Lanarkshire, Scotland, grew from a population of 742 people in 1831 to 30,000 in 1891. In contrast, in 1871 only 15% of the Irish population lived in cities of more than 5,000 people (though Ulster, in the north, was urbanizing).[16] In 1890, 48% of the population of the United Kingdom (Great Britain and Ireland together) lived in cities of 20,000 or more people; the United Kingdom was now truly urban.

In 1911, England and Wales had a population of 36 million, Scotland and Ireland each had about 4.5 million, and the population of London was over 7 million, more than the entire population of England and Wales in 1700.

As Victorians worried about the rise of the city, the countryside remained extremely important. While population was concentrated in urban spaces, these were very small compared with the countryside; in 1911 only 3.3% of the acreage of Wales and England, and far less of Ireland and Scotland, were given to urban space, and as late as 1950 only 9.7% of the land in England and Wales—and only 2.5% of the land in Scotland—was urban. Even in the later Victorian period, Wales was divided into an industrialized southeast and a rural north. Similarly, Scotland was dominated by a rural industrial society characterized by farm servants, tenant farmers, public service workers (who ran the post office, railway, and the like), tradespeople, and the local gentry family. One observer called the entire United Kingdom "an empty country dotted with small crowded spots called towns."[17]

The living conditions of the rural poor remained sparse. A report from the 1890s notes that even a two-storied cottage was only a living room and a small back kitchen downstairs, and then a staircase—often little more than a ladder—to two bedrooms upstairs. Lack of space meant that there was little furniture, perhaps one dresser or chest, a table, and a few wooden chairs (families could not usually all sit together for a meal). Outdoor toilets were shared by two or more houses, and many kitchens lacked ovens and sinks; women might bring pies or roasts to the local baker to bake for them, but otherwise cooked when they could in single pot over the living room fire. Bread, lard, and weak tea dominated the menu, with vegetables from the family garden and some bacon and cheese for flavor. Fast-growing nostalgia notwithstanding, the homes of the rural poor were anything but idyllic.

The capital, London, grew unplanned. Observers of the British capital frequently contrasted London's piecemeal development—the result of its decentralized political structure—with the grand urban planning called "Haussmannization" (after Baron Georges-Eugène Haussman (1809–1891)) that produced late nineteenth-century Paris. Yet London retained a fairly well-defined core and a clear status as a national and imperial capital. Its massive size—by 1881, over 10% of the population of Great Britain lived in London, and many more visited, courtesy of the railways—meant that life in London was both unique and a common experience. London's center was characterized by national and imperial politics at Buckingham Palace and the Houses of Parliament; entertainment and shopping in the Regent Street, Oxford Street, and Leicester Square; financial, commercial, and legal transactions in Lincoln's Inn and the City. Other key areas included Trafalgar Square and Hyde Park as sites of public gatherings and speeches; the Strand, the street on which most newspapers and periodicals were published, from which many travelers started their tours of the city, and South Kensington, site (after the Great Exhibition) of the South Kensington Museum and the Natural History Museum, with their massive displays of imperial science and culture.

City centers were massively developed during the later Victorian period and represented the best of what a city had to offer. Major provincial cities such as Birmingham and Leeds, and smaller towns such as Burslem in the Midlands and Merthyr Tydfil in Wales, had well-developed centers with entertainment, shopping, business, and commerce. These grew as their middle classes used city development to assert their identities. If London proclaimed its imperial identity to the world, smaller cities proclaimed their more modest status on a regional and national level. These cities developed elaborate civic and cultural infrastructures. Frequently, these centers were built by the growing middle classes, who not only proposed and funded key projects but used the city center as a stage on which to proclaim their importance and perform their identities. This was particularly true in provincial cities such as Manchester, which grew along with and because of their middle classes. One newspaper proudly declared that the warehouses of Manchester were "huge stone guardians watching over the morals and health of the city" that had a "humanizing, educating influence."[18] In Birmingham, Leeds, and Manchester, central spaces and civic identity were erected around such structures, which were central to the identities of these towns and their prosperous middle classes. In 1888, Thomas Greenwood (1851–1908), a tireless promoter of museums and libraries, argued that every town should have both, because "a Museum and Free Library are as necessary for the mental and moral health of the citizens as good sanitary arrangements [and] because the existence or absence of a Museum and Free Library in a town is a standard of the intelligence and public spirit manifested in that town."[19] The middle classes hoped that museums would elevate working-class visitors, and despaired when they acted rowdy, loud, casual, or insufficiently reverent in them, and when they felt entitled to rather than overwhelmed by them.

The central spaces and civic identity of these cities were also built around public cultural events such as the Hallé music concerts at the Free Trade Hall in Manchester. These were classical music concerts, organized by well-known pianist Charles Hallé (1819–1895), for which season and cheap single tickets were available; similar series existed in Leeds and Birmingham. These concert series established classical music as something run by middle-class civic leaders, but part of a public sphere of art available to the whole urban community. Also central to the public culture of the middle class were a seemingly endless succession of public pageants and ceremonials marking the openings of new buildings, the unveiling of new statues, the funerals of civic leaders, and royal coronations and visits. As refuges from and within these quintessentially public city centers, elite and middle-class men founded gentlemen's clubs. Cared for by staff, members could read the papers, socialize with one another, eat, drink, or even entertain guests. Clubs were thus both comfortably domestic and resolutely male spaces. While they had reputations as centers of illicit assignations, more often men went to them not to flee domesticity but to find it. Late marriage meant that men in their twenties and thirties were usually unmarried; clubs provided domestic space for them. For married men, clubs were an alternate domestic space; they could relax, not at home surrounded by wife, children, and familial responsibilities, but in clubland, the oasis of home in the city.

Urban slums continued to be areas of concern, both because of the terrible poverty in which their inhabitants lived and because they were so near to "respectable" areas. Social investigator Charles Booth (1840–1916), created "Maps Descriptive of London Poverty" (1898–1899) that were colored to indicate to income and class of inhabitants of every street in the capital. They revealed not only widespread poverty but worrying proximity between classes. Writer Walter Besant (1836–1901) claimed, in his study of *East London* (1901), that London's East End was home to fully one-twentieth of Britain's total population; it was also within walking distance of the fashionable West End. In the northern provincial cities, commercial centers were ringed by slums; in smaller cities the high streets were backed by slums. This pattern was of juxtaposition was replicated in other aspects of city life: pubs were often next to churches and, in the latter part of the century, middle-class women (who were shopping) and prostitutes (who were working) often wore similar fashions and walked in the same high streets, albeit for different commercial purposes. One response to this spatial proximity was a constant effort—through urban planning, public health schemes, political interventions, and rhetorical strategies—to maintain the center and the slum as two distinct zones rather than as the single multivalent areas they were, or to eradicate slums altogether. Another response to slums was an attempt to contain them rhetorically rather than geographically. Descriptions of slums and their inhabitants—styled "slumland"—were central to characterizations of the modern city. Slumland sensationalism made for popular reading, and newspapers did it to sell papers, but also to establish spatial boundaries. Just as Disraeli had done in *Sybil* in 1845, writer J. Cuming Walters described slums as foreign lands in his *Scenes in Slumland* series in the *Birmingham Daily Gazette* in 1901—though worryingly, they were foreign without being far-off. Slum homes were often described using words for animal dwellings such as rookeries, dens and hides. Slums were described as "dark and grim," full of diseased and stinking air full of "vapours that assail the lungs like poison"; the streets were depicted as crowded with dirty children; slum dwellings were portrayed as chaotic, with rooms that were used for multiple and conflicting functions. Slum inhabitants were repeatedly described as aimless, sleepy, and stagnant, with "trollops . . . idl[ing] around" and "groups of men . . . hanging about listlessly."[20]

From the 1860s, there were various pushes to solve the problem of slums and their miasmas, though housing and sanitary reform were very disruptive and so were often greeted with more resistance than receptivity by slum inhabitants. The Great Stink resulted in the quick passage of an Act to dig new sewers in London and to build an embankment along the Thames. Major housing acts and public health acts were passed in 1868 and 1875. In many cities, slums were demolished, and replaced by broad new roads. More affordable houses, called bye-law houses, were built; rising wages and falling food prices helped to make them affordable. Birmingham, under radical Liberal mayor Joseph Chamberlain, became a model of progress, with improved gas and water provisions, fewer slums, healthier housing, and broad shopping streets. However, in most cities slums were torn down without adequate planning for housing those who had lived in them. The original slums disappeared, but rather than being offered better options, the urban poor were squeezed even more tightly into nearby areas. Some observers realized that urban poverty was as likely to be caused as alleviated by urban reform schemes. By the 1880s, recognizing the negative and traumatic effect of all these reforms on the working class and the poor was so common that it had become a journalistic cliché. Housing reformers became disillusioned, and convinced that urban poverty and criminality were sociobiological and not amenable to reform.

Some chose to visit or even live in slums. From mid-century, "slumming" became popular among those portions of the upper and upper middle classes that traditionally did philanthropic visiting. Slums were simultaneously familiar and foreign; they were also attractive and repulsive, and, for many slummers, sites of sexual titillation and exploration. Slummers were also developing new governmental bureaucracies of social welfare, such as factory inspection, and emerging professions such as social work. Many were devout Christians who sought to love the poor as Jesus had. Some slumming was casual, intermittent, or even touristic; by the 1890s, guidebooks to London included tips for those who wished to see a slum as part of their visit to the capital. Others had sustained commitments to tackling the problems of poverty and to the people with whom they worked. Slumming had multiple purposes and effects beyond the stated one of learning about and aiding the poor. The practice helped to create cultural and geographic boundaries, establishing slums as conceptually distant from slummers' comfortable homes.

As traditional markers of class began to break down, middle-class Victorians were plagued by worries about authenticity and recognition, how to tell who was who on the crowded and anonymous city streets. From about 1870, the growth in working-class leisure time and the availability of fashionable mass-produced clothing—especially cheap crinolines and ready-made suits—rendered neither leisure nor dress reliable indicators of class. Of course, to the working class, this was not a problem but an opportunity. Lower middle-class clerks and salesgirls, working-class women, or prostitutes might now command the same respect as middle-class women out shopping; they all walked the same streets, wearing the same fashions. Young men of marginal status, the "mashers," "counter-jumpers," "swells," and "gents" who dressed fashionably, could be taken for established gentlemen. The provincial satirical press delighted in exposing and mocking these parvenus, but this did not solve the problem or close off the opportunity. City centers remained exciting spaces of consumption and leisure that were, simultaneously, problematic spaces of counterfeit identity and personal danger; negotiating these challenges became ever more difficult.

Some of the fiercest important debates were over women's presence in city centers. After 1870, women of various classes gained many urban freedoms, as lower middle-class women began working as clerks and salesgirls, as middle-class women began frequenting the department stores that made shopping a leisure activity, as slumming increased in popularity, and as activist women began working as social investigators of urban problems. Better transportation

[handwritten margin note:] the gap between the classes are closing so well that it is getting harder to tell which class someone is placed.

allowed women to come into the center; department stores that were safe and full of conveniences, such as toilets and cafés, allowed them to stay all day. But crowds, mud, the threat of sexual danger, and the humiliating possibility of being mistaken for a prostitute meant that respectable women's spatial freedoms were curtailed by a sense of lurking danger. Prostitution, the "great sin of great cities,"[21] was a central preoccupation, discussed at length by philanthropists, social purity activists, public health officials, feminists, the legal and law enforcement communities, and politicians in Parliament and elsewhere. Of course, prostitutes did not consider themselves sinners; they were women who had limited employment options and were making a difficult choice. Many worked as prostitutes only when they had to, and remained accepted members of their working-class communities. Many observations about prostitution were worries about space and spatial order. In 1877, a Birmingham periodical commented on the many prostitutes who gathered near the Midland Hotel as the theatres were closing. According to commentators, prostitutes who solicited in public streets tempted the unwary and introduced disorder into the public space of the streets. Ideally, prostitutes acted as a form of intestine or sewer, conduits by which sexual immorality was flushed from the city, but bodily metaphors could easily go wrong, so that there was also the fear that prostitutes who plied their trade in parks infected the city's lungs. Prostitutes who appeared at society occasions mixed with and could be confused with respectable women. Most Victorian attempts to regulate prostitution (notably the 1860s Contagious Diseases Acts) aimed not to stop prostitution but to contain it spatially, in specific urban areas or in brothels outside the city centers. Such regulatory schemes, which allowed the police to accost women merely on suspicion of prostitution or venereal disease, not only limited prostitution to specific areas, but limited the ability of all women to move freely in public.

Looking at urban life after 1870, some historians have emphasized the dangers of urban life; others, the fun of negotiating these new spaces. Peter Bailey emphasizes the opportunities for real or imagined adventure that were created by liminal spaces such as railway carriages. Judith Walkowitz stresses various dangers—especially to women—and the ways in which threats of sexual danger such as the Jack the Ripper murders in London in 1888 were used to restrict middle-class women's movements by establishing whole areas into which women who wanted to remain safe would not venture. People were in part defined by the spaces through which they could legitimately or safely move. This was especially apparent when people transgressed spatial boundaries, as when prostitutes mingled at high society gatherings, or workers protested in the fashionable West End, attracting attention and outrage. As working hours declined, where and how working-class people spent their leisure time became a matter of concern to their social betters. This led to the rational recreation movement, which unsuccessfully tried to impose on the working class middle-class standards about how leisure time ought to be spent.

The movement to provide city parks continued. The 1875 Public Health Act allowed local authorities to acquire and maintain land for recreation. Many, including housing reformer Octavia Hill, believed that contact with nature would help the lower classes accept their station in life. Park promoters believed that physical activity in parks would lead to an "increase in the mental powers" and a "decrease in crime, drunkenness, and immorality." They were the ideal place to provide the poor and downtrodden with "amusements of the right sort . . . [so] that the better influences will gradually displace the bad."[22] Others worried that the poor would resist redemption and would ruin any green space into which they were allowed. Between 1848 and 1885, 158 parks were opened in cities and towns throughout England. London's Hampstead Heath was established as a public park by the Metropolitan Board of Works in the 1880s. This was a major event in the lives of lower-income Londoners; by the turn of the century, one contemporary estimated that over a hundred thousand Londoners flocked there on every bank (public) holiday.

The openings of parks continued to be festivals of middle-class self-congratulation; when Burslem Park was built in Staffordshire in 1894, the town's bourgeois civic elite participated in laying foundation stones and inaugurating buildings, and later listened to speeches, planned and participated in an inaugural procession, and attended an exclusive "public" luncheon when the park was opened. Local manufacturers presented the city with inscribed fountains, shelters, and benches. The park was a celebration of the local middle class. But rather than engaging in new rational recreations, working-class people often replicated their existing leisure patterns inside the parks. Many working-class people complained about the conditions on which green space was made available. For example, in 1889 the populist *Reynolds's Newspaper* complained that Regent's Park, St James's Park, and Kensington Gardens, all technically open to the public, allowed entry only to those who were "well-behaved and properly dressed"; as public property, the parks should be open, Reynolds argued, to Londoners of all classes, not restricted to "fashionable promenaders."[23]

The suburbs continued to develop. In the late nineteenth century many middle-class people lived in suburbs if they could afford it. Furthermore the "workmen's trains" that from 1864 ran between cities and suburbs allowed some lower middle- and working-class families to move out to the suburbs and commute to work (George and Weedon Grossmith's famous *The Diary of a Nobody* (1892) depicts life in a lower middle-class suburb of London). By the end of the nineteenth century, one in every eight clerks who worked in London lived in the suburbs of Camberwell, Peckham, Holloway, Walthamstow, Wood Green, and Hackney. Historians once thought that workmen's trains were affordable for and used by only the upper working class and lower middle class. However, recent work on London's suburbs has revealed that this was not the case. From the 1880s many workers below the upper working class lived in the suburbs and used the workmen's trains, including unskilled male laborers, men who had only irregular employment, and even women and children, who earned very low wages. (The suburbs remained out of the reach of poorest sections of the working class, who had only casual employment and walked to work.)

At every economic level, families chose where they lived as carefully as their means allowed, including urban working-class families; for example, in early twentieth-century Wapping in east London, one resident recalled that "If you crossed the Dock Bridge, or lived beyond it, you were said to be 'on the other side.' . . . They were a community on their own and so were we, although we were all in one parish." One street might have a "rough" and a "respectable" end, and working-class families would sometimes move down the street or one street over when they could afford to.[24] After 1870, Irish and immigrant workers and casual laborers (who were especially low-paid) were least likely to leave the central housing districts, which often developed reputations as dens of foreignness in the middle of English and Scottish cities. Hundreds of thousands of Irish immigrants lived in the industrial cities of western Scotland and in the city of Dundee on the east coast of Scotland. They were concentrated in low-paid, unskilled jobs and lived in segregated neighborhoods that were maintained by their Scottish-born children.

In more elite homes, privacy and segregation of space continued to be more important than how crowded the home or the rooms were, the size of each space, or the flow of the houseplan. Houses that architect Robert Kerr (1823–1904) designed always had many specialized rooms—kitchen, scullery, pantry, larder— even when these were tiny, cramped, and difficult to work in. In Kerr's book *The Gentleman's House, or How to plan English residences from the parsonage to the palace* (3rd edition 1871) he ranked privacy as more important than either comfort or convenience. Shirley Foster Murphy, author of *Our Homes, and How to Make them Healthy* (1883) cautioned that "each room must be carefully planned with a view to its special occupation or use."[25] In her 1889 book on *The Art of Housekeeping*, journalist and interior decoration expert Mrs. Haweis even disapproved of writing in bedrooms. In the late nineteenth century, when middle-class homes got plumbing, space segregation also means separate rooms for the bathtub and the toilet. Middle-class home decoration had become a relentless pursuit; by the late Victorian period middle-class couples redecorated approximately every seven years. In between redecorations, they also purchased smaller items constantly; the clutter that we associate with Victorian interiors was a feature of the late nineteenth century. While middle-class men remained committed to domesticity, some historians argue that they retreated from home decoration after 1895 in part because Oscar Wilde's trial created an uncomfortable link between aesthetic pursuits and effeminacy.

In the working class, a home's size and cleanliness were important indicators of status. Two rooms were the minimum for achieving respectability. From 1870 rising real wages and cheap workmen's trains meant that some working families were able to afford a through terraced house that, though it had no front garden or hallway, had a living-room, kitchen or scullery, and perhaps even a parlor downstairs, and two or more bedrooms and perhaps a bath upstairs. Some could think about purchasing a small piano with which to decorate the parlor and impress the neighbors. However, two- and four-room back-to-backs remained common in many cities. Neighbors carefully scrutinized one another's homes to see how clean they were. This meant that women had great power: their housekeeping skills determined their families' respectability. It also meant that they spent hours keeping hearths swept, stoves blacked, curtains starched, front steps, door sills and even milk chutes whitened—any part of the house open to public scrutiny was kept scrupulously clean. In spite of rising wages and housing reform, overcrowding remained a problem. In 1891, overcrowding was defined as more than two adults per room; children under ten years of age counted as half of an adult, and babies under one year of age did not count at all. Under this definition, a three-room house could be home to four adults, four children, and any number of babies, without being overcrowded. Even so, the 1891 census indicated that 11.2% of the population of England and Wales was living in overcrowded quarters; in 1911 that figure was still 7.8%.

Working-class people, like middle-class people, furnished their homes with care and with an eye to display. Indeed, working-class wealth was put often put into items that could be displayed and could shore up the family's respectability. These included Sunday best clothing and elaborate funerals, but also included home decorations, such as figurines that were displayed on the mantelpiece (which might cycle in and out of pawnshops, weekly or in times of difficulty).

Working-class homes remained places of work for women and children. Women would bring home partially manufactured items to finish, such as "large bundles of umbrella frames . . . to be covered . . . cages full of hats, which yet want the silk and the binding," and the like.[26] In addition, very small houses and flats meant that working-class home life often spilled out into stairways and streets in a variety of ways; children played outside, using landings, stairs, and balconies, as well as the street. They were collectively supervised by the community and could be disciplined by their own mother or a neighbor. The street constituted a semi-domestic space. While displays of respectability and status such as pianos were done for the benefit of judgmental neighborhood eyes, the neighborhood was also a crucial unit of space and community for the working class. Neighbors were bound by ties of mutual assistance, both casual and formal. One woman from Barrow, an industrial town, remembered that women were in and out of each other's homes, asking "Can I borrow a cup of sugar? Have you a bit of margarine?" and that such debts were always carefully repaid. Neighbors kept an eye on one another's children and helped out in times of sickness or a death in the family. In some working-class areas, most married couples were from the same parish, and many had even been raised on the same street.[27]

[margin annotation: Neighbors help out of societal rules]

Middle-class commentators were deeply troubled by the fact that the rooms in working-class homes were multi-purpose. Families might take in lodgers (even middle-class families did this) or live in lodgings; both were choices made out of economic necessity that eroded the privacy and the boundaries of the home. Kitchens doubled as dining rooms; bedrooms were shared by parents and children, or by children of different sexes. Furthermore, working-class homes themselves were multi-purpose. Since so many working-class mothers did some sort of paid work at home, usually finishing mass-produced items, kitchens and parlors were crowded with partially completed shirts or umbrellas. This mixing of home and work space was very distressing to middle-class observers, but was an untroubling fact of life to ordinary working people. So was the lack of clear boundaries separating homes and their occupants from public space.

***

For much of the Victorian period, Britain prided itself on being an urban, industrial nation, although that description was as aspirational as it was real. England, the most urban of the four nations, could only be called urban from 1851, and even then only nominally so; Wales, Scotland, and Ireland were still decisively rural societies. By the early twentieth century Britain (though not Ireland) was an urban society. The British rejected urbanity and industrialization as false and ugly and began to identify the "true" Britain as rural, characterized by pastures and fields, folk music, and half-timbered pubs. This veneration of an idealized rural life tells us much, not about where Britain was going, but about the distance it had travelled during the Victorian period.

Notes

1   Quoted in Simon Gunn, "The Spatial Turn: Changing Histories of Space and Place," Simon Gunn and Robert J. Morris (eds), *Identities in Space: Contested Terrains in the Western City since 1850* (Aldershot: Ashgate, 2001), p. 1; emphasis added.
2   Anthony Trollope, *Dr Thorne*, Chapter 1.
3   "The Municipal Elections," *Birmingham Daily Post*, October 16, 1877, p. 8; "Birmingham Municipal Elections," *Birmingham Daily Post*, October 14, 1908, p. 11, quoted in Alan Mayne, *The Imagined Slum: Newspaper Representation in Three Cities, 1870–1914* (Leicester: Leicester University Press, 1993), pp. 158, 150.
4   *Liverpool Argus*, May, 1878, quoted in Hazel Conway, *People's Parks: The Design and Development of Victorian Parks in Britain* (Cambridge: Cambridge University Press, 1991), p. 208.
5   "The Moral Influence of Decoration," reprinted from the *Queen*, in *Furniture Gazette*, August 21, 1875, p. 105; Revd. F. Barham Zincke, "A Dishomed Nation," *Contemporary Review* 38 (August 1880): 179–180; quoted in Deborah Cohen, *Household Gods: The British and Their Possessions* (New Haven, CT: Yale University Press, 2006), p. 28.
6   Andrew J. Croll, "Civilizing the Urban: Popular Culture, Public Space and Urban Meaning, Merthyr c. 1870–1914." Dissertation, University of Wales, Cardiff, 1997, p. 20.
7   Peter Mandler, *The Fall and Rise of the Stately Home* (New Haven: Yale University Press, 1997), p. 72. *Murray's Shropshire, Cheshire and Lancs.*, 1870 edition, pp. 107–108, and *National Sunday League Record*, August 1858, pp. 277–278, quoted in Mandler, pp. 84–85.
8   *Daily Telegraph*, April 2, 1858, p. 5, quoted in Lydia Nead, *Victorian Babylon: People, Streets, and Images in Nineteenth-Century London* (New Haven, CT: Yale University Press, 2000), p. 86.
9   Patrick Joyce, *The Rule of Freedom: Liberalism and the Modern City* (London: Verso, 2003), p. 233.
10 *West Briton,* 2 February 1849, quoted in Andy Croll, "Street Disorder, Surveillance and Shame: Regulating Behaviour in the Public Spaces of the Late Victorian British Town," *Social History* [London] 24 (1999): 250–268, p. 262.
11 Benjamin Disraeli, *Sybil: Or, the Two Nations*, introduction by R.A.B. Butler, edited by Thom Brain (Harmondsworth, UK: Penguin Books, 1908), p. 96.
12 Michelle Allen, *Cleansing the City: Sanitary Geographies in Victorian London* (Athens: Ohio University Press, 2008), pp. 22, 117.
13 *Select Committee on Drunkenness*, BPP, vol. VIII, 1834, p. 328, quoted in Conway, p. 31.

14 Quoted in Judith Flanders, *Inside the Victorian Home: A Portrait of Domestic Life in Victorian England* (New York: W.W. Norton, 2003), p. 37.

15 Gilbert James French, *The Life and Times of Samuel Crompton, Inventor of the Spinning Machine Called the Mule* (London: Simkin, Marshall and Co., 1859), pp. 91–92.

16 Paolo Malanima and Oliver Volckart, "Urbanisation 1700–1870," Center for Economic Policy Research, 3rd RTN Summer Symposium, 26–28 October 2007. Available online at: www.cepr.org/meets/wkcn/1/1679/papers/Malanima-Volckart-Chapter.pdf (accessed April 22, 2011).

17 L.G. Chiozza Money, *Riches and Poverty*, 2nd edition (London: Methuen & Co, 1906), p. 79.

18 *Freelance*, September 19, 1873, quoted in Gunn, p. 42.

19 Thomas Greenwood, *Museums and Art Galleries* (London, 1888), p. 339, quoted in Kate Hill, "'Thoroughly Imbued with the Spirit of Ancient Greece': Symbolism and Space in Victorian Civic Culture," in Alan Kidd and David Nicholls (eds), *Gender, Civic Culture and Consumerism: Perspectives on Middle-Class Identity in Britain, 1800–1940* (Manchester: Manchester University Press, 1999), p. 103.

20 Quoted in Mayne, pp. 170, 176, 167.

21 "Birmingham Cribs," *Lion*, May 10, 1877; quoted in in Simon Gunn, *The Public Culture of the Victorian Middle-Class: Ritual and Authority and the English industrial City 1840–1914* (Manchester: Manchester University Press, 2000), p. 64.

22 Francis Fuller, "On our Paramount Duty to Provide Wholesome and Pure Recreation and Amusement for the People, and the Dire Results and Dangers which Attend our Neglect Of It," *Transactions of the National Association for the Promotion of Social Science* (1874): 747; Lord Reginald Brabazon, "Open Spaces and Physical Education," *National Review* 8 (1886): 488; both quoted in Nan H. Dreher, "The Virtuous and the Verminous: Turn-of-the-Century Moral Panics in London's Public Parks," *Albion* 29.2 (Summer 1997): 253.

23 *Reynolds's Newspaper*, April 28, 1889, p. 3, quoted in Peter Thorsheim, "Green Space and Class in Imperial London," in Andrew C. Isenberg (ed.), *The Nature of Cities: Culture, Landscape, and Urban Space* (Rochester: University of Rochester Press, 2006), p. 30.

24 Paul Johnson, "Conspicuous Consumption and Working-Class Culture in Late-Victorian and Edwardian Britain," *Transactions of the Royal Historical Society*, Fifth Series, Vol. 38 (1988): 40, 33–34.

25 Murphy, p. 85, quoted in Thad Logan, *The Victorian Parlour* (Cambridge: Cambridge University Press, 2001), p. 26.

26 Quoted in Sally Alexander, "Women's Work in Nineteenth-Century London: A Study of the Years 1820–50," Elizabeth Whitelegg et al. (eds), *The Changing Experience of Women* (Oxford: Martin Robertson, 1982) p. 37.

27 Andrew August, *The British Working Class 1832–1940* (Harlow: Longman, 2007), pp. 104, 97.

Relevant fiction that students might enjoy

Emily Eden, *The Semi-Attached House* (1859)
George Gissing, *New Grub Street* (1891)
George Gissing, *In the Year of Jubilee* (1894)
Flora Thompson, *Lark Rise to Candleford* (1945)

Further reading

Simon T. Abernethy "Opening Up the Suburbs: Workmen's Trains in London 1860–1914," *Urban History* 42, 1 (2015): 70–88.

Peter Bailey, "Adventures in Space: Victorian Railway Erotics, or Taking Alienation for a Ride," *Journal of Victorian Culture* 9, 1 (2004): 1–21.

Deborah Cohen, *Household Gods: The British and Their Possessions* (Cambridge, MA: Yale University Press, 2006).

Hazel Conway, *People's Parks: The Design and Development of Victorian Parks in Britain* (Cambridge University Press 1991).

Andy Croll, *Civilizing the Urban: Popular Culture and Public Space, Merthyr c. 1870–1914* (Cardiff: Univ. of Wales Press, 2000).

Anna Davin, *Growing Up Poor: Home, School, and Street in London, 1870–1914* (London: Rivers Oram Press; Concord, MA: Paul and Company, 1996).

Andreas Fahrmeir and Elfie Rembold (eds), *Representation of British Cities: The Transformation of Urban Space, 1700–2000* (Berlin: Philo, 2003).

Judith Flanders, *Inside the Victorian Home: A Portrait of Domestic Life in Victorian England* (New York: W.W. Norton, 2003).

Judith Flanders, *The Victorian City: Everyday Life in Dickens' London* (London: Atlantic Books, 2012).

Simon Gunn, *The Public Culture of the Victorian Middle Class: Ritual and Authority and the English Industrial City 1840–1914* (Manchester: Manchester University Press, 2000).

Seth Koven, *Slumming: Sexual and Social Politics in Victorian London* (Princeton: Princeton University Press, 2004).

Thad Logan, *The Victorian Parlour* (Cambridge, UK and New York: Cambridge University Press, 2001).

Alan Mayne, *The Imagined Slum: Newspaper Representation in Three Cities, 1870–1914* (London: Leicester University Press, 1993).

Amy Milne-Smith, "A Flight to Domesticity? Making a Home in the Gentlemen's Clubs of London, 1880–1914," *Journal of British Studies* 45 (October 2006): 796–818.

Judith R. Walkowitz, *City of Dreadful Delight: Narratives of Sexual Danger in Late-Victorian London* (Chicago: University of Chicago Press, 1992).

Online resources

Subject guide—urban history on British History Online: www.british-history.ac.uk/using-bho/urban-guide

History in Focus—The City: www.history.ac.uk/ihr/Focus/City/websites.html

Centre for Urban History at Leicester: www2.le.ac.uk/departments/urbanhistory

Atlas of Urban Icons: http://journals.cambridge.org/fulltext_content/supplementary/urban_icons_companion/index.htm

The Victorian Society, campaigning for Victorian and Edwardian architecture: www.victoriansociety.org.uk/

Parks and Gardens UK: www.parksandgardens.org/

Museum of London: www.museumoflondon.org.uk

UCL Bloomsbury: www.ucl.ac.uk/bloomsbury-project/

Martin Daunton on "London's 'Great Stink' and Victorian Urban Planning" for the BBC: www.bbc.co.uk/history/trail/victorian_britain/social_conditions/victorian_urban_planning_01.shtml

Emma Griffin on "Manchester in the 19th century" for the British Library: www.bl.uk/romantics-and-victorians/articles/manchester-in-the-19th-century

Victorian City Centre—Liverpool: http://public-art.shu.ac.uk/other/liverpool/index.html

Charles Booth Online Archive: http://booth.lse.ac.uk/

The Rowntree Society—Seebohm Rowntree and Poverty: www.rowntreesociety.org.uk/seebohm-rowntree-and-poverty/

2 "Discussions on the subject of reform"

Politics

Introduction

"Politics" is often defined as the art, science, and practice of governing. But to focus only on these is to study only those who governed. Such a narrow focus is problematic, especially at the start of the Victorian era, when that group was extremely small. We would do better to use historian Rohan McWilliam's much broader definition of politics as "the ways in which the distribution of power within society is understood and debated,"[1] which allows us to see more clearly the connections between the powerful and the obscure, the rich and the poor, elected officials, voters, and the disenfranchised. The majority of the Victorian population, while they did not participate in the formal political institutions of law-making, governing, or even voting, often cared a great deal about the ends to which power was used by those who possessed it. In 1914, the two political parties were more internally cohesive and more distinct than they had been in 1820; the House of Commons was more decisively the seat of power; many more people were able to directly participate in and influence formal politics than had been in 1820; and the government intervened in many more aspects of life.

This chapter seeks to lay out some of the principal Victorian political debates and events. It treats the Victorian era in three parts: the early Victorian period, from 1820 until 1850, during which politics was marked by the extension of the franchise to most middle-class men and by an increasingly formal, organized national politics; the mid-Victorian years, from 1850 until the mid-1880s, which saw the passage of two major Reform Acts that enlarged the electorate and saw the development of political parties and party leadership in their modern incarnations; and the late Victorian period, from the mid-1880s until the start of World War One, which saw major unrest in the unresolved areas of working-class and female political power and the Irish question, and a constitutional crisis. We focus here on national electoral politics, rather than local or regional politics—important as they were to so many lives on a day-to-day basis—except as they impact the national level.

***

the balance of the British government

The British constitution, unlike the constitution of the United States, is not a single document. It is made up of laws, convention, and tradition, both written and unwritten, which dictate the form of government and the limits of power of its various branches. Britain's government includes both monarchy and Parliament, whose powers are defined and limited by the constitution. Since the late seventeenth century, the balance of power between the two had been tipping away from the monarch and towards Parliament. During the nineteenth century, the monarchy would become symbolic. Parliament's lower house, the house of Commons, would definitively come to be the center of government, while its upper house, the House of Lords, remained important into the twentieth century, before being reformed in 1911.

Parliament (on which the United States' Congress was modeled) consisted of two houses. The upper house, the House of Lords, was populated principally by several hundred noblemen who sat for life by virtue of their aristocratic titles. The lower house, the House of Commons, consisted of about six hundred men called members of Parliament, or MPs, who were elected to represent the counties and boroughs of England, Scotland, Wales, and Ireland. England had many more representatives than the other three countries, because of its status as first among these four equals. In practice, MPs, like members of the House of Lords, were wealthy landed men (not least because MPs received no salary). Many were the sons or brothers of men who sat in the Lords.

The most famous Victorian analysis of the roles and responsibilities of the various parts of government was Walter Bagehot's 1867 book *The English Constitution.* Bagehot argued that the best way to understand the balance among the various parts of the government was not to think about the checks and balances that existed between the legislative, executive, and judicial parts of government, but rather to understand that government had—and needed—two parts, the dignified and the efficient. The dignified parts were more apparent, and the efficient parts were more active, but both were necessary. The dignified parts of the constitution—the monarchy, and to a limited degree the House of Lords—legitimated governmental authority without exercising much of it; the efficient parts of the constitution—the House of Commons—exercised effective authority and combined executive and legislative functions. The monarchy and House of Lords were critical to the English constitution because they were dignified and therefore revered, and so made government legitimate in the eyes of the people. The House of Commons was vital because it legislated, expressed the will of the nation, and appointed the cabinet (or executive).

The world of formal politics was extremely limited in 1820. The monarch and members of the House of Lords held their positions by virtue of noble birth. (Similarly at the local level, which was far more central to day-to-day life for most people than Westminster, magistrates and Justices of the Peace came from local elites.) MPs were elected, by the 516,000 elite men who had the vote in a population of 21 million. Elite families controlled (through a variety of mechanisms relating to property ownership and voting rights) so many of the seats in the House of Commons that many MPs were in effect appointed rather than elected, in spite of the appearance of an electoral system. Voting privileges were highly restricted, according to a number of criteria. At the most basic level, the basis for the vote was the ownership of land. Voters had to be substantial property owners, because owning property indicated one's place in the social hierarchy; property meant that you had a stake in society and deserved a voice in the governing of the nation. Others, the theory went, had "virtual representation"—that is, voters voted not only on behalf of themselves but on behalf of their dependents (women, children, male lodgers). Until 1918, when a Representation of the People Act gave the vote to all men over the age of 21 and all women over the age of 30, property-holding—and the respectability and independence it implied—was the foundation of political rights. This is perhaps the most fundamental difference between Victorian political culture and our own.

There were other qualifications as well. Voters had to be men, because almost everyone in Britain, Europe, and the United States agreed that women were not sufficiently rational or educated to be political actors. Voters had to be members of the Church of England. This last is difficult for twenty-first century Americans to understand. Britain's Anglican Church was an "established church," that is, it was the official state religion (see Chapter 13), to which stated allegiance was a requirement of citizenship. This does not mean that Britain was a theocracy, a state governed by its religion, but it does mean that the church was part of the government and that Victorian Britons had no sense that church and state were or should be in any way separated. Those who chose to practice other religions, whether other forms of Protestantism, collectively referred to as nonconformity, or Roman Catholicism or Judaism, both of which were seen as even more oppositional, were also placing themselves in opposition to the state and could not be citizens.

Small as the electorate was, the world of true political power was smaller. The world of politics in the decades before the early nineteenth century was often referred to by radicals as "Old Corruption." The term was coined by radical William Cobbett (1763–1835) to describe a system of government (originally constructed to wage wars during the eighteenth century and the Napoleonic era) that was parasitical and that allowed the elite to grab power and money at the people's expense. Old Corruption, then, was the radical claim that the nation was ruled inefficiently and to the benefit of the rulers rather than the ruled. Elites monopolized political power not for the purposes of governing wisely but rather to enrich themselves. Politicians and officials obtained their posts through patronage and connections, not ability. Government was rife with sinecures, large undeserved pensions, and fraudulently awarded government contracts.

While there was a degree of truth in these accusations, the concept of Old Corruption was one promoted by radicals in part for their own ends. During the Victorian era, reforms replaced Old Corruption with a much smaller, less expensive government that was self-consciously committed to public service and the public good. Until recently historians believed radicals' claims about the degree of corruption in Old Corruption, and further believed that Old Corruption was substantially attacked only from the 1830s, and only because of radicals' agitations. Recent research has emphasized that critiques of Old Corruption came from within as well as without government, and that reforms were taking place long before 1830, the date often cited as the start of an "age of reform." A full generation before 1830, politicians were cultivating a governing style of disinterested public service and avoiding any appearance of impropriety and favoritism. Over the course of the first half of the nineteenth century, various reforms reduced the size of the state—which had become large and expensive during the frequent wars of the eighteenth century—and convinced the public that government was now a public trust. Successive governments introduced administrative reforms, reduced the tax burden on the poor, and redistributed taxation upwards. A desire for administrative efficiency, the rise of evangelical beliefs among some parts of the ruling elites, and calls for a more economical style of government all contributed to this shift, which was already in process when our period began in 1820 and continued through periods of reform in the 1830s (by a Whig government), the 1840s (by a Conservative government), and the 1860s and 1870s (by a Liberal government).

The combination of economic reforms and an effort by the landed elites who governed to represent themselves as disinterested came together to reduce both the perception and reality of Old Corruption; the phrase was far less frequently used by the mid-1840s. Where late Georgian government was large, bloated, expensive (largely because of military costs), and shot through with patronage and corruption, by the mid-Victorian period government was smaller, cheaper, less corrupt, and spent far less on the military and far more on social upkeep and reforms. While this reform was admirable, it was also undertaken in part by the elites to stave off revolution or more drastic reform, and in this it was successful, allowing them to survive as ruling elites in a largely intact system.

During the Victorian period, the main political parties increasingly came to be known as the Liberal and Conservative parties. The terms "Whig" and "Tory," which were used during the Victorian period as synonyms for the Liberal and Conservative parties, or parts of them, were originally insulting terms for the opposing sides in the Glorious Revolution of 1688, indicating the long history organized political parties have in Britain. But this history hides the fact that parties were not always the same, were not always important in politics, and were not always ideologically consistent. Because the formal political world was, before mid-century, so small and so elite, connections, locality, and patronage could have more political weight than party affiliation, and in any case Whigs and Tories agreed on many issues in substance, disagreeing only at the level of emphasis or nuance. In general until the end of the Victorian period, parties were broad coalitions without narrow consistent doctrines or discipline: the Liberal and Conservative parties both suffered divisions during the Victorian period (the Tories in 1829 over Catholic Emancipation, in 1846 over the repeal of the Corn Laws, and in 1905 over tariff reform, and the Liberals in 1886 over the issue of Irish Home Rule). During the first half of the nineteenth century, party organizations helped parliamentary leaders win power, but had little meaning at the local or electoral levels. Indeed many Victorians were suspicious of the whole idea of organized political parties, believing that they were a bar to political independence and led to opposition and conflict for their own sakes.[2]

The Liberal and Conservative parties sound as if they might correspond to the American Democratic and Republican political parties, but they do not. The Liberal party grew out of and was dominated for decades by the Whigs, a group of moderately progressive aristocrats. The Whig–Liberal coalition—in which the Whigs were strong in the 1830s, with the Liberals becoming dominant thereafter—favored reform, albeit to a limited degree and at a moderate pace. Whigs were aristocratic and so in many ways shared a position with wealthy landed Tories. Whigs believed themselves to be the champions of the people's best interests. Later the aristocratic Whig coalition of the early nineteenth century was replaced by a much larger, more middle-class, more serious Liberal Party. The Liberal party included middle-class and working-class radicals and free-traders. Liberals were open to hearing and responding to popular grievances, and stressed the integration of all four countries that made up the United Kingdom into a unified whole. They believed in gradual progress and the gradual expansion of democracy. They had questions about the morality of empire, but not about the morality of free trade. They championed temperance and opposed personal excess.

Politicians across the Whig–Liberal spectrum agreed that the constitution was above all a model of balanced interests in which balance created freedom and liberty (from which the term "liberal" derived) and prevented any one branch of government from becoming overly powerful or despotic. They saw the Anglican church's position in government as historical but not intrinsic to the constitution, and favored bringing nonconformists into the political nation. Liberals saw themselves as the party of people across spectrums—across the class hierarchy, across religions, across the four countries of Britain. Liberals, who dominated from the 1840s, favored limited government, believing that the "invisible hand of the market" was more efficient than state intervention. Classical Victorian liberalism was articulated by John Stuart Mill, particularly in his 1859 essay *On Liberty*, which was concerned with how much authority government could wield over the individual—via the passage of laws and the provision of social services, but also via social pressure and public opinion—before it became unacceptably despotic. Mill valued original thought and individuality, and argued that the latter, far from being in tension with social needs, was the best path to an ideal society. Following on Mill's ideas, liberalism stressed progress, individual responsibility, and the centrality of character; it recognized the need for social reform and for government intervention, but insisted that government aid tended to limit individuals' freedom and motivation to succeed, and therefore to increase sloth and poverty to the detriment of the nation. Liberalism in this guise was the dominant ideology of the Victorian period. The party also favored Parliamentary power, religious tolerance, industrial wealth, gradual reform, *laissez-faire* economics and individual liberties.

Conservatives believed in tradition and in hierarchies. They favored monarchical power, the Church of England, landed wealth, and protectionist economic policies. Tories saw both hierarchy and the Church of England as validated by and ensconced in the constitution. They held that the landed elite were the proper rulers of society, and that it was their responsibility to care for the poor. Tories rejected abstract notions, especially Enlightenment ones regarding the rights of man; they stood in stark opposition not to Liberals—at least not until 1867—but to radicals. As the period progressed they came to celebrate empire and union with Ireland, but on a national level they favored English over British interests and identity. Put another way, while the Liberals had a British base, the Conservatives were an English-based party. Indeed they were almost entirely unsuccessful in Scotland, where they did not win a majority of House of Commons seats even once between 1832 and 1900. The Conservatives were more ideologically unified and bureaucratically organized than the Liberals, but spent little time in power before 1885. Before the 1860s they were resistant to popular politics and beholden to the landed interests that dominated the party. They were pragmatic. They were committed to an Englishman's right to leisure and to pleasure, making them the party of the pub rather than of abstemiousness.

The political world was neither small nor confined to Parliament. Vast amounts of evidence that indicate that people who did not technically have political power were nonetheless interested in and engaged in politics. For example, while aristocratic women did not share their male relatives' right to vote or sit in Parliament, formal politics were suffused with their influence (sometimes derided as "petticoat politics"). Aristocratic women canvassed, visited, and influenced patronage, and operated as political hostesses. During the social Season in London parliamentary and other politicking took place in social settings managed by women. During election years, female relatives of candidates for office, or female patrons who controlled seats, visited with the female relatives of voters and dined with aldermen.

Less elite men and women also cared about politics. While MPs were elected by a very small cadre of relatively elite voters, elections were elaborate ceremonial affairs that involved the entire community. Electoral rituals involved not only speeches but brass bands, handbills, posters, and the ringing of church bills. Candidates "treated" locals, including but not limited to voters, by putting on breakfasts, dinners, and more. People would dress in symbolic items (such as French Revolutionary cockades) or in party colors. Candidates aimed their messages on significant political issues towards the entire community, not just electors. In 1820, election rituals included canvassing, treating dinners, picnics, bonfires, banners, drums, speeches, and the chairing of the victorious candidate. Electors and non-electors alike partook in all of these; as historian Frank O'Gorman emphasizes, "[a]lthough most of the adult population were *not*, of course, formally entitled to vote, they clearly assumed that it was their birthright to participate in the election in other ways, and this they proceeded to do."[3] The vote that was finally cast by the voter was only one aspect of a much larger event. While this festive electoral culture began to decline in the 1830s, its existence demonstrates that the right to vote was only one aspect of political participation, and that the size of the electorate is not necessarily an accurate measure of political participation.

Beyond elections themselves, the disenfranchised majority also cared about other issues, including the abolition of slavery and free trade. Many had radical ideas; for example, early utopian socialists called Owenites (supporters of the radical Robert Owens (1771–1858)) envisioned a "new social order" character-ized by cooperative living in a world free of class- and sex-based oppression; they critiqued the institutions of property and marriage and endorsed religious free-thought and popular education. The most pressing political issue for those Britons without formal political power was political power itself, from the problem of political corruption to demands for a more democratic Britain. Political radicals consistently attacked the aristocracy as undeserving of its power, corruption as a stain on British politics, and the franchise as inadequate (there was even a republican call, strongest in the early 1870s, to abolish the monarchy). While hier-archy and class deference was one political reality in the Victorian period, popular distrust of aristocracy and government was another. The latter remained constant through the Victorian period, and helped to change the constitution in 1911.

Formal and popular or out-of-doors politics did not exist in separate realms; the interaction between them was constant and complex. Victorian print culture—the world of newspapers, pamphlets and books—was growing rapidly, with news-papers devoting much of their space to reporting parliamentary business for the public to follow. This vibrant print culture combined with the growth of the middle class to create something new called "public opinion"—in the early part of the period largely the opinions of middle-class men, later something much broader—which was to become a political force in and of itself.

1820–1850: New players in the political arena

In 1820, at the start of our period, Britain was a country in economic and political transition. The economy was growing and beginning to shift from an agrarian to an industrial and commercial base. There was increased dissatisfaction with the monarchy, and in particular with George IV, who had ruled as Regent during his father's last decade on the throne, and now began his own reign as king. In addi-tion there were more and more calls to reform Parliament, which (like the king) was seen as bloated, corrupt, and unresponsive to the people. The years after 1815 saw a spirited revival of extra-parliamentary radicalism, particularly mass radical platforms, in which crowds would gather to demand universal male suffrage, annual parliaments, and a secret ballot. These came to a violent end at the hands of the government in 1819, when the cavalry charged into the crowd at a meeting at St Peter's Field, Manchester, and 11 people were killed.

The Queen Caroline Affair of 1820 serves as a good political start date to the Victorian era because it exemplifies the degree to which unenfranchised groups could engage with high politics in ways that were both old and new. The Prince of Wales and his wife Caroline were unhappily married, and Caroline lived on the continent from 1814. In 1820, when her husband was to be crowned King George IV, she returned to England to claim her title as his queen. The unpopular king tried to stop her by accusing her of adultery and divorcing her, but the House of Lords acquitted the queen of any wrongdoing (though she was still barred from the king's coronation and died a year later). The Queen Caroline Affair was famous throughout Britain; political journalist William Hazlitt was struck by the breadth of interest in the affair, writing that it was "the only question I have ever known that excited a thoroughly popular feeling. It struck its roots in the heart of the nation."[4] Thousands of women empathized with the Queen and signed addresses sent to her. The celebrations that followed Caroline's acquittal by Parliament included fireworks, bonfires at Seven Dials and St Giles, and the illumination of much of London for three nights running.

The Queen's trial was described and debated in pamphlets, articles, ballads, chapbooks, and political cartoons. The Queen was supported by radicals and some Whigs in Parliament, who opposed the King and Old Corruption. She was also supported by a wide variety of disenfranchised groups. One was the middle class; middle-class public opinion saw the affair as proof of aristocratic immorality that contrasted with middle-class morality, respectability, and domesticity. Working-class radicals and their allies supported the Queen as a way of attacking the institutionalized corruption they saw in government. Many women of various stations empathized with Caroline as a wronged wife who could do little to defend herself from her husband's moral slurs and legal and economical assaults. The arguments of radicals and women (and of women radicals) were countered by popular conservatism, which attacked the Queen's sexual morality. Portrayals of the affair were replete with celebrations of liberty and the constitution and the condemnations of despotism and corruption. It was represented to and by the nation in the genres of melodrama and pornography, both of which included stock characters and plots and both of which resonated with very wide audiences.[5] The Queen Caroline Affair was short-lived; its main impact may have been simply the fact of the widespread agitations. However, its occurrence reveals how broad and how deep the political nation was—it was hardly confined to the electorate, let alone to Parliament—and the degree to which a single event could arouse multiple reactions. Furthermore, the calls sounded here for middle-class sobriety as superior to aristocratic immorality would resonate for the entire period.

From the late 1820s, the formal political arena opened to new groups. The confessional state—one that had a state church and was specifically Anglican and aristocratic—was demolished in a process that made way for the liberal state that would dominate the Victorian period. That process began with non-Anglicans. In 1828, the Repeal of the Test and Corporation Acts granted otherwise qualified nonconformists (men who were Protestant but not Anglican, and who owned sufficient property) the vote. This was a crucial moment in the development of liberalism, which rejected the narrowly confessional state that Tories embraced.

At the same time, the Catholic Association agitated for the same right for Catholics, most of whom were Irish. The relationship between Ireland and Britain had been fraught since the first English invasions into Ireland in the twelfth century. Ireland was overwhelmingly agrarian (in contrast with industrializing England), with a poor Irish Catholic majority of tenant farmers and a wealthier Anglo-Irish Protestant landowning minority. An unsuccessful 1798 Rebellion against British rule (inspired in part by the American and French Revolutions) prompted the 1801 Act of Union, which brought Ireland under tighter control by denying it its own legislature. The Act of Union, which politically and administratively unified Ireland and Great Britain into a United Kingdom of Great Britain and Ireland, abolished the Irish Parliament in Dublin, and added 100 seats for Irish MPs in the Westminster Parliament.

The first nineteenth-century calls for Irish independence were made by Daniel O'Connell (1775–1847), founder of both the Catholic Association, which from 1823 agitated for reform of Ireland's electoral system and church, and for tenant farmers' rights, and the Repeal Association, which in the 1830s and '40s agitated for the Repeal of the Act of Union. In 1829, one year after nonconformists got the vote, Catholic Emancipation was passed, under Prime Minister the Duke of Wellington, who opposed it but feared Irish unrest (as did many). It opened Parliament and most public offices (but not universities) to Catholics, and O'Connell was able to take the seat in Parliament to which he had been elected. Formal politics were now open to Anglicans, nonconformists, and Roman Catholics. This was a major contrast with the formerly confessional state. A decade later, when Prime Minister Robert Peel tried to assuage Irish complaints by increasing government aid to a Catholic seminary in Maynooth, Ireland, the move was so unpopular that it helped to end his government. The intense politics surrounding the Maynooth Grant, which seem puzzling today, give us a sense of how intertwined politics and religion were, how intense anti-Catholic feeling was, and how serious the "Irish Question" would prove to be. While nonconformists were being fully accepted into the political nation, Irish Catholics continued to be seen as foreign and not entirely trustworthy.

The formal political nation was also broadened in 1832 by the first major Reform Act. However participatory and popular politics were before 1832, the franchise was very small, and the distribution and system of representation was outmoded. Calls for the reform of both franchise and Parliament had become louder over the 1820s, as Parliament and the franchise both seemed unfair to many. When the new king, William IV, replaced Wellington as Prime Minister with the more reform-minded Whig Earl Grey in 1830, reform seemed possible. There was much to do. The counties and boroughs MPs represented had been established in the fourteenth century, and many were obsolete. Formerly prosperous but now virtually deserted towns such as Old Sarum, a village in Wiltshire, still sent members to Parliament (these were called "rotten" boroughs). Other members were chosen by a single aristocratic family (in "pocket" boroughs), or by the government (as "placemen"). Meanwhile, more recently populated areas, cities such as Manchester in the North and Birmingham in the Midlands, had no representation at all. The qualifications for voting were inconsistent and varied widely from place to place. The growing middle class wanted the vote (though in some constituencies they had it already), and argued that middle-class men were respectable and responsible enough for the privilege. Those in northern cities protested their lack of representation. Reform groups such as the Birmingham Political Union and other political unions across the country petitioned and spoke out in favor of reform. There were reform riots in London, Bristol, and Bath (in addition food riots in Ireland, in Limerick and Roscommon, contributed to a general sense of unrest and the need for reform). Even many conservatives, fearful of more revolutionary change and cognizant of the violent example of the French Revolution, endorsed the notion of parliamentary reform.

These issues were addressed in the 1832 Reform Act, the first major reform of Parliamentary representation in centuries. There was fervent support for and opposition to the 1832 Reform Bill, which was finally passed only after much debate, politicking, and royal threats to the Peers who resisted it. Once law, the 1832 Reform Act, formally titled the Representation of the People Act (1832) but subsequently known as the "Great" Reform Act, made many changes. It redistributed 100 obsolete seats to reflect existing population distribution; many rotten and pocket boroughs were abolished, while new industrial towns such as Manchester gained representatives for the first time. (Irish seats were unaffected.) It made voting requirements consistent across Britain (with the result that those scattered working-class men who had had the vote in their constituencies now lost it). It widened the franchise to include middle-class men. This was accomplished by broadening the notion of what it meant to possess sufficient property to claim a voice in politics. Rather than the outright ownership of land, the 1832 Act recognized the ability to rent land or a home worth £10 as a form of property ownership, at least insofar as status and political participation were concerned. It decreed that most adult males who owned or leased land or a home worth £10 could vote. As a result the electorate grew from 516,000 to 1.75 million, or 14% of adult men (7% of adults).

The intent and effect of the £10 franchise was to extend voting privileges to most middle-class men, but to deny them to most working-class men, a result by which many were bitterly disappointed. In contrast to the working class, perceived as dangerous especially after the violence of the Captain Swing riots in 1830, the middle class was seen as safe and respectable, and therefore as safe recipients of the privilege of voting. The division the Act created between the respectable middle class and the working class shaped popular politics thereafter (in part because the working class felt betrayed by the middle class). Various working-class groups, in particular the growing trade unions, strove to demonstrate that working-class men deserved the privilege of citizenship by adopting middle-class standards of behavior and proving the respectability of the working-class man.

The new franchise also included men while excluding women. In principle and by tradition, the vote had always been for men only, but there is evidence of women voting before 1832, and the English bill specified for the first time that voting was a male privilege (though its Scottish counterpart did not). The ideas about political responsibility on which the extension of the franchise rested were explicitly gendered. This did not mean that women were or were rendered apolitical; enfranchisement is only one route to political participation, and women of all classes were and remained political. Middle-class women bore a new relationship to formal politics by virtue of their class and family ties, and women of all classes continued to act as auxiliary supports and social organizers of political movements they cared about, such as Chartism. More men than ever before could be citizens, but however much they identified with the nation, women categorically remained subjects, not citizens. Most were legally barred from owning property, and even for those who could, no amount of property owned could qualify a woman to vote.

The Reform Act reflected and re-inscribed the belief that the Irish were incapable of responsible political behavior. (This suspicion did not extend to members of the Irish aristocracy, who sat in the House of Lords.) During the 1820s and early 1830s, the situation in Ireland was a topic of sustained Parliamentary enquiry and debate. Catholic Emancipation had just passed in the face of bitter opposition. Food and other riots in Ireland reinforced the belief that the Irish were uncivilized. The franchise expanded less in Ireland than in England and Wales, where one out of five men now had the vote, or in Scotland, where the figure was one in eight: in Ireland only one in 20 men now had the vote.

Historians are divided about the impact of the 1832 Reform Act; the Act has received far more scholarly attention than the Repeal of the Test and Corporation Acts and Catholic Emancipation, which were arguably more important. At the time, and for over a century afterwards, most observers called it the most important event in British political history, one that brought the middle class into the political nation and ushered in an age of democracy. Parties began to organize, at the local level and to some degree at Westminster. Public opinion became more politically important, as Parliament came to understand the need to respect and respond to it. But many historians have stressed the limits of the Act. Some rotten boroughs were left standing, prosperous southern England remained better represented in Parliament than Wales, Scotland, Ireland, or the north of England, electoral rights were still unevenly granted. Men from the working class, which made up the majority of the population, remained unenfranchised. Eighty percent of MPs still came from landed backgrounds. Electoral corruption actually increased by some measures, and corruption would be a central political issue for the remainder of the nineteenth century.

The Great Reform Act was passed by a Whig government, and during the 1830s the Whigs remained in power and turned their attention from political reforms to broader social reforms. The aristocratic Whigs were hardly radical. They remained committed to the notion that only the propertied should have a say in governing. They favored gradual reform in part as a way of staving off revolution. The prominent reforms they passed have led to the 1830s being seen as the first of many Victorian decades of social reform. Perhaps the most important was the new Poor Law of 1834. Under it, the system by which the British government provided assistance to those who needed it changed radically. Since the sixteenth century every parish had been responsible for its own poor. By the early nineteenth century many non-poor Britons perceived the poor as lazy and poor relief as encouraging their indolence; middle-class urban employers also disliked the fact that rural agricultural wages were subsidized. In addition, political economist Thomas Malthus (1766–1834) warned that resources could not meet demand unless population growth was checked (via birth control, delayed marriage, and celibacy), particularly among the poor, and that the current relief system did not serve as an adequate disincentive. Under the New Poor Law, poor relief was to a large degree nationally organized, though still locally distributed, and wage supplements were abolished. The Poor Law was harsh, and in Ireland was even harsher. In line with the writings of influential utilitarian philosopher Jeremy Bentham (1748–1832), who endorsed publicly provided relief but wanted it to be designed in such a way that it neither offered disincentives to work nor became too expensive, conditions in the workhouses were deliberately designed to offer subsistence without comfort. Those able-bodied poor who needed government aid were required to leave their homes and enter a parish workhouse; "outdoor" government relief (i.e. outside the workhouse) became illegal (although it persisted in some places). Conditions in the workhouses were unpleasant—the food was bad and the work was back-breaking—and generations of working-class Britons made it their goal to keep their families out. Poor Law Guardians in each parish (usually prominent citizens) collected poor law taxes, supervised the workhouse, and reported to the Central Poor Law Commission. The passage of the Poor Law made private philanthropy, of which there was much in Victorian Britain, even more important.

Another key Whig reform of the 1830s was the Factory Act of 1833, which sought to establish a regular and limited working day for children who worked in textile factories. For workers under the age of 18, work could not start before 5:30am, had to end by 8:30pm, and was limited to 12 hours per day; those aged nine to 13 could work only nine hours per day, and children under nine could not work in textiles at all. These limitations seem minimal at best to twenty-first century eyes, but at the time they were a significant limitation on working hours and a demand that factory owners take responsibility for their workers' well-being. More broadly, the Factory Acts were an attempt to temper the excesses of *laissez-faire* capitalism with state responsibility for the health of all Britons. Over the course of the century many more Factory Acts would be passed, which applied limits to women's work, further limited working hours, and required that child workers be educated. Adult male workers remained relatively unprotected and continued to work very long hours and through the night. Gas lighting allowed employers to keep production going around the clock, and the sight of these large, lit-up buildings in a society where few buildings were artificially lit at all gave rise the image of "dark satanic mills"[6] marring the landscape. Factory Acts were poorly enforced, but their passage indicates the commitment of liberal Victorian Britain to at least some degree of protection for those workers seen as most vulnerable.

Third, the Whig government of the 1830s abolished slavery in the British Empire. The British slave trade had been abolished in 1807, but promised improvements in the treatment of those already enslaved failed to materialize. Abolitionists therefore continued their longstanding campaigns, which resulted in slavery being abolished and slaves being gradually freed between 1833 and 1838. While historians remain divided about whether abolition passed for humanitarian or for economic reasons, the fact of abolition remains and was a key Whig reform.

These key Acts were the start of the Victorian period as an age of reform. They helped to position the Liberal party—which included the moderate aristocratic Whigs, free-traders, and radicals—as the party of progress, one which was in office for 42 of the 55 years between 1830 and 1885. Liberal governments focused on reform and accomplished much, including establishing a civil registry of births and deaths, establishing examinations for civil service positions, abolishing tariffs on grain, produce, and manufactured goods, and increasing the power of local government.

During this period, Sir Robert Peel (1788–1850) transformed the former Tory party into the modern Conservative party, which functioned principally as an opposition party. Once the Conservatives had accepted the reality of the Reform Act, they supported bills that appealed to middle-class voters, and there was real electoral support for the Conservative Party during these years of Liberal hegemony. During these years the parties became more distinct in their outlooks, with the Conservatives favoring a paternalistic style of governance that included state intervention, and the Liberals preferring utilitarian political theory and *laissez-faire* economic policies.

While middle-class men were now part of the formal polity, working-class men were not. The key working-class response to the 1832 Reform Act was Chartism, a mass movement for democracy. Chartists leaders included Fergus O'Connor (1762–1834), William Lovett (1800–1877), Bronterre O'Brien (1805–1864), and Ernest Jones (1819–1869). Chartists agitated in the 1830s and 1840s for the passage of their six-point "People's Charter," endorsed in 1838. The charter demanded equal constituencies, annual Parliaments, a secret ballot, the abolition of the property requirement, the institution of salaries for members of Parliament, and—perhaps most importantly—universal (male) suffrage. The Chartists worked to convince Parliament to consider their demands by collecting signatures on petitions and presenting these to Parliament. Three petitions were presented, in 1839, 1842, and 1848, accompanied by large rallies and marches. While the Chartists did not see their demands met in the 1840s, over the nineteenth century all of their points, save annual elections, were made law.

Chartism was more than a political movement; it had a strong social aspect as well. There were local Chartist associations all over the country, which held meetings and social events such as teas, dinners, and dances. Chartists banded together in "exclusive dealing" schemes in which they patronized only those shops whose owners supported the Charter. Not all Chartists agreed with one another. There were divisions between physical-force Chartists (those who endorsed violence as a means of achieving their ends) and moral-force Chartists (those who rejected violence), and between those who looked nostalgically back to small farms as the solution to workers' problems (and founded a National Land Company towards this end, which was supposed to buy land, divide it into small farms, and give these to shareholding Chartists) and those who did not.

During the 1840s, Chartism moved away from informal, local, and confrontational actions towards centralized, formal approach that focused on London and national politics. This made the movement more politically respectable, but also drained it of its vigor, not least because the shifts made it difficult for Chartist women to participate. At the same time, Chartists embraced middle-class notions of domesticity and sexual respectability. They began emphasizing the domesticity of the working-class family and demanding a breadwinner's wage, thereby aiming to achieve political status for working-class men (via the franchise), and apolitical status for working-class women (via the economic ability to choose unpaid domesticity over paid work outside the home).

In some ways, the most important political divide in the 1830s and 1840s was over tariffs, with the more middle-class Liberal party favoring free trade, and the more elite Conservative party favoring protective tariffs that kept the price of grain and the value of land high. One expression of the political ascendancy of the middle class was the success of the Anti-Corn Law League (ACLL), founded in 1838 and headed by radicals Richard Cobden (1804–1865), John Bright (1811–1889) and J.B. Smith (1794–1879). "Corn Laws," which would be called "grain laws" in American English, were tariffs that artificially raised the price of imported foreign grain, thereby giving domestic grain (and the landowners who profited from it) an economic advantage. Britain's protectionist tariffs on foreign grain favored aristocratic landowners and rural interests, and so were at odds with the middle-class men who dominated the commercial and manufacturing sectors and were local and urban leaders. Middle-class commercial manufacturing interests wanted to abolish the tariffs so as to promote free trade, the economic doctrine that was almost a religion in Victorian Britain. The ACLL—which was a coalition of a range of working-class and middle-class interests—was formed to lobby for an end to protectionist tariffs on foreign grain. It was therefore an early expression of popular liberalism, or the belief in the free market as both natural and the road to prosperity, and in moderate reform as desirable and necessary. If the Queen Caroline Affair was one opportunity for the expression of anti-aristocratic political feeling, the ACLL with its demands for pro-middle-class free trade rather than pro-aristocracy protectionism was another. The ACLL was a national movement that effectively used propaganda and electoral pressure. It was cohesive and well-funded, in part because it engaged many women, who held ACLL social and fundraising events such as the famous ACLL bazaars, one in Manchester in 1842 that raised £10,000, and one in Covent Garden in 1845 that raised £25,000.

In the mid-1840s, Conservative Prime Minister Robert Peel surprised his party, which traditionally protected landowners' interests, by embracing free-trade principles. In the Great Famine, which began in 1845, blighted potato crops in Ireland led to mass starvation and to a population decline of as much as one-fourth (from a combination of starvation and famine-induced emigration, principally to Liverpool, Glasgow, London, and the US). Many Irish felt that the effects of the blight were exacerbated by protectionist tariffs. Together the Irish Famine and Peel's support ensured the repeal of the Corn Laws in 1846. (Though not without consequences: Peel lost his office and divided his party). While modern economic historians are skeptical about repeal's role in the prosperity of the 1850s and 1860s, most contemporaries credited the repeal of the Corn Laws and free trade more generally with the prosperity that followed. Britain's political world was no longer an exclusively aristocratic one.

1850–1885: Ireland, parties, and working-class voters

The period after 1850—though it has been called an age of equipoise—was characterized not only by a degree of stability but also by conflicts with and over Ireland; the continuing nationalization of the two major political parties, headed by charismatic leaders William E. Gladstone (1809–1898) and Benjamin Disraeli (1804–1881); and by two Reform Acts that enlarged the electorate and changed the nature of politics.

In the 1850s radicalism declined in British politics. Until recently many thought that Chartism ended with the rejection of the third Chartist petition in 1848, and that radicalism did not reemerge until the growth of socialism in the 1880s. But historians now agree that aspects of the Chartist organization and platform persisted for another decade or more. In addition many British radicals focused on and supported the unification of Italy as a liberal-democratic nation state. Radicalism changed, deemphasizing class warfare and emphasizing nationalism and patriotism. Radical working-class groups embraced middle-class standards of domesticity, respectability, and self-reliance. These shifts were in part a response to developments in formal politics. Reforms undercut the traditional radical message of a monarchy which could only be reformed from without and a hopelessly corrupt elite. Victorian radicalism never disappeared, but by mid-century it was weakened by the trends towards domesticity on the one hand, and more formal, nationally-oriented politics on the other.

From the late 1850s, the wave of nationalist movements that swept Europe touched the multi-national United Kingdom in the form of Irish nationalism. In 1858, following the Irish Famine, the nationalist Irish Republican Brotherhood (IRB), also known as the "Fenians," was founded as a group committed to achieving Irish independence through violence. The IRB began abroad, amongst emigrants who had fled the famine, and promoted violence in both Ireland and Great Britain (principally England). The IRB staged an uprising in 1867, which the British government easily put down but certainly took note of. From the mid-1860s the problem of Ireland's political status in the United Kingdom dominated British politics. Indeed in some ways the two parties came to be defined by the Irish Question, as the Liberal Party became the party of Home Rule and the Conservative Party became the Unionist party. Inspired by Irish nationalists, Scottish nationalists—predominantly from the Highland areas of Scotland, which from the 1850s suffered from famine, overpopulation, and poverty—also agitated. From the 1870s, many Scots also protested the growth of state schools, which taught children in English and contributed to the decline of Scottish Gaelic.

During this period, each party came to be defined by a strong leader. Gladstone (1809–1898) was the leader of the Liberal Party from the mid-1860s until his death in 1898. He was a high-minded evangelical Christian whose strongly held moral beliefs informed his politics. He also had a complex relationship to sex and social purity, and would associate with prostitutes because of his involvement in rescue work, and then castigate himself (throwing into doubt his political rival Benjamin Disraeli's remark that Gladstone did not have "a single redeeming defect").[7] He began his political life in Peel's Conservative ministry and was Chancellor of the Exchequer (which is a very important post, equivalent to the American position of Secretary of the Treasury) twice in the 1850s before serving as Prime Minister four times starting in 1868. Gladstone's Liberal party was broad-based and committed to progress and to reform. In all of his ministries, he promoted sweeping bills on contentious topics, believing that they united the party and legitimized parliamentary rule. However, he was not unreflexively reformist and opposed many reforms introduced by his own party. Over his career, he became committed to the cause of a self-governing Ireland, a commitment that would increasingly drive his political life and in 1886 reveal the fissures in the coalition party he led.

Gladstone's political foe, Disraeli, was a very different man. He was a political pragmatist who despised Gladstone for his lofty moral goals and made no pretense of having any of his own. He saw politics as a game, one goal of which was to have fun. He was Anglican, but of Jewish descent, which made him an outsider in English society. Many saw him as a foreigner and as a Jew. Throughout his career he was mistrusted and seen as unprincipled, by allies as well as foes. Originally a novelist (he wrote several "silver fork" novels of high life as well as *Coningsby* (1844) and *Sybil* (1845)), he entered politics in the 1830s. Throughout his career he worked to protect and defend the landed interest. During the decades that the Conservative Party was out of power, he helped to promote it as a centrist, popular party of reform and of pride in empire. He had a hand in many major reforms, including the second Reform Act, and led a government that introduced many moderate reforms affecting industrial regulations and public health, but was opposed to radical changes to established British institutions and practices. He believed strongly in empire and focused on improving and solidifying Britain's position as a world power.

Both Gladstone and Disraeli participated in different ways in the passage of the second Reform Act of the Victorian era. Gladstone was a strong supporter of franchise reform. Disraeli wanted to make his party appeal to the masses, whilst wresting the mantle of reform from the Liberal party, and argued that a broader franchise could work to the party's advantage, despite the perils of democracy. Though the Conservative party was the party of the landed aristocracy, Disraeli was confident that he could shape it to appeal to working-class voters, and he was right. As we have seen, the passage of the 1832 Reform Act did not satisfy demands for electoral reform. Liberals and radicals of various stripes wanted a larger electorate, a secret ballot, and an end to corruption; some Conservatives wanted to ensure that new working-class voters were grateful to the Tories for the privilege. In the 1860s calls for reform intensified. The moderate middle-class National Reform Union (f. 1864) called for household suffrage (which would retain property qualifications). The radical working-class Reform League, led by John Bright (formerly of the ACLL), argued that the skilled male head of a respectable working-class household deserved the vote and sought universal male suffrage and the secret ballot (both Chartist demands). Events abroad during the 1860s also inspired calls for reform. These included the Civil War (1861–1865) in the United States, liberal reformist Italian politician Giuseppe Garibaldi's visit to Britain, and the unification of Italy into a liberal nation-state with a parliamentary democracy (1860s).

The notion of a Second Reform Act suddenly became politically realistic in 1865, when the leader of the Liberal party, Lord Palmerston (1784–1865), died. Palmerston was a brilliant parliamentary strategist, the dominant political figure of the 1850s, and twice Prime Minister. He had promoted a vision of social harmony in an urbanizing and industrializing age and led the country during the Crimean War. However, he had been opposed to extending the franchise, and his death cleared the way. It was widely expected that the progressive Liberal party, led by Lord John Russell and Gladstone, would pass a Second Reform Act. But when Gladstone introduced the government's reform bill in March 1866, the Liberal government was brought down by opposition from Conservatives and conservative Liberals (many of them aristocrats), who opposed the notion of working-class voters. The working-class Reform League responded in July 1866 by holding a demonstration in Hyde Park, London. When the police attempted to prevent the demonstration, the crowd broke down some railings, and demonstrators fought with the police. The "Hyde Park Riots," as the event came to be known, were brief and quickly put down, but they convinced Liberal and Conservative politicians alike that working-class political demands could not be ignored and that electoral reform was inevitable.

With the Conservative Party now in power, Disraeli introduced his party's reform bill in March 1867. He successfully exploited rifts in the Liberal party, argued that Conservatives were the true reformers, and passed the Representation of the People Act (1867), popularly known as the Second Reform Act. In June 1868 a Reform Act for Scotland that was substantially the same as the English and Welsh Act passed, as did a bill for Ireland.

Like the Great Reform Act, the Second Reform Act enlarged the electorate by enlarging the definition of what it meant to own property. The Acts gave the vote to male working-class householders in borough constituencies (urban areas)—effectively, to skilled workers, also known as the "labor aristocracy." The Second Reform Act recognized the "respectable working man" as someone who, while he might not own or rent much property, was deserving—based on his comportment of himself and his responsibility for others—of the vote. All male heads of household in borough constituencies now had the vote, the argument being that their status as upstanding heads of households made them citizens. In addition, male lodgers who paid £10 per year for unfurnished rooms also had the vote, on the logic that they too were on some level "independent." Renting a very cheap room, a furnished room, or living with one's parents after the age of 21, meant a man was too poor or too much a dependent (on parents or landlady) to vote. Renting an unfurnished room, however, suggested that his room was his home, to do with as he saw fit. The Second Reform Act also continued some of the work of the 1832 Act by abolishing more rotten boroughs and redistributing more seats. It increased the size of the electorate from 1.4 million to 2.5 million in a population of 35 million; somewhere around one third of men (one sixth of adults) could now vote. Its effects were striking in Wales, where a new rural middle class, which had been forming since 1850, asserted itself by voting overwhelmingly for the Liberal party in the 1868 elections. From 1880, Welsh politics were dominated by the Liberal party.

As with the 1832 Act, the changes the 1867 Act made had limits. Ireland's rural nature, along with persistent suspicion of the Irish, were both reflected in the fact that one in six men in Ireland—versus one in three men in England, Wales, and Scotland—could now vote. Certain types of men remained voteless. Working-class political pressure groups, led by trade unions, had promoted the skilled male head of a household. Perhaps as a result of this, the Act excluded many young and unmarried men, who did not head households or families. Trade unions (who generally did not organize unskilled workers, women, or immigrants, whom they saw as a threat to British "family men") remained powerful; in 1868 the Trades Union Congress (TUC) was founded and created a Parliamentary Committee to lobby Parliament. The Act also excluded women. One MP called the 1868 debates on women's suffrage a "pleasant interlude ... interposed to the grave and somewhat sombre discussions on the subject of Reform,"[8] and the women's suffrage amendment that radical MPs John Stuart Mill and Henry Fawcett introduced to the 1867 Bill was defeated by 123 votes. In spite of this inauspicious beginning, the movement for women's suffrage had begun. The feminist movement became increasingly focused on the vote, and from 1867 pro-suffrage women tried to persuade politicians and the public of the rightness of their cause, and to introduce women's suffrage into Parliament.

British politics remained, as they had after 1832, dominated by aristocrats, notions of deference and hierarchy, and local concerns. Men of privilege continued to dominate the House of Commons and the cabinet. Radical and popular attacks on aristocratic privilege and corruption persisted and even intensified, and included moral, economic, emotional, and political attacks; accusations of elite sexual misconduct were especially popular and common ways to attack the aristocracy as immoral. But overall the Second Reform Bill was extremely significant. The franchise had been significantly broadened. The enlarged electorate commanded respect from Parliament and in the cabinet. The parties also recognized the scope of the shift and began to create clubs and other organizations through which to register voters and win their loyalty. Parties had already started to become more organized, and this process now intensified. Independent back-bench MPs became rare as a clear association with a party and its message became necessary in Parliament. Similarly, outside of the Parliament contingent, locally-oriented political organizations were replaced by local branches of the national parties that answered to centralized and increasingly bureaucratized parties.

Even this list does not adequately convey the shocking degree to which the 1867 Act changed the basic nature of politics in Britain. Britain's political system under Old Corruption had been, at its heart, not so much corrupt as a system of, by, and for elites. The business of politics was the business of elites, and when parties reached out they did not have to reach very far. This system was modified by the Great Reform Act, but in substance persisted. The Second Reform Act brought this to an end by moving Britain into an age of mass politics. Where the Great Reform Act was the beginning of the end of Old Corruption, the Second Reform Act was the beginning of a new era entirely. To garner support from a large electorate the parties needed to be organized. They did this by becoming more distinct from one another and by presenting themselves to the electorate as very different options. The parties also became more important to the political process; more and more, everything was done by or through one of the two parties.

Party leaders and Prime Ministers Gladstone and Disraeli exemplify the growing contrast between parties. Gladstone, like his party, was well-intentioned but serious to the point of humorlessness; both leader and party sought to do what was right, not what was fun, tried to reflect deeply on every decision, and were convinced of their own moral superiority. Temperance—a good idea for alcohol-soaked Britain, but hardly appealing on its own merits—was a central Liberal cause. Disraeli, like the Tories more generally, celebrated empire unapologetically, saw politics as entertainment even as he took it seriously, and believed in the pursuit of pleasure and in an Englishman's right to a pint. The Tories' openness to alcohol and to fun, more than their political platform, made them the party of much of the working class after the Second Reform Bill. Popular Toryism maintained a strong sense of loyalty to traditional institutions, from the monarchy to the pub, and to the social hierarchy.

Following the passage of the Act by Disraeli's Conservative government, Gladstone—dubbed "The People's William" by the *Daily Telegraph*—became Prime Minster for the first time in December 1868. In this, his most effective government, the Liberal Party worked to improve society, to reform key institutions, and to address the Irish question. As Ireland's main complaints concerned religious and economic oppression, Gladstone addressed these, in 1869 by the disestablishment of the Anglican Church in majority-Catholic Ireland, and in 1870 with an Irish Land Act, which improved the terms on which tenant farmers occupied their lands (an 1873 attempt to reform Irish universities did not pass). However, these left Irish groups unsatisfied, and Irish nationalism grew stronger in the 1870s. In 1874 the new Irish Home Rule Party won 59 of the 103 Irish seats in Parliament. In other areas, Gladstone's government passed a major Education Act (1870) that created free state elementary schools for all children, reformed the civil service (1870) and the military (1871), abolished religious tests for entrance to Oxford and Cambridge Universities (1871), strengthened trade unions (while denying them the right to strike) (1871), reformed the judiciary (1873 and 1875), and introduced the Secret Ballot (1872), which was resisted though finally passed by the House of Lords.

Disraeli came back into power in 1874, in part because of his work since the 1850s of positioning the Conservative Party as popular, populist, and pragmatic. His Conservative Party had taken the working class seriously and had worked to educate and socialize working-class people (after 1867, working-class voters) into the political process. The result was that after 1867 they enjoyed quite a bit of electoral success at the polls, especially in older boroughs such as Bristol and York. While some historians claim that the Conservative Party patronized the working class and manipulated its members into voting against their own interests, many working-class people had genuine conservative political feelings. Popular conservatism was characterized by patriotism, support for empire and for monarchy, and adherence to tradition (as well as to some degree of xenophobia and racism). It rejected self-denial in favor of an unembarrassed embrace of pleasure in the form of drink, gambling, football, and the music hall. The Conservative Party welcomed and was able to tap into all of these (as the Liberal and later Labour Parties, committed to reform, progress, and sober and rational recreation, were not).

During Disraeli's second government, which lasted until 1880, he sought to position his party as centrist and as the party of empire. In addition the Tory Party in the 1870s sometimes positioned itself as standing as a bulwark against the dangers of continental socialism. Fears of socialism were especially acute after the Paris Commune of 1870, in which working-class radicals briefly controlled and ruled Paris in defiance of the French government. In the domestic realm Disraeli extended modest and uncontroversial reforms regarding factory regulation, public health, and education, among others. His main focus was on foreign policy: he negotiated peace in the near East (at the 1878 Congress of Berlin) and prosecuted wars in Afghanistan (1877) and South Africa (Zulu Wars, 1879). He died in 1881, and Lord Salisbury, whose focus was also on foreign policy, became the Conservative leader.

While out of office, Gladstone had attacked Disraeli's foreign policy; when he began his second administration in 1880, he tried to limit imperial expansion and to promote self-rule for Ireland and Scotland. The Irish problem continued to plague British politics. The 1870s and 1880s saw significant agrarian protests collectively referred to as the Land War, in which tenant farmers protested unfair rents and absentee landlords and demanded that peasants own the land they worked. From 1879, the fight for Home Rule was led by a rising star in Irish nationalist politics, Charles Stewart Parnell (1846–1891). Parnell was a charismatic leader who headed a variety of organizations, including the Land League, which spearheaded the Land Wars, and the Irish Parliamentary Party (IPP), before he was brought down by a divorce scandal in 1889. When Gladstone began his second administration in 1880, he tried to address Irish discontent by passing a second Irish Land Act, but it (like its 1871 predecessor) angered Whig landowners without satisfying tenant farmers or placating nationalists. Both the Whig and radical wings of the Liberal party were exasperated with his increasing focus on Ireland. Beyond foreign policy and empire, Gladstone continued his work of reforming society by reforming institutions. His biggest accomplishment here was the trio of electoral reform acts passed in 1883, 1884, and 1885.

The 1884 Reform Act applied the same standards to counties (rural areas) that the 1867 Act had applied to boroughs (urban areas). Rural men who were adult householders or who paid £10 as lodgers now had the vote. Historians have said less about this Act than about the two previous reform Acts, and it is true that by 1884 only about one quarter of the population lived in the countryside. But the notion of granting the vote to a new group was always fraught for the Victorians. In this instance, contemporaries were quite anxious about the notion of giving the vote to the male agricultural worker, who was personified in the press in the illiterate and unkempt figure of "Hodge" and who by the 1880s was known to very few Victorians in person. There was quite a bit of fear that rural folk were not sophisticated enough for this privilege; many Liberals believed that rural people would vote Conservative (they assumed the same about women), at least until they had been properly educated.[9]

The 1884 Reform Act is best seen as part of a tripartite reform that included the Corrupt and Illegal Practices Act of 1883 and the Redistribution Act of 1885. Together these extended the work of the first two Reform Acts to such an extent that Britain became a mass democracy. The Corrupt and Illegal Practices Act addressed problems that, as radicals and reformers frequently pointed out, continued to pervade the electoral process. It made bribery illegal, limited the amount spent on any election, and required party canvassers to be unpaid. Of course the many forms of influence that were subtler than bribery persisted, with many large employers supporting local football clubs and other organizations in expectation that their employees' votes would be swayed. However, more direct forms of corruption were addressed. Candidates' expenses, which had reached ridiculous heights by 1880, plummeted immediately. The number of petitions to examine elections for corruption also fell, from an average of 67 per election between 1832 and 1880 to only 9 per election between 1885 and 1910. The 1884 Reform Act increased the electorate to 5.6 million men out of a population of 36 million; two thirds of English and Welsh men, three fifths of Scottish men, and half of Irish men could now vote. The 1885 Act redistributed Parliamentary seats so that each seat in the House of Commons represented approximately the same number of voters and rural and urban areas were represented equally. It gave most constituencies only one member, rather than two, making elections cheaper and easier to contest. Since 1832 almost half of elections had been uncontested, but after 1885 the number of contested seats rose above 90% for the first time, which suggested that winners were not pre-determined and that democracy was working.[10]

As with the Reform Acts of 1832 and 1867, some features of the political system remained in place. Elite men retained much political power, and middle-class men were far more likely than working-class men to be registered to vote.[11] The resolutely undemocratic House of Lords retained political power in the face of increasing democracy. The vote remained tied to property, so that almost 2 million men, most of them young or living in lodgings, remained disenfranchised. Complete male suffrage would not come until 1918. In addition, women still could not vote, and the vote now seemed based on gender rather than on property. More than that, the 1884 Reform Act was a very serious problem for feminists pursuing votes for women. It was clearly the final suffrage bill that would be passed for some decades; that it excluded women left suffrage supporters with no larger Reform bill onto which they could add a women's suffrage amendment. It was clearer than ever that suffrage would not be gradually extended to women, as it had been to middle-class and then working-class men; there would have to be a fight. Women did attain suffrage at the local level—which many saw as housekeeping writ large rather than Parliamentary politics writ small—with the passage of the 1894 Local Government Act. It allowed otherwise qualified (i.e. propertied) married women to vote in local elections, and by 1900 women made up 13.7% of voters in local elections. But many remained unpersuaded that responsible local voting was any indication of women's fitness for national voting.

What the 1883–1885 Acts did do was to begin a new political era of mass politics by posing a real challenge to aristocratic political power. By virtue of scale, they revolutionized the system that had been reformed from 1832. The electoral system that had been created for elite landowners became one beholden to urban and suburban interests and dominated by working-class male voters, who by the turn of the twentieth century were the majority of voters. The modern system of party politics that began after these Acts was a response to mass political participation. After 1885, British elections were general and national in scope, were fought by cohesive national parties, and were voted in by a party-oriented electorate.[12] Because the 1883 Act made paid electioneering illegal, parties now relied on volunteer workers, and to this end party organizations formed that were meant to encourage socializing, coherence, and loyalty. Liberals, socialists, and conservatives all formed social wings of their parties. The largest and most successful was the Conservative Party's Primrose League. The Primrose League, which encouraged members to socialize across class lines, was very effective in welcoming women and working-class members and training them to work as political volunteers. Promoting imperialism, welcoming Catholics as well as Protestants, and sponsoring many respectable social events, by 1900 the League claimed 1.5 million members. Similar in purpose were the Liberal Associations. These worked well at the Parliamentary and electoral levels, but were never as effective as a social organization as the Primrose League was, in part because women were isolated in auxiliary Women's Liberal Associations. There were also socialist groups; the Social Democratic Federation had a separate Women's Council, and the Labour Party, formally established in 1906, had a Women's Labour League (WLL).

1885–1914: Labour, lords, women, and Ireland

Though Gladstone had been voted out of office in 1885, he returned in 1886 committed to bringing about a self-ruled Ireland. There was no movement for a self-ruled Scotland, but Scottish demands for political power led to the creation in 1885 of the Scottish Office and the post of Secretary for Scotland. Parnell still led the Home Rule movement. Irish nationalism had taken on a cultural aspect, with attempts to revive Irish language and culture through such organizations as the Gaelic Athletic Association (GAA). In 1886, Gladstone made Home Rule part of the Liberal Party platform and introduced the first Home Rule Bill (which was

Figure 2.1 1886: A mob kicking British Prime Minister William Ewart Gladstone in the
air over the contentious Home Rule Bill in a cartoon called "Away with Him,"
accompanied by the line from Tennyson "The wild mob's million feet will kick
you from your place."

defeated, as the second would be in 1893). Gladstone's decision ended his ministry and split the Liberal Party. Liberals who opposed Home Rule, and more generally supported the British Empire, left the Liberal Party (which became far smaller, poorer, and more radical) to found the Liberal Unionist party. Led by Lord Hartington and Joseph Chamberlain (until it splintered again in 1903 over free trade), the Liberal Unionist Party combined Liberal principles with support for the British empire and often worked with Lord Salisbury's Conservative Party. Together these Conservative and Liberal defenders of Union and empire formed the political right.

From 1886 until 1905, radicalism and reform both entered a period of relative decline, as many Britons turned their attention from domestic reform to issues abroad, including naval and colonial competition from Germany and the state of the empire. With the Liberal party divided by Home Rule the Conservative party, which had been out of power for most of the previous half century, ruled Britain for much of this period.

Since Disraeli's death, the party had been led by Lord Salisbury, who like Palmerston was uninterested in and resistant to social and electoral reform. He was an aristocratic elitist (the last politician to sit in the House of Lords while Prime Minister) who believed strongly that the constitution supported the Anglican church and had difficulty in conceptualizing a non-Anglican citizen.[13] Salisbury disliked the idea of an overwhelmingly working-class electorate, had resigned in protest over the 1867 Reform Act, and opposed Tory democracy, the strategy of appealing to working-class voters using patriotism and social reform that Disraeli had used so effectively. Salisbury preferred instead to consolidate his party's alliance with (and 1912 absorption of) the Liberal Unionist party. He focused on foreign policy: indeed whilst Prime Minister Salisbury did not take on the cabinet post of Lord of the Treasury, as was typical, and instead served as Foreign Secretary. Regarding continental Europe, he pursued a policy of what has been called "Splendid Isolation," characterized by a determination to avoid any European entanglements in favor of a focus on protecting and expanding the empire. For example, he successfully asserted British over French interests in the River Nile in the Fashoda crisis of 1898.

But while Salisbury was uninterested in pandering to the working class, his party nevertheless enjoyed its support. The Conservatives opposed a large government and kept both taxes and state intervention to a minimum (at least until the outbreak of the South African War). Many working-class voters (more numerous and more important than ever after 1884) were, it turned out, conservative in their political outlook, particularly in their opposition to a large or interventionist government. In addition many were also strong supporters of empire. These two political outlooks meant that many working-class voters supported the traditionally wealthy and landed Tory party. Salisbury's focus on empire proved less successful when he led Britain into the Second South African War (1899–1902), a drawn-out and humiliating conflict in which the mighty British empire took three full years to conquer a much smaller enemy force, revealed its population to be unfit for military service, and earned the world's contempt for its use of concentration camps. Salisbury stepped down soon after the war ended, succeeded by his nephew Arthur Balfour.

The political left continued to focus on reform. Between 1886 and 1905 the rump Liberal Party worked with the powerful Irish Home Rule MPs. They were also joined on the left by socialists; the 1880s saw a revival of British socialism, inspired in part by the emergence of Marxist socialist groups in continental Europe. Its mostly middle-class leaders included Marxist H.M. Hyndman (1842–1922), who founded the Social Democratic Federation and the National Socialist Party, sexologist Edward Carpenter (1844–1929), artist William Morris (1834–1896), and the members of the Fabian Society, a group of intellectuals including Beatrice (1858–1943) and Sidney Webb (1859–1947) who sought to enact socialism through gradual reforms. Late nineteenth- and early-twentieth century socialists tried to appeal to the working class and to rescue not only work regimes but leisure time from capitalism and commercialism by offering leisure options that made socialism a way of life. This goal seemed especially important in a period when commercialized leisure pursuits such as music halls, football, and vacation (holiday) packages were quickly expanding. However socialists' typically middle-class humorless determination to improve the working-class, who saw them as elitist outsiders, was not successful. The "rational recreation"—cycling, lectures and the like—they offered was didactic and unappealing; they managed to attract only a small group from the upper working class and lower middle class. A more authentic expression of working-class interests was the trade union movement. In spite of laws prohibiting workers from organizing or striking, trade unions were stronger and had a longer history in Britain than in the rest of Europe, and had been a force in politics since before the Second Reform Act. From the 1880s trade unions expanded, with membership rising from 750,000 in 1888, to slightly under 2 million in 1900. This was largely because new union tactics focused on organizing unskilled workers. Gas workers were unionized, as were matchmakers (whose 1888 strike was the most famous example of female labor agitation in the period) and there were many episodes of labor unrest, including the 1889 London Dockers' Strike.

From 1905 until after World War One, Britain was governed by Liberal governments. It also saw major changes in the political rights of the working class and women, the political status of Ireland, and in the constitution itself. In government, Balfour's Conservative government passed the 1902 Education Act, which added secondary education (what Americans call high school) to the elementary schools that had been established in 1870. While this was a reform that helped the working class, the clearest sign of the political power of the working class was the founding of a British Labour party in 1906 (the Scottish Labour Party had been founded in 1888). The first chair of the party, Keir Hardie (1856–1915), was a trade union leader, and trade unions and their members were a powerful majority in the Labour party. Compared with its European counterparts, the British Labour party was fairly conservative, largely because it needed the mass working-class support that the powerful but cautious trade unions could provide. While the older, Chartist-flavored, democratic radicalism that emphasized such ideas as adult suffrage and the abolition of the House of Lords persisted, it was not dominant. The Labour Party was an important party and a significant formal expression of working-class political feeling from its founding.

One reform issue that was ignored by much of the political left was women's suffrage. In the early twentieth century the feminist movement, which had agitated for employment options for women, legal rights within marriage, and an end to the Contagious Diseases Acts, became focused on the vote. Feminists had been agitating since the 1870s for votes for women, but with little success. One enormous barrier was the fact that until very late in the century, married women (that is, most adult women) could not legally own property, which was central to the right to vote. Another was the longstanding belief that women's portfolio in society did not extend to national politics. A third was the Liberal party's fear that women would vote Conservative, which led many Liberal politicians to oppose votes for women. In 1903, Emmeline Pankhurst (1858–1928) and her daughter Christabel Pankhurst (1880–1958) founded the militant Women's Social and Political Union (WSPU), which—in contrast to suffragists, who pursued various legal and legislative options—staged performative demonstrations that called attention to the cause of suffrage. The WSPU was controversial, but it unquestionably invigorated the suffrage movement. From 1907 major suffragette and suffragist demonstrations were held in London and other cities. Posters and other images arguing for and against suffrage flooded public spaces.[14] Women would finally get the vote in 1918.

There were problems abroad as well. The Cabinet was feeling increasingly nervous about Germany, because of its industrial progress and increasing naval strength. Britain's extensive military commitments to its colonies rendered it unready for European conflict, but it became increasingly convinced that it had to subsume colonial issues to the emerging problem of the conflicts and balances among European powers. Britain and France began to explore an alliance together against Germany, via a 1904 Entente and other consultations. By 1906, government fears had spread to the public, and stories and scares of German spies and invasions abounded. In 1907, an Anglo-Russian Entente was signed as a way of defusing a Russian threat. Britain, France, and Russia were now aligned with one another in a "Triple Entente" that stood against the comparable "Triple Alliance" of Germany, Austria-Hungary, and Italy. From 1909 the Liberal government tried to build up the British navy, while the German government responded in kind.

The Liberal party, working in alliance with the nascent Labour party, returned to power in 1906 in a landslide that would turn out to be their last major electoral victory. One effect of this victory was to divide the houses of Parliament, with Liberals dominating the House of Commons and Conservatives controlling the House of Lords. The new government passed Acts that reserved school places for children too poor to pay school fees, began programs of medical examinations and meals in schools, and set minimum wages in sweated trades. The introduction of a limited system of old age pensions (what Americans call social security) for the poor was an ambitious and expensive extension of the public safety net. In part to offset this cost, the Liberals' most ambitious attempt at reform came in the form of the budget proposed by Prime Minister Asquith's Chancellor of the Exchequer David Lloyd George in 1909. This budget came to be known as the "People's Budget" because while it maintained a Liberal commitment to free trade, it aimed to redistribute wealth away from the richest citizens and towards the working-class majority of the British population through a combination of social programs—including national unemployment insurance—and progressive taxation that distinguished between earned and unearned wealth.

The Conservative Party vehemently opposed this budget; they preferred to pay for rising state costs via tariffs, not taxes. The House of Lords saw the People's Budget as a step too far. The distinction between earned and unearned income seemed a radical step and was looked on with horror by a landed class whose income had fallen steeply because of falling rents, particularly in Ireland but across the United Kingdom. The Lords, which by tradition never blocked financial legislation, blocked the People's Budget, and thereby set off a constitutional crisis.

A number of politically complex moves followed. The Liberal government used traditional opposition to the aristocracy to attack the Lords. The Lords passed the People's Budget in March 1910, but by this time the Liberal party, led by Asquith, was determined to use the moment to limit the power of the Lords. The Liberals held a second general election in 1910, which was widely seen as a mandate for the change they wanted. Edward VII died and was succeeded by his son, George V; the new King was forced to agree to cooperate with the Liberal party and to threaten the House of Lords with the creation of hundreds of Liberal peers. Ultimately, the result was the passage of the 1911 Parliament Act, which drastically and permanently reduced the power of the House of Lords in the British constitution. Peers lost the power to address financial legislation in any fashion. They also lost the power to prevent the passage of any other legislation (though they could delay a bill's passage for up to two years). Furthermore the Parliament Act introduced annual salaries of £400 a year for MPs, which would allow many more people to stand for office, and shortened the maximum length of a parliamentary session from seven years to five years.

By limiting the powers of the House of Lords the Parliament Act made explicit what had become fact over the course of the nineteenth century—that the House of Commons was the center of the British government. While it remained rare for the House of Commons to pass a bill over the objections of the House of Lords, the symbolic import of the new Act was clear. The House of Lords was the most obvious and most material symbol of the power of the aristocracy; changes to its political status made clear the growth of democracy and the decline of the real political power of the aristocracy, in theory since 1832 but in practice since the mid-1880s. Attacks on the unfair power enjoyed by the upper house were also connected to the long tradition of popular and radical distaste for the aristocracy and attacks on it as unfairly ruling and as unfit to rule. In contrast to the 1820s, by the early twentieth century anti-aristocratic feeling was separate from anti-monarchical feeling; indeed the monarchy was fairly popular at this point.

The several years after this constitutional crisis saw the continuation and intensification of labor, Irish, and feminist unrest. Trade union membership continued to grow quickly, from 2.3 million in 1909 to 4.1 million in 1913. However trade unions continued to imagine the ideal member as a skilled, native, male head of household. Trade unions remained hostile to immigrant labor and did organize unskilled or female workers, and union membership was 90% male. There was profound labor unrest, with 70 million working days lost because of strikes between 1911 and 1914. The largest and most famous strikes were of coal miners, in Wales in 1910 and 1911, nationally in 1912, and in Yorkshire in 1914; of cotton workers and jute workers in 1911 and 1912; of transport workers in 1911; and of dock workers in 1911 and in London in 1912. Trade unions won many concessions from the government regarding wages, hours, and the right to collective industrial action.

The Irish question remained unresolved and increasingly tense. In 1905, Irish nationalist Arthur Griffith (1872–1922) had founded a new Irish nationalist party called Sinn Féin (Ourselves Alone). The third Home Rule Bill was introduced in 1912, and was, like the two before it, vociferously opposed by the unionist Protestants who lived in Ulster, in the north of Ireland. They responded by founding a paramilitary group, the Ulster Volunteers (later the Ulster Volunteer Force, or UVF), who were much like the paramilitary Catholic groups in the south such as the IRB. Delayed by the House of Lords, the 1912 Home Rule Bill was slated to become law in 1914, but its enactment was suspended when World War One began. In the middle of the war, the unsuccessful but highly symbolic 1916 Easter Rising, led by Sinn Fein members, changed the terms of the Irish problem and made Home Rule a political impossibility. After the war, in 1919 the southern majority of Ireland was granted complete independence from Britain, and became the Republic of Ireland; it immediately plunged into a civil war that lasted until 1921. Northern Ireland—the northernmost six counties, which had a unionist Protestant majority—remained a part of the United Kingdom. This partition of Ireland continues to plague Irish and British politics.

World War One is widely known to have begun with the assassination of Austrian Archduke Franz Ferdinand by Serbian nationalist Gavrilo Princip in Sarajevo on July 28, 1914. At first, most British politicians saw this act as local and Balkan in nature. However, by early August Russia had decided to support Serbia, Germany had decided to support Austria, and France had been drawn in. Only days afterwards, Asquith's government committed Britain to the war. While the war may have been a welcome distraction from domestic chaos, the Liberal government was opposed to the war and entered it reluctantly. In the event the war—widely expected to be over by Christmas, but in fact over four years long—only interrupted the domestic political developments we have explored here.

Notes

1 Rohan McWilliam, *Popular Politics in Nineteenth Century England* (Oxford: Routledge, 1998), p. 2.

2 Rohan McWilliam, "Victorian Political Cultures," in Martin Hewitt (ed.), *The Victorian World* (London: Routledge, 2012). Many thanks to the author for sharing this essay prior to its publication.
3 Frank O'Gorman, "Campaign Rituals and Ceremonies: the social meaning of elections in England, 1780–1860," *Past & Present* 135 (1992): 92.
4 William Hazlitt, "Commonplaces," no. 73 (November 15, 1823), in P. Howe, *The Complete Works of William Hazlitt* (Toronto: J.W. Dent, 1934), 20: 136, quoted in Thomas W. Laqueur, "The Queen Caroline Affair: Politics as Art in the Reign of George IV," *Journal of Modern History* 54.3 (1982): 417–466, p. 417.
5 McWilliam, *Popular Politics*, p. 12.
6 William Blake, "And did those feet in ancient time" (1808), line 8.
7 William S Walsh, *Handy-Book of Literary Curiosities* (Philadelphia: J.B. Lipincott and Co., 1892), p. 356.
8 Representation of the People Bill, House of Commons Debates, May 20, 1867, c. 838, quoted in Sophia Van Wingerden, *The Women's Suffrage Movement in Britain, 1866–1928* (Basingstoke: Palgrave Macmillan 1999), p. 11.
9 Patricia O'Hara, "Knowing Hodge: The Third Reform Bill and the Victorian Periodical Press," in Laurel Brake and Julie F. Codell, *Encounters in the Victorian Press: Editors, Authors, Readers* (Basingstoke: Palgrave Macmillan, 2005), pp. 103–118.
10 Matt Cole, "Democratic Watershed for Britain?" *Modern History Review* (February 1999): 6–7.
11 Robert Self, *The Evolution of the British Party System 1885–1940* (London: Longman, 2000), p. 18.
12 Self, p. 3.
13 McWilliam, "Victorian Political Cultures," p. 3.
14 Lisa Tickner, *The Spectacle of Women: Imagery of the Suffrage Campaign 1907–1914* (Chicago: University of Chicago Press, 1988), p. 48.

Relevant fiction that students might enjoy

G.W.M. Reynolds, *Mysteries of London* (1844)—now available in full text online.
Benjamin Disraeli, *Coningsby* (1844)
Anthony Trollope's "Palliser Novels"; *Can You Forgive Her?* (1864), *Phineas Finn* (1869), *The Eustace Diamonds* (1873), *Phineas Redux* (1874), *The Prime Minister* (1876), and *The Duke's Children* (1879)
George Eliot, *Felix Holt* (1866)
The 'Condition of England' or 'industrial' novels—Benjamin Disraeli's *Sybil* (1845), Elizabeth Gaskell's *Mary Barton* (1848) and *North and South* (1855), Charles Kingsley, *Alton Locke* (1850), Charles Dickens' *Hard Times* (1854)

Further reading

Catherine Hall, Keith McClelland, and Jane Rendall, *Defining the Victorian Nation: Class, Race, Gender and the Reform Act of 1867* (Cambridge: Cambridge University Press, 2000).
Part 3: Politics, in Martin Hewitt (ed.), *The Victorian World* (Abingdon, UK: Routledge, 2012).
Rohan McWilliam, *Popular Politics in Nineteenth Century England* (Abingdon, UK: Routledge, 1998).
Frank O'Gorman, "The Culture of Elections in England: From the Glorious Revolution to the First World War, 1688–1914." In Eduardo Posada-Carbó, (ed.), *Elections before*

Democracy: The History of Elections in Europe and Latin America (Basingstoke and London: Macmillan, 1996), pp.17–31.

Part II Politics and Government, in Chris Williams (ed.), *A Companion to Nineteenth-Century Britain* (Oxford: Blackwell, 2004).

Online resources

University of Cambridge Electronic Resources for British political and constitutional history, 1700–1914: www.hist.cam.ac.uk/seeley-library/online-resources/e-resources/part-i-paper-5

University of Cambridge Electronic Resources for British political and constitutional history since 1867: www.hist.cam.ac.uk/seeley-library/online-resources/e-resources/part-i-paper-6

UK Parliament website: www.parliament.uk

Politicians in The Parliamentary Archives—William Ewart Gladstone: www.parliament.uk/business/publications/parliamentary-archives/archives-highlights/archives-images-of-gladstone/

Chartist Ancestors: www.chartists.net/

3 Ruling the world

Imperialism

Introduction

Umbopa understood English, though he rarely spoke it.

"It is a far journey, Incubu," he put in, and I translated his remark.

"Yes," answered Sir Henry, "it is far. But there is no journey upon this earth that a man may not make if he sets his heart to it. There is nothing, Umbopa, that he cannot do, there are no mountains he may not climb, there are no deserts he cannot cross . . . if . . . he holds his life in his hands counting it as nothing, ready to keep it or lose it as Heaven above may order."

I translated.

"Great words, my father," answered the Zulu—I always called him a Zulu, though he was not really one—"great swelling words fit to fill the mouth of a man."

For the next ten minutes we trudged in silence, when suddenly Umbopa caught me by the arm.

"Look!" he said. . . . I followed his glance, and some two hundred yards from us perceived what appeared to be a hole in the snow.

"It is the cave," said Umbopa.

"By Jove! I believe it's full of diamonds," he said, in an awed whisper; and, indeed, the idea of a small goat-skin full of diamonds is enough to awe anybody.

"We are the richest men in the whole world," I said.[1]

This scene comes from *King Solomon's Mine*, by H. Rider Haggard. The bestselling 1885 adventure story was only one of thousands of Victorian publications that depicted white Britons as leaders, explorers, and heroes across the globe, many miles from the British Isles. Why were such stories conceivable? How did they come to be so popular? The answer is the British Empire, which was first established in the sixteenth century, remained largely intact until after World War Two, and continues to have profound ramifications today. During the Victorian period, Britain, a very small country, was the most powerful imperial nation on earth. Thousands of people from the empire settled in Britain, millions of Britons settled in, travelled to, made their living by, read about, sang songs about, and saw plays about empire, and hundreds of millions of people around the world found their lives impacted by British imperialism.

In 1820, when our period begins, Britain had lost most of its North American colonies, but it still had many others. Between 1820 and 1914 it expanded dramatically. The late nineteenth and early twentieth centuries saw the rise of anti-colonial nationalist movements that challenged the validity of British rule. Then in the decades after World War Two, Britain's colonies declared their independence and the empire ended. Decolonization began with Indian Independence in 1947 and was often violent; while it lies outside the chronological boundaries of this book, it is a key focus of historians of imperialism.

British imperialism and the British Empire are huge topics. Indeed, this chapter is the only one in this book on a topic to which entire undergraduate courses are routinely dedicated, in the US, the UK, and elsewhere. (This is not to say that undergraduate courses specifically on space, consumption, sexuality, or religion in Victorian Britain would not be fascinating, only that they are rare. Undergraduate courses specifically on Victorian high politics do exist, though they usually claim to be general history courses.) The British Empire was huge; by 1914 it comprised one quarter of the world's population and one fifth of its land. And the British Empire is huge: it is its own field of history—indeed, it is several fields of history—and it has become a more popular topic of scholarship in recent decades. This chapter will not attempt to narrate all of the events that occurred in all of the areas of the British Empire. Instead, it will introduce readers to the field of British imperial history, and to some of the key questions historians currently ask about the British Empire. It will then present a brief sketch of the British Empire between 1820 and 1914.

Arguing about empire

We should start with a definition. *The Encyclopedia of Empire*, a project overseen by prominent historian of the British Empire John MacKenzie, concisely defines an empire as "an expansionist polity which seeks to establish various forms of sovereignty over people or peoples of an ethnicity different from (or in some cases the same as) its own."[2] Victorian Britain was certainly such an imperial nation. During the Victorian period (and before and after it) the British state continually worked to expand the territories, peoples, and cultures that it governed, controlled, or influenced. It was the largest empire on earth.

The formal study of the history of the British Empire can be dated to 1882. In that year, Sir John Seeley (1834–1895) published a set of lectures he had developed for Cambridge University undergraduates as a book entitled *The Expansion of England*. Seeley proposed that scholars integrate the history of Britain's empire and the history of Britain. His new approach to imperial history mapped onto a new imperialist approach: western powers were beginning to practice a "new imperialism," in which Britain and other imperialist European powers rapidly claimed large parts of Africa, south Asia, and East Asia. After World War Two, empire became a standard part of the undergraduate history curriculum. The impetus for this change came in part from the work of historians Ronald Robinson and John Gallagher, who co-authored a series of influential works that stressed the power, reach, and influence of Britain on its colonies. They focused on the policies of the British governing elite ("the imperial mind"), on the role of local and indigenous "collaborators" in the governing of empire, and on "informal" as well as "formal" empire, that is, on places and polities Britain controlled via economic domination, even if it had no formal political presence. The Robinson–Gallagher school dominated the study of empire for generations, as imperial historians focused on high politics, the economy, and the role of the military in the expansion of empire.[3]

However, since the late 1970s imperial history has changed dramatically. This is due to several developments, including the rise of area studies and subaltern studies, the rise of postcolonial theory, the imperial turn, and the emergence of "the new imperial history." As decolonization progressed, scholarship began to decolonize and to nationalize as well. Rather than studying the British Empire in its entirety, scholars began to study the histories, geographies, and literatures of particular regions of the former empire, such as the Caribbean or South Asia. These new interdisciplinary or multidisciplinary approaches to culturally-, politically-, or geographically-defined areas were dubbed "area studies." Area studies focused on experiences at the ground and on the periphery, that is, on the experience of formerly colonized peoples rather than on those of British imperial officials. As such, they spoke to the determination of people in new nations to write their own histories. Also important was the rise of Subaltern Studies, led by the Subaltern Studies Group (SSG). This was a movement of scholars determined to treat South Asians as people with agency, rather than as passive recipients or victims of imperial policies, and to focus on South Asian peoples' political and cultural subjectivity and agency.

Another important new academic movement to emerge was "postcolonialism." Postcolonial theory emerged out of literature departments and literary criticism; its most important scholar is Edward Said (1935–2003), author of *Orientalism*.[4] Postcolonial scholars focus on the long-term cultural effects of imperialism that persist after formal imperialism has ended. Many imperial historians criticize postcolonial scholars for being overly theoretical and insufficiently archival or empirical. Others, including Dane Kennedy and Durba Ghosh, have argued that more traditional empirical work on imperial political history can be enriched by postcolonial approaches, including a close attention to language (also called "the linguistic turn" or "discourse analysis") and by an openness to cultural history (also called "the cultural turn").

Third, from the 1990s, many historians who had previously focused on Britain enlarged their remit to study its empire. They rejected the Robinson–Gallagher assumption that influence flowed only from Britain to its empire, and began to investigate the complex relationship between Britain and its empire. In particular, historians who took "the imperial turn" discovered that while the metropole influenced the empire, the reverse was true as well. In historian

Antoinette Burton's words, the empire was a "fundamental and constitutive part of English culture and national identity at home."[5]

All of these new trends came together to create "the new imperial history." The new imperial history turns away from political, military, and economic history to focus on cultural, social, and intellectual history. It is particularly concerned with race, gender, and sexuality, along with science, technology, consumption, and the environment. It eschews Robinson and Gallagher's top-down approach, preferring a bottom-up perspective. It pays close attention to the creation and exchange of material goods, but also of knowledge and information. The new imperial history emphasizes networks and exchanges, and the fact that influence traveled from colony to metropole as well as vice-versa. It holds that empire constituted not only the identities and cultures of the colonized, but those of the colonizers as well. Furthermore, recent new imperial historical work has emphasized that influence could also travel around the periphery, with colonies influencing one another. Where "old" imperial history might study leading administrators of British India and the policies they implemented, new imperial history might trace the rise of white domesticity in British India, the move from a society in which white men in India were encouraged to have non-marital sexual relationships with Indian women to one in which white men were expected to marry white women and bring them to India (and how that shift was repeated in other imperial sites). Where "old" imperial history would look at the tactics and strategies employed during the Second South African War, new imperial history might concern itself with representations of concentration camps in the international press during the same war.[6]

The new imperial history has reframed the questions that historians ask. Some practitioners of new imperial history have sought to de-center empire, to see it as a network that had no single center, of geography or of power. Others have engaged in comparative work, comparing pre-colonial to colonial societies, or the British Empire to other empires. Such works have created connections between imperial history and world history—as well as disagreements over how central the British Empire was to global historical change. In recent years some historians—not all of them aligned with the new imperial history—have nominated other terms or categories that might be more helpful than "British Empire," such as the "British world" or "British world system." John Darwin uses "empire project" and "unfinished empire" to stress the fact that empire-building was always in progress and never completed. James Belich argues that migration and settlement were the key forces that transformed the globe, and that we should think about an "Anglo-World" that includes the United States. Public intellectual and political conservative Niall Ferguson, author of *Empire: The Rise and Demise of the British World Order and the Lessons for Global Power*, has coined the term "Anglobalization."

There are two current debates in about the British Empire that we should note. The first is about how much empire mattered at home. Historians have been arguing for some time about whether typical people living in Britain were affected by, aware of, or proud of the empire. This debate is connected to the new imperial history and its differences with traditional approaches. A central claim of much new imperial history—that empire was constitutive of Britain—rests on the assertion that, if we look closely, we can see that nineteenth-century Britain was awash in imperially-generated wealth, imperial foodstuffs, imperial products, imperial narratives, and imperial images. Yet more traditional scholars, led by historian Bernard Porter, argue that most people in Britain were unaware of and relatively unaffected by empire. Some of this debate revolves around timing, with new imperial historians arguing that empire was central to Britain from the eighteenth century or earlier, and others arguing that empire was not a part of most people's consciousness until the late nineteenth century if it ever was.

In this debate, this book sides with the new imperial history and with John MacKenzie, whose influential 1986 book, *Imperialism and Popular Culture*, was the first work to argue that empire was integral to popular culture in Britain. It seems clear that in Victorian Britain, empire was all around, in a wide variety of ways. Empire was present in Britain in the form of people travelling in all directions. The empire was visited by, or home to, many British people. Where they went and what they did depended on their class and their goals and resources. Upper-class people took posts at the very top of the imperial bureaucracies. Middle-class people became civil servants abroad or in imperial departments. Lower middle-class and working-class women found work as servants, in factories, or as prostitutes (usually with military men as their clients). Prostitutes were often subjected to various regulations, and white women who served nonwhite clients were looked on with contempt. Lower middle-class people frequently went abroad as missionaries. (The Baptist Missionary Society (BMS) was quite successful at converting Jamaican slaves. Missionaries to India, however, were only ever able to convince a very small minority of Indians to convert to Christianity; they were a bit more successful in the South Pacific and Africa (a popular destination for female missionaries), but not until the twentieth century. Missionaries were often socially isolated, because they were rejected both by natives who were unreceptive to their message, and by higher-class colonial officials and ruling elites.) Working-class people moved to imperial places because they served in the military, worked on large projects such as railways, or emigrated to various parts of empire in search of a better life. Many sought the opportunity to become small farmers, something that was no longer possible in Britain.

Emigration created a permanent awareness of imperial spaces for those family and friends who remained in Britain. It also linked those in Britain to the empire via money, as many emigrants sent funds home. For instance, Christmas brought a slew of "American letters," sent from young adult Irish emigrants to their parents in Ireland, which contained £1 million annually and were vital to many in western rural Ireland. (Following the famine, many Irish young adults expected to find work in the United States, not Ireland.) Many Cornish miners emigrated to South Africa (to mine gold and diamonds); in the early twentieth century every delivery of mail from South Africa brought £20,000 to £30,000 to families back in Cornwall.[7] And emigration was not always permanent—as many as 40% of those who emigrated from England and Wales between 1870 and 1914 resettled in Britain, further entwining Britain and empire. Britain was visited by many imperial subjects, both nonwhite and white, with a constant stream of travelers, students, and others arriving, settling, and departing. Former slave Mary Prince (c.1788–1833?) was well-known on the lecture circuit in the early 1830s; leader of the Hindu reform movement *Brahmo Samaj*, Rammohun Roy (1772–1833), travelled to England in the 1830s. In the 1880s, social reformer Pandita Ramabai (1858–1922) came to England to train as a doctor, and Indian independence movement leader Mohandas Gandhi (1869–1948) studied law. Empire was largely responsible for the presence of small but vibrant non-white populations within Britain. Though Britishness and whiteness were often conflated, the population of nineteenth-century Britain included thousands of nonwhite people, most of whom lived in London or in port cities such as Bristol, Liverpool, Chester, Dartmouth, and Plymouth. These included African or Afro-Caribbean men who were former slaves, former servants, or sailors; they often married white working-class women, who were thought to find African men particularly virile and desirable. They also included the biracial children of white Caribbean planters and white East India Company employees. As technologies of communication and transportation improved, more Africans and Asians came to Britain (where they probably remained concentrated in urban port areas). Nonwhites were rarely considered truly British, even if they had been born in Britain.[8]

Another way in which empire was present in Britain was via a constant and dynamic flow of things and images: of raw imperial materials that were processed in Britain, such as Indian jute, processed in Dundee; of British goods consumed in empire, such as calico cotton cloth; of imperial goods consumed in Britain, such as tea and curry powder. Empire transformed British interior decoration, gardening, fashion, and diet; the British ate and drank Indian tea, Nigerian chocolate, New Zealand lamb and butter, and South African apples, grapes and pears. Eliza Acton's *Modern Cookery* (13th edition, 1853) and *Mrs Beeton's Household Management* (1861) both provided recipes for the curries that *memsahibs* (middle-class wives of British officials in India) had made popular in Britain. Some items (such as authentic Kashmiri shawls) were expensive, but many were not; after 1870 working-class Britons considered at least two imperial items, tea and sugar, to be staples. Representations and narratives of empire were everywhere. Until 1870, missionaries' tales of their exploits abroad were many Britons' primary source of information about the empire. These they encountered in weekly church services and fundraising efforts and in periodical literature (from the *Church Missionary Gleaner* to more general magazines like *The Leisure Hour*), in which they read missionary biographies, fiction, anecdotes, and articles. There were also stories about explorers and other virile, intrepid adventurers; descriptions of the travels of David Livingstone, who crossed the entire African continent in 1853, and of Richard Burton, who travelled in Africa and Asia, were very popular. India was the frequent location of melodramatic plays. Photographs of India, Burma, China, and North Africa were available in England from the 1850s. Imperial images, narratives, and rhetoric were available throughout the Victorian period and saturated Britain from about 1870. Wilkie Collins' novel *The Moonstone* (1868) and the Sherlock Holmes novel

The Sign of Four (1890) both have plots linked to the British presence in India. Displays of exotic colonial peoples and animals, painted panoramas and dioramas, and museums also created imperial knowledge for the British public, as did official exhibitions such as the Colonial and Indian Exhibition of 1886, where for only 6d. attendees could purchase booklets on the "History, Products, and Natural Resources" of all the colonies and dominions. Empire was a subject of celebration in music halls. Programs that expressed imperialist-nationalist sentiments had titles like "Indianationality," "Britannia," and "Grand Military Spectacle." Popular songs such as *Soldiers of the Queen*, and *Sons of the Sea*, and *By Jingo!* celebrated imperial military exploits abroad. In the twentieth-century, cinema newsreels covered colonial events like the South African War in a new and dramatic medium. Celebrations of Queen Victoria's new title of "Empress of India," and of her Golden and Diamond Jubilees, served as celebrations of royalty and empire. The Queen was the imperial symbol of an imperial nation. Children were inundated with empire. Textbooks such as *A Student's History of England* assured readers that "England cannot but perceive that many things are done by the natives of India which are in their nature hurtful, unjust, or even cruel, and they are naturally impatient to remove evils that are evident to them."[9] Popular boys' story papers such as the *Boy's Own Magazine* (1855–1875) and *Boy's Own Paper* (1879–1967) depicted empire as a place of adventure, conquest, and character formation. Adventure stories by G.A. Henty (1832–1902) and Rider Haggard (1856–1925)—one of which began this chapter—had imperial settings. Boys and girls could send, collect or swap picture postcards featuring frontier warfare, imperial heroism, and indigenous peoples. They could play with imperially-themed toy soldiers, board games, and jigsaw puzzles. From 1904 they participated in celebrations of Empire Day.

The capital city, London, was an imperial city, marked everywhere by signs of Britain's military victories and imperial status. The Colonial Office was in Whitehall. Imperial goods were unloaded at the docks and railways every day. A statue of Field Marshal Hugh Rose, later Lord Strathnairn, who put down the Indian Rebellion, stood in Knightsbridge. Port towns, where goods arrived from or left for empire, also had a strong imperial awareness. But these interactions extended further, into less obvious places such as Birmingham. Birmingham is not a port; it was famous in the Victorian period as a manufacturing center, and visitors would tour factories and workshops to gaze in awe at British industry. But Birmingham was also imperial: Australia and New Zealand were both important markets for Birmingham doorknobs, India welcomed Birmingham padlocks, Australia and India needed Birmingham-made cut nails, chains, cables, and anchors, and Birmingham's wrought-iron hinges sold well in the Caribbean, Canada, New Zealand, and South Africa. Birmingham's newspapers reported on and editorialized about events in empire. For example, the weekly *Birmingham Journal* published articles on emancipated slaves, the Sikh war, the Morant Bay rebellion and the Eyre controversy, troubles on the Cape, and challenges emigrants to New Zealand faced, among many other imperial topics.[10]

The second current debate we must note is about how big and how important the British Empire was in the first place. Was it developed, maintained, and ruled by design, a well-run, powerful, and mighty behemoth? Or was it a patchwork, so diverse that it was more a collection more than a plan, something managed but never really ruled, created by accident, and run on the cheap? MacKenzie has dubbed this the "ramshackle or rampaging" debate.[11] The ramshackle side is associated with famous phrases, that the British had "conquered and peopled half the world in a fit of absence of mind" (the phrase is Seeley's), that they were "reluctant imperialists" who were surprised to find an empire thrust upon them, dealt with it as best they could, and dissolved it as soon as was practical. It includes historians Bernard Porter and John Darwin. On the other (rampaging) side are most new imperial historians, who hold that the empire, however diverse it might have been, wielded such a huge amount of power over such a large number of human lives and societies and square number of miles that we need to take it and its effects seriously. We cannot minimize it or absolve it of responsibility for its effects. Historians MacKenzie, Ghosh, and Catherine Hall all belong to this school of thought. Connected is a debate about whether the British Empire was a typical or an exceptional empire. Those who see the empire as ramshackle also tend to see it as exceptional; those who see it as rampaging are more likely to compare it to other empires. Both debates are also about whether the British Empire was, fundamentally, a good thing or a bad thing, whether the British today should celebrate it or apologize for it. Political conservatives— professional historians and others—are more likely to celebrate empire; Ferguson is a good example. Those whose politics lie more on the left of the spectrum are more likely to see the empire as powerful, damaging, and apology-worthy. Kennedy points out that current discussions of the British Empire are often actually discussions about something else. In the UK, he argues, debates about the history of empire are really debates not just about Britain's past but also about deepening anxieties about its future. In the US, they are a vehicle for discussions of America's own role as a global power—many would say an empire—today. Here again, this book sides with the new imperial history. The British Empire had huge effects on the world, and the British went to great lengths to keep it. There was nothing accidental about any of this. While many see the diversity of forms of imperial control as evidence that the empire was ramshackle and reluctant, we can just as easily argue that this diversity is evidence of a commitment to empire and determination to maintain it. As historian Philippa Levine remarks, given the enormous size of the empire, and the difficulty and expense of administering it, the notion that the British were at all reluctant is "not awfully persuasive."[12] Whether they were reluctant or not, there was nothing timid or partial about the mark they made on the world.

1820–1870: The turn to India, the end of slavery, the rise of emigration

When our period began in 1820, Britain had experienced a significant recent change to its empire in the form of the loss (in the late eighteenth century) of most of its North American colonies. This loss marks the end of the "first British

Empire," and was followed in the late eighteenth and early nineteenth centuries by the emergence of a "second British Empire" that lasted until the twentieth century. As the empire's second iteration began, the British Empire became less focused on the Atlantic world and more oriented towards South Asia (this was made easier by the decline of the Dutch, Spanish, and French as imperial powers). Even in 1820, Britain had extensive holdings from which it derived much wealth and geopolitical power, with territory in North America, the Caribbean, South Asia, South Africa, and the South Pacific. Between 1820 and 1870, the British Empire expanded, shifted its orientation eastwards, and increased its number of non-white subjects. It acquired parts of India, the Straights settlements (Singapore, Penang and Malacca, in 1826), western and southern Australia (in the 1820s), the Falklands Islands (in 1833), and Hong Kong (in 1841). It also became a powerful force in the economies of China, Siam, Argentina, and Brazil. All of this was not accomplished without force: between 1820 and 1870 Britain put down the Indian and Morant Bay Rebellions and fought the Afghan, Opium, Sikh, Xhosa, Anglo-Burmese, Maori, and Taranaki Wars.

Some colonies were considered settlement colonies, to which British people moved and settled permanently; Canada, Australia, and New Zealand were all settlement colonies. Others colonies, sometimes called dependent colonies, had much smaller British populations; British people were expected to move there only to work (in military or civil service, the extraction industries, and the like) and to return home to Britain. Jamaica and India were dependent colonies. In dependent colonies, the British recognized that there were indigenous populations with which they had to coexist. In contrast, the British often represented settlement colonies as empty lands, waiting to be filled by white Britons, although this was not the case; Canada, Australia, and New Zealand all had thriving indigenous populations.

Central to the empire in the late eighteenth and early nineteenth centuries was the Atlantic slave trade. While slavery was not new in human history, the Atlantic slave system was distinctive in its focus on agricultural labor, its racial specificity, and its enormous scale: by the late nineteenth century 12 million African people had been shipped to the Americas as slaves. Life for enslaved people in the British Caribbean was very difficult, in part because sugar production there combined exhausting agricultural work with exhausting factory work to grow and process sugar. Violence, including sexual violence against women, was endemic to the slave system. On the backs of the enslaved, many planters in the 14 sugar colonies, of which Jamaica was the largest, made vast fortunes selling slave-grown sugar to the British public, who quickly developed a taste for sugared tea and for "puddings" (desserts).

The British anti-slavery movement was very active in the late eighteenth and early nineteenth centuries. Britain abolished its slave trade—but not slavery itself—in 1807. It then abolished slavery in the British Caribbean, Mauritius and the Cape in 1833, though on terms that were very gradual and very favorable to enslavers. Enslaved people were told that they had to work as "apprentices" for their enslavers for seven more years, until 1840 (though in the event this scheme was so unsuccessful that it was ended in 1838). Furthermore, enslavers were compensated by the government the enormous sum of £20 million.

The success of the abolition movement and the end of slavery meant that in the 1820s and 1830s the sugar colonies' plantations became far less profitable than they had been, and the Caribbean sugar trade stopped being the source of easy wealth it had once been. Together with the loss of the North American colonies, the end of slavery led to Britain shifting its imperial energies towards Asia and the Pacific.

Two important colonies, Australia and New Zealand, were in the Pacific. Both were settler colonies, valued for their sheep, farm land, timber, and flax. These areas had been explored from the eighteenth century; many "new" plants and animals were "discovered," and scientific discovery became linked to exploration and imperial expansion. Between 1787 and 1868 over 160,000 people (60% English, 34% Irish, and 5% Scottish, and predominantly male) convicted of capital crimes had their sentences commuted and were instead "transported"—that is, forced to emigrate—to Australia. (Until 1776 penal convicts had been transported to British America, but after the American Revolution the British government was forced to find a new place to send them.) While transportation gave Australia a reputation as a nation of criminals, most convicts were working-class people who had committed only small property crimes and were as skilled and as literate as others in the working class. Australia also welcomed many voluntary migrants, mostly working-class people attracted by the free passage and cheap land offered by colonial governments and emigration societies from the 1830s. Australia's British population grew quickly in the Victorian period. In 1820, there were 32,000 colonists in Australia. By 1850, the white population of Australia's two colonies was 400,000, including both convicts and emigrants. The Australian gold rush (which started in 1851) attracted male immigrants who sought adventure and immediate success through luck rather than a punishing work ethic. In the 1850s and 1860s there was also a movement to have unmarried women emigrate, to solve the so-called "redundancy crisis" (the belief that the census of 1851 had revealed the problematic existence of as many as a million more women than men in England who were "surplus" and would never marry) and the gender imbalance in Australia in one fell swoop. Some women emigrated, though in smaller numbers than men, seeking jobs, husbands, or both. By 1868, when transportation to Australia ended, approximately 350,000 Britons— convicts and emigrants in equal numbers—had travelled to Australia. As the white population grew, the indigenous population suffered. The number of Aboriginal people—seen as primitive by white Britons—in Australia declined from about 300,000 in the eighteenth century to only 80,000 by the late nineteenth century. Whites controlled Aboriginals through violence and poor treatment, even though they relied on Aboriginal labor and knowledge to settle Australia.

White emigration to New Zealand began in 1839, much later than emigration to Australia; by the early 1840s there were 10,000 whites in New Zealand. From the 1840s, the Maori and the white settlers were at war, mostly over land ownership, as the whites (called *Pakeha* by the Maori) took over Maori lands and geographically marginalized the Maori. As with the Aboriginals in Australia, the indigenous population declined, from 200,000 in 1840 to 100,000 by the end of the nineteenth century. In North America, Canada, valued for its fur and timber trades, followed a similar pattern of decimation of the native population. By the 1860s, Canada, Australia, and New Zealand had all been granted "responsible self-government." Many political powers remained centered in the metropole, but these colonies were seen as capable of governing themselves, and as miniature Britains across the ocean, central to the idea of a British Commonwealth. Colonial whites often considered themselves British even if they had never set foot in England, Scotland, or Wales. Once in Britain their skin color allowed these "fictive Europeans" to move across Britain more freely than people of color, but their colonial accents marked them as socially subordinate, and the British often did not consider white colonials British.

In India, the British Empire's shift from the Atlantic world to Asia and the Pacific meant even more attention to a colony that had been an important source of income, exploration, and scholarship since the seventeenth century. The Indian subcontinent became more important for the wealth it offered via cotton, silk, indigo dye, tea, and opium, and the geopolitical power it gave Britain. And succeeding in India became an important symbolic counterbalance to failing in America. In 1820, there were only about 45,000 white Britons in India (and 150 million indigenes). Technically, British India was ruled not by the British government but by a private company, the East India Company (EIC) (which had been chartered and granted this right by the government). However, by the nineteenth century this was virtually a technicality; one historian describes the nineteenth-century EIC as a department of state. From the early nineteenth century, and especially in the 1840s under Governor-General Lord Dalhousie, the EIC moved from a eighteenth-century Orientalist and non-interventionist approach, in which whites declined to interfere in Indian cultural practices, to a more judgmental interventionist approach that tried to replace a wide range of Indian practices with English ones. The goal was to make Indian culture less barbaric and more English. Often the imposed changes related to women. For example, in 1829 Governor-General William Bentinck declared *sati* (the burning of a widow on her husband's funeral pyre) illegal, a move that revealed a misunderstanding of Indian society (*sati* was confined to elite families and was not at all widespread). In the 1840s and 1850s, the British westernized India by building railways, creating a postal system, allowing Hindu widows to remarry, and revamping land inheritance laws and the terms of military service for Indian men. All of these changes were represented as improvements on non-European culture. Yet at the same time, the British were actively engaged in opium trading. A large portion of Britain and the East India Company's profits came from its sale of Indian opium in China (in spite of Chinese anti-opium laws). When the Chinese government sought to block this illegal trade in their own country, the British successfully fought the Opium Wars from 1839 to 1842 (thereby acquiring Hong Kong) and from 1856 to 1860 to ensure its "right" to sell opium (and spread opiate addiction) in China.

These and other actions on the part of the British were unpopular, and dissatisfaction with them was partly responsible for a military uprising that grew into the Indian Rebellion of 1857. The Rebellion was an expression of widespread Indian anger at multiple aspects of British rule. In addition to the changes noted above, the British had expanded their territories, annexing the Punjab in 1849 and Oudh in 1856. In the Indian Army, new regulations (including some requiring travel) angered high-caste Hindu *sepoys* (Indian troops). Then, in 1857, came the last straw. A new weapon, the Enfield rifle, was introduced to Indian troops. A rumor quickly spread that the cartridges of the new rifles were greased with a mixture of beef and pork fat (offensive to both Hindus and Muslims). Soldiers in the Bengal Army mutinied. Though the British tried (well into the twentieth century) to minimize the conflict by calling it the Sepoy Mutiny, in fact the soldiers' disobedience quickly developed into a much larger rebellion that included both soldiers and civilians. This surprised and upset many Britons who saw Indians who they thought were their devoted servants leave them to join the rebellion. However, while Indians had much pent-up anger, they had no leader or clear political goal.

The Indian Rebellion was fought across the north and northwest areas of the Indian subcontinent for over a year, and was marked by looting and killing of civilians on both sides. The British public at home was kept well-informed about Indian "atrocities" such as the massacre at Cawnpore (now Kanpur), in which 200 British prisoners (mostly women and children) were thrown down a well and left to die. However, it heard little or nothing of comparable acts committed by the British, such as the brutal mistreatment of rebels at Ajnala, where over 200 were shot and 45 died of crowding and exhaustion awaiting the same fate. The massacre at Cawnpore was considered horrific by the British, particularly because women and children had died. In addition there were many rumors of Indian men raping and torturing English women at Cawnpore and elsewhere. The popular press was full of allusions to "unspeakable" and "atrocious" acts, that is, rapes of white British women by nonwhite Indian men. Although no personal accounts of rape survive and all reports were later discredited by official inquiries, the myth of the 1857 rapes persisted and became a key part of the collective imperial memory.

The rebellion was put down by the end of 1858, and that same year the British government passed the Government of India Act, which dissolved the EIC. The EIC was replaced by a new Indian civil service and direct rule of India by the Crown, and India became the only colonial possession that had its own government department, the India Office, to whom the Viceroy of India (a new post) reported. Announcing its implementation, the Queen gave a speech, her Proclamation to India, in which she promised her Indian subjects her affection and respect, and equality under British law.

The post-Rebellion rule of India is referred to the British Raj. In principle, then, Britain's control over India took on an entirely new form after the rebellion. New policies regarding criminal law, civil law (in particular, property inheritance) and census-taking were put into place. In practice, however, much stayed the

Figure 3.1 A British depiction of the 1857 "Massacre at Cawnpore," from *The History of the Indian Mutiny* published in 1858 (engraving) by English School (nineteenth century).

Private collection/Ken Welsh/The Bridgeman Art Library.

same. Lord Canning, who was Governor-General of India when the rebellion broke out, became the first Viceroy of India in 1858. Officials and soldiers of the EIC became officials and soldiers of the Crown. From the perspective of Indian subjects, the main change after 1858 was a huge increase in the number of white soldiers stationed in India, to 60,000, fully one third of the entire British army. Stability was reestablished, but British Indian society became more racially and culturally divided and Indian resentment and dissatisfaction persisted.

The Indian Rebellion was soon followed by wars with the Maori in New Zealand from 1861 to 1865, and then by another major colonial revolt, this time in Jamaica. Jamaica was governed by colonial administrator, Edward John Eyre. While the island was technically a representative democracy following the abolition of slavery in 1838, in practice most Jamaican blacks were small farmers who could not vote because they were too poor to pay their poll tax. Struggles over land ownership and cultivation, labor conditions, and electoral law led to increased dissatisfaction among black Jamaicans. In October 1865, following an unpopular legal verdict, several hundred Jamaicans rioted outside the Morant Bay courthouse. Governor Eyre declared martial law, and over the next month—despite the lack of any organized resistance—British troops executed hundreds of Jamaicans, flogged others, and burnt over 1,000 homes. Paul Bogle, the leader of the rebellion, was hanged, as was George William

Gordon, a mixed-race member of the Jamaican House of Assembly suspected of involvement. The House of Assembly was abolished, as blacks were clearly unready, the British claimed, for representative government. Debate raged for months over whether Governor Eyre had been justified in the amount of force he had used. While he had the support of the Colonial Office, protests from abolitionist and dissenting groups resulted in a Royal Commission which in mid-1866 concluded that Eyre's response had been excessively violent and unnecessarily prolonged. The Eyre controversy split Britain's liberal intelligentsia. Eyre Defence Committee members included John Ruskin, Charles Kingsley, and Charles Dickens, while the opposing Jamaica Committee was led by John Stuart Mill and included Charles Darwin, Thomas Huxley, and Herbert Spencer. Proceedings against Eyre were started three times, but he was never tried. In 1866, public opinion in Britain was against Eyre (white Jamaicans supported him), but by 1868 he enjoyed broad popular support in Britain. Overall, the combination of the Indian Rebellion, the Maori Wars, and the Morant Bay Rebellion had convinced the white British public and government that nonwhite natives were inherently violent, and that governing them with a firm hand was more important than protecting their political rights.

In 1866 and 1867, as Jamaicans lost their representative government, Canadians saw their right to responsible self-government confirmed: Canada was granted Dominion status. Canadians were white (and increasingly were British rather than French), and thus were perceived as people who could govern themselves as violent black Jamaicans could not. During these same years, Britain experienced a series of anti-Irish riots, and Fenians—those in favor of Irish Home Rule—were labeled as terrorists rather than political activists, a way of stating that neither their cause nor their methods were valid. 1867 was also the year that the Second Reform Act separated respectable from unrespectable working-class men, granting the former but not the latter the vote. All of these took place at the same time, and all happened in the context of the others, as groups were deemed respectable and politically valid or not. The imperial conflicts of the 1850s and 1860s, together with unrest in Ireland and political reform in Britain, re-inscribed race, gender, class, and respectability as critical indicators of who was deserving of self-government and participation in political processes.

1870–1914: Colonial expansion and anti-colonial challenges

Some historians see contrasts between earlier and later Victorian imperialism. They stress that, in the later period, the British were facing new rivals in the form of Germany, now a major colonial power (following its creation as a nation in 1870), and of the United States. Britain was also suffering from an economic depression (which began in 1873, see Chapter 4), which impacted imperial policy. Other historians emphasize continuities across the entire nineteenth century, noting that both emigration and territorial expansion continued apace, and that London's position as the center of international commerce and finance helped to maintain Britain's influence in international trade in spite of the depression.

Emigration to Australia and New Zealand continued, and in the late nineteenth century and early twentieth century many lower middle-class and working-class people emigrated to Canada and South Africa as well. By 1885, approximately 375,000 people had emigrated from Great Britain and Ireland to New Zealand; by 1900, over half a million people had emigrated from Great Britain and Ireland to Australia. Starting during the Irish Famine and continuing for a half a century, emigration from Ireland was extremely high. Emigration from Scotland was also very pronounced and contributed to the low Scottish population. For example, Jean Burns was born in Dundee, Scotland in 1895 and worked in a carpet factory from the age of 14. At 18, hoping for a better life, she arranged passage to Ontario, where she married and raised four children. Between 1820 and 1930, 4.25 million people left Britain and Ireland for the United States alone; between 1870 and 1914, a total of approximately 10 million people emigrated from Britain to Canada, the United States, Latin America, South Africa, Australia, and New Zealand. Both of these statistics support Belich's argument that when we think about migration we should think in terms of one large "Anglo-World" that encompasses Britain, the settler colonies, and the United States.

Aggressive territorial expansion continued, helped by new technologies including faster ships across the oceans, railways across continents, and telegraphy across both. In the decades after 1858, Britain claimed new territories on the Indian subcontinent, and used the Suez Canal to ship textiles between Britain and India. We also see deliberate expansion in the changing dynamics between the British and Ottoman empires. The once-powerful Ottoman Empire was, by the nineteenth century, quite weak. The British had generally been respectful of Ottoman territorial claims and supportive of the Ottoman Empire, seeing it as a useful bulwark against the French and the Russians. However, in 1878, when the British felt that they needed a supply line to the eastern Mediterranean, they changed tacks and took the island of Cyprus from the Ottomans, declaring it a British protectorate. We see a similar tactical shift regarding Egypt, which was also part of the Ottoman Empire. Egypt's Suez Canal opened in 1869. Shipping through the Suez Canal was cheaper and faster than overland transport across India and so was very important to the British textile industry. From the mid-1870s most of the goods shipped through the canal were British, and Britain owned 44 percent of the canal. Given its importance to British industries, an 1882 nationalist uprising in Egypt was a serious economic concern for Britain. Britain tried unsuccessfully to gain informal control of Egypt, and in the end occupied and claimed Egypt as part of its empire. In only four years, Britain had taken two key possessions from its alleged ally, the Ottoman Empire.

The colonization of Egypt was quickly followed by the so-called "scramble for Africa," which many consider the most notable imperial development of the late nineteenth century. Starting in 1884 (with the Berlin Congress), over a dozen European colonial powers including Britain, Germany, France, and Belgium spent 20 years "scrambling" to lay claim to large swaths of the African continent, for palm oil and prestige and to prevent other powers from gaining territory. Traditionally, the scramble for Africa has been seen as a period of distinctively rapid territorial conquest. However, historian Christopher Bayly has recently argued that as aggressive territorial conquest was a feature of the whole nineteenth century, the scramble for Africa was not a particularly distinctive period in British imperial history. The centrality of enslaved Africans to British and European imperial wealth earlier in the period reveals that British and European interest in Africa as a source of wealth was nothing new. What we see in the scramble for Africa is, instead, a shift from humans and the west coast to palm oil and the interior as wealth producers.

   The late nineteenth century was not a period of uninterrupted triumphs for the British Empire. On the contrary, difficult colonial conflicts continued: in 1879 alone the British suffered losses in Afghanistan and at Isandhlwana (against the Zulus). The conflict most damaging to Britain's international reputation was the South African or Boer War (1899–1902). The British had established their first colonial presence in South Africa in 1795, when they seized the Cape Colony from the Netherlands, taking over the governance of the white Afrikaners, called Boers, who lived there. In the 1830s and 1840s, many Cape Colony Boers chose to migrate further inland on what came to be called the "Great Trek" and established two Boer states—the Orange Free State and the Transvaal Republic—independent of British control. However, the discovery of gold and diamonds in those regions in the 1860s and 1870s sparked British interest. Thousands of British prospectors came from the Cape Colony and Britain to the Transvaal, and as these British settlers (called *Uitlanders*) came to outnumber Boers in the Transvaal, friction between Britons and Afrikaners rose. The failed Jameson Raid (1896)—in which British mining interests attempted to spark an uprising amongst the British gold prospectors in the Transvaal—increased tensions, as did disputes over the political status of the *Uitlanders*. The British declared war in October 1899. While many Liberal party leaders opposed the war, it was at first extremely popular in Britain, enjoying broad support across class lines and in particular among young lower middle-class men. Large crowds gathered to see off soldiers going to fight in South Africa, singing *Rule Britannia* and *God Save the Queen*. There were public celebrations when British forces lifted the siege of Mafeking in May of 1900. However, from September 1900 until the end of the war almost two years later, the war went poorly for the British. The Boers, who knew the terrain well, used guerilla tactics, and the mighty British army suffered a series of humiliating defeats at the hands of the tiny rural Boer republics. Desperate to defeat the Boers, the British employed a scorched earth policy and moved Boers, whose homes, farms, and villages they had destroyed, into "concentration" camps. The British were attacked in the international press for the poor conditions in these camps, which were unsanitary and lacked adequate food and housing, and in which thousands of Boers (and black Africans, who were put in separate camps) died. The increasingly unpopular war finally ended in the spring of 1902. The British made a number of concessions and reparations, and the Boer republics were absorbed into the British Empire but granted a limited autonomy that ultimately led to the establishment of a dominion state, the Union of South Africa, in 1910. (That dominion became the Republic of South Africa in 1961, and maintained legally enforced racial segregation via its system of "apartheid" until 1994.) Because of its long duration in spite of Britain's vastly larger military and international castigation of the "concentration" camps, the South African War was a terrible blow to the prestige of the British Empire.

One result was the Haldane Reforms to the Army, which were a response to the military's poor performance in the war. These reforms sought to centralize military strategy across the empire and created an Expeditionary Force trained to fight in overseas wars. In civil society, both masculinity and femininity were thrown into crisis during the Boer War. Many of the working-class men who volunteered to fight were found to be physically unfit for duty (urban men especially had health problems). The poor physical condition of potential recruits inspired fears about racial deterioration, leading to demands that Britain raise stronger and more virile men. Boys were encouraged to be physically fit through such organizations as the Boy Scouts. Critics scolded middle-class women for "shirking" motherhood in favor of education or career, or by limiting family size. They chastised working-class women for the poor health of their sons, and after the war began to provide mothering classes for poor women. A committee that investigated the health of recruits published its Report of the Inter-Departmental Committee on Physical Deterioration in 1904, which inspired some of the social reforms that the 1906 Liberal government instituted, such as school meals and medical examinations for poor children.

The most significant new aspect of the British Empire after 1870 was the rise of anti-colonial nationalist movements. Ireland was also pressing for political independence during the late nineteenth and early twentieth centuries. While resistance to British imperialism was not new, these organized political movements, which challenged the legitimacy of British rule and asserted the rights of indigenous groups to their own nation-states, were a feature of the late nineteenth century. In their use of nationalist rhetoric they reworked European nationalist ideology, which had helped to create the nations of Italy and Germany in the 1860s and 1870s, in various local contexts. They also used British notions of political representation to challenge their own lack of political voice. In the twentieth century, British attempts to suppress local demands for representation led to the swift growth of anti-colonial agitations across large portions of the empire. Many would gain energy during World War One, as colonies questioned the policy by which they supplied troops without being consulted on strategy.

The Indian independence movement first took hold (in some areas of India) in the 1880s. The notion of an independent nation of India was especially popular with urban professional middle-class Indians, who chafed at Indians' lack of a political voice. Anti-colonial feeling was especially strong in Calcutta (a large city in Bengal and the nineteenth-century capital of British India). The Indian National Congress (INC) was founded in 1885 by socially elite middle-class high-caste

Hindus. The INC was not the only organization committed to a postcolonial India but it led the movement for independence. In 1906 the INC declared its commitment to a self-governed India. During the early twentieth century, Indians resisted British rule using both violent and nonviolent means (boycotts were one tool).

Conclusion

While the key characteristic of the nineteenth-century British Empire was expansion, the key characteristic of the twentieth-century empire was contraction. After World War Two, anti-colonial nationalist movements, along with the weakened state of Britain, led to the demise of the British Empire. Decolonization began with British India, which in August 1947 was partitioned into two "dominions," India and Pakistan, but the partition of India was only the first of several stages of post-war decolonization.

Today what remains of the British Empire is a voluntary association of 54 states—including 51 former colonies and the United Kingdom of Great Britain and Northern Ireland—called the Commonwealth of Nations. Member states describe themselves as "free and equal members of the Commonwealth of Nations, freely co-operating in the pursuit of peace, liberty and progress"; they do not swear allegiance to the British crown, but Queen Elizabeth II serves as the head of the organization. Member states include Australia, New Zealand, Canada, South Africa, India, Pakistan, Bangladesh, Sri Lanka, Jamaica, St Lucia, St Kitts and Nevis, and Cyprus.

But this is not to say that the British Empire, or its effects in the present day, is in any way as straightforward or as uncontroversial as the Commonwealth's stated goal of promoting "democracy, rule of law, human rights, good governance and social and economic development." The British Empire was very large, very powerful, and very influential, and the fact that it no longer exists does not mean that its effects have dissipated.

Notes

1 H. Rider Haggard, *King Solomon's Mines* (1885), excerpts from Chapters 5, 6, and 17.
2 John M. MacKenzie, et al. (eds), *The Encyclopedia of Empire* (Oxford: Wiley Blackwell, 2015), quoted in John M. MacKenzie, "The British Empire: Ramshackle or Rampaging? A Historiographical Reflection," *The Journal of Imperial and Commonwealth History* 43.1 (2015): 99–124, p. 101.
3 Durba Ghosh, "Another Set of Imperial Turns?" *American Historical Review* 117.3 (June 2012): 772–793, p. 775.
4 Edward Said, *Orientalism* (New York: Pantheon Books, 1978).
5 Antoinette Burton, *After the Imperial Turn: Thinking with and through the Nation* (Raleigh: Duke University Press, 2003), pp. 2–3.
6 Stephen Howe, "Introduction," in Stephen Howe (ed.), *The New Imperial Histories Reader* (London: Routledge, 2010).
7 Andrew Thompson, *The Empire Strikes Back? The Impact of Imperialism on Britain from the Mid-Nineteenth Century* (Harlow, Pearson Longman, 2005), p. 61.
8 For a recent example of this phenomenon in British culture, see Zia Haider Rahman's opinion piece "Oh, So Now I'm Bangladeshi?" *New York Times* April 8 2016.

9 Samuel Rawson Gardiner, *A Student's History of England: From the Earliest Times to 1885* (London: Longman, Green and Co., 1892), p. 954.
10 Catherine Hall, *Civilising Subjects: Metropole and Colony in the English Imagination 1830–1867* (Chicago: University of Chicago Press, 2002), pp. 271–275.
11 John M. MacKenzie, "The British Empire", pp. 99–124.
12 Philippa Levine, *The British Empire: Sunrise to Sunset*, 2nd edition (London: Routledge, 2013), p. 92.

Relevant fiction students might enjoy

Jane Austen, *Mansfield Park* (1814)
Charlotte Bronte, *Jane Eyre* (1847)
Charles Dickens, *David Copperfield* (1850)
H. Rider Haggard, *King Solomon's Mines* (1885), *She* (1889)
Rudyard Kipling, *Kim* (1901)
Joseph Conrad, *Heart of Darkness* (1902)
E.M. Forster, *A Passage to India* (1924)
George Orwell, *Burmese Days* (1934)

Further reading

Jamie Belich, *Replenishing the Earth: The Settler Revolution and the Rise of the Anglo-World, 1783–1939* (Oxford and New York: Oxford University Press, 2009).
Niall Ferguson, *Empire: The Rise and Demise of the British World Order and the Lessons for Global Power* (London: Allen Lane, 2004).
Durba Ghosh, "AHR Forum: Another Set of Imperial Turns?" *American Historical Review* 17.3 (June 2012): 772–793.
Stephen Howe, *The New Imperial Histories Reader* (London: Routledge, 2010).
Stephen Howe, "Review Essay: British Worlds, Settler Worlds, World Systems, and Killing Fields," *The Journal of Imperial and Commonwealth History* 40.4 (November 2012): 691–725.
Dane Kennedy, "The Imperial History Wars," *Journal of British Studies* 54.01 (January 2015): 5–22.
Philippa Levine, *The British Empire: Sunrise to Sunset*, 2nd edition (Oxford: Routledge, 2013).
John M. MacKenzie, "The British Empire: Ramshackle or Rampaging? A Historiographical Reflection," *The Journal of Imperial and Commonwealth History* 43.1 (2015): 99–124.
Andrew Thompson, *The Empire Strikes Back? The Impact of Imperialism on Britain from the Mid-Nineteenth Century* (Harlow: Pearson Longman, 2005).

Online resources

Legacies of British Slave-ownership: https://www.ucl.ac.uk/lbs/
National Archives of India: http://nationalarchives.nic.in/
Digital South Asia Library: http://dsal.uchicago.edu/
Historical maps of India: http://homepages.rootsweb.ancestry.com/~poyntz/India/maps.html
History in Focus: Empire: www.history.ac.uk/ihr/Focus/Empire/web.html
British Documents on the End of Empire: http://bdeep.org/
Invisible Australians—Living under the White Australia Policy: http://invisibleaustralians.org/

4 Wealth and poverty, growth and slumps

The economy

Introduction

A children's book about the Great Exhibition of 1851, in "describing the beautiful inventions and manufactures exhibited therein," told its readers about many items of British origin:

> an immense map of the busy city of Manchester; and there is a huge railway carriage; and still further on, there is an iron wire, one mile long. At a little distance stands a magnificent bed and bedstead, fit for the Queen to sleep in. It came from Edinburgh, and is made mostly of materials which can be produced in Scotland. And in this direction, we can see a set of beautiful mantelpieces and fenders, from Sheffield, all decorated in the most elegant manner. . . . Here is a pair of scissors made in Sheffield, and ornamented in the most beautiful way, with a crown for a handle; and yonder are a pair of cotton stockings from Ireland, spun so fine that they look exactly like silk, and indeed you would be likely to mistake them for silk, if you were not told they were merely cotton.[1]

Not completely true?

The Britain this book describes is a prosperous country full of expertly-produced goods, and indeed this was many Victorians' image of their nation (if not of their own lives). How did these maps and carriages and mantelpieces and scissors come to be? One of the most important features of Victorian Britain was its growing economy. With the earliest phases of the "Industrial Revolution" behind it, from 1820 the British economy expanded to become the richest country in the world. All sectors of the economy, including finance, industry, agriculture, and service were transformed in various ways. Overall, Victorians were better off than previous generations; they had adequate food and shelter and, after mid-century, had extra income to spend on discretionary items such as alcohol, leisure pursuits, and holidays. Some decades were times of plenty, others of want. Some fields of work and some areas of the country fared better than others: handloom weavers suffered as their skills became obsolete, while those who lived in Lancashire had job and income opportunities in factory work.

The critical precursor to the Victorian period was the process of industrialization that took place in Britain—the first country in the world to industrialize—roughly between 1760 and 1840. Traditionally this process has been referred to as the "Industrial Revolution"; the term implies sudden and drastic change, but today while most historians remain convinced that the changes industrialization wrought were dramatic, they also stress that the process occurred very gradually, affected Britons unevenly, and was more an evolutionary than a revolutionary process. Britain's agricultural sector, which during the early modern period had become more efficient, produced more food using fewer workers. This is why Malthus's dire predictions of mass starvation as food supplies failed to keep pace with population growth did not come to pass. The efficiencies of the agricultural revolution rendered his predictions incorrect. Even so his work influenced many Victorian reformers including Edwin Chadwick (1800–1890), who believed that social policies such as the Poor Law ought to be structured to provide disincentives for the poor to have too many children.

At the same time, several new inventions and new modes of work organization, including the spinning jenny, the flying shuttle, the steam engine, and the factory, emerged. These came into use at different times: for example, the steam engine was invented in 1769, but was not in widespread use until well into the nineteenth century. They changed some industries more profoundly than others: cotton textiles were made in factories from the late eighteenth century, but many types of manufacture remained in workshops and homes. They affected some regions of Britain more than others: throughout the period, and especially before 1870, Britain and Ireland were quite regionally varied. Regional variations in various economic indicators such as population growth and the types of employment available are often hidden by national statistics, but they reveal important differences in people's lives. For example, while the national population increased by 120% between 1841 and 1911, the populations of Glamorgan and Monmouth, in Wales, increased by almost 400%; the population of Essex, one of the Home counties of England, increased by almost 300%; the population of industrial Lancashire increased by 186%; and the populations of Dumfries and Galloway, in the Highlands of Scotland, of Rutland in the Midlands, and of Huntingdonshire near Cambridge, all declined in absolute terms. Generally speaking over the whole period from 1841 until 1911 there was a relative loss of population in the counties of East Anglia and the southwest of England, North and West Wales, and Grampian and the Highlands in Scotland, and a relative gain of population in southeast England (that is, London and the Home Counties), Cheshire, Lancashire, the West Riding, Durham, and Glamorgan and Monmouth in Wales. Stafford saw population gains, but only between 1841 and 1861, and Hampshire gained only after 1881.

Different parts of the country were dominated by different sectors of the economy. One economic historian argues that there were four distinct types of regions: rural areas that experienced little or no growth; the textile-oriented regions of Lancashire, the West Riding of Yorkshire, and Tayside; the mining and metal-working regions, principally Durham, Northumberland, Glamorgan and Monmouth; and the greater metropolitan area, London and the surrounding

"Home Counties," which were service-oriented.[2] The English Midlands, the North, and parts of Scotland became highly industrialized, but Ireland and the southeast of England remained largely agricultural, and the economy of greater London was based on service. In Ireland, the number of workers in the manufacturing sector actually decreased, because the Irish textile industries, which were dominated by linen production, contracted after the famine. Textile manufacture was the principal form of employment in Lancashire, Tayside and the West Riding. It was also strong in Cheshire, Central and Fife, and Nottingham, in Derby, Leicester, and Strathclyde early in the Victorian period, and in the Borders region later in the period. Mining dominated the economic landscapes of Durham in England and of Glamorgan and Monmouth in Wales. Cornwall was a mining area in the 1840s and 1850s, Stafford was in the 1860s, Northumberland was from the 1880s, and Derby and Central and Fife in Scotland were from the 1890s. Mining dominated the economy of mining areas more than textiles dominated the economy of textile areas. The economy of the southeast of England was dominated by service industries and the manufacture of consumer-oriented goods, especially luxury goods. Two-thirds of the jobs created in this area between 1841 and 1911 were in services; one economic historian calls the southeast of England "the world's first large-scale consumer society."[3] These regional differences were extremely important: those who lived in Cheshire could work in cotton factories, but not mines, while the situation was reversed for workers in Durham, and workers in London would almost certainly find themselves in some service industry.

So far i'ust discusses what form of economy dominates what area of Victorian Britain.

Historians question the notion of an industrial "revolution" because the large factories that are said to have characterized industrialized England were unheard of in 1760 and rare in 1800; in the first decade of the nineteenth century factories were the rule only in the cotton industry, and as late as 1850 most consumer goods were still produced by hand in small workshops. Historian Raphael Samuel observed that even by the middle of the nineteenth century, when the process of industrialization is thought to have been completed, "there were few parts of the economy which steam power and machinery had left untouched, but fewer still where it ruled unchallenged."[4] Throughout the Victorian period, while many goods became factory-produced, many others were still made in small workshops or in homes by skilled craftspeople. And although we tend to talk about urbanization and industrialization as twinned processes, much industrialization relied on rural populations for workers and needed access to rural forms of power such as streams.

Given the uneven nature of industrialization, not all Britons were affected at the same time, in the same way, or to the same degree. For those that were, however—working-class people living in or around Manchester or Preston, in the north, would have been in this group—life and the world around them changed dramatically. Before industrialization, spinning had been quintessentially a female task, performed by women all over England at home, by hand, between other chores. But the invention of the spinning jenny allowed a single spinner simultaneously to work eight spindles, then 16, and, by 1800, 100 spindles. At first, jennies were used by women in their homes. Then, women moved into cotton factories to work larger jennies. Finally, as spinning jennies were replaced by mulespinners, women were pushed out of spinning, which was now a factory job called "minding" done (mostly in south Lancashire) by men. Weaving was mechanized soon after spinning, with power looms first appearing in cotton factories in the 1820s. Weaving had been a highly skilled male task, but handloom weavers found their artisanal craft made obsolete and their social status and earnings capacity destroyed by the new powerlooms, which like mulespinners were located in factories. Within two generations, then, the north of England was transformed into a place of factories and factory work where none had existed before. Most young people expected to migrate from the countryside to the nearest large city or large industrial area to work. They did not always go far—70% of those who migrated to the industrial town of Preston to work had done so from fewer than 30 miles away. In some rural areas spinning and weaving remained home-based practices, and even most factories were small, family-owned concerns, in which workers all worked in a single room and all knew one another. But enormous factories out of the gates of which hundreds if not thousands of workers—a large proportion of them women and children—streamed every day at the sounding of the whistle also existed, and, for more and more people, work now involved a separate place of work, a time-conscious regimen, and long hours of hard but unskilled work. Britain's landscape was transformed by what Blake saw as "dark, satanic mills." In Mrs Gaskell's industrial novel *North and South* (1855), the heroine Margaret Hale, who is from the south of England and has "a repugnance to the idea of a manufacturing town," is overwhelmed by what she sees when she comes to live in the north, in the fictional manufacturing town of Milton, in the unsubtly-named county of Darkshire, which Gaskell based on Manchester:

> For several miles before they reached Milton, they saw a deep lead-coloured cloud hanging over the horizon in the direction in which it lay. . . . Nearer to the town, the air had a faint taste and smell of smoke. . . . Quick they were whirled over long, straight, hopeless streets of regularly-built houses, all small and of brick. Here and there a great oblong many-windowed factory stood up, like a hen among her chickens, puffing out black "unparliamentary" smoke, and sufficiently accounting for the cloud which Margaret had taken to foretell rain.[5]

Based on the factories corrupting the land.

None of this is remotely familiar to Margaret; it will take the entire novel before she is able to perceive any beauty or nobility of character in the industrial north. As uneven as it was, the process of industrialization was certainly a critical and significant precursor to the Victorian economy, which was a mix of agriculture, industry, service, finance, and the fiscal state. Between 1820 and 1850, Britain's economy was growing in a rapid and unregulated way. Growth was swift, but conditions could be very harsh, and there was little or no state regulation. The following years, from 1850 until 1873, were more prosperous and less harsh, because of the introduction of state controls on growth and the treatment of workers.

The final decades of the Victorian period saw an economic depression from 1873 until 1896, and then by modest recovery until the start of the First World War.

National income was growing quickly. That might suggest that people were better off. In fact one of the biggest debates in Victorian economic history is the "standard of living" debate, an argument about whether the quality of life got better or worse for the average worker. The answer depends in part on whether scholars decide to measure wages, real wages (wages considered in terms of their purchasing power), working conditions, leisure time, life expectancy, height, or something else. For example, in 1820 wages were higher than before, which would indicate a higher standard of living, but work was more difficult and more dangerous, which would indicate a lower standard of living. While economic history seems at first glance to be amenable to objective or scientific analysis, interpretation and argument remain central.

too many factors to tell

In addition to and connected to growth, a second critical feature of the Victorian state was the fiscal role of the state. This was being rebuilt as the British state worked to re-legitimize itself as a body that could tax moderately and spend wisely. What historian John Brewer called the "fiscal-military" state of the eighteenth century reached its most extreme pitch during the Napoleonic wars that preceded the Victorian era.[6] The government imposed high taxes, including an income tax, to support its expensive military operations. Government spending was very high—indeed by 1810 it had soared from an eighteenth century average of 8 to 10% to 23% of the gross national product (GNP, the market value of all products and services produced in the nation in a year). But as government spending rose, public acquiescence to high taxes, and public confidence in the government's right to tax and spend and ability to spend wisely, all fell. Opposition to taxes and to government spending contributed to the hatred of Old Corruption that we saw in Chapter 2. Even the expiration of the income tax (in 1816) and the establishment of a gold standard for British currency failed to resolve the situation, in part because the national debt was now so high, in part because the fiscal system was seen as inequitable. Over the Victorian period, the state became associated with free trade, the gold standard, and equal treatment of social classes. It was able to rebuild public consent to taxation and public trust in the government's ability to spend tax money wisely. The gold standard became linked to tax policies, was adopted by several other countries in the late nineteenth century, and became widely accepted as part of British political culture and as a sign of civilization.

The government built public trust via real and rhetorical attacks on "waste" that included: lower government spending; the gradual development of a political culture of fair and balanced tax policies that favored direct over indirect taxation, most importantly by reintroducing an income tax in 1842; and the enacting of administrative reforms that included simplifying government accounting, keeping interest groups out of the budget process, and making Parliament an auditor of expenditure. By 1900, tax revenues had been reduced back down to 9% of GNP. The creation of public trust in government and its taxes was the principal fiscal accomplishment of the Victorian state, and was critical to Victorian peace and prosperity.

1820–1850: Rapid growth

Between 1820 and 1850 Britain had a fast-growing economy that was increasingly less agricultural and more industrial, urban, and financially stable. There was still a thriving agricultural sector, and the majority of the population lived in rural areas. Urban populations had already grown since 1800, and would continue to do so. The censuses tell us that London's population had been about 1 million in 1801 but was 1.4 million in 1821. Manchester and Birmingham's populations had been about 70,000 each in 1801, but were about 106,000 by 1821—a jump of 50%—and they would rise to 145,000 each by 1831. In the 1820s and 1830s, rapid growth occurred in all sectors of the economy. But the 1840s were difficult years for most workers: bad harvests, trade slumps, high unemployment, and in Ireland, the famine, came together to render the decade the "hungry forties." The famine was the result of a failure (due to a fungal infection) of the potato crop that made up a large part of the Irish diet. The British government made some attempts to provide emergency rations, but these were insufficiently urgent and inadequate. Approximately 1 million people living in the richest empire on earth died of starvation or disease. Hardest hit were the rural poor, whose diet depended on the potato, and particularly those in the counties of Roscommon, Sligo, and Mayo, in Connaught, and Cavan, Fermanagh, and Monaghan in Ulster. Some counties, for example Wexford, were barely affected. But the social geography of Britain, Ireland, and the world was affected over the next 25 years, as 3 million Irish people fled the famine and its effects and emigrated.

Economic growth was made possible in part by a reliable banking system. In contrast to continental Europe, Britain had a sophisticated banking system by the eighteenth century, and, after the Napoleonic wars ended in 1815, London was the financial center of international trade. The British banking system played a key role in Victorian industrialization and economic growth because it was extremely efficient at providing short-term credit. Because industrialists could get short-term credit from banks, they used their own funds for long-term investment in their industries. Because merchants could get credit, they could offer credit to industrialists, which also enabled the economy to grow. Yet even as public credit developed and modernized, private credit—the small amounts of credit routinely extended by shopkeepers and others to their customers—was more useful in most people's lives and adhered to a more traditional model that relied on reputation and personal networks. From 1821 the banking system was headed by the Bank of England (f. 1694), which was privately owned but connected to the government, and which was beginning to function as a central bank (the Bank Charter Act of 1844 strengthened this role). The Bank of England held most of the government's funds (for example, money collected for taxes), serviced the national debt, discounted bills of exchange, and provided short-term loans to the government, merchants, and others. Other financial institutions included private London banks, smaller provincial banks, and bill-brokers. The banking system remained vulnerable to cyclical fluctuations and to speculative bubbles, but overall was stable. And while the Victorian period is usually characterized as an industrial age, in which factory, mill, and mine owners became wealthy through industrial profits, far more wealth was created in the world of finance, chiefly banking and insurance.

Transportation, including railways, roads, and ocean shipping, was an important aspect of the Victorian economy. One entirely new arrival on the economic landscape was the railways, first built in 1825. Railways transformed transportation and the landscape. They spelled the demise of inland canals. However, they also created both demand for new things—steam, coal, and iron—and new demand for older things, especially horse-drawn travel, which brought people to and from railway stations in both rural and urban areas. The number of commercial, horse-drawn vehicles on the road increased from 100,000 in 1811 to 161,000 in 1851, mostly because of the growth of rail travel. Railway building began slowly, but a boom in the 1840s helped to create the prosperity of the 1850s and 1860s. Railway building also created jobs and human mobility, the values of which are hard to measure but easy to underestimate. Overall the development and expansion of railways—in Britain and abroad, where British investors frequently put their money—allowed many other economic sectors to expand too, and so was very important.

Farming grew during this period. A series of advances in agricultural efficiency (such as the adoption of crop rotation) during the early modern era had made British farming more efficient and more productive. In Ireland, land was leased to tenant farmers on disadvantageous terms that kept them in poverty. Land would remain a source of political conflict in Ireland throughout the Victorian period. Southern England (outside of London) was dominated by agricultural workers who lived in rural areas. By the early nineteenth century, each British farm worker produced a third more than his or her French counterpart did, and more than twice what his or her Russian counterpart did. Early Victorian agriculture was characterized by large farms of 200 acres or more, especially in the southeast. Although owned by wealthy aristocratic or gentry families, they were farmed by tenant farmers and hired laborers who worked very long hours (though in Wales, Yorkshire, and Scotland, small family farms remained common). In 1846, when the Corn Laws that protected British grain prices by imposing tariffs on imports of foreign grain were abolished, many farmers turned to animal husbandry. Through 1860 the agricultural labor force continued to grow as a proportion of the GNP, and agricultural output rose to meet the demands of the growing population.

Industrialization relied on and was part of a rural economy. Agricultural efficiency freed rural people to work in factories and mills, which relied on rural sources of power such as streams. Cotton textiles were an important part of the British economy: the first factories were in the cotton textile industry in Lancashire, Cheshire, and Scotland, and cotton cloth was one of Britain's main exports. By 1831, cotton dominated, forming over one fifth of British industry, and between 1820 and 1851 the textiles industries grew at a rate of over 4% per year. Manchester and Glasgow competed for the moniker "Cottonopolis" (which Manchester won by mid-century because of its higher-quality cloth). The first innovations in textile

[margin handwritten note:] Britain was still not the most agricultural compared to other countries and nations of the time

manufacture, including the spinning jenny and the mule spinner, were used both inside and outside factories, often in rural homes (where spinning and weaving supplemented farming income). They preceded steam power, which was applied to textile manufacture in the 1830s and 1840s. Once steam-powered production was introduced into industry, its use grew quickly. By 1840 twice as much steam power was in use as had been in 1800. Steam power allowed factories to be located in or near large cities, and so contributed to the combined industrialization and urbanization that Britain was undergoing. It made factories more productive but louder, faster, and more dangerous places to work. By the 1840s, while many workplaces were small and outwork remained pervasive, large factories—the most recognizable symbol of industrialized England—were common, especially in cotton and iron. There were over 3,000 textile factories in Britain. The largest employed several hundred workers; cotton and worsted woolen mills employed an average of about 170 workers, and the median was about half that. In London and the southeast, factories were rare, but labor was beginning to be divided; a cabinet would be made not by one skilled cabinetmaker but by various workers who specialized in sawing, turning, polishing, and upholstering, and tailors paid women low wages to sew seams or make buttonholes. These seamstresses were among the poorest of the poor, and were known for being forced out of desperation into prostitution.

Although industrialization gave many people jobs, it took away many jobs as well.

The coal and iron industries had also undergone advances in the late eighteenth and early nineteenth centuries, including the adoption of coke in blast furnaces, and the puddling and rolling of pig iron. From 1820 the iron industry grew; there was a boom in the Scottish iron industry in the 1830s, and as the economy overall grew, and as new uses were developed for cast and wrought iron—in machines, water and gas pipes, beams in buildings, iron bridges, the first iron ships, and railway rails, locomotives, and other equipment—the coal and iron industries expanded rapidly. Much of the iron industry was centered in Lanarkshire, Scotland. As coal and iron became important sources of power and building material, mining—principally of coal for steam power and iron for steel—did too. The largest extractive industry was coal; as its consumption rose, coal production and distribution did too. The British used 30 million tons of coal per year by 1830, and 70 million tons per year by the early 1850s, far more than any other country. Mines created jobs, railways, ships, and much wealth; they also created dangerous workplaces and ruined environments. Iron mining transformed southeastern Wales, which became highly industrialized. Wales's Swansea valley was spattered with copper mines. The gigantic Cyfarthfa and Dowlais ironworks each employed over 5,000 men, and in 1851 14 works had over 350 workers, though many firms employed only about 50 workers. There were tensions between management and labor: one of the largest early strikes was the 1844 coal miners' strike.

Service—everything that is not manufacturing, mining, or agriculture, and as such includes domestic service, retail sales, the clergy, all professionals from teachers to doctors to bankers, and much more—is important in all societies, but industrialization creates especially keen demand for services. By 1841 there were 1.7 million Britons employed in services; by 1911 that number had ballooned to

6.2 million. Innovations across the service sector—from transportation and communications to finance and distribution—helped to create an integrated national marketplace and made service an important agent of economic change and growth. The large shops (including department stores) that characterized nineteenth-century retailing were beginning to emerge, as was the funeral industry, which was very important in working-class culture.

While the economy grew in all of these sectors, and wealth was created, most working people were not benefiting. While Britain as a country got richer, most people's standard of living actually decreased between 1820 and 1850. Working-class Britons earned no more in 1832 than they had in 1792; even when real wages went up slightly in the mid-1830s, they did not compensate for harder work, more work days, and urban disamenities. Infant and child mortality rose between 1820 and 1850, most sharply in northern cities such as Manchester and Glasgow. Life expectancy for native Glaswegians fell six years between 1820 and 1840, and those born in Manchester lived 16.4 fewer years than other Britons. Reformer Edwin Chadwick's 1842 *Enquiry into the Sanitary Conditions of the Labouring Population of Great Britain* revealed that rapid and unregulated industrialization produced enormous, dirty, unhealthy cities and industrial areas in which thousands of men, women, and children worked extremely long hours under dangerous conditions for low pay and lived without sufficient space or adequate sanitation. Chadwick wrote that "the annual loss of life from filth and bad ventilation are greater than the loss from death or wounds in any wars in which the country has been engaged in modern times."[7] The solution for which he agitated was to supply the poorer parts of large cities with clean water and adequate sewage systems. German factory owner Friedrich Engels, who would go on to write *The Communist Manifesto* with Karl Marx, wrote in his book on *The Condition of the Working Class in England* that working-class Manchester was a mass of "filth, ruin, and uninhabitableness [in] defiance of all considerations of cleanliness, ventilation, and health" and marveled at "how little of civilization [a worker] may share and yet live."[8]

As a result of these problems, a debate arose about the "Condition of England," which intensified during the hungry forties. The term was coined by Thomas Carlyle (1795–1881), one of the major thinkers of the Victorian era, in an 1839 essay on Chartism. Many politicians, intellectuals, and leaders questioned the moral condition of a nation that had both a growing economy and a large number of poor people, and called on government and employers to take responsibility for the industrial poor. In 1832, a Parliamentary Committee led by MP Michael Sadler (1780–1835) interviewed child factory workers. One typical interviewee explained that he was "most generally awoke or lifted out of bed, sometimes asleep, by my parents," so as to arrive at work by 6:00am, that he worked fourteen- to sixteen-hour days, and that he was beaten "very severely" if late.[9] In 1843, Carlyle published an essay entitled "Past and Present," which excited intense interest and sold a thousand copies almost immediately. In it, he compared medieval with industrialized Britain and found the latter sadly wanting. In his view, industrialized, free-market Britain created individual poverty of both body and spirit in the midst of profit and plenty. It forced workers to spend their lives

* These accusations were true.

supporting profit and earning wages, without any freedom of choice or any opportunity to enjoy or be proud of their work. He warned that "the condition
and disposition of the Working Classes is a rather ominous matter" about which
"something ought to be said, something ought to be done."[10] Another Committee,
this one convened in 1842 by Lord Ashley, the Earl of Shaftesbury (1801–1885) to
study working conditions in the mines, heard from such workers as Isabel Wilson,
who at age 38 said that she had worked "below 30 years," as had her husband,
who was "getting touched in the breath now," and that when she "was a carrier of
coals, [the work] caused me to miscarry five times from the strains." Investigators
discovered that she, her husband, and their seven living children—all of whom
worked in the mines from a young age—"sleep in two bedsteads, and the whole
of the other furniture consisted of two chairs, three stools, a table . . . and a
few broken basins and cups."[11] No wonder Disraeli famously claimed in *Sybil, or
the Two Nations*, that England had become

> two nations between whom there is no intercourse and no sympathy; who
> are as ignorant of each other's habits, thoughts, and feelings, as if they
> were dwellers in different zones, or inhabitants of different planets: the rich
> and the poor.[12]

In response, the Victorian state began to attempt to regulate the worst excesses
of capitalism and to protect its citizens. The wave of reform legislation, started
in the 1830s, limited the number of hours women and children could work
in factories, required that children who worked in factories be educated, and
established the new Poor Law. But state intervention was limited because of the
Victorian fidelity to the principles of *laissez-faire*, which dictated minimal state
control of the market. The repeal of the grain tariffs in 1846 symbolized and
crystallized Victorian culture's commitment to the economic doctrine of free
trade. In the mid-1840s, when real wages began to rise and the quality of life
began to improve, many contemporaries saw free trade as the cause. In addition
free trade and the gold standard worked together to connect the interests of the
middle and upper classes. By 1850, Britain was a noticeably different country
from the one it had been in 1820. Real wages were about 28% higher than they
had been in the 1760s. Most working-class people now had enough money for
food, shelter, and clothing, though not much more. Cities were cleaner and healthier. The country was characterized by many large workplaces, employing one
hundred people or more, in industries including textiles, railways, shipbuilding
(especially thriving in Clydeside, Scotland), iron, and steel, which at their mid-
century peak employed 40% of the workforce; by a growing rail system; and by
a flourishing service sector.

One point of tension during the early Victorian period was the re-introduction
in 1842 of an income tax, the first ever imposed outside of wartime, by Tory
Prime Minister Robert Peel. The tax was introduced as a three-year measure; it
was extended to aid with funding of railways, and though theoretically temporary
even today has been collected ever since. Peel had originally opposed an income

tax, but turned to it when faced with empty government coffers and a large deficit. The income tax, of slightly under 3%, was imposed only on those with annual incomes above £150, so it affected only the middle and upper classes and did not tax the working-class majority. In addition, Peel reduced the customs duties on many items. The result was a more progressive tax structure that benefited the working class and contributed to an increase in trade. Nevertheless, the income tax was hotly opposed by radicals and by free traders and protectionists alike, and remained contentious for a decade after its introduction.

1850–1873: Prosperity

The period from 1850 until 1873 was a time of economic growth accompanied by social stability. Following the rapid economic and political change of the late eighteenth and early-nineteenth centuries, and preceding the economic depression of the last quarter of the century, it is sometimes referred to as the age of "equipoise" or "complacency." While recently historians have challenged this notion, arguing that any equipoise was either overstated or the temporary result of uneasy compromises, this was nonetheless a prosperous period. It was also a time of population growth: a high birth rate meant that even with significant emigration to the United States and to the British colonies, the population of Britain grew quickly, from nearly 21 million in 1851 (and another 6 million in Ireland) to 26 million in 1871 (with another 5.5 million in Ireland). That population also became more affluent.

1851 witnessed two milestones: the census and the Great Exhibition. The first reflected, and the second celebrated, Britain's economy and its place in the world. According to the census that year, Britain was now an urban nation, with the majority of people living in cities (though, as we saw in Chapter 1, a town needed a population of only 2,500 to count as a city). The largest cities were now extremely large: London had a population of 2,500,000, Liverpool of 376,000, Manchester of 303,000, and Birmingham of 233,000. These four along with four others—Bristol in the west and Leeds, Sheffield, and Bradford in Yorkshire—had populations of over 100,000, and were home to fully one quarter of the British population. In the same year, less than one fifth of France's and Germany's populations, and only one third of Belgium's and the Netherlands' populations were urban. The United States' population would not become mainly urban until 1921. This critical shift, of which Britons were made aware via the census, seemed to demonstrate that Britain was irretrievably "modern": advanced, industrial, urban. The census led to new attention being paid to urban planning, architecture, transportation, sanitation, and other key factors in health and well-being. While Britain continued to think of itself—and to some extent still does, even today—as at heart a rural nation that loved its countryside above all, the fact of urbanization was clear.

The second important event of 1851 was the Great Exhibition, an enormous international fair that showcased the industrial and technical abilities of many nations. Organized by Prince Albert and other members of the Royal Society for the Encouragement of Arts, Manufacture, and Commerce, it was intended as a display of Britain's supremacy on the world stage. The Great Exhibition took place in the architecturally impressive Crystal Palace, which was designed for the event by architect Joseph Paxton. 1848 feet long and 454 feet wide, it was made entirely of glass and cast iron. The more than 100,000 objects displayed by 14,000 exhibitors (13,000 of them from the UK) were viewed by over 6 million people.[13] (After the Exhibition they became the collections of the new Museum of Manufactures, which in 1899 was renamed the Victoria and Albert Museum.) The Great Exhibition included exhibits of raw materials, machinery, manufactured goods, and fine arts, and has been extensively studied by historians of industry, design, mass production, taste, architecture, display, culture, and class. With the Great Exhibition, Britain was declaring its economic, industrial, and manufacturing prowess and supremacy, to itself and to the world. The exhibitions of British heavy machinery, described by the *Official Catalogue* of the Exhibition as "the most direct representation of one of the principal sources of the industrial success and prosperity of Britain," were the most popular with visitors. They included a room containing a series of cotton textile machines from Hibbert, Platt and Sons that allowed viewers to appreciate in detail the mechanized production of cotton cloth.[14]

Britain was now the richest nation on earth. *Chambers' Encyclopedia* confidently (and correctly) stated that "[i]n point of national industry, England stands unrivalled by any other country on the globe."[15] Until 1873 its economy grew even more quickly than before, expanding at an average annual rate of 3%. Of course the economy remained volatile and growth was not consistent: there was a slump in 1852, a boom in 1853, slumps in 1857 and 1862, a boom in 1864, and another slump in 1867. But Britain's national income rose from £523 million in 1851 to £916 million in 1871. In 1860, per capita income was £13 in Germany, £21 in France, but £32 in Britain.[16] While Britain's trade balance seemed to indicate a weak economy—imports exceeded exports by about £100 million per year—it was balanced out by re-exports and by overseas investments, mostly in railway construction in the United States, South America, and India. These soared from £225 million in 1850 to £1 billion in 1875.

The standard of living was rising. The middle class, which had more disposable income and a higher standard of living than the working class, expanded. Average heights, which seem to be more closely tied to the quality of life than to average incomes, had fallen in the early Victorian period, but now began to rise, suggesting that children lived in healthier environments and were better fed than in the previous generation. Wages increased faster than prices, so that "real" wages rose steadily (even with cyclical and temporary unemployment taken into account). Work hours and child labor both decreased and life expectancy began to improve (though the rural and the wealthy lived longer than the urban and the poor, and men lived longer than women, principally because childbirth remained so dangerous). And while Britain was still suffering strains that were the result of uncontrolled urbanization and industrialization, a number of Factory Acts (in 1850, 1853, 1864, 1867, and 1874) ameliorated the worst abuses.

In my opinion, all of this is important.

One reason for prosperity was the continued strength of the banking system. There was a rash of speculation in the 1860s, but overall British finance prospered. London solidified its position as the financial center of the world, with the majority of international transactions arranged and financed there. Critically important was the introduction of limited liability, the principle that shareholders and investors had their liability limited to what they had invested in a corporation; their other wealth was not in danger even if the venture was unsuccessful. Scotland had enjoyed limited liability for shareholders since the early eighteenth century, but the freedom to establish limited liability companies was only introduced into English and Welsh law in the late 1850s and early 1860s. Limited liability turned investors into shareholders, with limited vulnerability, rather than partners, who were vulnerable to personal bankruptcy. This made raising capital easier and made those with money to invest more adventurous, and so spurred investment and economic growth. It also prompted a rapid expansion of joint-stock banking and bank branching. Larger joint-stock banks amalgamated with one another, absorbed smaller provincial banks, and opened branches. By 1880 there were 2,712 branch banks in Britain.[17]

Also important was a growing acceptance of the income tax. In 1853, Chancellor of the Exchequer William Gladstone gave a speech defending the income tax—and its extension to Ireland and to annual incomes of £100 and above—and in particular the fact that it was a flat-rate tax (meaning that the percentage of income taken as taxes was the same regardless of income level), by asserting that government must be not only "minimal" but "integrative." The speech, and the budget it introduced, helped legitimate the income tax. So, too, did the fact that between 1850 and 1890 government expenditure (both local and central) grew at a slower rate than the rest of the economy, and so shrank as a proportion of the economy. (Over time, the system of national taxation continued to evolve, but the system of local taxation did not. The inflexibility of local taxation systems, and their inability to meet the needs of an increasingly modern democratic society, were one reason that local government shrank and central government grew over the second half of the nineteenth century.) Public spending would not rise until the start of the Great War.

Well, duh. → Another reason for mid-Victorian prosperity was manufacturing. Cotton, coal, steel, railways, and shipbuilding all did well. While the majority of workplaces remained small, large factories and mines were now extremely large: in 1875 the largest factory in the textile industry, Platt's of Oldham (which manufactured textile machinery), had 7,000 workers. Paisley was the center of cotton thread production. Dundee shifted its textile production from linen to jute; by 1900 the city would be the world center of jute production (one historian has dubbed it "Juteopolis"), employing 35,000 workers. Innovations in work organization and processes improved production, as did the application of steam power to industries beyond textiles. By 1870, Britain used 2 million horsepower of steam every year, half of it in the textile industry. By 1907, steam power had replaced water power. Steam was especially important in shipping, where the British merchant fleet now ruled the waves, carrying the country's foreign trade plus a large proportion of foreign goods destined for British and other ports, with German merchant ships its only rival. Furthermore, the growing use of standardized, interchangeable parts in manufacturing consumer and other goods made previously expensive manufactured goods—such as pianos—affordable for middle-class and even some lower middle-class families.

In the 1850s the textiles industries were growing at the steady rate of 2.3% per year. The 1850s were a decade of strong production and profits (in spite of Factory Acts which many factory owners had insisted would spell economic disaster). British cotton was an international industry, with all raw materials imported and most cotton thread and cloth exported. This could be an advantage; for example, India, the jewel in the imperial crown, bought 23% of English cotton exports in 1850, and 31% in 1860. But it could also mean vulnerability to global events: in the mid-1860s the American Civil War caused a "cotton famine" by interrupting supplies of raw cotton. Cotton workers found themselves unemployed and cotton textile consumption plummeted.

The metals industries—principally iron and steel, but also copper, tin, and lead—expanded to become a larger proportion of British industry than textiles. The main area of expansion was production for domestic use (though exports of pig-iron, iron, and steel grew from 783,000 tons in 1850 to 3,383,000 tons in 1872). Three new processes (developed by Bessemer in 1858, Siemens in 1861, and Gilchrist and Thomas in 1879) allowed steel to be produced cheaply and in large quantities. By the early 1870s Britain produced over 500,000 tons per year of steel, and dominated international trade in iron and steel. Scottish iron producers were particularly efficient at using new techniques to reduce costs.

Railways were growing quickly. The first railway lines had been laid in the 1820s, but in the 1850s and 1860s railways became pervasive parts of the landscape, economy, and culture. Between 1850 and 1870 railways became the principal mode of transportation for goods of all kinds. Seven thousand miles of track were laid, and shipping rates became affordable. As early as 1846 a government official declared that "the railways can always carry cheaper,"[18] and as railways replaced canal and coastal shipping of iron ore and of coal the canals fell into disrepair and became obsolete. Railways carried not only goods but information: the Post Office sent letters by rail. Telegraph lines followed railway lines.

Railway travel became common for passengers, too. In 1850, 68 million passenger journeys were made, and by 1871, 322 million passenger journeys were made. In *The Diary of a Nobody*, the main character Charles Pooter and his wife Carrie take train journeys as a matter of course, as, for instance, on "Christmas Day.—We caught the 10.20 train at Paddington, and spent a pleasant day at Carrie's mother's."[19] Extensive branch lines ran to every town and village, reaching even remote rural areas. Horse-drawn journeys to and from railway stations continued to grow, with 702,000 commercial horse-drawn vehicles on the road by 1901. Fares became affordable: in 1844 Parliament mandated that all railway companies provide penny-per-mile third-class service on all of their lines, and in the 1860s cheap fares for workmen were introduced. Before penny-per-mile fares, few working-class people would have been familiar with train travel. However,

Figure 4.1 Charing Cross Railway Station, engraved by the Kell Brothers, late 1860s (chromolitho) by English School, (19th century). The growth of railways was central to and symptomatic of Britain's economic growth.

National Railway Museum, York, North Yorkshire, UK/ The Bridgeman Art Library.

many working-class people continued to live near their places of work, whether rural or urban, and did not commute (in part because the schedules for cheap trains did not accommodate their work schedules) until the 1880s. Casual laborers, who showed up every morning at the docks or a construction site hoping for a day's work, had to live close to their places of work and never commuted. But to some degree low fares remade city geographies: by making commuting more affordable, they contributed to the building of modest suburban areas for working-class and lower middle-class families. As commuting became a common form of rail travel, the average journey shortened from 16 miles in 1850 to nine miles in 1890. At the same time, rural young people used railways to travel to towns seeking work, so that railways accelerated both the growth of suburbs and urbanization. Railways also impacted leisure by making day trips to the countryside and longer holidays at the seaside possible (see Chapter 7).

The service sector also grew and contributed to prosperity. Domestic service, the largest personal service sector in 1851, grew rapidly (reflecting the growth of the servant-employing middle class), so that by 1871 fully one third of working-class women were servants. While some service workers, such as women who were maids of all work, were relatively unskilled, others were skilled male workers such as engine mechanics, telegraph operators, piano teachers, and, at the upper end

*[handwritten margin note: * to service jobs were in g very important and great demand, but offered very little in return.]*

of the service scale, professionals such as doctors. As the economy became more specialized, and as people became more urban and more affluent, the service sector grew because more people had the wherewithal and the desire to pay for services they might have performed themselves in earlier generations, such as clothing-making and food preparation. Urbanization prevented most people from producing food and led them to rely on others; rising wages allowed people to spend money on leisure pursuits as the such theatre or music hall, gambling, drinking, and retail shopping. Working-class men and boys were especially fond of football, both playing and watching professional games; gambling on horse racing was also popular. Working-class men had more leisure time and money than women, but women found time for leisure too: poor women in London visited pubs such as the Phoenix Pub and the Sun Pub in Lisson Grove (near Regent's Park) with female friends or their husbands.

The one exception to all this prosperity was agriculture. Agriculture grew until 1860, but then went into a decline which—while it was dotted by a few bright spots—never reversed. Agricultural output decreased, and agriculture declined as a proportion of the gross national product. While all western industrialized nations experienced a decline of their agricultural sectors as they industrialized, Great Britain was the only country to experience this transformation during the nineteenth century. The number of people working in the agricultural sector began to decline in 1860 and was down fully 10% by 1881. Those who remained in farming found it difficult to make a living as farm work mechanized and food prices dropped. Imported food became a larger part of the British diet. Some farmers survived by focusing on the needs of an urban society; for example, some dairy farmers did well by supplying fresh milk to urban areas (with the help of the railways). However, overall, the picture for farmers was one of decline.

1873–1914: Growth slows

The period between 1873 and 1896 was one of stagnation, followed by a degree of recovery from 1896 until the start of World War One. The population rose from 26 million in 1871 to 41 million in 1911. Most people—65% of the population in 1871, and 79% in 1911—lived in urban areas. Indeed, by 1911, 55% of Britons lived in cities of 100,000 or more. But from 1873 there was a dramatic change as Britain—along with the United States and most of Europe—entered an economic depression that lasted for over 20 years. Rents and prices fell almost 20% between 1873 and 1896 (and then rose 18% between 1896 and 1914). Unemployment rose. Bankruptcies became more common, with only 1,906 in 1870, but 5,161 in 1893. The British economy was still growing, but more slowly than before and more slowly than its new industrial competitors, Germany and the United States. And while these nations were establishing higher technical education institutions whose researches had industrial applications, such as Berlin's Royal Technical College of Charlottenburg (f. 1879), Britain's growing private educational sector continued to focus on educating men to become gentlemen. The redbrick universities, which provided higher education that was local and industrially-oriented, all opened between 1900 and 1909 (see Chapter 14). Britain's first university of technical education, Imperial College in London, was founded in 1907 (partly in response to calls for a "London Charlottenburg"). Furthermore as many countries began to adopt neo-mercantilist policies that included protective tariffs, Britain's strict adherence to free trade put it at a disadvantage in international trade. All of these factors came together to create a long period of economic sluggishness and difficulty that until 1929 was referred to as the Great Depression.

Historians have tried to explain the depression in various ways. Many point to the declining manufacturing sector as the main cause. One of the most famous arguments about late-Victorian economic failure is Martin Weiner's. Weiner argues that economic failure had cultural causes: rather than focusing on the skills and long hours at work that had made them prosperous, middle-class businessmen aspired to an aristocratic lifestyle that was at odds with a middle-class work ethic. Instead of embracing the qualities that had made them rich and made Britain great, they foolishly rejected these for the very aristocratic culture—with its emphasis on public schools and classical learning rather than scientific or practical skills, its horror of hard work, and its disdain for manufacture and industry— that had failed to create wealth without them. The middle class made the mistake of educating their children in public schools, marrying their children to aristocrats, and buying their own country estates, and in the process ruined Britain.

While Weiner's attention to the persistence of aristocratic status is interesting, most economic historians think that Weiner's explanation of Britain's industrial decline is overstated. The British middle class was never predominantly manufacturing and industrial, but always commercial and service-oriented. Public schools taught mathematics as well as classical learning, and their aristocratic students did not always disdain middle-class classmates' families or wealth. And while many young middle-class men chose commercial rather than manufacturing careers after 1860, this was probably not because they were rejecting their middle-class roots and seeking status, but because commerce seemed more secure and more promising.

overstating the facts?

Others question whether there was any failure to explain. Many argue that the very notion that Britain was a nation in industrial decline is overstated. While the British economy now had a rate of growth that was slower than its competitors', and was slower than it had had previously, growth persisted. The problem was less outright failure than a certain absence of dynamism. Manufacturing exports remained the core of the British economy. The British economy remained the center of the world economy. It was hardly "failing."

While the nation's economy was weaker, typical—that is, working-class— Britons were actually better off than they had been before. For a decade after 1873 prices for food, clothing, and housing fell significantly, and these falling prices (caused in part by increased industrial efficiency), coupled with rising wages, gave consumers higher real wages. Staples were cheaper and more affordable. Tea and sugar became cheap enough to become staples rather than luxuries; the soap and chocolate industries flourished too. Mass production meant low prices that

✱ Although Britain has not as prosper nes and growing as it once has doesn't mean that it's worse off.

allowed the working class to purchase discretionary items such as fashionable clothes and sporting accessories. People also had more leisure time; the average worker's work week shortened from 60 hours in 1870 to only 55 hours in 1900. Even when prices began to rise after 1896, wages kept pace, so that the working class did not suffer serious reverses, and the early twentieth century was a stable period for the working class and a prosperous period for the upper and middle classes. The thriving business that music-halls and professional football clubs did from the 1880s is testament in part to the working class's increased leisure time. A football ticket cost between 3d. and 6d. (1s. for a championship game), which meant that upper working-class and lower middle-class men could afford tickets at least occasionally. Even less affluent working-class men could even afford a railway ticket to attend a distant away game on occasion: the *Northern Review* newspaper complained in December 1887 that "the dangerous class of rough turbulent boys . . . fought their way into the [railway] carriages" to attend a match in Sunderland. One man at the Pavilion music hall in Leicester said proudly, "I never miss a Friday night a' all, and haven't done these 15 years."[20] Middle-class families often prospered too, as is evidenced by the growth in middle-class sports such as tennis and golf at the end of the century.

Finance continued to be central to economic growth. In banking and finance, the City of London still acted as the center of international finance, even more after 1880 than before. The London Stock Exchange expanded beyond the government and railway securities it had focused on. Banks continued to consolidate and to add branches. Between 1891 and 1902, over 100 amalgamations took place, and of the resulting large banks, two had more than 100 branches, and three had more than 500 branches. From the 1880s, hydraulically-operated elevators (and later, steel-framed construction) made tall buildings with upper-floor offices possible, and these were erected in city centers all over the country. (These technologies were applied to other sorts of buildings as well, such as London's Ritz Hotel, which was built in 1904.) Government spending continued to decline as a proportion of the economy, and the state was generally regarded as trustworthy on economic problems. In the early twentieth century, government spending on both social welfare programs and on the military—possible because of the long nineteenth-century process of government retrenchment—began to rise, gradually at first, and then sharply when the Great War began. The widely accepted British income tax meant that Britain was in a strong fiscal position when the war began. This was a sharp contrast to Germany and France, where income taxes introduced in 1913 and 1914 failed to gain the public trust and produced political tensions.

Manufacturing remained strong in the traditionally largest industries of cotton, coal, steel, shipbuilding, and railways. Factory architecture developed, with steel-framed, multi-story factories enjoyed a heyday from 1880 until after World War One.[21] Scottish industry was particularly strong, and by some measures was the strongest part of the British manufacturing base. By 1900 the Scottish coal industry, which in 1800 had employed 9,000 people and made up 15% of British coal output, employed 103,000 people and accounted for 27% of British coal production.

The industrial focus on these older fields meant that Britain ceded primacy in newer industries such as chemicals, motor cars, and electricity, to Germany and the United States. However, the older industries still made large profits, and newer industries remained small. Gas lighting (used in the new Houses of Parliament that were built in 1859, but uncommon in homes) was still the rule for most buildings and streets. It was not until the very end of the nineteenth century that electric lighting began to replace gas lighting, and as late as 1907 electricity powered only 10% of British industry.[22] In cotton textiles, the "cotton famine" of the 1860s was followed by a depression in the late 1870s, but the industry revived in the 1880s. Labor costs were increasing as fewer children worked and as women's wages rose, but the efficiency of Lancashire's cotton workers compensated for this; three of them could operate 1,000 spindles, a task that required six or more workers in continental Europe. The United States, India, and Japan all used ring-spinning and cheap labor, or both, to undercut British prices and threaten the British cotton industry. But cotton textiles remained profitable, and as late as 1911 still employed 1.5 million people, who were 16% of the industrial labor force. Overall, the problem in manufacturing was a lack of technical education for the next generation, and a concurrent lack of innovation that left British industry to stagnate.

Iron and steel were a slightly different story. The British iron and steel industries were changing, with older districts exhausting their resources and new districts emerging near Durham in the northeast, Cumberland in the northwest, and in the Midlands. But overall the picture was of declining production and exports. After 1873, Germany and the United States took the lead in iron and steel production. By 1900, Britain produced only a third of the steel that Germany and the United States together did, and by the eve of the First World War Britain made only half as much as Germany, and a quarter as much as the United States. Similarly, Britain's share of the international trade declined; indeed, after 1895 Britain imported iron and steel, and, by 1913, was one of the world's biggest importers of them.[23]

Railway construction slowed after 1870, though there was modest growth into the twentieth century. Railway companies began to merge and become more efficient; in 1904 14 companies owned about 85% of the tracks in the country. By 1913, when the railway system was at its peak, 1.5 billion passengers travelled every year on 20,000 miles of track, railways carted almost three quarters of the goods that circulated in the economy, and over 832,000 commercial horse-drawn vehicles made journeys to and from railway stations. In the 1890s, as rising rents in the cities and the inner suburbs forced workers to live ever farther from their jobs, the average railway journey lengthened from nine miles in 1890 to 17 miles in 1913. A series of laws passed between 1888 and 1894 controlled fares and suggested that railways were a public service first, a profitable enterprise second. Steam-powered ships replaced sailing vessels. The latter reached a peak in the 1890s but were then overtaken; by 1913 most merchant ships were steam-powered, and almost half had been built since 1905. Telephone service arrived in Britain in 1877, but Britain's excellent postal service made demand low, so phone service lagged (Americans and Germans were appalled by British phone service).

By 1895, Britain had 2,500 miles of trunk lines, but it was never a leader in telephone technology or usage.

The service sector was still growing: some say that by the 1890s Britain, which at the start of the nineteenth century was the world's first industrial nation, had become the world's first service nation. By 1900, the average middle-class and upper-class family spent one third of its income on services—principally on domestic service, motor cars and other travel, entertainment (including betting), and medical care. (Motor cars were extremely expensive: at £385 in 1900 they cost many times the average worker's annual salary.) The average working-class family spent one-tenth of their income on services, in the form of railway and tram travel, medical care, life insurance, funerals, and entertainment. As non-domestic service jobs such as a telegraph or telephone operator or typist became available, working-class women overwhelmingly preferred these jobs to domestic service, and the number of servants in Britain began to decline. State school teaching also grew quickly; in 1871, 261,158 children attended voluntary primary schools, and by 1911, 6 million children attended school, and they needed teachers. London hired 990 new teachers in 1871 alone.[24] Service workers provided and enjoyed many of the urban leisure activities that were such a feature of late Victorian Britain. One Italian visitor to London was astonished to find streets, shops, and audiences full of

> shopgirls, milliners, dressmakers, typists, stenographers, cashiers of large and small houses of business, telegraph and telephone girls . . . who avail themselves of the liberty allowed them by custom . . . to wander alone at night from one end of London to the other, spending all their money in gadding about, on sixpenny novels, on magazines, and above all on the theatre.[25]

The growing service sector, combined with more spending power for most, created this milieu.

The agricultural sector suffered terribly during the depression, and its proportionate contribution to the Gross National Product continued to decline. So did the percentage and number of workers in agriculture: in 1841, 22% of Britons were employed in agriculture or fishery, but, by 1911, only 8% could say the same. Grain farmers were the worst hit, while cattle and dairy farmers fared somewhat better. By the turn of the twentieth century, there was not a single county in England or Wales whose economy was more made up of more than 45% agriculture. Not only was Britain an urban nation, but almost every county in it was as well—the only agricultural regions left were a few in rural Scotland and Ireland. By 1914, Britain relied on imports for over half of its food—the only country to do so at this time—and agriculture was no longer an important part of the national economy.

Fiscal policy continued to develop as well. In the late Victorian and Edwardian periods, Liberal governments changed the flat-rate income tax system by introducing both differentiation—the principle of taxing income from earnings at a lower rate than income from investments—and graduation—the principle of taxing higher incomes at a higher rate. From 1906 until the start of the First World

War in particular, Liberal governments implemented reforms that broke with the previous insistence on minimalist tax policies.

Poverty persisted. A 1913 study revealed that 11% of urban working-class households lived in poverty. But while that sounds high, it was a proportion lower than Britain had in 1850, and lower than most other European countries had in 1913. It was also lower than the rates which prevail in the United States and in Britain today. Liberal governments were interested in creating more structural safety nets. In 1908, they instituted old age pensions (which had already been instituted in Germany in 1889 and in New Zealand at the turn of the century). Further plans to ameliorate the challenges of industrialized urbanized life—which had begun with the Condition of England debate in the 1840s—were halted by the start of the First World War.

Notes

1 *The World's Fair; or, Children's Prize Gift Book of the Great Exhibition of 1851. Describing the Beautiful Inventions and Manufactures Exhibited Therein; With Pretty Stories About the People Who Have Made and Sent Them; and How They Live When At Home* (London: Thomas Dean and Son [1851?]).

2 C.H. Lee "Regional Growth and Structural Change in Victorian Britain," *Economic History Review*, New Series, 34.3 (August 1981): 438–452.

3 C.H. Lee, "Regional Growth and Structural Change in Victorian Britain," *The Economic History Review* 34.3 (August 1981): 451.

4 R. Samuel, "Workshop of the World: Steam Power and Hand Technology in Mid-Victorian Britain," *History Workshop Journal* 3.1 (1977): 19.

5 Gaskell, *North and South*, Chapter 7. The smoke is "unparliamentary" because it does not comply with the 1848 Public Health Act, which sought to improve the quality of air and water in towns.

6 John Brewer, *The Sinews of Power: War, Money and the English State, 1688–1783* (London: Unwin Hyman, 1989), p. xvii.

7 Edwin Chadwick, *Report to Her Majesty's Principal Secretary of State for the Home Department, from the Poor Law Commissioners on an Inquiry into the Sanitary Condition of the Labouring Population of Great Britain* (London: W. Clowes and Co., for H.M. Stationery Office, 1842), p. 369.

8 Friedrich Engels, *The Condition of the Working-Class in England in 1844* (London: Swan Sonnenschein Co., 1892), p. 53.

9 Mr Matthew Crabtree's evidence to the Sadler Committee, in *The Sadler Committee Report* (1832), available online at: www.victorianweb.org/history/workers1.html (accessed December 26, 2015).

10 Thomas Carlyle, *Chartism* (London: James Fraser, 1840), p. 1.

11 Isabel Wilson's evidence to Lord Ashley's Mines Commission, in *Children's Employment Commission (Mines) 1842 report* (1842), available online at: www.victorianweb.org/history/workers1.html (accessed December 26, 2015).

12 Benjamin Disraeli, *Sybil: Or, the Two Nations*, introduction by R.A.B. Butler, edited by Thom Braun (Harmondsworth, UK: Penguin Books, 1980), p. 96.

13 Jeffrey Auerbach, *The Great Exhibition of 1851: A Nation on Display* (New Haven: Yale University Press, 1999), p. 91.

14 *Official Descriptive and Illustrated Catalogue* (London: Spicer Brothers, 1851) 209, quoted in Auerbach, p. 104.

15 William Chambers and Robert Chambers, *Chambers' Information for the People*, Volume 2 (Edinburgh, 1849), p. 213.

16 Martin Pugh, *Britain Since 1789: A Concise History* (New York: St Martin's Press, 1999), p. 73.

17 Francois Crouzet, *The Victorian Economy* (Columbia: Columbia University Press, 1982), p. 331.

18 J.H. Clapham, *An Economic History of Britain, Volume II, Free Trade and Steel 1850–1886* (Cambridge: Cambridge University Press, 1932), p. 199, quoted in Mark Thomas, "The Service Sector," *The Cambridge Economic History of Britain, Volume 2, Economic Maturity, 1860–1939* (Cambridge, Cambridge University Press, 2004), p. 103.

19 George and Weedon Grossmith, *The Diary of a Nobody* (London, 1892), Chapter 13.

20 On railway, *Northern Review*, December 10, 1887, quoted in Mike Huggins and John Tolson, "The Railways and Sport in Victorian Britain: a critical reassessment," *Journal of Transport History*, 3rd ser., 22:2 (2001): 99–115, p. 108; on music hall, quoted in J. Crump, "Provincial Music-Hall: Promoters and public in Leicester, 1863–1929," in Peter Bailey (ed.), *Music Hall the Business of Pleasure* (Milton Keynes, UK: Open University Press, 1985), p. 65.

21 Peter Scott, "The Evolution of Britain's Urban Built Environment," in Martin Daunton (ed.), *The Cambridge Urban History of Britain, Volume 3 1840–1950* (Cambridge: Cambridge University Press, 2000), p. 506.

22 Roderick Floud, *The People and the British Economy, 1830–1914* (Oxford: Oxford University Press, 1997), p. 118.

23 Crouzet, pp. 239–241.

24 Dina Copelman, *Class Acts: London's Women Teachers 1870–1930* (London: Routledge, 1996), p. 69.

25 Mario Borsa, *The English Stage of To-day* (New York: J Lane, 1908), pp. 112–113.

Relevant fiction that students might enjoy

Charles Dickens, *Hard Times* (1854)
Anthony Trollope, *The Way We Live Now* (1875)
H.G. Wells, *Tono-Bungay* (1909)
Arnold Bennett, *Clayhanger* (1910)

Further reading

Martin J. Daunton, *Wealth and Welfare: An Economic and Social History of Britain, 1851–1951* (Oxford: Oxford University Press, 2007).

Roderick Floud, *The People and the British Economy, 1830–1914* (Oxford: Oxford Paperbacks, 1997).

Roderick Floud and Donald McCloskey, *The Economic History of Britain since 1700* (Cambridge: Cambridge University Press, 1994).

Eric Hopkins, *Industrialisation and Society 1830–1951* (Oxford: Routledge, 2000).

Joel Mokyr, *The Enlightened Economy: An Economic History of Britain, 1700–1850* (New Haven: Yale University Press, 2009).

Martin Weiner, *English Culture and the Decline of the Industrial Spirit* (Cambridge: Cambridge University Press, 2004).

Online resources

University of Cambridge Electronic Resources for British economic and social history, 1700–1914: www.hist.cam.ac.uk/seeley-library/online-resources/e-resources/part-i-paper-10

5 "Bristling with shops"
Consumption

Introduction

In 1905, journalist T.W.H. Crosland was amazed at the ubiquity of shopping. He wrote that the streets, especially of suburban towns:

> more or less bristled with shops . . . to buy at a shop, or, in the chaste cant of the time, to go "shopping," is a popular suburban amusement. . . . All the shop-windows that ever were have been pranked, tricked out, decked, and dressed. . . . There are gold rings, hall-marked, at five shillings apiece; there are fat gold watches, hall-marked, at thirty shillings apiece; there are gold sleeve-links at three and sixpence a pair, and guinea gold wedding-rings at half a guinea.[1]

Surely a practice that marked public spaces so drastically, and incited at least one writer's vitriol, is worthy of examination. Yet historians did not used to study shopping. Economic historians focused on production and labor—how goods were manufactured, transported, marketed, and sold, the workers who were paid to make them, the profits gleaned—but ignored consumers and their purchases, even though sellers need buyers. Historians of leisure concentrated on sports, drinking, and gambling, as well as attendance at the theatre, opera, or music hall. They did not consider the shopping opportunities near entertainment venues, even though theatrical and shopping districts were often contiguous if not identical, suggesting that many people did both in one outing. But in the past two decades, historians have come to appreciate consumption as an important activity by which individuals and groups forged their identities, and historians of the economy, leisure, gender, class, and the city now study various aspects of consumption.

When scholars discuss consumption—the selection and purchase of goods—they refer not to the act of buying necessaries such as food but to acquisition that is on some level discretionary—fashionable clothes, decorations for their homes, accessories for specific leisure pursuits. In a "consumer society," most people have the desire and the ability to shop, choosing among various non-essential goods and services, and re-categorizing previously discretionary items as essential.

Approaching a society as a "consumer society" involves exploring the centrality of shopping and material possessions to people's identity. (This may have negative connotations: those who describe our modern society as a "consumer society" often imply that we have been reduced from informed citizens to mindless shoppers.) Agreed that a "consumer revolution" took place, and that Britain was transformed into a "consumer society," historians argue about when, why, and how this occurred. One scholar drily notes that historians of various periods insist that Britain emerged as a consumer society "in the seventeenth century, in the eighteenth century, in the second half of the nineteenth century, between the two world wars, in the years following the Second World War, and during the 1980s."[2]

Until about 1850, consumption patterns looked very much as they had in the late eighteenth and early nineteenth centuries. The elites and the growing middle class indulged in discretionary purchases, but they did so in small stores where the merchandise was kept behind the counter and presented to them by the shopkeeper. Working-class people indulged in occasional discretionary purchases—usually clothing or housewares—but could do so only rarely. Then from about 1850 until 1875, Victorian scholars argue that a "retail revolution" took place, one which centered on the rise of the department store. During this period, as the middle class and middle-class incomes grew dramatically, their demand for more things to buy and more ways to express themselves through their purchasing choices fueled many of the changes we see in the nineteenth century. From the 1870s, the working classes, too, began to engage in consumption. The rise in real wages increased disposable income and meant that consumption was frequent and common at every level of society. A wide range of domestic and personal manufactured items—clothes, furniture, lace, ornaments, souvenirs, bicycles, books, pianos—became affordable to a large portion of the population (this was exciting for some groups, threatening for others). By the turn of the century even the young enjoyed discretionary income that they spent on items that helped them define who they were or who they hoped to be. Only the elderly and the very poor, hampered by their lack of mobility and options, tended to be left out.

The mid-Victorian retail revolution was, then, a turning point. It was characterized first by the qualities of its material culture: industrially-produced, ready-made merchandise that was easily and frequently replaced. Second was its style of shopping, which featured goods displayed for browsing, fixed prices (rather than haggling), cash sales (rather than infrequently paid accounts that left shopkeepers unable to bring in new merchandise), and branding and advertising. Finally, it created a broad-based retail culture: more and more, people at all socioeconomic levels partook of consumption on a regular and ongoing basis. Early modern historians point out that many of these allegedly new Victorian practices are discernible in the eighteenth century (or even earlier). Very few eighteenth-century Britons spun the cloth they wore; most purchased it, and some ready-made clothing was available as well. Many also bought small, stylish, discretionary items—lace to trim a cap, or an earthenware teapot—whenever they could afford to; they were not strangers to discretionary retail purchases. Fashion, with its ability to lure people into the marketplace, was familiar even to working people.[3]

characterizations and changes of the "consumer revolution"

Some of these marketing practices however, were already present before the "revolution".

Eighteenth-century plebeians cared about fashion and wanted stylish clothes; young adults especially would save their wages to buy a suit of best clothes, distinct from their work clothes. In the mid-eighteenth century, Sheffield plateware—tableware and ornaments made of silver-plated copper that was attractive and much cheaper than solid silver—was sold for cash only, at fixed prices. By the late eighteenth century ceramics, carpeting and cotton textiles for home decoration had become affordable to middle-class people. There were shops in central London that allowed consumers to browse without purchasing. Branding and advertising already existed. From this perspective, the Victorian retail revolution was neither Victorian nor revolutionary.

And yet it was: the mid-Victorian revolution's individual attributes may not have been new, but their combination and ubiquity gave the era distinctive features. Eighteenth-century Britons bought cloth, but they then brought it to their tailor or mantua-maker to be cut and assembled. (Only sailors and soldiers bought ready-made clothing—uniforms.) In contrast, Victorians purchased much of their clothing ready-made and off the rack. While early modern Britons attained some of their clothing through retail purchases, much of the clothing that early modern plebeians wore was supplied to them by their betters, as when servants were presented with clothes by employers; by the Victorian period these practices were rare. In the eighteenth century, young working people prided themselves on having "saved hard," in one apprentice's words,[4] to buy a stylish outfit, or even more than one, but such outfits were expensive—clothing constituted a good part of many people's total wealth—and tended to be long-worn and frequently repaired. Furthermore, styles, at least those worn by the non-wealthy, changed little over the course of the eighteenth century and even into the early nineteenth century. In contrast, Victorian shoppers were far more likely to own a higher number of less expensive goods, which they wore for only a season or two before discarding them; lower quality and quickly changing fashions (along with higher real wages) came together to create a culture of constant shopping. The "rapid turnover of material possessions"[5] that characterizes consumer societies was a feature of Victorian consumption.

While browsing, fixed prices, cash sales, and branding and advertising can all be found in the early modern period, they were limited to specific areas or industries. Sheffield plateware was sold for cash at fixed prices, but that was unusual, and in any case the plateware was purchased only by the solidly middle-class. Shops that permitted obligation-free browsing were rare (and all in London), and only for the wealthy. Advertising was confined to proprietary (quack) medicines. It was only in the Victorian period that all these things came together, were applied to all realms of marketing, and together created a new and different culture of consumption.

Over the course of the Victorian era, new developments in manufacturing, transportation, and marketing started to make new shopping options and experiences possible. For example, new methods of manufacturing meant that shoes were now made in standard sizes, often with rubber soles, machine-sewn uppers, and mechanically riveted soles. This made a wide range of affordable choice possible. When C. & J. Clark Shoes was founded at the start of our period, in the

1820s, they offered fewer than 30 styles of men's shoes. But in 1863—during the explosion in Victorian retail—they were able to offer 334 different styles in a wide range of sizes, and by 1896 that number had more than doubled to 720.[6]

We see a similar progression in larger, more durable items, such as the piano. Before the Victorian period, pianos were found only in the homes of the wealthy. From the 1820s the piano had become the key status item in the typical middle-class home and had replaced the dining table as the most expensive object house. Then in the 1860s, pianos spread even further down the social scale, because aspiring lower middle-class families could afford inexpensive, German, machine-made pianos. And by the start of the twentieth century, better-off families in the urban working-class could afford pianos and accommodate them in their homes. While their pianos were, of course, smaller and of lower quality than those in upper-class homes, they would have been sources of pride and envy in working-class neighborhoods, marking their owners as financially stable and as cultural leaders in the neighborhood. One man, describing life in the early twentieth century, recalled that "if you were keeping up with the Joneses, you had a piano and had your front door open so that people could hear."[7] Owning a piano also implied that a working-class family pursued its leisure at home, not at the pub, and perhaps partook in rational recreation.

[handwritten margin note: References to the introductory chapter of the book]

As the example of the piano suggests, over the course of the Victorian period shopping became on some level democratic. In the early Victorian period, workers shopped as much as they could, but low wages and high food prices meant that most people had little disposable income before 1870. The non-wealthy majority enjoyed buying earthenware pots and clocks for their homes, new patterns of fabric for their clothes, but they could only do this infrequently. In contrast, in the late Victorian period consumer culture was shared by more and more people, virtually regardless of geography or class. Victorian England was a nation not only of shopkeepers, but of shoppers.

1820–1860: The rise of shopping

At the start of our period, while some cities did have central shopping streets, the shops on them tended to be specialized and expensive, aimed at aristocratic and polite shoppers. Most people favored smaller, traditional, local options. Every neighborhood had its own general shop that sold a wide variety of goods, plus more specialized stores such as the draper's (which sold cloth). Most shops were small (in villages, they could even be a front room of someone's home). Shop owners could be manufacturers of the items they sold: many shops were workshops in the back, retail sales counters in the front. Items were rarely on display, and customers did not browse; they described their needs and were presented with items by the shopkeeper. Store owners often extended credit to their customers, who they knew personally, and went for long periods without being paid. Itinerant hawkers and peddlers went door-to-door selling an odd variety of household goods and clothing. (They were often called "Scotch drapers" or "Manchester men," because of ethnic stereotypes that associated Scottish and Jewish people with cheap goods and the clothing industry.) Outdoor markets, some of which were on weekly or monthly, others seasonally or even annually, featured a variety of small producers who sold wares from stalls set up in the streets. There were also charity and commercial bazaars, in which a hall was set up to accommodate stalls selling jewelry, fancy work, and other ornamental items.

Over the earlier Victorian period more and more cities featured central shopping districts. Established towns such as Bath and Bristol developed central shopping areas. So did new and industrial towns: in the 1820s, Dale Street in Liverpool and Market Street in Manchester were widened. In the 1830s, Newcastle's Grey Street, a particularly refined shopping street, was established. In London, Regent Street was finished in 1820, and New Oxford Street was finished in the 1840s. These central areas were characterized by broad new streets (often made possible by slum clearance) that could accommodate public transport and large crowds.

Among newer stores, the earliest form, permanent indoor covered markets—also called bazaars—emerged between 1815 and 1840. (The term "bazaar" is Persian in origin, and reminds us both that the notion of marketplace overflowing with goods seemed exotic, and that many of the consumer items that Britons purchased were imported, from the empire and elsewhere.) Bazaars were in part a response to street markets, which, with their growing number of stalls and customers, were becoming a nuisance in central shopping areas. Other influences included Parisian *passages* and fundraising bazaars such as the gigantic Anti-Corn Law League bazaar put on in Covent Garden in 1845. Like these, indoor markets had small walkways lined by rows of individual shops. Small indoor markets in Oxford and Bath were soon outdone by the first large bazaars, which appeared in the north, in Liverpool (f. 1821) and Newcastle, whose renowned Grainger market (f. 1835) was the largest in England (until 1899, when it was overtaken by one in Leeds). In London, the Soho Bazaar (f. 1815) the Oxford Street Bazaar, and Exeter Change in the Strand were extremely popular. At bazaars shoppers could find jewelry, watches, hats, lace, books, china, work baskets, and so on; the Soho Bazaar advertised itself as specializing in "light goods, works of art, and female ingenuity."[8] While bazaars' stalls were individually owned, they often had a unified aesthetic—along with a pleasurable feeling of spectacle, plenty, and distraction for shoppers. In 1844, *Punch* advised, "in bazaar-shopping, beat each stall separately. Many patterns, colours, novelties, conveniences, and other articles will thus strike your eye, which you would otherwise never wanted or dreamt of."[9] By the 1840s both charity bazaars and fixed commercial bazaars provided entertainments (such as jugglers, tableaux, or a puppet show) to their shoppers. Bazaars were very important through the 1860s, and then declined in the late Victorian period, with London's Soho Bazaar emblematically replaced by a department store in 1889. Charity bazaars were organized by women's groups, and all bazaars tended to feature items thought to appeal to women. Also in the 1840s and 1850s, cooperative ventures emerged as attempts to combat the high price of staples. One of the first, the Rochdale Pioneers (f. 1844), sold food and clothing to working-class people at affordable prices, and distributed profits to its members

as dividends on what they had spent. By 1851 there were over 100 such cooperative ventures, and by the 1860s the movement was national, with Co-op stores
opening in Newcastle, London, Leeds, Liverpool, Huddersfield, Cardiff, and elsewhere. Cooperative stores had their working-class members' interests, not merely
profit, at heart; they were considered to offer a moral form of shopping and
were a key way in which working-class people participated in consumerism.

Class and income were, of course, principal factors in where and how various
Britons shopped. From 1820 until the 1850s, the shopping habits of all classes
of people looked much like they had in previous decades. Lower middle-class and
working-class people had very little disposable income and did not shop much.
At the other end of the socio-economic spectrum, wealthy customers had dressmakers and the like come to their homes, or else sat outside a store in their
carriages, to which salespeople would bring goods out for consideration. Polite
middle-class women shopped accompanied by a servant, male relation, or other
chaperone; they did not appear in public alone. This was partly because the
middle-class domestic ideal fit poorly with the figure of the urban consumer,
and partly because early Victorians believed their cities (especially London) to
be ugly, dirty, and uncomfortable, and so unsuitable for middle-class women.
And since most cities had no eating or drinking establishments into which polite
women could safely and comfortably enter, and no toilet facilities for them,
shopping time was limited.

1860–1914: Disposable income and department stores

From the 1850s, the world of Victorian consumption began to look and feel
markedly different. Changes in transportation, advertising, and spectacle were
integral to the success of new retail developments that emerged from 1850;
most important was the rise of the department store, starting in the third quarter
of the nineteenth century. Even so, traditional forms of shopping persisted.
Older, rural, and poorer shoppers tended to shop at older forms of stores and
markets, while younger and urban dwellers were more likely to have access to,
and to take advantage of, newer ways to shop.

From the 1850s, shopping habits began to change. While working-class people
had little disposable income before the 1870s, they still participated in the world
of discretionary consumption. Food was a necessity, but people still made telling
choices about what to eat. Milk, bread, and potatoes were seen as basics; more and
more, so were tea and sugar, which had been considered discretionary items in
the eighteenth century. Most Victorian working-class families also indulged in
luxuries such as eggs, fruit, and fish when they could. Clothes were a necessity,
but Sunday best clothes were a choice. A skilled worker might be able to wear a
fob watch along with his Sunday outfit. Other clothing choices were regional; in
Craigneuk, outside of Glasgow, a working-class mother would carefully choose the
shawl in which she wrapped her baby for its outing.[10]

The wealthy began shopping more publicly than they had before. This meant
the new practice of going into stores and browsing through goods on display,

like other consumers; while they might be aided by a salesperson, they wandered through large department stores and down exclusive shopping streets full of expensive boutiques, shopping in public. Every city had its fine shops for those who could afford to patronize them, but London's West End had special significance. It was known that "ladies" shopped in the West End, and between 1850 and World War One the West End shopper was, in most minds, a wealthy woman. Knightsbridge was for the wealthiest shoppers. Regent Street, Old and New Bond Street, the Strand, Piccadilly, and the Burlington Arcade were also popular.

Wealthy

Middle-class shopping habits changed too. Profit-hungry Victorian retailers were determined to overcome the barriers that kept middle-class women from spending the day shopping. Department stores began to provide lavatories and cafés at which middle-class women could safely and comfortably rest and refresh themselves, and then continue shopping. Outside of department stores, too, new places of refreshment for shoppers began to proliferate in central urban shopping areas. These appealed especially to middle-class women, who were highly conscious of their respectability and the spatial challenges involved in upholding it. Comfortable refuges were a new form of urban public space for middle-class women that differentiated them both from men and their pubs and from the prostitutes who frequented many shopping districts. From the 1860s urban shopping was a safe and comfortable experience over which women with money to spend could linger. For middle-class men, too, shopping for items that adorned their persons and their homes was important. Advertisements, catalogs, and articles aimed at them indicate that they were interested and active shoppers, and married and unmarried men alike took an interest in home decoration.[1] Even for the more modest middle class, the mid-Victorian period brought a new era of consumption. What disposable income they had was spent on the key status markers of dress and home decoration—furniture, books, and household ornaments were especially popular.

Middle-class

One aid to these changes was the rise of convenient mass transport to and within cities. From the 1850s, affordable and frequent suburban railway lines, horse-drawn busses, and streetcars made it easy for people to leave their neighborhoods and suburbs to shop in the city center; in the 1860s, journalist Henry Mayhew described suburban mothers and daughters streaming to Oxford Street in central London to shop. Middle-class suburban women could take the train into the city to spend the day shopping in indoor markets, arcades, or department stores; middle-class city dwellers could travel from their residential neighborhoods to growing central shopping districts. These continued to develop—in London, Victoria and Southwark Streets were built in the 1860s, and Shaftesbury Avenue and Charing Cross Road in the 1870s and 1880s. Also in the 1880s, the industrial midland city of Birmingham laid out Corporation Street, intended to transform the city into the retail center of the Midlands. Working-class people, however, while they might well work as salespeople in such stores, were still more likely to shop near home than to travel to the fancier and more expensive stores in the city centers.

Working-class

A second important development was the spread of advertising from quack medicines to other areas. While a slight tinge of disrespectability clung to advertising and to sales, which were associated with cheaper and less reputable stores, by the end of the century both were common even at very expensive shops. More and more over the course of the century, hundreds of consumer items that appealed to all income levels were heavily advertised, as were sales; stores and brands pursued customer loyalty. High-end retailers often emphasized the foreign origins of the goods they sold, trumpeting their Egyptian cigars and Spanish leather. Mass marketers were more likely to emphasize that their goods were British-made, and in the late nineteenth century liked to associate their goods (with or without consent) with the royal family. During Queen Victoria's Jubilee in 1887, hundreds of manufacturers used her image or her insignia, and associated the queen with diverse objects including perfumes, soap, jewelry, dolls, jump-rope handles, spoons, and bookmarks.[12]

Visually appealing advertisements were part of the growth of spectacle in Victorian Britain. Writer Edward Bulwer Lytton called Britain the "Staring Nation,"[13] and the taste for spectacle is evident in various arenas, from entertainment to scientific displays to courts of law. As the Victorian era progressed, shop-owners worked harder to provide visual and other stimuli that would tempt shoppers to enter and remain in shops. Two mid-century technologies, large plate glass windows and gas lighting, made elaborate displays possible and window shopping more exciting and safer later at night. (Later in the century, department stores were among the first places to introduce electric lighting.) To walk down a commercial Victorian street was to be surrounded by artful displays of tempting goods. Precedents for this sort of pleasurably overwhelming plenty included pleasure gardens, bazaars, French department stores, and the Great Exhibition, at which hundreds of items were displayed in the largest glass and iron structure in the world. Consumer spectacle reached its apex at the end of the century at the grandest London department stores, Harrods (which became a large department store in the 1880s) and Selfridges (f. 1909), which featured large glass windows, ornate architecture, and art nouveau facades. The latter was founded by American entrepreneur Gordon Selfridge and used American managerial and selling techniques that would go on to become popular in Britain. (The television show *Mr Selfridge* dramatizes the founding and running of the store.)

Given the spectacle and excitement of Victorian shopping, it was inevitable that shoplifting was a common crime. But while working-class and poor women who stole were labeled criminals, upper-class and middle-class women caught stealing were considered to be suffering from "kleptomania"; the medicalization of theft absolved them of any moral or legal wrongdoing. When Mary Ramsbotham, the wife of a wealthy doctor, was caught shoplifting four handkerchiefs from a drapers in 1855, her lawyers and supporters insisted that she was not a criminal but was suffering from a stealing mania and succeeded in having her freed.[14]

Transportation, advertising, and spectacle all supported the most important mid-Victorian development, the rise of the department store. Department stores were related to earlier developments: Bainbridge's, the first department store, originated as a draper's stall in Newcastle's Grainger Market. Like bazaars, which offered varied goods from many different stall owners under one roof, early department stores also offered varied goods under one roof, but in a single large store with many departments. In the 1860s, Whiteley's drapers in Westbourne Grove, Bayswater, London, transformed itself into a department store, and had so many departments that it called itself the Universal Provider; Whiteley boasted that his store sold "everything from a pin to an elephant."[15] As Whiteley and others expanded, they took over neighboring storefronts: in its first decade, Whiteley's acquired ten storefronts. Lewis's started in Manchester in 1877 with six departments, and by 1884 had taken over the entire block. The stores tempted customers with lavish displays, and used fixed prices and cash sales to keep costs and prices down. T.W.H. Crosland (with whom this chapter began) remarked slightingly that a "fine window display traps the suburban [woman] in precisely the same manner that a piece of cheese traps the fatuous mouse."[16] In these early decades, a key inducement to shopping in department stores was savings: cash sales and large scales allowed them to offer high-quality goods for prices about 20% lower than were offered elsewhere.

Following the success of the department store in northern cities, much larger department stores emerged in London—first in Bayswater, then Kensington High Street and Knightsbridge for the wealthiest London shoppers, Oxford Street for others—and then elsewhere. (Not all cities developed department stores: Leeds and Birmingham favored arcades.) These took as their models the grand French stores, especially the Bon Marché (after which several English stores were named). The Bon Marché set new standards of size and spectacle which brought hundreds of potential shoppers in every day. France also provided a model of employee relations, in which the largest shops had dormitories in which sales assistants lived under tight surveillance. (One French innovation that British stores did not quickly adopt was salesperson-free browsing, until Fenwick's opened in 1898 with its "silent assistants.")

As department stores became common, so did negative commentary on female shoppers, especially middle-class ones, and the proprietors who tempted them (aristocratic women had been associated with spending even in the eighteenth century). Women were seen as either expert shoppers who used their skills for the good of their families, or as overexcited shoppers, easily seduced by displays of merchandise, especially if it was on sale. Men were seen as indifferent to shopping, henpecked by their wives, and incompetent when they attempted to shop alone. Of course, there was plenty of evidence that men enjoyed shopping and could do it well, and that women were able to keep their heads while they shopped, but the stereotypes persisted: our own association of women with shopping, both expert and reckless, comes to us from the later Victorians. Supporters of women's new consumption habits saw shopping as liberating and a form of access to the public sphere, critics saw it as corrupting, but both claimed it was a new and an important aspect of middle-class women's lives. (The debate over whether shopping was liberating or ruinous for Victorian women has been replicated in the scholarship about them, with some scholars arguing that consumerism was inherently

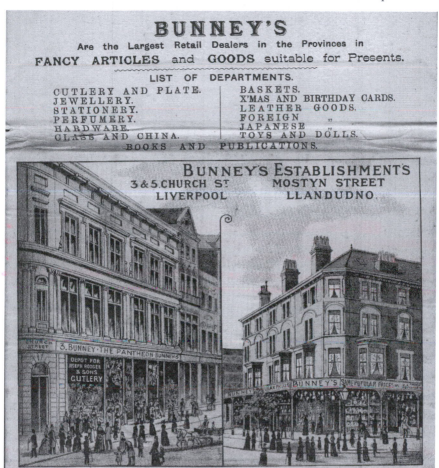

BUNNEY'S

Are the Largest Retail Dealers in the Provinces in
FANCY ARTICLES and GOODS suitable for Presents.

LIST OF DEPARTMENTS.

CUTLERY AND PLATE.   BASKETS.
JEWELLERY.   X'MAS AND BIRTHDAY CARDS.
STATIONERY.   LEATHER GOODS.
PERFUMERY.   FOREIGN   ,,
HARDWARE.   JAPANESE   ,,
GLASS AND CHINA.   TOYS AND DOLLS.
BOOKS AND PUBLICATIONS.

BUNNEY'S ESTABLISHMENTS
3 & 5. CHURCH ST   MOSTYN STREET
LIVERPOOL   LLANDUDNO.

Figure 5.1 A department store: Bunney's Establishments in Liverpool and Llandudno.

© Amoret Tanner/Alamy.

liberating and helped women to achieve public authority, others that it was oppressive and deflected women from politics.[17]) Shopping was often represented in the popular press as liberating for women; new forms of consumption allowed suburban middle-class women new access to the public realm, so that the ideal middle-class woman was seen as wholly domestic, yet not out of place in the urban marketplace. Critics argued that with so many amenities, women were ensnared into shopping all day, and that this "excessive shopping . . . was calculated to play all kinds of unpleasant things with the peace of families."[18] Still others worried that shopping was the only kind of public engagement allowed to women. In March 1912, when suffragettes broke the plate glass windows of Liberty's, Marshall & Snelgrove, and other stores on Oxford and Regent Streets, they were proclaiming that access to the public realm of consumption was not enough, and demanding access to another public realm, that of politics.

A good example of the debates over women and shopping is the one that took place around Whiteley's department store in Westbourne Grove, London in the 1870s. To attract lady shoppers, the "Universal Provider" offered first a refreshment room, and soon thereafter larger dining rooms, reading and writing rooms, lavatories, and entertainments. Competitors and critics were especially enraged in 1872 when William Whiteley applied for a license to serve wine and beer in the refreshment room. He (and others who applied for similar licenses) stressed that he was responding to customers' requests "for a glass of wine and a biscuit," not titillating them into new desires, that his customers were respectable, and that it was safer and more respectable for them (and of course more profitable for him) to remain in his store than to leave it and enter places of ill repute in search of a drink. But critics such as Henry Walker, the editor of the local *Bayswater Chronicle*, argued that making a place for women in public transformed them into public women. Given that shopping brought ladies into close physical proximity to prostitutes, and that both groups were involved in commerce and in pleasure, the additional similarity of drinking seemed to him too dangerous. Walker argued that a refreshment room that served wine to respectable ladies could all too easily allow women "dressed to represent ladies" to use it as "a place of assignation."[19] Furthermore, the availability of wine would encourage respectable women to drink, which might in turn transform them into drunkards or even prostitutes. As more stores provided amenities and encouraged respectable women to stay all day—turning a visit to a department store into less an excursion into the public sphere than a sanitized and domesticated experience—opinion remained divided over whether such stores were safe, innocent, and pleasurable, even liberating, or dangerous and destructive of womanhood and by extension society itself. Throughout the period, attacks on female shoppers as avaricious, uncontrollable, or sexualized—as sellers of, rather than buyers of adornments for, their own bodies—indicated an ongoing discomfort with the public middle-class woman.

During the late Victorian and early Edwardian years shopping opportunities for the upper and middle classes continued to expand. London's West End was now famous for the best shopping in all of Europe. The rise of fashionable ready-to-wear clothing allowed men to express themselves through their clothing choices. For example, the 1903 Harrods catalogue devoted 37 pages to "Gent's Outfitting," and featured accessories such as socks, collars, and neckties, and ready-made dinner suits, dress suits, lounge suits, shooting suits, frock coats and morning coats, and more.[20] By the end of the century, the largest department stores were large and imposing institutions with enormous staffs; the largest, such as Harrods in London, employed over one thousand people. The first custom-built store, a Bon Marché in Brixton, was said to have cost a staggering £70,000 to build.[21] In 1881, Whiteley's moved to a purpose-built building in the Queen's Road, which even former critics admired. These stores strove for a feeling of glamorous luxury that would tempt the middle-class woman; they became known for the many amenities that they provided rather than for low prices. Their gorgeous window displays and profusion of items delighted and overwhelmed shoppers. By 1900 every large city had a range of shops, with the most expensive and most spectacular stores in city centers, and more modest stores in outlying neighborhoods and suburbs.

By the 1880s, as well-appointed department stores and solo female shoppers both became typical, criticism of women shoppers died down. By 1912, the *Lady's Pictorial* could complacently note in a piece on "Our Shopping Habits" that shopping was "a national pastime," that the English excelled at making "a kind of pleasurable outing of our shopping" and that "we may certainly congratulate ourselves on our shopping methods and manners."[22] However, female shopping remained contested, as depictions of Christmas shopping reveal. Extended shopping for the family's presents (a new task, as mid-Victorian Christmases were small private affairs that involved only a bit of marketing on Christmas Eve) gave women an opportunity to assert their public authority: they were seen as praiseworthy because they used their shopping expertise and braved crowds to find the best prices on the nicest presents, all for the good of their families. In the 1890s, *Punch* and the *Pall Mall Gazette* depicted men as incompetent Christmas shoppers who were tricked by shop assistants into buying overpriced out-of-fashion items. Magazines were full of portrayals of ridiculously passive husbands who trailed helplessly behind their intensely focused wives.

During the post-Christmas sales, though, there was a backlash, as women were put in their place by representations of women as irrational sales shoppers. Journalist Clarence Rook wrote in 1907:

> Whence comes the woman's passion for a bargain? During those weeks at the turn of the year, I have been shoved off the pavement by rabid ladies in High Street Kensington; and I have seen the bargain sales in Chicago. The women of the world are struggling to get a remnant at cost-price.[23]

Representations of women sales shoppers as irrational sapped shopping of its positive connotations. Though men were not seen as shoppers, the *Lady's Pictorial* made a point of observing in 1912 that "Englishmen are really very much keener on shopping than they allow, or, perhaps, even realize."[24] Though men were demonstrably quite invested in certain types of shopping, this was seen as merely symptomatic of interests, hobbies, or forms of expertise, which happened to involve purchases, rather than as "shopping" per se. In the eighteenth century, elite men spent huge amounts of money on wine, luxury foods, leather goods for horses, dogs, and coaches, and on their own clothing and related male accoutrements.[25] In the nineteenth century, wealthy men continued this tradition, shopping for luxury items such as wine and tobacco products, and for formal clothing. They also took up antique collecting, a pursuit that required money, education, and taste. Cardiff pharmacist and antiques collector Robert Drane warned that distinguishing "cheap, mechanical and false" pieces from beautiful ones required expertise and innate taste.[26] Writer Desmond Coke (1879–1931) never married and commented that "if I had not always spent a good third of my yearly income on antiques . . . I might have had . . . a limousine, a week-end cottage, and a pot-belly."[27] Towards the end of the century, specialized hobbies that required knowledge, skill, or both, became popular areas for masculine consumption at all socioeconomic levels. Hobbies that required specific journals, guides, and tools, including do-it-yourself home improvement projects and sports, grew in popularity and became established as firmly masculine interests in which shopping was seen as incidental.

Men were as interested as women in home decoration, and in many families choosing and purchasing major household items was the man's responsibility. This, too, was an expansion of eighteenth-century households' spending patterns, in which men dominated costly household refurbishment projects in families that could afford them. Many men in the upper and upper middle classes kept abreast of women's fashion; one debt court judge's praise of a husband before him as one of the "few men of sense in this world . . . who don't care a farthing for what their wives wear" suggests that most husbands were keen or at least willing to have fashionably turned-out wives.[28] Men also cared about their own clothing: from the mid-nineteenth century, men's clothes became standard and ready-made and were heavily advertised. Advertising and amenities indicate that retailers believed that men were invested in shopping: Whiteley's famous amenities included free shaves for male customers who patronized the hairdressing department, and a department store in Blackpool had a reading room for men stocked with newspapers, cigars, and coffee. Men's consumption could be an opportunity to perform masculinity. For example, during the South African War military khaki was a runaway civilian fashion, with khaki neckties, handkerchiefs, and hats all selling briskly. Mass production meant that this new craze touched men of all social levels. By the late nineteenth and early twentieth centuries, men of all classes were invested in the purchase and use of consumer items, including clothing, and in how these could be part of their crafting of their social identities.

But the most important late Victorian development in consumption concerned the working and lower middle classes: rising real wages and falling work hours meant that they saw their options expanding. Lower middle-class shoppers faced the challenge of appearing middle class on incomes not quite adequate to the task. This was one reason that bi-annual sales—well-established by the 1870s, and common even in top stores by the 1880s—were such important economic and social events for lower middle-class shoppers.[29] One thing that helped those lower on the socio-economic scale become consumers was the emergence of chain stores. These were related to cooperatives but emerged in the 1880s alongside department stores. The first and most famous chain was Marks & Spencer, which started in 1884 when eastern European Jewish immigrant Michael Marks opened a stall in Leeds' indoor market, Kirkgate. Over the next ten years he opened stalls in markets across Yorkshire, Derbyshire, and Lancashire, and then—in partnership with cashier Thomas Spencer—began to open stores. Chains (and cooperatives) differed from department stores in that they focused on offering low prices to lower middle-class and working-class shoppers: to achieve this they had multiple outlets, sold a narrow range of goods, offered few services, used their size for buying power and low prices, and adhered to fixed prices and cash sales. Both were aimed principally at lower middle-class and working-class consumers (though chains sought only profit, while cooperatives offered dividends and a socialist approach).

Thus the urban lower middle and working classes entered the world of consumption beyond the necessaries. This might mean more expensive food; Margaret Loane, a district nurse who wrote about the London poor, observed in 1908 that "schoolchildren are constantly forbidden to tell one another what they have had to eat—unless . . . there may be something to boast of."[30] Turning to more durable items, the prices of mass-produced items—especially ready-made clothes, personal accessories, furniture, and home décor, but also ornaments, souvenirs, bicycles, newspapers, and books, and the all-important piano—were now in the range of working-class budgets. Consumer items related to literacy and to music—books, newspapers, sheet music—became more common in working-class homes. Working-class Britons continued to rely on older retail forms such as bazaars and neighborhood shops, especially since small local traders were more responsive than larger stores to working-class customer's needs and preferences. For example, they kept their stores open late, recognizing that their working-class customers shopped in the evening, after a work shift or a pub visit. (In the 1840s, when the first large department stores had supported the Early Closing Association, it was to prevent this competition, not out of any concern for their workers.) *working-class*

Decorating the home was central to late Victorian working-class culture and consumption. Those lucky enough to have a parlor filled it with covered chairs, framed paintings, large mirrors, and of course a piano if one could fit and they could afford it. Families who lived in two-room tenements would often display, on a chest of drawers, their cups and saucers and some artificial flowers under a glass shade. Even very poor families could distinguish themselves by planting window-boxes of flowers and putting up curtains. A middle-class observer of the homes of casual workers in Liverpool—among the poorest in the working class—noted disapprovingly that "dust-collecting knickknacks often abound in houses from which the more pawnable articles of useful furniture have been stripped," but such families clearly valued those ornaments and made sacrifices to afford them.[31]

Young, single, working-class and lower middle-class men and women embraced consumption. As yet unmarried and with no children to support and no houses to furnish, they had relatively high incomes compared with their needs and often spent money on fashionable clothing, accessories, and other items. Lower middle-class men in particular were known—and mocked—for their commitment to fashion. Urban journalist George Sala described them thus:

> If the morning be fine, the pavement of the Strand and Fleet Street looks quite radiant with the spruce clerks walking down to their offices. . . . Marvellous young bucks, some of them are. These are the customers, you see at a glance, whom the resplendent wares in the hosiers' shops attract. . . . These are the dashing young parties who purchase the pea-green, the orange, and the rose-pink gloves; the crimson braces, the kaleidoscopic shirt-studs, the

shirts embroidered with dahlias, deaths' heads, racehorses, sun-flowers, and ballet-girls; the horseshoe, fox-head, pewter-pot-and-crossed-pipes, willow-pattern-plate, and knife-and-fork pins. These are the glasses of city fashion, and the mould of city form, for whom the legions of fourteen, of fifteen, of sixteen, and of seventeen shilling trousers, all unrivalled, patented, and warranted, are made.[32]

As Sala's contempt makes clear, one middle-class reaction to lower middle-class culture was satire and criticism. In his early twentieth-century commentaries on lower middle-class suburbia, for instance, Crosland depicted the married lower middle-class man as "pitiful," with a "preposterous air," while his wife shopped at stores where "cheapness and flaringness and vulgarity run riot."[33] To the lower middle classes themselves, of course, things looked quite different. They shopped at less expensive stores or the sales, looking for fashion at an affordable price. They enjoyed shopping as an outing; lower middle-class shoppers could not afford the tony restaurants in the best department stores, but could patronize the Lyons or ABC cafés, or in Scotland and Wales, the Italian cafés and ice cream parlors, that now dotted shopping streets.[34]

By the late Victorian period, then, every class partook in the world of consumption. This democratic aspect was liberating to some, worrying to others. One of the major anxieties of the Victorian era was that of the impostor or impersonator, and this fear was exacerbated—perhaps even created—by the new world of consumption. Anyone could enter a department store and browse for hours without shopping. Cheap and expensive clothes could look almost identical. Fashionably-dressed middle-class women frequented the same central urban areas as fashionably-dressed prostitutes, sometimes at the same time of day. Salesmen and women in fine department stores could, when their shift ended, be mistaken for their customers—the derogatory term "counter jumper" was an attempt to put them back in their proper place.

In the eighteenth century, fashions might have traveled from high life to low or low life to high; nevertheless clothing instantly revealed whether its owner was rich or poor. The late Victorian era was quite different. The press was full of articles on the problem of distinguishing people by class now that clothes and public comportment, previously reliable indicators, had become far too similar. This problem was crystallized in the oft-mocked figure of the pathetically aspiring "masher" (also called the "swell" or "gent") who tried to imitate his betters by wearing similarly extreme but far cheaper fashions. Newspapers depicted the swell as ridiculously done up, with slick hair, a mustache, and a tight-fitting jacket. Critics claimed that the masher always gave himself away in spite of his best attempts. *Punch* abounded with cartoons mocking "The Height of Masherdom" (1905), and one of its most popular and enduring creations was "'Arry," a vulgar cockney masher. Just before World War One there was even a suburban version of the masher, called the "knut." But the term "masher" was always a relative one: mashers were, to the upper classes, middle-class poseurs, but to the middle class, working-class poseurs. Ultimately, then, the term "masher" reveals that by the end of the Victorian era consumption and fashion were key arenas in which identity was performed and only provisionally upheld, and that every class was conscious of and threatened by the one below it.[35]

Notes

1 T.W.H. Crosland, *The Suburbans* (London: John Long, 1905), Chapter 14, pp. 129–130.
2 John Benson, *The Rise of Consumer Society in Britain, 1880–1980* (Harlow: Longman, 1994), p. 2.
3 John Styles, *Dress of the People* (New Haven, CT: Yale University Press, 2008), pp. 6, 8.
4 Styles, p. 1.
5 Styles, p. 321.
6 Judith Flanders, *Consuming Passions: Leisure and Pleasure in Victorian Britain* (London: HarperPress, 2006), p. 93.
7 John Langley, *Always a Layman* (Brighton, 1976): 11, quoted in Paul Johnson, "Conspicuous Consumption and Working-Class Culture in Late-Victorian and Edwardian Britain," *Transactions of the Royal Historical Society*, Fifth Series, Vol. 38 (1988): 27–42, p. 40.
8 Flanders, p. 108.
9 *Punch* 1844, quoted in Peter Gurney, "'The Sublime of the Bazaar': A Moment in the Making of a Consumer Culture in Mid-Nineteenth Century England," *Journal of Social History* 40.2 (Winter 2006): 385–405, p. 391, which notes it as quoted in *The Times*, September 26, 1844, p. 8.
10 Johnson, p. 35.
11 Deborah Cohen, *Household Gods: The British and Their Possessions* (New Haven, CT: Yale University Press), p. 90.
12 Thomas Richards, *Commodity Culture of Victorian England: Advertising and Spectacle, 1851–1914* (Stanford: Stanford University Press, 1991), pp. 87, 91.
13 Edward Bulwer Lytton, *The Siamese Twins, A Satirical Tale of the Times*, Book I, Chap III, p. 50.
14 Tammy C. Whitlock, *Crime, Gender, and Consumer Culture in Nineteenth-Century England* (Aldershot: Ashgate, 2005), p. 196.
15 Dorothy Davis, *Fairs, Shops, and Supermarkets: A History of English Shopping* (Toronto: University of Toronto Press, 1966), p. 289.
16 Crosland, pp. 129–130.
17 Christopher P. Hosgood, "'Doing the Shops' at Christmas: Women, Men and the Department Store in England, *c.* 18801–914," in Geoffrey Crossick and Serge Jaumain (eds), *Cathedrals of Consumption: The European Department Store, 1850–1939* (Aldershot: Ashgate, 1999), p. 98.
18 Quoted in Erika Rappaport, *Shopping for Pleasure: Women in the Making of London's West End* (Princeton, NJ: Princeton University Press, 2001), p. 37.
19 Quoted in Rappaport, p. 31.
20 Brent Shannon, *The Cut of His Coat: Men, Dress, and Consumer Culture in Britain, 1860–1914* (Athens: Ohio University Press, 2006), p. 66.
21 Flanders, p. 113.
22 "Our Shopping Habits," *Lady's Pictorial*, November 23, 1912, p. 828.
23 Clarence Rook, in *The Reader*, January 12, 1907, p. 308, quoted in Hosgood, p. 111.
24 "Our Shopping Habits," p. 828.
25 Amanda Vickery, *Behind Closed Doors: At Home in Georgian England* (New Haven, CT: Yale University Press, 2009).
26 Cohen, *Household Gods*, p. 157.
27 Desmond Coke, *Confessions of an Incurable Collector* (London: Chapman & Hall, 1928), pp. 241, 18–21, quoted in Cohen, *Household Gods*, p. 160.

28 Deborah Cohen, "Review: Buying and Becoming: New Work on the British Middle Classes," *Historical Journal* 46.4 (2003): 999–1,004, p. 1,003.
29 Christopher Hosgood, "Mrs Pooter's Purchase: Lower Middle-Class Consumerism and the Sales, 1870–1914," in Alan Kidd and David Nicholls (eds), *Gender, Civic Culture, and Consumerism: Middle Class Identity in Britain 1800 to 1940* (Manchester: Manchester University Press, 1999), p. 156.
30 Johnson, p. 32.
31 Johnson, pp. 36–37.
32 George Augustus Sala, *Twice Around the Clock, Or, The Hours of the Day and Night in London* (R. Marsh, 1862; Original from the University of Michigan, Digitized March 31, 2006) p. 83.
33 Crosland, pp. 24, 38, 133.
34 John K. Walton, "Towns and Consumerism [1840–1950]" in Martin J. Daunton (ed.), *The Cambridge Urban History of Britain, Volume 3: 1840–1950* (Cambridge: Cambridge University Press, 2000), pp. 735–736.
35 Shannon, p. 144.

Relevant fiction that students might enjoy

George Sala, *Twice Round the Clock* (1859)
George Eliot, *Middlemarch* (1871–1872)
Emile Zola, *Au Bonheur des Dames* (The Ladies' Paradise) (1883)
George and Weedon Grossmith, *The Diary of a Nobody* (1892)
H.G. Wells, *Kipps: The Story of a Simple Soul* (1905)

Further reading

Judith Flanders, *Consuming Passions: Leisure and Pleasure in Victorian Britain* (London: HarperPress, 2006).
Peter Gurney, "'The Sublime of the Bazaar': A Moment in the Making of a Consumer Culture in Mid-Nineteenth Century England," *Journal of Social History* 40.2 (Winter, 2006): 385–405.
Christopher Hosgood, "'Doing the Shops' at Christmas: Women, Men and the Department Store in England, c.1880–1914," in Geoffrey Crossick and Serge Jaumain (eds), *Cathedrals Of Consumption: The European Department Store, 1850–1939* (Aldershot: Ashgate, 1999), pp. 97–115.
Christopher Hosgood, "Mrs Pooter's Purchase: Lower Middle-Class Consumerism and the Sales, 1870–1914," in Alan Kidd and David Nicholls (eds), *Gender, Civic Culture, and Consumerism: Middle Class Identity in Britain 1800 to 1940* (Manchester: Manchester University Press, 1999), pp. 146–163.
Erika Rappaport, *Shopping for Pleasure: Women in the Making of London's West End* (Princeton, NJ: Princeton University Press, 2000).
Brent Shannon, *The Cut of his Coat: Men, Dress, and Consumer Culture in Britain, 1860–1914* (Columbia: Ohio University Press, 2006).

Online resources

A history of the department store: www.bbc.com/culture/bespoke/story/20150326-a-history-of-the-department-store/index.html

6 "Born into the lower-upper-middle"
Class

Introduction

In one of P.G. Wodehouse's stories about the wealthy Bertie Wooster and his personal manservant Jeeves, Bertie's aristocratic Uncle George (Lord Yaxley) intends to propose to Rhoda Platt, until he discovers that her aunt, Maud Wilberforce, is the barmaid he loved and lost, and proposes to her instead. Discussing both women in the course of the story, Bertie and Jeeves have the following exchanges:

"I gather that this Miss Platt is not of the *noblesse*."
"No, sir. She is a waitress at his lordship's club."
"My God! The proletariat!"
"The lower middle classes, sir."
"Well, yes, by stretching it a bit, perhaps. Still, you know what I mean."
"Yes, sir."
"But Jeeves!"
"Sir?"
"[Mrs Wilberforce] *is*, as you remarked not long ago, definitely of the people."
He looked at me in a reproachful sort of way.
"Sturdy lower middle class stock, sir."
"H'm!"[1]

To Bertie, the difference between working class and lower middle class is either imperceptible or unimportant; to Jeeves, it is neither. To twenty-first century American eyes, the positions of both men—Bertie's that, although he considers himself broad-minded, the difference between the aristocracy and all of the lower orders is undeniable, and Jeeves', that the precise distance between Lord Yaxley and these women matters quite a lot—are somewhat perplexing. But these sorts of fine-grained distinctions were (and are) important in British society. In *The Road to Wigan Pier*, George Orwell famously reflected on the British class system, explaining:

I was born into what you might describe as the lower-upper-middle class. The upper-middle class [was] the layer of society lying between £2,000 and £300 a year: my own family was not far from the bottom. You notice that I define it in terms of money, because that is always the quickest way of making yourself understood. Nevertheless, the essential point about the English class-system is that it is not entirely explicable in terms of money. Roughly speaking it is a money-stratification, but it is also interpenetrated by a sort of shadowy caste-system; rather like a jerrybuilt modern bungalow haunted by medieval ghosts.[2]

Orwell was a perceptive guide to the class system; furthermore like Jeeves, he could make very fine distinctions amongst those near him in class status.

Class was important in Victorian Britain to a degree that is difficult for people living in the twenty-first century to comprehend. Today Americans in particular are uncomfortable discussing or identifying class disparities. Wealthy Americans identify themselves as "comfortable," not "upper class"; commentators prefer the more generic "working Americans" to "working class." Over half the adults in the United States identify themselves as "middle class." This self-identified "middle class" includes 40% of those with annual incomes below the poverty line of $20,000, and 33% of those whose annual incomes above $150,000 make them members of the wealthiest 5% of American households. In Britain, too, many claim to be beyond class. However, about half of Britons today identify themselves as working class, and in a 2010 newspaper piece entitled "Of Course Class Still Matters—It Influences Everything That We Do," columnist Will Hutton argues that while "[n]obody wants to believe that British society is as class-bound as it is ... the social truth will out."[3] For Americans, a better parallel to class in Victorian Britain is race in the United States. In both instances, there is a long and complex history that is characterized by hierarchy, by institutionalized inequity, and by a strong feeling on the part of most people that people of different classes and races are fundamentally unlike one another.

Victorian Britain was a deeply classed society; everyone was aware of class, admitted that it was a meaningful social reality, and identified themselves as a member of a class. As a result, understanding class is fundamental to understanding Victorian Britain. In some ways the organization of British society by class started in the Victorian period. This is not to say that pre-Victorian Britain was devoid of social hierarchy or wealth disparities—far from it—but that an understanding of social difference as organized specifically by something called "class" was a feature of the industrializing nineteenth century. Eighteenth-century Britons were likely to talk about such groups as "the middling sort" or "the lower ranks." From the late eighteenth and early nineteenth centuries Britons began to use the terms "class" and "classes" to describe how society was organized (though the intended group could be as broad as "the laboring classes" or as narrow as "the class of tenant farmers"). Many schemes of class organization have been proposed, by both contemporaries and historians. Some scholars suggest that it is wiser to think about Victorian society in terms of status and hierarchy, which overlapped with but were not identical with class; for example, a village schoolteacher or parish priest both had statuses that far outweighed not only their income but their class. Historian Patrick Joyce rejects class as an overarching category, stressing that while class may have been important to people's work and professional identities, that in other arenas populist rhetoric and values— suspicious of aristocracy and government, alert to oppression and injustice on the part of either—were more important than class.[4]

Class can refer to people's income levels; to their relationship to the means of production—whether they enjoyed the profits of the process in which they were involved, or were paid a wage that did not reflect their entire contribution; to socioeconomic standing, which includes educational level and employment type; to cultural choices; to values. In Victorian Britain class is related to, but not defined by, income, which tells us how much money people had, but not how or where they spent it. Some upper working-class families had higher incomes than some lower middle-class families, but did not consider themselves middle class. A wealthy middle-class father might send his sons to an elite school in a bid to have them accepted as upper class as adults. Some members of the aristocracy were happy to socialize with wealthy middle-class people whose incomes were as high as their own, but some scorned them because of their class origins.

The different factors to consider when determining one's class.

British society was fiercely hierarchical; hierarchy was one aspect of class, and class was one aspect of hierarchy. People believed that society was organized hierarchically, so that some groups and individuals had more wealth than others and had power over others. Even more importantly, the vast majority of Victorians accepted, even endorsed, this system. Most people sought not to break barriers or rise as high as possible, but to find happiness at the level at which they found themselves. People at all levels of society believed that the rich and the poor were different beings. For example, while it is true that rural villages were small and close-knit communities, that sense of community existed only among rural workers and did not extend to farmers and landowners, whether large or small. The locally powerful—who included magistrates and priests as well as the well-off—were entitled to respect, but were fundamentally other. Gradations of rank between different gentry families were important in those circles, but while perceptible from below they were not terribly significant.

While class remains complex, most Victorianists hew to a three-class model of working, middle, and upper classes, in which, following early nineteenth-century political economist David Ricardo (1772–1823), the working class got its income from wages, the middle class from salaries and profit, and the upper class from property, rent, and interest. Marxist historians saw class as dictated by one's relationship to the means of production and as a form of political consciousness that predicted an historical trajectory. According to Marx, the industrial working class, or proletariat, would come to be aware of itself as a class whose interests were opposed to those of the middle class, would rise up, and would create a class-less, communist society. The social history that dominated historical practice in the 1960s and 1970s was generally shaped by the Marxist model, though not all social historians of that era saw class conflict as primary, or saw a working-class revolution as inevitable. Today, most aspects of the Marxist scheme of history have fallen out of interpretive fashion. In particular, class is no longer seen as part of an inevitable historical trajectory towards revolution and a classless society. Furthermore, class conflict is no longer seen as inherent to a class system. Indeed, Victorian Britain was defined by class, but not by class conflict.

Furthermore, the individual's relationship to the means of production—the fact that a worker received a wage, and that his or her employer made a profit—is no longer seen as the only important factor in his or her identity. Class was not the only salient feature in economic or social organization in Victorian Britain. People understood themselves as parts of groups other than their class. Status was central; a schoolteacher had higher status than a manual laborer. Religion mattered: members of the Protestant majority saw themselves as very different from Roman Catholics, whose ability to be patriotic they suspected. Members of the Church of England were different from those who worshipped at Methodist chapels. People could be defined by race, and often were. People of African and Asian descent were considered to be of a different race, and many were convinced that this made them incapable of being fully British or fully patriotic, regardless of where they were born or how many generations of their families had lived in Britain. Jews were certainly a separate and suspect race, one that lacked the Christian beliefs that many saw as an aspect of whiteness, and in addition had what seemed a bizarre international aspect. The Irish, whether in Ireland or Liverpool, were of a different race too, in part because they were Catholic. Indeed many European nationalities were seen as separate races, especially if like the Irish they were Catholic—the Italians and the French are good examples. Overall, many differences that today would be described as cultural were understood by Victorians as racial. Gender was another important social category; in every class, male and female roles were different, and in some situations—for instance, the situation of being pregnant—women of different classes had more in common than men and women of the same class. So too was region: northern factory workers and miners and poor Londoners could have contempt for each other. Furthermore, much rhetoric about class had political and other goals that we need to take into account when we interpret it.

Class, then, was not merely an income bracket or a relation to the means of production, nor was it the only way that people understood themselves or others. So what was it? In Victorian Britain, classes were simultaneously economic, cultural, and discursive. They encompassed income, educational level, occupation, domestic standards and styles, politics and leisure. Classes were dynamic, not static, and could be inclusive as well as exclusive and went well beyond the economic. This book takes as a central premise the notion that class, however complex or discursive, did exist in Victorian Britain. It was one important way in which Victorians attempted to understand themselves and their society, one that affected every level of society from the individual's understanding of him- or herself to national government policy.

***

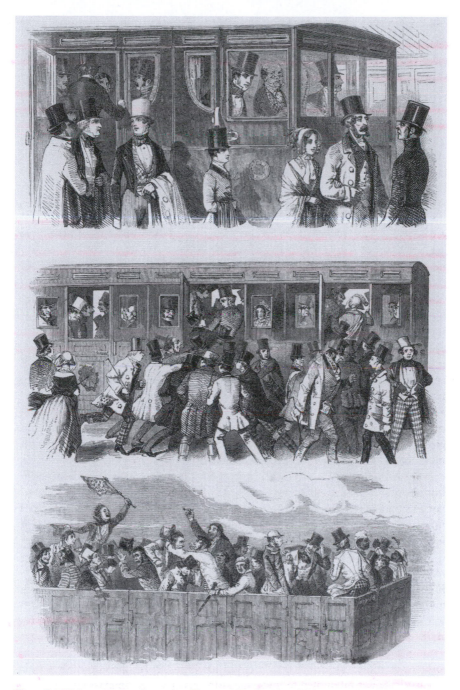

Figure 6.1 This engraving from the *Illustrated London News* (Volume 47/1, p. 328) depicts class distinctions through the division of rail travel into first, second, and third class, with the first-class passengers in their spacious carriage, the scramble for seats in the second class, and an open wagon carrying the third-class passengers, caricatured here as a rowdy uncouth mob.

Most Victorians saw their society as divided into the working, middle, and upper classes, with divisions within each of these. In 1820, the working class comprised about 80% of the population. Their family income, derived from wages, was usually under £100 per annum, but could go as high as £300 per annum. The middle class were about 15% of the population, and were growing both in absolute terms and as a proportion of the population throughout the Victorian period. They made up almost one quarter of the population by 1850, and between 1851 and 1871 the number of solidly middle-class families doubled. This growth was in large part because of the expansion from about 1860 of clerical and sales work, which allowed aspiring upper working-class men and women to become lower middle class. Middle-class family income, derived from commerce, manufacturing, or the professions, could be from £100 to £1,000 per annum. The remaining 5% of the population were upper class, with family incomes of at least £1,000 per annum, and often many times that: philanthropist Angela Burdett-Coutts (1814–1906) was worth almost £2 million, and William Cavendish, the seventh Duke of Devonshire (1808–1891) took in over £130,000 per year from rents and dividends alone. This class, whose incomes derived from rents of their landed estates or from investments, included the royal family, the titled peerage, and the gentry. Wealthy upper middle-class families often socialized with the local gentry, especially in provincial areas, and together these two classes formed a single social group—"polite" society.

The classes were complex and broad, lacking consistency or unity, so that some historians prefer the more capacious terms "working classes," "middle classes," and "upper classes." All of these classes were fluid—changes in fortune, marriage, education, and ambition all made moving up in class status a possibility (though a remote one) and made slipping down an ever-present danger (one reason that many people so despised those just below them).

The working class was the majority of the population, but was ignored by historians for many years prior to the 1960s. Social history in its early years defined itself by its focus on working-class, peasant, or subaltern groups. Social historians used statistical analysis to reconstruct the experiences of those who left few textual or intimate records. They often strove to celebrate the working-class lives they recovered, focusing on men, on large workplaces, especially factories and mines, and on unions. More recently, historians of the working class have broadened their remit to include women and immigrants as workers, smaller workplaces, the service sector, domestic service, white-collar forms of work, working-class conservatism, and working-class homes and leisure. While working-class people were often seen by those above them in the social hierarchy as uneducated, unrefined, and passive victims of their fates, in fact, the working class had a thriving and class-specific culture (or cultures) and a high degree of agency.

The middle class emerged in the eighteenth century, grew rapidly during the nineteenth century, and has attracted much scholarly attention ever since. This is in part because it lends itself to study: middle-class Victorians were educated and literate, and so left many written sources. Because they tended to form and join a wide variety of clubs and voluntary associations, we have minutes of meetings, newspaper coverage of public lectures, and other records. Many middle-class Christians also left spiritual journals and autobiographies. When women's history emerged in the 1970s, it focused on middle-class feminists. For much of the twentieth century, research on the middle class focused on ascendancy: on the growth of the middle class, the rise of middle-class professions, the rise of middle-class political power, the rise of the middle class as moral leaders of society. Recent research on the middle class has broadened to include evangelical religion, the large and important lower middle-class, provincial urban culture, and consumption.

The upper class was small—probably the smallest and wealthiest in Europe—and powerful. (The legal doctrine of primogeniture, in which estates and titles passed only to the eldest son, meant that Britain did not have the large but often impoverished aristocracy of many European countries.) Members had either titles, wealth, land, or all three. Historian of the aristocracy, David Cannadine, favors the term "the British landed establishment," including the aristocracy and the landed gentry, because it emphasizes land ownership and political power and conveys the economic, political, and social importance of the country's elite.[5] The top portion of the upper class, the titled aristocracy or peerage, consisted of the 400 to 500 men who sat in the House of Lords and bore the titles of baron, viscount, earl, marquess, or duke, and by implication their immediate families. These families spent half the year in London, participating in the parliamentary and social seasons, and half the year at their country estates. Below them was the gentry, which included baronets (the lowest title) and untitled large landowners and probably numbered several thousand people. Members of the gentry were not active in national politics and could not afford establishments in London. They did, however, have landed estates; while they led provincial lives, they were wealthy and influential within these and were active in local politics, often serving as Justices of the Peace. Together, the aristocracy and gentry owned most of Britain.

Before
1820–1870: Class and respectability

In the early Victorian period, more than anything working-class people were engaged in a daily struggle not only to survive but to do so with dignity. This meant working long hours to feed, house, and clothe self and family. In addition, it meant maintaining a home, family, and public face that fell on the right side of the all-important divide in working-class culture between the "rough" and the "respectable." The resources that supported these goals included work, family, community, political and other associations, and religion. Many, especially those who were Methodists, took their religion very seriously; for many working-class women, especially, religion was a key site for agency and self-expression. In 1820, there were probably about 200,000 committed Methodists in Britain, and perhaps as many as one million people who were in some ways influenced by Methodist theology and culture, and over 60% of them were members of the working class.

Most working-class people began working—in the household, on the farm, or for wages—at the age of about 11 or 12, and worked 12 or more hours per day, six days per week, for most of their lives. Most working-class work was manual: whether or not it required skill (however defined), it was physically taxing and often dirty. It was frequently also dangerous: men especially, who were not protected from danger or long hours by Factory Acts as women and children were, spent their entire lives exhausting themselves earning a living, and were often injured or died young. Work was extremely varied. Work could be artisanal or industrial, skilled or unskilled, rural or urban. It might be seasonal, on a small family farm, or year-round, as a domestic servant, in a one-room workshop, or in one of the enormous textile factories that were common in Lancashire and Cheshire from the late eighteenth century. Some received relatively high wages for skilled work in permanent positions; most got much lower wages and lived from week to week. Many industries were seasonal (many women who worked as prostitutes did so only during the off-season of some other industry). Most workers earned an hourly or piece wage, paid in cash at the end of the week, but some received some remuneration in kind; agricultural laborers might get some vegetables or cheese, and domestic servants sometimes got last year's clothes as hand-me-downs in addition to room and board. Many workers could find only "casual" work; they would turn up at the docks or at a farm every morning hoping to be given one day's work. Day laborers and their families, called the "casual poor," were never sure of an income from one day to the next, and lived precarious and difficult lives.

Ideally, working-class men worked full-time and year-round at respected jobs that earned a "breadwinner's wage," sufficient to support a family. In practice, however, much work was part-time, seasonal, occasional, precarious, unskilled, or poorly paid. Men's work included artisanal craft work, work in large factories, small workshops, and mines, work in the service sector, especially in urban areas, farming and domestic service (though both of these declined for men over the period), and low-level white-collar work (though this was only available to those with some education). The dangerous and fatiguing nature of most men's work was one reason that parents were so eager to vault their children into the lower middle class; even if the pay was not always better, the life was. From the 1840s, many working-class families hoped that the female head of household would be able to eschew waged work, but this was another ideal that was rarely realized in practice: most working-class women worked for wages for at least part of their lives. Women's work included factory work, domestic service (especially before marriage), piece work done at home, and work in the service sector. Married women who did not work outside the home for wages often did piece work to earn money at home, or took in boarders to generate income. And although giant factories and mines dominate our mental picture of the nineteenth century, the majority of workers were employed in small workshops or factories, worked at home, or worked in the homes of others (domestic service being one of the largest occupational groups of the era).

Working-class people usually delayed marriage until they felt they could afford it (though they married at slightly younger ages than the middle class and upper class); in 1816, the average age at marriage was at a historical low, but it rose through the mid-1840s, until most working-class people married at 23 to 25 years old. Of course, there were significant variations; for example in post-Famine rural Ireland, very late marriage became the rule, and a large proportion of the population never married. Once they married, couples were expected to establish their own household. Contraception was not considered respectable and in any case was not reliable, so many working-class women spent the two decades or so after marriage pregnant, breastfeeding, and/or caring for small children.

Before the passage of the 1870 Education Act working-class children did not necessarily go to school. A lucky few got rigorous educations at "National and British" schools run by philanthropists. Others attended ragged schools, factory schools, or workhouse schools. Some in rural areas got no schooling at all. Most popular were working-class private schools (also called dame schools), which consisted of a few children in a neighbor's home, being cared for while their parents were at work and learning some basics, and Sunday schools, which for many constituted their entire education and were responsible for whatever literacy they achieved. Given this, literacy rates were impressively high (though female literacy was always lower than male literacy) in 1840, between two thirds and three quarters of working-class people had achieved rudimentary literacy. Literacy was not a dividing line in working-class culture; literate and illiterate people socialized with one another and often married one another. The literate read aloud to the illiterate, in homes, workplaces, and leisure spaces such as pubs and coffeehouses. Education and literacy were generally best in Scotland, where one 1855 survey indicated that female Scottish literacy was higher than male English literacy, and worst in Wales, Ireland, and rural England.

Working-class people strived for respectability, but the standards by which this was defined—as regarded domesticity, sexual behavior, drinking habits, and the like—were specific to working-class culture (they were not simply laxer versions of middle- and upper-class standards). Respectable or not was probably the most important social distinction in working-class society. However, many families slid from one to the other or socialized across the divide, and in any case respectability can be seen less as a fixed status than as a performance, one that many chose to perform or refrain from performing for different audiences. Respectability meant status in the community—"independence" and "character" for men, and good housekeeping and mothering skills for women. Adult women spent an inordinate amount of time figuring out how to keep their families fed and clothed on a small budget. Men worked even longer hours than women, and the best husbands gave their Friday pay packets to their wives right away, rather than drinking away half of it on Friday nights.

Respectability was usually judged by the neighbors, and the criteria were multiple, complex, and varied. Neighbors noted how conscientious a woman was about returning borrowed items; whether a husband worked steadily or not, drank to excess or not, beat his wife or not; whether a couple was legally married; whether a family had a parlor in which to entertain company; whether the children were sent to Sunday school; whether the family had Sunday-best clothes or enjoyed a

A little grey area when it comes to respect amongst the working-class.

Sunday dinner together; whether they could afford a proper funeral.] Those deemed respectable usually had good relations and good credit with the local grocer; they might also have an understanding with the pawnbroker (some working-class communities saw pawning as rough, others as potentially respectable). Some working-class families prided themselves on never accepting charity or entering the workhouse; others relied on these often and without shame. But while neighbors could be judgmental, they were also a source of aid, with families helping one another when there was need, usually by passing a purse around into which each able family would place a penny or two. Working-class people also gave to institutional charities, usually to their churches' missionary funds.

What the working class called rough and respectable, the middle class perceived as the "deserving" and "undeserving" poor. This distinction—which, of course, working-class people could manipulate through their behavior in front of charitable middle-class visitors—was fundamental to all Victorian charity. Middle-class and upper-class Victorians were extremely charitable, but also immensely anxious that their support go only to those who deserved it and would use it wisely. They were always on the lookout for signs of feigned distress, of poverty that was the individual's own fault, and for sexual impropriety. They gave food, clothes, bibles, and even money frequently, but usually insisted on dispensing advice along with these. After 1834, when the new Poor Law created workhouses that the many working-class strove to avoid, philanthropy, the rough–respectable divide, and the deserving–undeserving divide, all became more important.

There were significant regional differences in working-class lives. Those in London almost certainly worked in the service sector. Those in the south and east of England and parts of Wales and Scotland were likely to be rural. They lived in cottages, worked on farms—often in family groups—knew their neighbors, and grew at least some of their own food. In the north, the Midlands, much of Scotland, and parts of Wales, people lived in either rural or urban areas, but they worked in the strong and growing fields of manufacturing and mining. This meant long hours away from home doing work that was segregated by sex, age, and skill level. In the north and Wales there was a lot of work available, so although the hours were long, the working-class was relatively well-off. In pockets all over Britain, service industries were also on the rise. For working-class women, domestic service in the town or city nearest to their birthplace was the most common job (before marriage). While some worked for wealthy families with many servants, the vast majority were "maids-of-all-work" and their employers' only servant.

Many working-class people were politically engaged. Working-class British politics ran the gamut from radicalism to conservatism. It also included apolitical-ism; then as now, many people did not engage in formal or national politics in any sustained way. For the Victorian working class, national engagement was often less important than local engagement; town, neighborhood, and the politics of every-day life, with its constant power struggles, remained primary to most working-class people. In the 1820s, many working-class people, women and radicals in particular, were (as we saw in Chapter 2) supporters of Queen Caroline. In the 1830s, many saw the 1832 Reform Act, and even more the 1834 new Poor Law, as betrayals of the working class. These helped to give rise to Chartism, in which working-class Britons demanded their constitutional rights to participate in government. Unionism was also important: although it was illegal to belong to a union until 1871, in 1850 a quarter of a million workers belonged to unions. As Chartism faded as a political force at mid-century, some working-class radicals worked with middle-class radicals; others aligned themselves with one of the two major political parties, Conservative and Liberal, even though working-class men could not vote before 1867. Unions gave workers a sense of solidarity and enabled them to bargain collectively with employers. However, unions tended to focus only on skilled male natives, shunning the unskilled, women, and immigrants, who they saw as threats to "real" workers.

Before 1870, working-class Victorians (especially women) had very little time or money to spend on leisure pursuits. There were local clubs—such as friendly societies or church- or chapel-based groups—that were sites of leisure. Drinking at the pub was a dominant form of working-class sociability. Over the first few decades of the period, pubs became the province of the working class, and alcohol consumption was high. In the 1820s and 1830s, men and women both went to the pub, but by the 1840s respectable women were rarely seen in pubs. They were more likely to snatch brief moments of sociability by chatting with neighbors between chores. There were also working-class people, especially women, who adopted and promoted temperance. Some were inspired by their Methodist faith; others sought an alternative to a life permeated by the poverty and violence that drink so often engendered. But temperance culture was only a small slice of working-class culture, and a beleaguered one at that; temperance men especially often found their masculinity questioned or challenged.

The Victorian middle class was distinguished not just by its income level but by its gender regime and its notions of domesticity. The Victorian middle-class espoused a doctrine of "separate spheres" that associated women with the private or domestic sphere, men with the public sphere. Also called "domestic ideology," it venerated the domestic sphere as a spiritual and familial refuge from the cruelties of the marketplace. This doctrine dictated that middle-class women were domestic creatures who were wholly focused on home, children, and religion and avoided politics and commerce. It was especially clearly articulated in middle-class evangelical Christianity, which was strongest from the late eighteenth-century until about 1840. Middle-class evangelical Christianity encouraged women to cultivate their godliness in domestic ways. Middle-class men were also domestic, though not exclusively: they left the home to work, but returned eagerly, valuing family and home above all else. If evangelical, they too had a domestically-oriented religious role, that of leading the household in prayer once or even twice each day. Of course, the notion of separate social roles for men and women was hardly unique to the Victorian middle class. However, separate spheres ideology dictated its particular division of abilities and responsibilities with special vigor, especially before 1860.

Middle-class men worked, but they did not do manual labor, eschewing dirty or physical work as working-class, and priding themselves on the fact that they dressed nicely for work. They were usually paid in salaries or fees rather than wages, in the fields of industry, civil service, local government, banking, insurance, commerce, and the professions (including teaching). As in the working class, there was a wide range of status and income. A family could be headed by a wealthy factory owner who was a major supporter of civic culture in his industrial town, or by a schoolteacher, or by a bank clerk; by the owner of a chain of department stores or his salesclerk. All of these men would be recognized as middle-class, but their status and wealth would be very different. In *The Diary of a Nobody*, Mr Pooter, a clerk, is middle-class, if just barely; so is his employer, Mr Perkupp, of whom he is in awe. Before 1870 middle-class women did not work for money (though they might give long hours to charitable work of all kinds). Middle-class work was higher status than working-class work not only because it was not manual but because it required education. At its upper ends, middle-class work used university education and expertise and carried with it significant social status: school head-masters, bankers, upper-level bureaucrats, doctors, barristers and solicitors were all highly educated and trained. The notion of professions, and professionalism in particular, was expanding in the Victorian period, and came to focus on train-ing, examinations, and professional associations. Professions became central to middle-class identity and helped to establish middle-class men's work as high status. Middle-class women were not supposed to earn money. This stricture was observed far more closely in the middle class than in the working class, but for those without family support or a husband, work could be a necessity. Before 1860, the only respectable paid options were governess or dressmaker, and both were poorly paid and low-status, leaving many middle-class women impoverished. For those who wanted work but did not need income, the only unpaid options were philanthropic endeavors.

Because standards for maintaining a non-working wife were so high in the Victorian middle class, men tended to remain single during their twenties; they married in their thirties or forties and they were more likely than previous genera-tions not to marry at all. Middle-class women married in their twenties; the result was an age disparity between husbands and wives that reinforced men's dominant position. Once a couple married, it could be very hard to keep up middle-class appearances: comfortably maintaining a family in a middle-class lifestyle required an income of at least £300 per annum, but a large number of middle-class fami-lies actually lived on only £100 to £300 per annum. As a result most families struggled to maintain the appearances that were necessary to their class status. Men worked to earn money, while women strove to make it go as far as possible. Small wonder, then, that *How I Managed My House on Two Hundred Pounds a Year* (1864) by Mrs Eliza Warren sold an astounding 36,000 copies in its first year of publication.

Schooling was more gendered in the middle class than in the working class. Before mid-century middle-class boys were educated by governesses and perhaps tutors, and then attended day or boarding schools. Some middle-class boys were educated into their station in life; others received an aspirational education that was intended to help vault them into the upper-class. They became more likely to attend university over the course of the period. Girls received far less education. They had only their governesses, and perhaps a year or two of finishing school, until girls' academic day or boarding schools were founded after mid-century. Ideally, a boy was educated into character and a profession; a girl, into an impeccable reputation and domesticity, with a particular emphasis on being a helpmeet to her husband and a loving inculcator of moral values to her children.

In the early Victorian era the middle class gained its first foothold into high politics. Even before 1832, some of Queen Caroline's most ardent supporters were middle-class women who defended her from charges of adultery. In 1832, the first Reform Act in centuries gave middle-class men the vote. This meant that middle-class men (and by extension, their families) were brought into the formal political nation. The class composition of Parliament and governing cabinets did not change, but candidates now had to appeal to middle-class voters. The success in 1846 of the Anti-Corn Law League in repealing the protective tariffs that favored land-based, aristocratic wealth was a triumph for one portion of the middle class—those who profited from manufacturing—and demonstrated not only the ability of the middle class to organize politically but the ascendancy of the middle-class doctrine of *laissez-faire* economics that would come to be almost a Victorian religion. Overall, however, the political ascendancy of the middle class should not be overstated: the middle class entered formal national politics, but certainly did not dominate it. The upper class maintained its wealth and political power through the nineteenth century, continuing to dominate the upper echelons of government, including cabinet positions.

Middle-class leisure was somewhat restricted before about 1860. As late as mid-century, many members of the respectable and often evangelical middle class saw leisure pursuits (even novel-reading) as moral temptations to be resisted. Many middle-class people believed that all time should be used wisely, for self-improvement, and this spawned a culture of rational and respectable recreation that smiled on family walks in the park and evening lectures, and frowned on theatre and in particular on the pub. Middle-class people used public culture, especially cultural events such as classical music concerts and civic ceremonies, to articulate themselves as a class, especially in industrial cities. Among men, social clubs, which were private and hence selective, and had the comforts but not the responsibilities of home, were popular.

The aristocracy was the smallest of the three classes. In theory, the upper class was open to newcomers, since anyone with money could buy land, and the Queen could create a peerage for anyone she chose. In practice, however, the vast majority of new Victorian peerages were given to members of the gentry, so there was little dramatic upward mobility. As with the other two classes, status and affluence varied. The wealthiest aristocratic families had annual incomes derived from land of £10,000 or more per annum, as did the 500 richest gentry families. Below this, the lesser gentry (and some aristocrats) had smaller incomes, though an income of at least £1,000 per annum was necessary to maintain even a small provincial estate. In light of the fact that most working-class families lived on a pound a week or less, and that most middle-class families lived on 100 to 200

• The higher in class you are, the less work you practically do.

136 *Class*

pounds per year, even this lower amount represented a lot of wealth, and the absence of a land tax for most of the century helped the upper class to remain wealthy. In addition, the upper class adapted to changes wrought by industrialization and commercialization, adding profits from mineral deposits, the development of urban land, and investments in banking and railways to their traditional streams of income.

Many members of the provincial gentry did business and socialized with the wealthiest upper middle-class people, who had incomes of several thousand pounds a year, sent their children to the same schools as the upper class, and partook of some of the same leisure pursuits (such as theatre and opera). Together, the lower gentry and the wealthy middle class formed what was sometimes called "polite" society, whose affluent members shared a culture defined by their lifestyle rather than their sources of wealth.

As upper-class people lived on their incomes from rents and investment profits, any notion of upper-class "work" must be a broad one. The upper class managed their estates, which included taking responsibility for the well-being of their tenants. They had to keep land and cottages in good repair to keep them profitable. They managed their agricultural holdings, their mines and factories, and their investments in the City. They also worked in politics, with men in appointed or elected positions and women behind the scenes. Many in the Victorian upper class had a strong sense of responsibility and of duty. They saw politics, whether national or local, as well as the military, as forms of service, and felt compelled to serve. Many were philanthropically active: Angela Burdett-Coutts gave away over £1 million during the course of her life, and Queen Victoria subscribed to many charities, as well as being a patroness of hospitals and other philanthropic endeavors all over Britain. On a smaller scale, aristocratic and gentry families took responsibility in a broad sense for "their" poor, staying aware of when families were experiencing an illness or were otherwise in need, helping daughters get first jobs in service, and the like.

For the upper class, marriage and domestic life were notable for the fact that husbands and wives existed in the domestic space together, and for the fact that home, work, and politics were so interwoven. The aristocratic home, with its dinners, parties, and meetings, was a site of political activity. Aristocratic men did not leave the home every morning for the workplace (although they attended Parliament when the family was in London), and men and women both worked at managing the household and the estate, directing servants, and hosting large parties of guests. As in the middle class, men tended to marry late, to younger women. Spouses usually had gender-specific responsibilities, but they often performed their intertwined tasks side by side. This is not to say that aristocratic marriages were all happy partnerships; extra-marital affairs were not uncommon, especially for aristocratic men, who often had illegitimate children whose parentage was widely-known though rarely acknowledged.

Upper-class children were almost always educated at home, by governesses and, for boys, by tutors. Boys were sent to boarding schools, which served critical social as well as educational functions; subjects such as Latin were more socially significant than useful, and throughout the century a high proportion of the nation's political, military, and imperial leaders had been schooled at Eton or Harrow (the Duke of Wellington is said, apocryphally, to have claimed that the battle of Waterloo had been "fought and won on the playing fields of Eton"). Similarly, most upper-class men went to Oxford or Cambridge University, not because they were especially academically inclined but because it was expected of their social class. Upper-class girls rarely went to academically-oriented schools or to university.

Aristocratic dominance of national politics makes it clear that while the 1832 Reform Act was important in welcoming middle-class men into the electorate, upper-class men remained the political leaders. Throughout the period, the upper class filled the House of Lords and dominated the House of Commons and Cabinet positions. Almost all the members of the upper house of Parliament, the House of Lords, held their seats by virtue of their aristocratic status. Members of the House of Commons, which was the center of government during the Victorian period, were elected, so theoretically middle-class men could serve. However, elections were expensive, and MPs were not paid until 1911, so only wealthy men who did not work could run or serve. Aristocratic men often entered the House of Commons at a very young age. Eldest sons often sat there until they inherited their titles and moved to the House of Lords, while younger sons could make it a career: the 1841 House had 199 members who were sons or grandsons of peers, and the 1865 House had 220 men who were either sons or grandsons of peers, or were baronets. Upper-class men formed the majority of the House of Commons through the 1860s. They also dominated the political life of rural areas; for example, by serving as Justices of the Peace.

Upper-class leisure was, like that of the other classes, class-specific. For the very wealthy, leisure pursuits were part dictated by which home the family found itself in. Countryside pursuits included fox hunting and shooting, while in London, opera, ballet, and theatre were popular. Wealthy families had a strong sense of responsibility regarding the tenants on their estates, and for much of the century participated in fairly dutiful sociability such as giving parties for tenants upon the heir's coming of age or for Christmas.

Free time depended on where you live

After 1870–1914: The rise of working-class comfort and lower middle-class aspirations

After 1870, the quality of life improved dramatically for most working-class people. Real wages rose, prices and work hours fell; some people even got holidays from work (what Americans call vacation time), albeit unpaid ones. All of this meant that for the first time, working-class Victorians had time and money to spend—on better food, on entertainment, on household furnishings, even on family vacations. (This was particularly true of the urban working class, far less true of the rural working class, which had contracted dramatically.)

Working-class people continued to work hard, and, compared with today, hours remained long. But one major change was the growth of low-level white-collar work—principally clerking and retail sales work—from about 1860. The growth of bureaucracy, the service industry, and consumption all came together to make many new, modestly paid but non-manual jobs available. The establishment of state-provided education from 1870 made more young working-class people eligible for these jobs. These two changes together opened up new opportunities for young working-class people to move, by virtue of their engagement in non-manual work, into the lower middle class (though wages were usually no higher than they would have been in manual jobs). Being lower middle-class was an opportunity, but also a constant challenge. It was difficult if not impossible to keep up even modest middle-class standards with a lower middle-class income. Yet most lower middle-class people were determined to maintain their status and to avoid manual labor. They strove to further educate themselves, for instance, by learning shorthand or typing to improve their earning power or by going to lectures on science or music. They made sacrifices to educate their children so as to prevent them from slipping down into the working class. They used their choice of neighborhood, their white-collar style of dress, and perhaps their choice of church, to proclaim their membership, however tenuous, in the middle class.

From about 1860 this new (albeit limited) class mobility was a striking new development. But the education necessary to move up into the lower middle class was beyond the reach of the poor, who remained numerous. At the end of the nineteenth century, famous social surveys of London in 1889 by Charles Booth and of York in 1899 by Seebohm Rowntree suggest that between one quarter and one third of the working class in those cities was living in terrible poverty, with families crowded into small living spaces and often going hungry. We can see, then, that the working class had significant socioeconomic and cultural strata within it. In some families, some members were highly paid skilled artisans, others had moved into the lower middle class by receiving a secondary school education and becoming clerks or elementary school teachers. In other families, members were employed sporadically if at all in unskilled fields, had little or no education, frequently pawned their belongings, relied on charity, or spent time in the workhouse.

The passage of the Education Act (also called Forster's Act) in 1870 had a profound influence on the working class. It set out a plan by which all children between the ages of five and ten had access to an "elementary" education. Local School Boards were created, which were charged with using tax money to create and maintain schools for working-class children. Once these state schools were introduced, working-class children became more and more likely to receive a formal, full-time, elementary education until the age of ten or 12. Whether or not to charge fees or to make state attendance compulsory was up to each local school board, which meant that in practice access to schooling remained uneven. In addition, most children missed several half days or days each week because they were helping at home. Secondary schooling remained less common, and university attendance unheard of outside of Scotland. There, before the late nineteenth century about 20% of university students were working-class boys who were mentored by their parochial schoolteachers and granted generous bursaries, or scholarships. Over the course of the nineteenth century, however, the Scottish educational system became more like the English in social exclusivity, and by the early twentieth century few working-class Scots attended university either. By the start of World War One, however, elementary education was both free and compulsory across England and Wales, and the British working class had achieved full literacy.

Keeping the family respectable remained a priority, at which women especially worked hard. They could be extremely resourceful; in Birmingham, working-class women would wait outside butchers' shops on Saturday evenings until they were about to close. With no refrigeration, the butchers could not keep what meat they had left, and began selling it at lower prices. One woman remembered that she would "wait and wait . . . [the butcher] used to start off with half a crown [two and half shillings, or 30 pence] parcels, you know. Come down to two bob [two shillings]."[6] Some married women found that constant cleaning, mending of clothes, careful shopping, budget-conscious cooking, and the like were so time-consuming that it made more financial sense to confine themselves to unpaid family labor. In this way they saved money on childcare and prepared foods and had evenings to devote to tasks other than cleaning. Indeed there was a saying among working-class women that "[b]etween the woman who works and the woman that doesn't there is only 6d. to choose at the year's end, and she that stays at home has it."[7]

Working-class political engagement continued to develop. After Chartism faded as a political force at mid-century, some working-class radicals worked with middle-class radicals; others aligned themselves with one of the three major political parties, and especially with Labour (after it was founded). Most importantly, working-class men were granted the vote: the Reform Act of 1867 gave the vote to almost 1 million, mostly urban, working-class men (and doubled the number of voters, to about 2 million). The Reform Act of 1884 enlarged the franchise to include rural working-class men as well, and increased the number of voters to over 5 million. (However one out of three men over 21—almost all of them working-class—still lacked the vote until 1918, either because they did not own property or because they were not heads of households.) Working-class men also continued to organize: in 1871 half a million workers belonged to unions. In the late nineteenth and early twentieth centuries, large strikes disrupted trade and life. New political attention to urban slums and the founding of the Labour party increased class-based politics and political conflict in the late nineteenth and early twentieth centuries.

While working-class Victorians worked very long hours, they did have some time for leisure, especially from mid-century as real wages rose and work hours declined. Music halls were popular in the working class, as was theatre. In addition, shorter work days and the railway came together to make holiday travel possible. In one of the most popular illustrated comics of the period, *Ally Sloper's Half-Holiday* (published 1884–1923), the main character has adventures in the countryside on his Saturday half-days off. Working-class seaside resorts such as

Blackpool were popular for longer holidays. Increased literacy and mass publication meant that light reading for pleasure became more widespread. Mass newspapers, including sporting papers, were widely read.

In the later nineteenth century, working-class leisure became more commercialized. Entrepreneurs expanded short and long-term holiday excursions into large businesses. Music halls were formed into syndicates with standardized programs. Professional football emerged to become a major preoccupation of working-class men and boys.[8] Throughout the period, and especially in response to commercialized leisure, middle-class philanthropists and socialist organizations offered alternatives in the form of uplifting "rational recreation" such as visits to the library or strolls (not football) in the park. However, the working class remained committed to pleasure in the form of luxury food, alcoholic drink, tobacco, and gambling, and music hall performances of which disapproving observers despaired. Some embraced rational and improving activities, but most did not.

The biggest changes for the middle class after 1870 were the rapid growth of the lower middle class and the expansion of educational and vocational options for women. Starting in the 1860s, and continuing until the start of World War One, Britain saw a huge increase in the proportion of the population that was lower middle class. This happened for a variety of reasons. First, economic shifts created more and more low-level clerical and service work, requiring more and more people to fill jobs as clerks, typists, and sales assistants. State-provided education meant that more people were achieving basic literacy and numeracy. The so-called redundancy crisis created calls to allow young middle-class women to do clerical, sales, nursing, or teaching work until—or if necessary, instead of—marriage. All of these factors meant that the growth of the middle class was in large part the expansion of the lower middle class.

Middle-class men's work after 1870 was largely consistent with their work before 1870: salaried work in industry, civil service, banking, insurance, railways, commerce (including finance and retail), and the professions (including teaching). To these were added a large number of low-level clerical and sales jobs. Even these lower-level middle-class jobs required literacy and numeracy, and were seen as distinct from working-class work, which made them compelling to many young people. Between 1870 and 1920 the number of men doing office work increased by a factor of five, and the number of women increased by a factor of five hundred, as both private and public concerns hired masses of clerks and assistants of all kinds.[9] In pursuit of respectability, young men often took jobs that paid less than the best working-class jobs, such as entry-level clerkships and retail sales positions. Male clerks might, however, assume that they would move up fairly swiftly, into higher-level and higher-paid jobs (in spite of the fact that the field was overcrowded).

Middle-class women, however, saw dramatic changes, as options opened up for them after 1860. In 1861 fewer than 200,000 women did white-collar work, but by the turn of the century that number had risen to almost 600,000. For those who did not need to earn money, but wanted meaningful employment, philanthropy was still a vibrant field; Poor Law Guardian and School Board official were also good options. For those for whom paid work was a necessity, options opened to include clerk, shop assistant, and hospital dispenser. Women also worked in civil service as government-appointed inspectors of workhouses, prisons, and work-places. More ambitious and more educated women could become teachers or nurses. While some of these posts, notably clerking, sounded the same as men's work, middle-class work was always carefully gender-segregated; women trained and then worked in women-only environments, such as girls' schools or women's floors of large bureaucratic concerns. Women were restricted to auxiliary tasks deemed female and unskilled, were paid less than men, and had little hope for career advancement. They also were required to remain unmarried and childless, as men were not. In contrast, women could rarely move much past the entry level. For upper working-class women, the chance to move into the lower middle class was an opportunity for social mobility; for middle-class women who needed (or wanted) to support themselves, these new clerical, sales, and teaching jobs meant they could maintain their class status and earn a sufficient (if modest) living. However, middle-class women still rarely worked once they married. (And middle-class marriage changed very little, though men's average age at marriage rose from 30 years at mid-century to 33.5 years in 1906.)

Education expanded for middle-class children, though not as dramatically as it had for working-class children. From the 1860s, girls in particular had many more options than they had had in the early Victorian period. Feminists founded secondary schools for girls that were academically-oriented, rather than simply teaching graceful comportment and finishing. They also worked to open university education to women, and the small number of women who attended university classes or even received degrees were, before 1914, almost exclusively from the middle class.

While the upper class continued to dominate politics at the highest levels, in the later Victorian period some middle-class men came to feature in formal national politics not just as voters but as politicians. In the 1850s about 20% of MPs had professional, commercial, or industrial occupations (and so were middle class). By 1874, 45% of MPs (314 members) were middle-class men, and by 1880 that number had increased to 65% (426 members).[10] Because MPs were unpaid, only the wealthiest middle-class men could afford to serve. And even when wealthy middle-class men served in the House of Commons, they did so relatively late in life, after retiring from actively running the family business, which meant that they had short parliamentary careers and rarely made it to the cabinet; partly as a result, upper-class men dominated every cabinet until 1905. In terms of party affiliation, the Liberal Party, which favored gradual progress and *laissez-faire* economics, was the party of the middle class. In 1886, one fifth of Liberal MPs were upper-class, while one half were professional middle-class men. But mid-century also saw the rise of middle-class urban and suburban Tories (called villa Tories after the suburban homes in which they lived). There were also a small number of middle-class radicals, many of whom were enamored of the heroes of Italian unification, and at the end of the century some middle-class socialists.

From the 1850s on, more middle-class people, even many evangelicals, grew more comfortable with leisure and the pursuit of it. Middlebrow literature flourished, expanding to meet the middle-class appetite for fiction and periodicals such as *Punch*. From mid-century, theatre was also popular; musical comedy, in particular the operettas of Gilbert & Sullivan, appealed to middle-class audiences. Clubs remained popular among married men; women used shopping in the new department stores as a form of leisure, a day out in the town center. Golf and lawn-tennis were popular, as were seaside resorts that catered to the middle class.

While it is tempting to look at the twentieth and twenty-first centuries and infer a decline in aristocratic power in the late nineteenth century, in fact the British aristocracy remained wealthy and powerful in the decades after 1870. For example, in 1873 more than 80% of the land in the United Kingdom was owned by less than 0.5% of the population, who were aristocrats. Many remained wealthy even as the economy changed dramatically.

The aristocracy remained politically powerful as well, and social events in upper-class homes were, in the words of novelist Anthony Trollope, "semi-social and semi-political."[11] Parties and other social activities were a key part of the milieu in which politicians operated. In the later nineteenth century, the Whig/Liberal Ladies Palmerston and Waldegrave, and the Tory Ladies Jersey and Londonderry, among others, were famous political and social hostesses. Emily Palmerston once received the news that votes were needed to support her husband's ministry with the spirited declaration "Stay! We will have a party!"[12] After the Home Rule split of 1886, the Unionist faction of the Liberal Party gathered at Devonshire House (home of the Dukes of Devonshire), while Tory ministers gathered at Lansdowne House (home of the Marquess of Lansdowne). Grosvenor House (home of the Duke of Westminster) was the base of operations for opponents of the 1909 "People's Budget" and House of Lords reform.[13]

But the wealth and political power of the aristocracy did decline in the later Victorian period. Economically, from the 1880s, agricultural and rent prices collapsed and taxes were imposed on inherited wealth. Many coped poorly: as rents fell, many upper-class families refused to adjust their lavish lifestyles and so ran up large debts. In addition many young aristocratic men in particular ran up huge gambling, drinking, and clothing debts, expecting that their fathers would settle these or (if they were younger sons) that they would marry into wealth that would solve their problems. Their leisure practices also became the less dutiful and more self-indulgent activities of "the pleasure class," in David Cannadine's words, rather than the "leisure class."[14] Such extravagance added to the middle class's conviction that their own creed of thrift, industriousness, and hard work was the answer to Britain's problems. By the turn of the twentieth century, wealthy middle-class businessmen outnumbered upper-class landowners, many of whom were awarded titles by the crown.

Politically, the aristocracy began to decline as well, though that decline should not be overstated. Aristocrats still dominated every cabinet before 1905. But aristocratic opposition to House of Lords reform failed, and the Parliament Act 1911 significantly reduced the power of the House of Lords (see Chapter 2).

And there would be more to come: in between 1958 and 2014 a series of Acts established life peerages, allowed women into the House of Lords, abolished almost all hereditary seats, and established that peers could be disqualified for non-attendance and removed for receiving prison sentences of a year or more. From the 1870s, upper-class men were no longer the majority in the House of Commons; however, they were still a disproportionate one third of the Commons well into the twentieth century.

Notes

1 P.G. Wodehouse, "The Indian Summer of an Uncle," in *Very Good, Jeeves* (New York: W.W. Norton Company, 2011), pp. 212, 231.
2 George Orwell, *The Road to Wigan Pier* (Orlando, FL: Houghton Mifflin Harcourt, 1958), Chapter 8, pp. 121–122.
3 Will Hutton, "Of Course Class Still Matters – It Influences Everything That We Do," *The Observer*, Sunday, January 10, 2010.
4 Patrick Joyce, *Visions of the People: Industrial England and the Question of Class 1848–1914* (Cambridge: Cambridge University Press, 1991).
5 David Cannadine, *The Decline and Fall of the British Aristocracy* (New Haven, CT: Yale University Press, 1990), p. xiv.
6 Andrew August, *The British Working Class 1832–1940* (Harlow: Longman, 2007), p. 102.
7 Quoted in Joanna Bourke, *Working-Class Cultures in Britain, 1890–1960: Gender, Class and Ethnicity* (Oxford: Routledge, 1993), pp. 173–174.
8 August, pp. 91, 139.
9 Gladys Carnaffan, "Commercial education and the Female Office Worker," in Gregory Anderson (ed.), *The White-Blouse Revolution: Female Office Workers since 1870* (Manchester: Manchester University Press, 1988), p. 82.
10 Michael S. Smith, "Parliamentary Reform and the Electorate," in Chris Williams (ed.), *A Companion to Nineteenth-Century Britain* (Malden, MA: Wiley-Blackwell, 2004), pp. 161, 169.
11 Anthony Trollope, *Phineas Finn* (Oxford: Oxford University Press, 1973), p. 355.
12 Quoted in K.D. Reynolds, "Politics Without Feminism: The Victorian Political Hostess," in Clarissa Campbell Orr (ed.), *Wollstonecraft's Daughters: Womanhood in England and France 1780–1920* (Manchester: Manchester University Press, 1996), p. 102.
13 Julia Bush, *Edwardian Ladies and Imperial Power* (London: Leicester University Press, 2000), p. 18.
14 Cannadine, p. 386.

Relevant fiction that students might enjoy

George and Weedon Grossmith, *The Diary of a Nobody* (1892)
Anthony Trollope's "Palliser Novels" (see Chapter 2)
George Eliot, *Middlemarch* (1871–1872)

Further reading

Martin Hewitt, "Class and the Classes," in Chris Williams (ed.), *A Companion to Nineteenth-Century Britain* (Oxford: Blackwell, 2004).

Part 2: Economy and Society, in Martin Hewitt (ed.), *The Victorian World* (Abingdon, UK: Routledge, 2012).

Rohan McWilliam, *Popular Politics in Nineteenth Century England* (Oxford: Routledge, 1998).

Online resources

University of Cambridge Electronic Resources for British economic and social history, 1700–1914: www.hist.cam.ac.uk/seeley-library/online-resources/e-resources/part-i-paper-10

Liza Picard on "The working classes and the poor" for the British Library: www.bl.uk/victorian-britain/articles/the-working-classes-and-the-poor

Liza Picard on "The Victorian middle classes " for the British Library: www.bl.uk/victorian-britain/articles/the-victorian-middle-classes

Charles Booth Online Archive: http://booth.lse.ac.uk/

Rowntree Society—Seebohm Rowntree and Poverty: www.rowntreesociety.org.uk/seebohm-rowntree-and-poverty/

7 "Oh, I do like to be beside the seaside"

Leisure

Introduction

Most Victorians worked long hours (in a variety of places—in a factory, at physically taxing domestic labor, on a city street or a farm, at a desk—and not always for pay). But even the reputedly conscientious and work-obsessed Victorians did not work all the time. In addition to working, eating, and sleeping, Victorians also played, watched, and gambled on sports (which the British call "sport," not "sports"), drank alcohol, went to concerts, music halls, and the theatre, read the latest best-seller, collected something or other, grabbed a few minutes for gossip with a neighbor, spent a day in the country, and took vacations (called "holidays" in Britain). Such pursuits—of pleasure, of relaxation, of connection with others, of fun—are collectively referred to as "leisure." And like politics, the economy, and class, leisure has a history and is part of history.

Many textbooks overlook leisure; indeed, until fairly recently the entire discipline of history ignored leisure. But while politics are certainly important, so are football games and vacations. (And of course the amount of money many of us spend on leisure pursuits—on purchasing tickets to games or concerts, on alcohol, on books and newspapers—reveals that the history of leisure is closely connected to both economic history and the history of consumption.) This chapter will explore some of the leisure pursuits that Victorians enjoyed, with sports, drinking, and vacations covered in this chapter, and arts, entertainment and print culture addressed in Chapter 11.

The scholarly history of leisure emerged in the 1960s. Early works had a defensive edge to them, with authors intent on convincing their readers that leisure was as important to study as the acts of monarchs or Parliament. A half century later, leisure history is a theoretically sophisticated field that is neither segregated nor antiquarian. Even now, most people cannot "conceive of alehouses and race horses on a par with the machinations of church and state,"[1] but many historians now understand that leisure is important. Historians of leisure seek not just to delineate the chronology and details of a particular leisure pursuit—which operas were most performed or how big a soccer field (which the British call a football pitch) was—but what a particular leisure pursuit meant to its practitioners. Leisure is seen to be a way in which people created, understood, expressed, and performed their identities. These could be identities based on class (a favorite), nationality, locality, gender, sexuality, or race. Often multiple identities could be in play; a man might use football to express both his masculinity and his national pride, or even to identify himself both nationally and locally, depending on the particular context.

What do historians of leisure study, or to put it another way, what exactly is leisure? It is surprisingly hard to say. Some people define it against work, so that leisure is the things people do in their discretionary time when they are not at work. This idea is peculiarly modern, since it rests on the notion that work takes place at discrete times and places—that people go to work, clock in, clock out, and leave work—which is a structure that emerged in the Victorian period. But it is also problematic, because work time and leisure time are not so easily separated. People could snatch moments of leisure at work, by leaving their posts for a cup of coffee or a smoke, or could combine work and leisure, by singing together while they worked. Conversely, not every moment away from paid work was spent on leisure—there were children to feed, houses to clean, church services to attend. Historian of leisure Peter Borsay argues that the intrinsic features of leisure are that it is symbolic (for instance, a horse might represent those who bet on it), that it is play, a self-contained activity without necessary or obvious significance (for instance, that a sports match is "just a game," and when the spectator leaves the stadium, s/he leaves that game behind), and that it is other, time or space apart from quotidian life (for instance, an evening at the music hall or a trip to the seaside).[2] Similarly, cultural historian Peter Bailey emphasizes that leisure above all involves playfulness, fantasy, and fun.[3] These positive definitions of leisure as freedom *to* (have fun), rather than negative definitions of leisure as freedom *from* (work), help us to see leisure as something that is part of human happiness and as something that can happen anytime and anywhere, but is also usually experienced at certain times (such as evenings and weekends) and certain places (such as the pub, the stadium, or the beach).

How did leisure change over the Victorian period? The orthodox narrative states that, until the early nineteenth century, Britain's leisure culture was vibrant, authentic, traditional, and popular. Most recreations were uncommercial, local, and shared by a wide range of people, with county gentry tolerating or even patronizing the leisure pursuits of the poor. Then in the early nineteenth century life changed. Industrialization, urbanization, and transportation separated work from home and work time from leisure time. Working-class Britons moved from the countryside to cities, where they worked long hours, had no discretionary income to spend on leisure, and saw their leisure pursuits attacked and dismantled by the increasingly powerful and humorless middle class. By the 1830s, all of this had created a "leisure vacuum," containing nothing but gin and despair. Then, from about 1870, the middle class relaxed, working-class wages rose and hours at work fell. Leisure was once again possible. People had time for an evening out, and money to spend on new consumables such as fish and chips and cigarettes. But traditional leisure had been replaced by modern leisure, which was nationally consistent, homogeneous, and commercial; where in the 1820s people gathered in pubs to sing together, in the 1870s they paid to watch performers in music-halls. This orthodox story stresses class conflict, disruption, and loss, in which inauthentic, top-down, purchased mass entertainment replaced authentic, truly popular traditional leisure.[4]

While there is some truth in this orthodox narrative, it tends to overemphasize modernity as a disruptive and negative force and to underemphasize the many continuities in nineteenth-century leisure. Recently, historians have begun to tell a more nuanced story. Leisure was never static and was always "modernizing." By the same token, "traditional" forms of leisure did not go extinct during the Victorian era; for example, blood sports such as cock-fighting persisted well into the late nineteenth century. And late nineteenth-century pubs, for all of their plate-glass and gas or electric lighting, share many features with late eighteenth-century beershops. Most leisure pursuits were class-specific; working-class leisure was a source of anxiety for middle-class reformers, and from mid-century the issue of leisure was often intertwined with fears about social disorder and hopes for civic standing. For all that, though, nineteenth-century leisure was not determined solely by class; gender, race, and respectability also mattered. Many forms of leisure became more commercial in the late nineteenth century, but commercialism had always been a factor; horseracing, prize-fighting, and cricket were all commercially-oriented by the late eighteenth century. In other words, historians no longer see the history of leisure as a history of discontinuities and attacks on working-class culture. Instead, they see a complex story characterized by gradual changes. (It is also a story with variations. For example, while all of Britain did not suffer through a "leisure vacuum" in the 1830s and 1840s, it is true that many industrial and iron towns in South Wales did; there were very few leisure options for their inhabitants in those decades.)

Leisure history first emerged as a subfield of social history, and since social history was at first mainly concerned with working-class men's lives and with class structure, leisure history was too. It focused on urban working-class men's leisure pursuits, especially those that were organized or institutionalized in some way. Most scholarly work analyzed leisure looking for signs of class conflict or class consciousness. Scholars looked mostly at football: watching it, gambling on it, playing it in local leagues and clubs. Also central were drinking in pubs and going to the music hall (see Chapter 11). These male working-class leisure pursuits—sometimes characterized as "clubbable and pubable"[5]—almost always featured an all-male atmosphere. Men played football together, without women present; men often drank together without women present. Even when men went to the music hall, which had a mixed-sex and mixed-class audience, they went as a group of men. In addition, many of these pursuits left records for historians to consult: professional football league's timetables, local football club minutes and finances, records of the number of pubs in a town. However, early leisure history tended to overlook women's leisure, middle-class leisure, and rural leisure. In recent years, leisure history has started to expand, but we still need to know more about the leisure practices of women, of the middle class, and of people living in rural areas. We need to know more about casual, intermittent, snatched forms of leisure, those that took place outside of organized clubs or groups. In many cases, these lacunae overlap: women were far less likely to take part in organized leisure. We need to use Borsay's notions of symbol, play, and other, to see more forms of leisure.

1820–1870: Drink, sport, gambling, and the seaside

Between 1820 and 1870, working-class people had neither the money nor the time to participate in much leisure. This was especially true during the "Hungry Forties," when many working-class families experienced real economic distress and had very little in the way of discretionary funds. They also had very little time: hours spent in mills, mines, and factories were extremely long, and domestic workers had almost no time away from work. During the mid-nineteenth century a series of parliamentary Acts limited work hours, giving people more time for leisure, and from about 1870 real wages rose, giving people more money for leisure. Before these changes, however, for most people leisure consisted of the occasional drink at the pub or the celebration of a birthday in the family of the local gentry. Some leisure was commercial—people went to pleasure gardens (see Chapter 1), and there were some fee-paying spectator sports. Much leisure was non-commercial; for example, the "free and easy" was a spontaneous event in which people played music, sang, and danced.

For upper-class people, who had discretionary incomes, things were different. Upper-class people had money to spend on trips to continental Europe ("the continent"), on second homes, on attending theatre and opera, on gambling at card games. They could afford to purchase pianos and to give their children sheet music and lessons. They could purchase the expensive accessories necessary for hunting, shooting, riding (horses), and other elite pursuits. Middle-class people also had some time and money for leisure, though they had different ideas about how to spend those. Middle-class men tended to have strong work ethics and to work long hours; middle-class women were usually busy with home and children. Mid-century middle-class evangelicals, and those who embraced strict notions of respectability, frowned on many public expressions of leisure, especially those that involved drink or rowdiness, that were favored by the working and upper classes. On the other hand, not all middle-class people embraced strict notions of respectability, and many middle-class men enjoyed a drink at the pub, a night at the music-hall, or gambling on horses or cards.

Drinking was a big part of Victorian leisure. Actually, alcohol is central to modern global history; it can be argued that alcohol, along with tobacco and caffeine, was a key force in the globalization of trade in the modern period.[6] Drink was central to Victorian society; one historian argues that before 1870, when working-class real wages became high enough for working-class people to spend money on leisure, that the main forms of entertainment for most people were drinking and gambling. However, while anti-drinking groups (such as the Temperance Society) and the business of drink (including the rise of pubs) are well-studied, drinking itself is not.

Victorians made and drank a variety of alcohol, typically either gin (or another spirit or "hard liquor") or beer. Alcohol was produced both commercially and in households, especially large or rural households. Wine was never very popular in Britain beyond the elite and, excepting a brief bump in the 1860s, wine consumption per capita was the same in 1915 as it had been in 1815. Gin was more popular and more controversial. Gin was very cheap; for the price of one good seat at the Adelphi Theatre in London, one could purchase five bottles of gin. Gin remained the most popular liquor by far until the late nineteenth century; rum was popular among sailors and in port towns, and as an ingredient in sweet punches. Brandy was popular among the wealthy. Whisky was the national drink of Scotland, and from the 1820s became more popular in the rest of Britain. Beer was a very widely-consumed beverage in England and Wales; it was less popular in Scotland and Ireland. Until the 1870s, the medical establishment held that moderate beer-drinking was healthy, and a relative lack of regulations made beer accessible. Beer was often cleaner than water (which was rarely drunk) and cheaper than tea (which was heavily taxed), though there were many complaints about diluted or adulterated beer. Beer was such an innocent and healthy drink that it was supplied in workhouses, even after the passage of the 1834 Poor Law, and was provided to patients in lunatic asylums as a reward and encouragement for good behavior and work until the 1880s. Women drank, as did children from a relatively young age. Many working-class men drank beer before and throughout the workday; male rural agricultural workers drank as much as two gallons of beer in the course of a workday.

Overall, the nineteenth century saw a trend towards more restriction and more regulation of drinking. Beer went from being a drink that all classes consumed with meals to being one that was drunk mostly recreationally and mostly by the working class. Licenses became more difficult to get, and pub opening hours were restricted. This was in part because of the temperance movement, which started in the late 1820s (the British Association for the Promotion of Temperance was founded in 1835) and saw first hard liquor and then all drink as a social evil. It was also because of middle-class and upper-class fears of a drunk and disorderly working class, in spite of the fact that heavy drinking was endemic to all the classes. But while temperance was a large and active movement, alcohol drinking remained widespread in Victorian Britain. Drinking alcohol was a cheap and easy way to relax, and drinking venues were seen as respites from the world of work and obligation. In addition, sites of alcohol were also sites of other social moments. Drinking spots were often the stopping places for coaches, and so were part of the pre-railway travel network; as railways developed, almost every station had a pub. Drinking venues were often connected to other forms of leisure such as gambling and playing pub games. Beershops and pubs were central for socializing; pubs were where darts was played and where bets were placed. They were sites of bear-baiting and other rough sports. They were also used as places to organize political movements, to seek work or workers, and to sing, dance, and hear music played.

The early Victorians drank alcohol in a variety of venues. Music halls, alehouses, beershops, and gin shops were where most non-elite people drank; taverns and inns were a bit swankier. Commercial spaces included "public houses" (the shortened term "pub" was not widely used until the 1850s), taverns, inns, gin shops, alehouses, and beershops (the latter a product of the 1830 Beer Act) all of which differed slightly. Gin shops began to feature ornate architecture and interior decorations, leading to the moniker "gin palaces." Music halls had their origins in drinking establishments and continued to offer alcohol even as the entertainment became the main feature. The sale of spirits was regulated, and gin could be sold only in public houses; this was a reaction to the eighteenth-century "gin craze" and an attempt to reduce the consumption of gin, which was seen as a social evil. In contrast, beer was available everywhere. The 1830 Beer Act, which remained in force until 1869, allowed any ratepayer (taxpayer) to buy a license to brew and sell beer for two guineas. The hope was that the Act would help wholesome beer replace dangerous gin. The Act was a tremendous success—in 1831 alone 32,000 licenses were granted—and gave rise to the beershop.[7] Over the course of the nineteenth century, rural domestic brewing faded out, and brewing became concentrated in the hands of fewer larger concerns that dominated the market and owned many of the pubs (and continue to do so).

Between 1820 and 1860, drinking spaces changed. Beershops became ubiquitous. Public houses adopted the decorating styles of gin palaces, including ornate fixtures and fittings, and became more uniform across Britain. At the same time, the middle and upper classes withdrew from the public house, preferring to drink in private homes and clubs. Working-class women withdrew too, as new codes of working-class respectability dictated that nice women did not drink in public. The term public house was shortened to "pub." By 1850, while people still drank in a wide variety of places, Britain was a land of pubs, which were relatively homogenous in appearance (red velvet upholstery and ornate gas fittings) and in clientele (working-class, mostly men). By 1869, there were almost 120,000 venues licensed to serve alcohol on the premises; most but not all were pubs. British alcohol consumption reached its peak in the 1870s.

For many working-class men, drinking was central to their identities. Drinking was associated with virility and masculinity (as was drunkenness and the physical violence that often accompanied it). Pubs were associated with community and conviviality; they could also be associated with occupational identity. In the middle and upper classes, the drinking of various beverages could be associated with relaxation at certain times of day, with entertaining, or with social status, as well as with drunkenness (which was certainly not confined to the working class).

Sports—playing, watching, betting—were a central form of leisure for boys and men. Play could be spontaneous, or organized and disciplined. In the Victorian period, team sports—rowing crew, playing cricket, playing rugby, and especially playing football—were taken up with enthusiasm in elite boys' public boarding schools. From the 1830s, athletics became central to these schools' curricula; team sports were thought to make boys virtuous, manly, and even Christian. Team sports solved problems: boys who were busy at or tired from playing sports would be less inclined to be rowdy in public or to masturbate in private. The cult of athleticism became a central feature of the boarding school experience.

Football games were popular across the socio-economic spectrum. Before the late nineteenth century the word "football" was a generic term for a range of games played all over Britain in various forms. There were many popular and folk football games, in which feet, hands, and balls connected in various configurations. The size of the field (the "pitch") varied, as did the number of players on the field. Over the early Victorian period, elite styles of play became more standardized. During the 1840s elite boys' boarding schools—first Rugby, then Eton—started to codify football. They created written rules that dictated the size and shape of the field, the number of players on a team, and the amount of physical violence that would be tolerated. At the same time, various forms of football were still played by working-class boys and men in most places through the 1830s, in some places through the 1850s, and in a few places (such as Lancashire and rural Oxfordshire) even later than that. There were also spectator versions of football and other games. From the late eighteenth century some localities saw the emergence of professional players and teams with established rules, published schedules, and fee-paying crowds. These declined somewhat around 1850, and would begin to flourish in earnest from the 1870s.[8]

By the 1860s, most players had adopted one of two now-distinct games: "association" football (soccer), in which the ball was kicked, and "rugby" football, in which players also held the ball in their hands (American football developed in the 1890s from rugby football). The 1863 founding of the Football Association (FA), an organization intended to oversee professional and amateur football, was a milestone in the history of football. However, the FA did not immediately change things for many players and spectators. We used to think that the FA created the distinction between "football" (soccer) and "rugby football" (rugby), but it may have just codified a division that was already clear. Furthermore many popular variants of football persisted among working-class players and spectators, probably into the 1890s, even as the newly-codified game gradually gained popularity. While the FA is now both enormous and central in British football, in 1863 it was founded to solve the very particular and very elite problem that upper-class boys who went to elite boarding schools became accustomed to their own school's rules, only to arrive at Oxbridge for their university educations and to discover that Eton's rules conflicted with Harrow's. The foundation of the FA and its adoption of the "Cambridge rules" (which were based in part on older, popular games) for all players, teams, schools, and universities, solved this problem. For these boys, the Football Association was important, as its new rules allowed them to come together at Oxford and Cambridge Universities and to play football together. But it had little impact beyond that for several years. Even when standardization of the rules created a single codified game—both for playing and for watching—this was as much the result of the larger forces of urbanization, industrialization, and modernization as it was of the foundation of the FA.[9]

Another important sport was boxing. Boxing was closely linked to the pub, to gambling, and to crime, and was a profit-oriented sport. Boxing was popular among many working-class male subcultures, in part because it was a sport in which men could demonstrate their toughness. English Jews including Dan Mendoza (1764–1836) were prominent in boxing; for poor Jewish immigrants, boxing was a way of integrating into the British working class. Early fights were actually bare-knuckle "prizefighting," but during the first few decades of the Victorian period prizefighting was replaced by the somewhat more refined gloved boxing. In 1867, the adoption of the "Queensbury Rules," which dictated the use of gloves and three-minute rounds and forbade all wrestling and hugging, rendered boxing somewhat less violent.[10]

Gambling was a widespread pastime and was linked to boxing and other sports. As with drinking, many opponents depicted it as a moral problem that afflicted only the working class, but gambling in a variety of forms was widespread among the elites too, as well as among certain portions of the middle class. Playing and betting on games of dice and cards were very popular. There was also a state lottery. Between 1820 and 1850, however, direct informal betting was replaced by gaming houses, run by bookmakers.

During the Victorian period, there were constant fears that gambling was immoral, and that it ruined working-class bettors who could not afford the habit. The state lottery was abolished in the 1820s because the government wished to distance itself from this immoral practice. Victorian gambling was character-ized by on the one hand, legislative and moral campaigns against "off-course" gambling (that is, gambling that took place off the racecourse itself, in shops and pubs) and on the other hand, a flourishing and increasingly commercialized culture of betting. While commentators insisted that gambling was ruining the working class, evidence suggests that while gambling was widespread among the working class, that most gambling was regular, moderate, and determined by income. Over the course of the Victorian period legislation was periodically passed that made forms of gambling more regulated or illegal. However, while the rising middle class disapproved of both working-class and upper-class gam-bling, legislation was aimed at the working class; upper-class betting was not inter-fered with. Following the abolition of the lottery in 1826, there was the 1853 Betting Houses Act, reinforced in 1874 and 1906. These made commercial betting shops and gaming houses illegal. (The betting shops that are a feature of every British high street (shopping street) today were made legal only in 1961.)

In spite of legislation, and of the middle-class perception that gambling was both immoral and ruinous, gambling was extremely popular throughout the Victorian period. (And there was a constant tension between "gambling," which was depicted as immoral, financial investment in the stock market, which was not, and speculation, which was the immoral version of stock investment. Commentators struggled to articulate why one was admirable and the others immoral, and to describe the dividing lines.) People bet on games of dice and cards (such as whist), on games played in pubs such as darts, on horse racing and dog racing, on "pedestrianism" or foot-racing, on prizefighting and boxing, and later on amateur and professional sports of all kinds. There were gaming houses and gambling clubs that served different slices of society; for the wealthy, the most popular club in London in the 1830s was Crockford's. Betting on horses was more respectable than betting on dog races. In Cumbria in the northwest, wrestling had a much higher status than prizefighting, even though both involved two men in physical combat and were accompanied by drinking and betting by spectators. Pubs were central to betting, as was print culture, with papers like *Bell's Life* and *Sporting Times* aimed at upper-class gamblers. Urban factory and mill workers patronized betting shops before 1853 (and placed the same bets, illegally, in the backs of pubs after 1853). Informal betting included games such as pitch and toss, card games, and betting on pigeon racing and on bowling. Street games such as pitch and toss were dominated by boys and young men (though girls did play), and were a way to demonstrate manliness and bravado (opponents stressed that the drive to prove oneself could easily lead to financial ruin that hurt women and children).[11]

Middle- and upper-class commentators of various stripes were constantly worried about working-class leisure. It was, they were convinced, not rational enough, not respectable enough, not moral enough. It cost too much, and involved too much drinking, violence, or sex. Of course, not all middle- and upper-class people worried about surveilling working-class leisure, and historian Mike Huggins has shown that some middle-class men participated in some very unrespectable forms of leisure.[12] But the elite impulse to discipline and control working-class leisure was a clear theme throughout the Victorian period.

This impulse was made apparent through a variety of organizations. Perhaps the biggest was the temperance movement. Temperance activists were intent on saving the working class from the evils that accompanied excessive alcohol use. They often painted vivid pictures of working-class wives and children left poor, hungry, and battered by drunken men. Temperance was a complex movement, and did not consist solely of middle-class scolds; indeed many working-class women were converts to temperance, precisely because alcohol abuse by men was a real problem in working-class life. But temperance certainly had its share of middle-class members who focused on the problem of drink in the working class. Another group was organized religion, and in particular the Methodist church (as well as other nonconformist churches), and later in the century the Salvation Army. There was also the rational recreation movement. Most middle-class people believed that all aspects of life, including leisure, had to be rational and uplifting, and many worked to impose this belief on others, through both public and private bodies that regulated the use of spaces (such as parks, which the middle class believed were for family walks, not rowdy football games) or provided "clean" alternatives to the pub (such as evening lectures). Some members of the working class embraced these alternatives; others resolutely rejected them.

Not all leisure involved clubs or records or took place during a discrete time. In particular, working-class and middle-class women with children tended to have no time away from their families. Men, though they worked very long hours, tended to see their time out of the workplace as their own, to spend on themselves and on leisure; no one saw women's time this way. Whether they worked outside the home or not, for wages or not, women did not have time off. While for men, informal leisure might mean a spontaneous drink at the pub, as opposed to a scheduled football match, for women, informal leisure was quite different and far more important.

Upper-class women might spend many hours in structured leisure pursuits—reading, playing piano, walking, or playing cards in the evening. Middle-class women might occasionally spend time reading, believing such an act to be self-improving. But for many women, and for working-class women in particular, daily life was a series of perpetual tasks; as they could never say that the working day—which might include paid work, housework, and childcare—was over, they felt guilty about having any free time or carving out any leisure time at all. Women had to find leisure in unexpected places—while out doing the shopping, or on their own front doorsteps. The only organized leisure that working-class women were likely to pursue was a local women's group, usually organized by their church or chapel. Groups such as the parish's Young Wives' Club or Mother's Circle would often have some stated religious or charitable function, so that women could permit themselves to attend, but would be largely social in nature. Middle-class and upper-class women also participated in religiously- or charitably-affiliated groups, the structure of which allowed them to justify the time away from home and family.

One of the principal forms of women's leisure was gossip. Historian Melanie Tebbutt defines gossip as information exchanged about the activities and behavior of mutual acquaintances. She points out that the term "gossip" is gendered as female; men are never described as "gossiping" even when they are engaged in the identical behavior. Working-class women would allow themselves to take a few moments for gossip—for example, in a quick gossip with the neighbors in the morning, after they had gotten everyone out of the house to work (or school) and before they began their own chores. Such gossip usually happened while standing at the front door, as sitting down in a friend's kitchen or taking a walk with a neighbor was too close to dedicated leisure time. (As a result there was a Dorset proverb that "standing gossips stay the longest.") These doorstep moments, snatched from a relentless workload, may not have been much in the way of leisure, but they were all that many working-class women got, and they were important. Moments of conversation in shops, with neighbors or the proprietor, or with door-to-door peddlers, were other opportunities for such interstitial leisure.[13]

The most geographically apparent form of leisure is a vacation, which the British call a "holiday." People going on holiday talk about "getting away," and some scholars argue that when people holiday, they literally leave their regular working lives in pursuit of leisure, and enter into a space where they can do things they would not be able to do at home; that holidays are an escape from responsibility and even from social norms. But as every parent who has exhausted themselves amusing a toddler away from home knows, traveling away from home does not always guarantee a change of lifestyle. In this vein, other scholars argue that holidays do not guarantee departures from routines or norms, that holidays for some are often work for others, and that social and political conflicts usually come along to holiday spots.

Before the mid-nineteenth century, holidays were mainly the prerogative of the well-off. Working-class and lower middle-class people had neither the time away from work nor the disposable income to travel away from home. The most common forms of holidays in the early nineteenth century were Grand Tours of "the continent" (continental or mainland Europe) and trips to British seaside resorts near London. The Grand Tour was an aristocratic tradition in which young men, after finishing their university education, would spend about two years travelling in Europe. They were often accompanied by a tutor or older family friend and, of course, by a retinue of servants. These trips emphasized visits to sites of classical antiquity, and as such were a way of rounding out a traditional university education, which stressed the classics. In addition, the well-off visited seaside resorts for sea-bathing, which was fashionable. These trips were for health: sunshine, seaside air, and sea water were all thought to be beneficial, particularly to invalids. Municipal authorities were well aware of this; for example, an 1840 advertisement urging people to holiday at the seaside town of Weston-super-Mare boasted of how easily visitors could "be accommodated with landaus, pony and other cars . . . as well as sedans and wheel chairs for invalids."[14] During the early nineteenth century these seaside resorts were extremely popular and grew as rapidly as the industrializing urban areas; tellingly, between 1821 and 1831 the fastest-growing towns in Britain were the industrial town of Bradford and the seaside resort of Brighton. Seaside resorts were so popular that inland spas, a staple of the eighteenth-century aristocratic circuit, began to decline. Even so, visitors to seaside resorts comprised only a small percentage of the total population before the late nineteenth century.

Between 1820 and 1860, before railway networks made the seaside easily accessible, upper-class invalids were joined at the seaside by middle-class people, mainly well-off men seeking to rid themselves of the over-civilization and sluggishness of city life. Middle-class holidays were made easier by better transportation, by stage coach in the 1820s, railway from the 1830s. Railways stimulated the growth of seaside resorts, first by making the journey to the coast cheaper, faster, and more comfortable for those already taking it, and later by making the seaside accessible for working-class holidaymakers, and this popularity grew steadily. This is not to underplay the abilities of stagecoaches and steamers, which in 1837 brought fully 37,000 people to the seaside town of Brighton. But by 1850, the railway made it possible for 73,000 people to come to Brighton every week—most of them middle-class or lower middle-class "daytrippers." Llandudno, in north Wales, had been a fishing and farming village, but from 1848 was accessible by railway and from 1849 was developed as a seaside resort for holidaymakers from Liverpool, Manchester, and the Midlands (a pier was added in 1878). In the 1840s and 1850s, as the railway network grew and railway companies began offering cheap "excursion" fares, some working-class people began going on organized holidays, organized by working-class Friendly Societies or by local employers. The railway was central to the rise of holidays, and in some cases seems to have been definitive; the tourist industry in Cornwall, in the far southwest of Britain, developed only after the area became accessible by railway in 1859. However, many accounts place too much stress on railway routes and fares, holding them largely or entirely responsible for the growth of holidays. Rising wages were also important as was the desire and ability of working-class people to plan and save for holidays, to demand (unpaid) leave from work, and to visit the seaside.

In the 1850s, the growth of cheap travel, commercial travel agents, working-class savings clubs, and days off of work all contributed to the growth of one-day and multi-day working-class holidays. The rise of modest, inexpensive, and family-friendly lodgings helped as well. There were also working-class people taking Saturday-to-Monday excursions, mostly from the cotton district. One of the biggest turning points here was the Great Exhibition of 1851, for which working-class people travelled across Britain to London in huge numbers. While we used to think that working-class attendance was a result of middle-class efforts to educate working-class people into respectable and educational forms of leisure, historian Susan Barton argues that the initiative for these day-trips—and for the holiday savings clubs that made them possible—in fact came from working-class people themselves.[15] Then following the Great Exhibition, workers, especially well-organized workers from northwest England, started pursuing seaside holidays. Some resort advertisements started aiming both at middle-class visitors, emphasizing health benefits and natural splendors, and at working-class families, emphasizing beaches, fun, and commercial entertainment, rather than trying to attract upper-class people in poor health. As the classes found themselves in proximity, tensions sometimes arose, especially around swimming (called bathing); upper-class and middle-class people bathed in machines, large contraptions that hid them from view, while working-class men often swam nude and in public.

In the mid-Victorian period, as middle-class families began to visit—*Punch* called Brighton during the high season "London *plus* prawns for breakfast and the sea air"[16]—seaside resorts developed their own distinctive modes of entertainment, which became central to leisure culture and to people's memories of childhood holidays. Itinerant entertainers traveled on a resort-town circuit. They offered minstrel shows and Punch and Judy shows. There were also vendors selling snacks and trinkets, and the rituals of donkey rides on the beach and promenades on the pier.

1870–1914: Sport on the rise, drink in decline, and the rise of working-class leisure

The late Victorian period saw a tremendous boom in sports. Playing and watching sports became an enormous and central part of British culture in ways that are still true today (the same can be said of American culture). This boom did not much affect upper-class people, who continued in their traditional sporting endeavors—riding and hunting in the country, spending time at the course betting on horse races, as well as football and other team sports (mostly determined by where they had gone to public school). The main participants in the sports boom were working- and middle-class men, for whom the relationship to the teams they played on and supported became central to their identities and for whom sport factored into most of their leisure time. In the late Victorian period, organized sports were one of the most important factors in many people's civic and local pride, and by 1900 almost every town had its own professional football team. Some middle-class women were also able to make inroads into sports culture; working-class women, however, lacked the time, the money, and organizational opportunities to participate in sports.

From the 1880s, spectator sports—football, rugby, and in the north of England, cricket—were large, commercial, and intertwined with the drinking industries (pubs and breweries). As professional sports expanded, they became central to much male culture. In addition, a gap developed between professional and amateur athletes, or more precisely between those who revered amateurism in sport and those who did not. For those who did—mostly upper-class and upper middle-class commentators—amateurism was superior. However this position excluded most working-class athletes, who could not afford to pursue a sport full-time without pay. The entire sport of rugby split over this issue. Professionalism grew fastest in football and in Lancashire, and was made legal by the FA in 1885.

The Cambridge rules of football had been established in 1863. From the 1870s, these rules became more important as football became more important. (In Ireland, where rugby and Gaelic football were popular, football spread more slowly.) Towns, cities, suburbs, Anglican churches, nonconformist chapels, and workplaces all sponsored football teams. City clubs developed rivalries with clubs from nearby towns. Associations were formed, all with their own cup competitions (the FA Challenge Cup was founded in 1871). By the early 1870s, pitches were fenced off and spectators had to pay to watch games; even so, the size of the crowds grew throughout the 1870s. Local men watched and supported as a matter of identity and pride. So not only did football become more widely played, it became part of men's individual, civic, and regional identities. Brad Beaven's work on Coventry shows that outside of wars, football was the main way that working-class men and boys expressed civic pride or national patriotism.[17]

Between 1885 and 1914 Britain saw the very rapid growth of football as an aspect of culture. The number of people—mostly men—who played football (whether casually, as organized amateurs, or as professionals), watched football, and wrote newspaper articles about football grew dramatically. The number of football clubs and competitions grew, too, as did their geographical reach. While there were regional differences, football (like many other aspects of commercial leisure) became a more uniform experience across Britain, as footballers at all levels adopted the Cambridge rules and played the same game. Most importantly, between 1885 and 1914 football became a central part of British leisure and British culture for men of all classes. As historian of football Dave Russell writes, "In 1875 [football] was still largely a game for a leisured elite; by 1914, it lay at the heart of much English male culture."[18] No other leisure pursuit drew such a large number of people together so regularly. And from the 1880s football became a pervasive part of British culture—in public parks, where games were played, in the press, and later on in radio and cinema newsreels.

Indeed, by 1900, the majority of the boys and men who played and watched football were working class, with the first professional players largely from the upper or skilled working class, many from Scotland or Wales but playing for English teams. The playing and watching of football developed its own culture, of club colors, scarves, drinking and drinking songs, rowdy crowds, noise, and excitement—that emerged from and contributed to British working-class culture more generally. When middle-class and upper-class men went to watched games, they often sat separately from the rest of the crowd. Older histories of football often portray football as an arena of social control, in which middle- and upper-class managers and owners controlled the working class, but more recent accounts tend to point out that working-class spectators and players created their own football culture on their own terms.

The growth of professional football and of league competitions was fastest in northern industrial Lancashire, and slowest in the south of England. It was hampered by the commitment of some middle-class and upper-class Britons to the notion of the superiority of the unpaid amateur, a notion that was strong in politics as well, where MPs were not paid a salary until 1911. The Football League, which organized league competition between professional football clubs in the north and the Midlands, was founded in 1888, and its competitions remained the highest in England and Wales until the formation of the Premier League in 1992. In 1894, a rival Southern League was founded, made up of teams in the south who were finally ready to embrace professionalism in football. The two leagues together made up elite professional football in England and Wales. In Scotland, the national league, called the Scottish Football Association or Scottish FA, was founded in 1873 and preceded the embrace of professionalization in the late 1880s. (Many Scots claimed that football was more a Scottish game than an English one.) There was never a British league. In Scotland and Ireland, rival leagues reinforced existing ethnic and religious sectarian divides. The league system was key in the growth of football's popularity; by the start of the twentieth century Britain had dozens of professional, semi-professional and amateur leagues that helped the game to spread. Amateur play flourished in local clubs, school games—in 1900 state schools adopted football as a wholesome form of exercise—casual street games (for working-class boys and men), and the Amateur Football Association, founded in 1907 to protect and promote amateur play. Much recreational and amateur football is unrecorded and hard to measure, and many clubs existed only for a few years or even a few games, so we cannot measure it precisely, but we know there was a lot of it. Playing and supporting both amateur and professional football became a central way for working-class boys and men to express their identities, and often to express multiple and even conflicting identities; for example, a man might support his team against its local rival, but support the rival team at the regional or national level. Civic celebrations for teams coming home from a win became a form of ritualized street theatre alongside comparable political displays.

As association football was established in the 1860s and 1870s, rugby became distinct from football. In 1871, the 20 local clubs in England came together and formed the Rugby Football Union. Rugby became a popular spectator sport, and a way of expressing Lancashire–Yorkshire rivalries; the Yorkshire cup in particular was a hugely popular spectator game. In the 1870s and 1880s styles of play began to diverge into a more southern and upper or middle-class style and northern and more working-class style. In 1895, rugby split into two separate styles of play: rugby union, which was played by upper- and middle-class boys (and in the later twentieth century, girls), and stressed amateurism, and rugby league, which was played by working-class boys and men and which permitted teams to compensate players (making it easier for working-class men to participate). In northern England and south Wales especially, rugby was popular both to play and to watch.

In the later Victorian period amateur boxing went from being a middle-class sport to a working-class sport. Boxing as a spectator sport moved from pubs to separate halls, where young working-class men paid entrance fees. While upper- and middle-class men continued to box at exclusive clubs, there were now also many opportunities for working-class boys and men to box: settlement houses, churches, and working men's clubs all offered boxing instruction and competition. Professional boxing was widely covered in newspapers, and both professional and amateur champions became heroes to working-class boys. Amateur boxing championships were held annually in England from 1881. There was also an Irish club, in Dublin, a Welsh club—Cardiff lightweight Harry Marks won the English championship in 1898—and in 1910 Scotland, Wales, and Ireland all started their own championships.

British alcohol consumption reached its peak in the mid-1870s, with beer consumption peaking in 1874 at 42 gallons per capita annually. Similarly, the number of "on-licenses"—venues that were licensed to serve alcohol on the premises— reached its high of 118,499 in 1869. Thereafter, the amount of alcohol consumed and the number of pubs in Britain both declined. By 1901 the number of "on-licenses" in England and Wales had dropped to only 103,000. Beer consumption also fell quickly; in 1886 it was down 20% from its 1874 high. However, we also see after 1870 the beginnings of mass marketing and branding of alcoholic beverages. Some advertised taste, quality, or strength; others claimed medicinal qualities for their brands, such as Barrett's Stout for Invalids.

Culturally, from 1870 the pub became less central to the lives of working-class people (particularly working-class men) than it had been. Of course pubs remained an important part of working-class culture. One Saturday night in March 1879, Ellen Grace and a friend went to a pub in Phoenix Street in their London neighborhood of Somers Town for a night out; both met the men they were to marry.[19] Some working-class men pursued respectability by joining private working-class men's clubs and drinking there. And as real wages rose and more leisure options developed, pubs competed (for both time and money) with many other options. Many working-class families chose to spend their money on more and better food or on tobacco. There were other leisure activities outside of the home such as sports, day trips, and holidays, as well as respectable in-home options such as hobbies and music; as pianos became more affordable, inviting the neighbors to gather round yours and sing became a form of both status and leisure.

When World War One began, the government began to discourage drinking, in part so that grain could be used to make bread rather than drink, in part because it feared that the now female-dominated domestic workforce would be a drunken one. It published propaganda that portrayed drinking as unpatriotic. New Acts were passed that reduced the strength of beer, and the well-entrenched British tradition of buying rounds, in which each member of a group would take a turn buying drinks for the whole group, was made illegal (though today rounds are once again common practice in Britain, and failing to buy a round is a social gaffe).

From 1870 gambling grew, in spite of the efforts of anti-gambling groups. Working-class people asserted the right of the individual as a "free-born English punter";[20] the idea was that it was the right of an independent and manly citizen to bet his own money, based on his own decisions, if he so chose. Gambling also shifted from a mostly informal culture into a commercialized mass market based on bookmakers and the sporting press. Gambling on horse races became more controlled during the 1880s as most racecourses were enclosed (so that all (legal) gamblers had to pay an entrance fee). Other new pastimes were also linked to gambling: pigeon-shooting, pigeon-racing (a competitive hobby among working-class men), and bowling. Betting remained an important part of working-class culture, and a way for people to demonstrate variously their intellects, expertise, or belief in luck. The "punter" or bettor was consistently seen as irrational and irresponsible by anti-gambling critics, but in fact working-class bettors had complex systems of beliefs and strategies, and usually gambled with restraint.

Middle- and working-class reformers continued to worry about working-class leisure. Leaders in the temperance movements, political movements, and the Salvation Army were all anxious that working-class people spend their leisure time doing respectable or self-improving things. They worried that working-class people spent too much time drinking, and that they used leisure spaces incorrectly. Yet at the same time, many middle-class-sponsored forms of leisure excluded working-class people—for example, museums were open only during working-class working hours. In spite of this, working-class leisure was very varied. Drinking was certainly popular, as were spending time in the pub more generally and gambling. But some working-class people also visited museums when they could and engaged in leisure pursuits that did not involve drinking or required intellectual effort, such as animal-breeding.

From the 1870s, the combination of rising real wages, increased time off from work, and railway accessibility made holidays widespread. The 1871 passage of the first Bank Holidays Bill (largely in response to demands for unpaid leave) created the first four "bank holidays" (what Americans call public or federal holidays), on which banks closed and most workers got time off from work. Holidays at seaside towns became a central feature of British culture. These were a new kind of seaside holiday—working-class and boisterous in nature, nothing like middle-class explorations of nature or upper-class commitments to health. In 1911, there were 145 resort towns in England and Wales. The largest resorts were Blackpool in the north (which attracted the northern working class), Bournemouth on the south coast (which tried to attract both working-class people and more affluent invalids), and Aberystwyth (in Wales). Many working-class people's clearest childhood memories were of family holidays to the seaside. Working-class Britons enjoyed their seaside holidays in very culturally specific ways. They went to areas that were accessible by an inexpensive railway journey and that featured affordable lodgings (usually at some distance from the beach itself). Sometimes they purchased packaged tours from Thomas Cook or smaller local providers; railway companies also offered deals for budget-conscious holidaymakers. Families crowded into lodgings that were small (though no smaller than their homes), but there was entertainment everywhere—and by the late nineteenth-century, resorts were so popular that entertainers could live in them and work year-round. Working-class families enjoyed commercial entertainment such as donkey rides on the beach, arcades, sideshows (freak shows were especially popular), Punch and Judy puppet shows, mixed and boisterous swimming, and drinking. (The tradition of working-class men swimming nude in the ocean, though widely castigated by polite observers, survived until the 1890s).[21]

The growth of working-class seaside holidays did not mean that the upper and middle classes adopted a working-class style of vacationing (or that the working class adopted an upper- or middle-class style of vacationing). While some

PUNCH AND JUDY AT THE SEASIDE

Figure 7.1 "Punch and Judy on the beach at Llandudno" by R. Barnes, an illustration in the periodical *The Graphic* in 1887. Britons on holiday would head for seaside towns such as Llandudno in north Wales, where they would gather on the beach to socialize and enjoy entertainments such as the Punch & Judy puppet show in the upper left; in the background are bathing machines (left) and a large hotel (right).

Private Collection/© Look and Learn/Illustrated Papers Collection/Bridgeman Images.

wealthier people began to seek out different kinds of holidays—to continental Europe, or to more remote coastal areas in western Wales—many continued to visit English seaside resorts. Resorts tended to cater to one part of the social spectrum or to have distinct areas that were priced to attract different social strata. Even when they vacationed in the same town, people of different classes probably experienced proximity but not real interaction. In many towns, there were constant battles over atmosphere and tone, and towns struggled to appeal both to middle-class people looking for a place with a quiet remote nature, and working-class people looking for a louder and more commercial sort of fun.

The later nineteenth century witnessed more and more social conflict at seaside resorts, largely between those who unashamedly pursued pleasure for its own sake and those who maintained that leisure had to have some uplifting, moralizing, or educational aspect. Especially at the edge of the water, there were conflicts between rowdy groups and more sedate groups of families and older people, between unruly daytrippers and others. We tend to assume that this conflict broke along class lines, with the respectable middle class in tension with the boisterous working class, but while there were class overtones to these tensions, class was not the dividing line; there was always some middle-class support for popular entertainments, and there were also working-class people (often members of the temperance movement and/or of Methodist or other nonconformist faiths) who were committed to sober and self-improving modes of leisure. By the turn of the twentieth century, this tension seems to have resolved, and conflicts declined.

In the twentieth century, and especially after World War Two, British vacationing habits changed again. Vacations at seaside resorts declined. Trips to less commercial, less developed, more natural parts of Britain—to undeveloped parts of the coastline, to more remote areas such as Cornwall in the southwest or rural Scotland in the north, and to cities of historical significance—became more popular. So, too, did trips to a new type of cheap beach resort: those that were abroad, and required a cheap flight rather than a cheap railway journey. Today in Britain, once-popular seaside resort towns such as Blackpool and Scarborough have a somewhat deserted, slightly down-at-heels feel, and busses are plastered with advertisements to cheap foreign beach destinations such as Tenerife (a Spanish island near Morocco).

Notes

1 Peter Borsay, *A History of Leisure: The British Experience since 1500* (London: Palgrave Macmillan, 2006), p. xiii.
2 Borsay, p. 6.
3 Peter Bailey, "The Politics and Poetics of Modern British Leisure," *Rethinking History* 3.2 (July 1999): 131–175, p. 157.
4 Andy Croll, "Popular Leisure and Sport," in Chris Williams (ed.), *A Companion to Nineteenth-Century Britain* (Malden, MA: Blackwell, 2004): 396–411, p. 396.
5 Borsay, p. 113.
6 D.C. Courtwright, *Forces of Habit: Drugs and the Making of the Modern World* (Cambridge, MA: Harvard University Press, 2002).
7 Paul Jennings, *The Local: A History of the English Pub* (Stroud: Tempus, 2007), pp. 57–62.

8 Matthew Taylor, *The Association Game: A History of British Football* (Harlow: Pearson Education, 2008), pp. 19–61.

9 Tony Collins, "Work, Rest and Play: Recent Trends in the History of Sport and Leisure," *Journal of Contemporary History*, 42.2 (April, 2007), pp. 397–410.

10 Michael Berkowitz, "Jewish Fighters in Britain in Historical Context: Repugnance, Requiem, Reconsideration," *Sport in History* 31.4 (December 2011): 423–443.

11 Mark Clapson, *A Bit of a Flutter: Popular Gambling and English Society, 1823–1961* (Manchester: Manchester University Press, 1992).

12 Mike Huggins, "More Sinful Pleasures? Leisure, Respectability and the Male Middle Classes in Victorian England," *Journal of Social History* 23.3 (2000): 585–600.

13 Melanie Tebbutt, *Women's Talk: A Social History of Gossip* (Aldershot: Scolar Press, 1995).

14 John Hassan, *The Seaside, Health and the Environment in England and Wales since 1800* (Aldershot: Ashgate, 2003), p. 33.

15 Susan Barton, *Working-Class Organisations and Popular Tourism, 1840–1970* (Manchester: Manchester University Press, 2005).

16 "Brighton," in *Punch*, Volumes 8–9 (1845): 158.

17 Brad Beaven, *Leisure, Citizenship and Working-Class Men in Britain, 1850–1945* (Manchester: Manchester University Press, 2005).

18 Dave Russell, *Football and the English: A Social History of Association Football, 1863–1995* (Preston: Carnegie, 1997), p. 30.

19 Andrew August, *Poor Women's Lives Gender, Work, and Poverty in Late-Victorian London* (Madison, NJ: Fairleigh Dickinson University Press), p. 127.

20 Clapson, p. 3.

21 Hassan, pp. 39, 59; John Walton, *The English Seaside Resort; A Social History 1750–1914* (Leicester: University of Leicester Press, 1983), pp. 157, 190.

Further reading

Susan Barton, *Working-Class Organisations and Popular Tourism, 1840–1970* (Manchester: Manchester University Press, 2005).

Peter Bailey, "The Politics and Poetics of Modern British Leisure," *Rethinking History* 3.2 (July 1999): 131–175.

Peter Borsay, *A History of Leisure: The British Experience since 1500* (London: Palgrave Macmillan, 2006).

Mark Clapson, *A Bit of a Flutter: Popular Gambling and English Society, 1823–1961* (Manchester: Manchester University Press, 1992).

Tony Collins, "Work, Rest and Play: Recent Trends in the History of Sport and Leisure," *Journal of Contemporary History* 42.2 (April, 2007): 397–410.

Andy Croll, "Popular Leisure and Sport," in Chris Williams (ed.), *A Companion to Nineteenth-Century Britain* (Oxford: Blackwell, 2004), pp. 396–411.

Mike Cronin, "Playing Games? The Serious Business of Sports History," *Journal of Contemporary History* 38.3, Sport and Politics (July, 2003): 495–503.

Judith Flanders, *Consuming Passions: Leisure and Pleasure in Victorian Britain* (New York: HarperPress, 2006).

David Hassan and Philip O'Kane, "Ireland" in S.W. Pope and John Nauright (eds), *Routledge Companion to Sports History* (Abingdon: Routledge, 2010), pp. 461–471.

Mike Huggins and J.A. Mangan (eds), *Disreputable Pleasures: Less Virtuous Victorians at Play* (London: Frank Cass, 2004).

Martin Johnes, "Great Britain" in S.W. Pope and John Nauright (eds), *Routledge Companion to Sports History* (Abingdon: Routledge, 2010), pp. 444–460.

Catriona M. Parratt, *"More Than Mere Amusement": Working-Class Women's Leisure in England, 1750–1914* (Evanston, IL: Northwestern University Press, 2001).

Matthew Taylor, *The Association Game: A History of British Football* (Harlow: Pearson Education, 2008).

John K. Walton, "The Origins of Working-Class Spectator Sport: Lancashire, England, 1870–1914," *Historia y Comunicación Social* 17 (2012): 125–140.

Online resources

See Introduction

8 "A common cause with all the females in this kingdom"

Gender

Introduction

As we saw in Chapter 2, the Queen Caroline Affair was a major event in British politics. Among all the remarkable things that happened in the Queen Caroline Affair, one was the outpouring of support she received from women all over Britain. An address from the "Females of Bristol" was signed by 11,047 women; another, from "the married ladies" of London was signed by 17,652 women. The "Ladies of Edinburgh" declared in their address that "your Majesty's case becomes a common cause with all the females in this kingdom." Why did thousands of women of all classes see themselves in common cause with a German princess who was fabulously wealthy and who had not even lived in Britain since 1814? The answer is lies in the power of gender in Victorian Britain.

"Gender" is best understood as a description not of reproductive and sexual organs but of social roles in relation to one another. Historians of gender explore the roles—in the workplace, the family, politics and law—that societies assigned to men and women. They also seek to uncover the assumptions past societies made about men's and women's respective abilities: what each were best fitted for, what each were incapable of. When we study gender we study not only particular men and women (or groups of men and women) but the categories of "male" and "female," seeking to distinguish between these and biology. The work that gender did to organize Victorian society was profound, complex, and variegated, and gender roles differed depending on a variety of factors (the primary one was class, but race, nationality, ethnicity, religion, and sexual orientation also mattered). In addition, feminine and masculine ideals changed over time and interacted with other critical forces such as the decline of working-class radicalism, the rise of political parties, and the emergence of popular imperialism.

This chapter considers gender in Victorian Britain before and after 1860. For each of these periods, it starts by exploring ideology, and then looks at gender across the lifecycle—how it helped to define childhood, schooling, work, and marriage.

1820–1860: Separate spheres

Ideas and laws

The central tenet of gender ideology in the early Victorian period was the "doctrine of separate spheres," which developed starting in about 1780 and reached its apex around 1850. The doctrine of separate spheres stated that men and women inhabited different roles in society. Men were essentially public creatures; women were private creatures. Men went out to do battle in the worlds of business and politics; their identities centered on being workers or professionals, husbands and fathers who were good providers. Women remained at home, in the domestic sphere, where they ran their households, raised their children, and cared for their husbands. Men were fundamentally independent; women were dependent. Men were by nature sexually predatory; women were sexually passionless. Men were socially and politically dominant; women were morally superior.

Central to separate spheres ideology was domesticity, the celebration and idealization of the home. Home was a refuge from the cruelty and rapaciousness of the workplace and the marketplace. It was a morally elevated and fundamentally comforting space. Women were responsible for the home. They were expected to confine themselves to the home, and to make those homes inviting refuges from the rough and tumble world outside. Here they were expected to focus on childrearing, an expectation that intensified with the influence of evangelical religion as the century wore on. Women were seen as naturally maternal and were expected to embrace mothering. From the late eighteenth century, mothering became more time-consuming as women bore more children and saw more of them live to adulthood than ever before. For men, on the other hand, domesticity was a highly permeable barrier, across which they traveled constantly. Men were often out of the house all day, returning only in the evening; for many families the day officially ended, and the evening officially began, when father arrived home from work. Men made the domestic sphere possible through their work, but were rarely physically present in it. Yet men were intensely domestic. Most historians agree that men came to embrace domesticity during the first part of the Victorian period, most intensely between about 1840 and 1870. While men did not clean house, shop for, prepare, or serve food, or take physical care of babies or young children, they were engaged with and identified with their families and their homes. While on paper men were public and not private, in practice they were deeply invested in home, even if they were not always present or doing daily chores.

Key to men's roles was "manliness." Codes of manliness were most highly articulated in upper-class and upper middle-class homosocial spaces, particularly elite public schools like Rugby and Eton. But manliness was not restricted to the comfortable classes. It was distinguished by several traits: an emphasis on independence, individualism, and personal integrity; a strong, even punishing work ethic; a restraint on physical aggression; and a perception of the home as a compensatory refuge and reward. "Character" was highly valued. "Manly" and "straightforward" were terms of high praise, as was the concept of "manly simplicity." Different men might express aspects of manliness differently—in particular, "independence" meant different things to property-owners, salary-earners, and wage-earners—but most men subscribed to its core values. They valued independence, which implied an ability to support and protect one's dependants as well as oneself without turning to others—including the state, and after 1834 its dreaded workhouses—for help. They valued their professional identities; work was conceptualized as masculine, and men were conceptualized as workers. They believed that men were defined by their work and should spend long hours at work. They earned wages or salaries with which they supported their dependants. They did not see public displays of physical violence as necessary to virility. Violence, which had been pervasive in the eighteenth century, from village brawls to duels between aristocratic men, was valued and widely practiced only by the rough portions of the working class. The rise of manliness was an aspect of the relative fortunes of the upper class (declining) and the middle class (rising) as moral arbiters. In the eighteenth century, the most admirable form of masculinity had been "gentlemanly politeness," which was characterized by elite social standing, sociability, and ease of manner. The replacement of gentlemanly politeness with manliness was a sign that middle-class values were ascendant. Manliness was constructed around the life experiences of middle- and working-class men and privileged their experiences, in particular their commitment to hard work. Upper-class men were now seen as soft and lazy rather than as admirably at ease. In the eighteenth century gentlemanly leisure and non-vocational learning had been admirable; in the nineteenth they came to seem like idleness and uselessness.

Domesticity and sexual modesty were key to women's roles. Women were expected to be private rather than public and therefore oriented around domesticity and children. Women needed to demonstrate or perform all of these qualities, but could also sometimes manipulate these roles to their own benefit. Women were, ideally, not economic creatures. They were expected not to work for wages or salaries, and once married could not legally own property, make contracts, or incur debts (though accounts with the grocer meant that the latter requirement was honored most often in the breach). Lacking economic independence, women were to remain dependent on men throughout their lives, moving seamlessly from the status of daughter to that of wife. Female effort, regardless of the skill required or the effort expended, was conceptualized as not "work" but something else—usually housekeeping. Neither childrearing, nor cooking, nor cleaning, were categorized as work when they were done for one's own family, even though they took expertise and effort, and even though many women performed similar or identical tasks before marriage as domestic servants in the homes of others.

Victorians knew that men wanted sex, and women did not. Men were expected to desire sex with their wives. They were also expected to have sufficient sexual desire that they were driven to have pre- and sometimes extra-marital sex with prostitutes, who served a regrettable but necessary purpose in society by preventing men from being driven to masturbation or sex with other men. At the same time, men were expected to restrain themselves from acting on their sexual desires. In contrast, women were expected to be, in a phrase coined by historian Nancy Cott, "passionless." They did not have sexual desire, and so did not have to restrain themselves from having illicit sex; on the contrary, they submitted to having legitimate—marital, procreational—sex when their husbands requested it. Prostitutes were perceived not as women who were making an economic choice, but as women so unfeminine as to have sexual desire.

The sexual double standard rested in part on a belief that there were important biological differences between men and women. Men were aggressive and were characterized by their physical strength. Women were passive. It was their natural destiny to give birth, and whether or not they did they were dominated by their reproductive systems, incapacitated by menstruation and pregnancy. They could not physically or mentally exert themselves too far or else they would drain needed energies from their wombs. Many commentators drew on perceived physical differences between male and female animals to justify social differences between men and women.

Separate spheres ideology and the sexual double standard stood in marked contrast to previous notions about gender. Before industrialization, home and workplace were identical or overlapping spaces and men and women worked side by side (though not at the same tasks); as a result the notion of "separate" male and female "spheres" of work and home could not have existed. Before the late eighteenth century, most people believed that women had more sexual desire than men (this was one reasons that widows were seen as a threat to the social order) and that men and women alike did and should enjoy sex. Separate spheres and the double standard arose alongside and were strengthened by the rise of evangelical religion, which elevated women as the moral and spiritual centers of their families.

While separate spheres ideology was just that—ideology, not lived reality—it was quite influential. Separate spheres and domestic ideology were most clearly articulated and most closely observed in and by the growing middle class, particularly its evangelical sections. Furthermore as the middle class grew and became more powerful, its notions of gender roles came to influence the ideas and even the behavior of some in the elites. For example, separate spheres ideology influenced parts of the working class, which from the 1840s embraced the (largely unattainable) goal of a breadwinning husband and his non-working wife.

The notion that men and women were fundamentally different was clearly apparent in the legal system. Laws passed in the 1830s, 1840s, and 1850s concerning work assumed that men were independent and not in need of protection, while women (who were often put in the same legal category as children) were vulnerable and in need of protection. During the same period, male workers struggled to assert themselves in rapidly changing work environments, in which the sexual division of labor was changing. Their efforts were dominated by exclusionary rhetoric, in which male workers identified themselves as true workers whose work could not be done by "protected"—juvenile or female—workers. They sometimes supported restrictions on hours for women and children in the expectation that these would reduce the incentive to hire women and children,

[margin handwritten note:] Men + women were percieved differently before industrialization and the late eighteenth century

and therefore increase the incentive to hire men.[2] The 1842 Mines Act prevented women and children from working underground at mines. Factory Acts passed in 1833, 1844, 1847, 1850, and 1853 did similar work, limiting the number of hours and children could work and the types of work they could do. For example, the 1850 Factory Act prevented women and children from working at night. Men were not seen as in need of such protection, even though many worked very long hours under very dangerous conditions. This notion privileged men's work and men's relationship to their work; men could more freely decide which work to take on. For better and for worse, they were neither hampered nor protected. The first law to address the long working hours of adult men was not passed until 1874. This meant that in the early Victorian period, men's work was hard and dangerous.

Legal differences were especially stark when it came to married women—that is, most adult women—who had very different legal rights from men and single women. Legal theorist William Blackstone explained that "the very being or legal existence of the woman is suspended during the marriage."[3] Others compared marriage to riding horseback together, where clearly "one must ride behind." When a woman married, everything she owned became her husband's; anything she acquired once she was married belonged to him as well, even if he had deserted her. Husbands could deny women access to their children. They could even go to court to have their conjugal rights legally enforced. The legal term for this state of affairs is the doctrine of *coverture*. The clearest effect of the doctrine of *coverture* was that married women could not own property; neither could they be party to any contract or incur any debt. This had critical political implications. In day-to-day life, the system of *coverture* was more flexible in practice than in theory. Wives were allowed to pledge their husbands' credit to buy household "necessaries," and their frequent appearances in small claims courts indicates that shopkeepers, judges, and juries alike saw them—not their husbands—as the true consumers of many goods and debtors regarding many bills, irrespective of what the law said. When shopkeeper Mary Beale sued Thomas Ellis and his wife for £9 in 1843, testimony that "Defendant's wife paid trifling sums on the account" and "Defendant's wife promised to pay the amount" make it clear that Mrs Beale had in practice extended credit to Mrs Ellis, not her husband, for the tea, candles, soap, and sugar she had purchased.[4] The laws concerning marriage, property, and gender could also weigh heavily on men—for instance, those whose wives ran up large household debts for which their husbands were legally responsible.

For those in happy marriages, in which financial decisions were reached mutually, the fact that the couple's resources and children were controlled by the husband was only a technicality. But for those in unhappy, conflictual, violent, or de facto ended marriages, the problems raised by *coverture* were grave. A poor or working-class woman whose husband had deserted her could work to support her children, only to see her husband return and claim her wages. (Affluent middle- and upper-class women used a special form of law called equity law to put women's property in trusts and out of their husbands' control.) The lack of a civil divorce procedure meant that divorces were virtually impossible to obtain before

1857; only 224 divorces were granted in the eighteenth and nineteenth centuries, only four of them to women. The problem was dramatized by Dickens in *Hard Times*, in which factory worker Stephen Blackpool cannot marry his longtime love Rachael; his wife is an alcoholic who has deserted him and ruined his life, but she remains his legal spouse. *Coverture* also had political implications. In British national politics, the right to vote was linked to property ownership. Since married women could not legally own any property, they could not attain the vote. Feminists pointed out that married women were doubly disqualified from voting—once as women, and once as people who owned no property.

A notorious marriage that brought some of these problems to the attention of the public was that of Caroline Norton (1808–1877), whose sad story and melodramatic writing style made her famous and helped to promote the cause of legal reform. Caroline Norton's 1827 marriage to George Norton was a disaster from the start. Norton drank and abused his wife; they separated several times, and in 1836 George Norton hid their sons from their mother, barred her from the family house, and sued for divorce (his case was dismissed). In protest, Caroline Norton published *Observations on the Natural Claim of a Mother to the Custody of her Children as Affected by the Common Law Right of the Father* (1837), which helped to prompt the passage of a Custody of Children Act in 1839 (amended in 1878 and 1886).

1820–1860: Lifecycle

Childhood was very different for boys and girls before 1860. The most significant difference was that boys received far more formal education. This did not make much difference in the working-class, simply because before the passage of the 1870 Education Act few working-class children received any sort of consistent full-time education at all. Boys and girls alike received on average four and a half years of schooling all told, often primarily at Sunday school (in some rural areas, poor children did not reach even basic literacy). When they were schooled, working-class girls and boys received relatively ungendered educations: both learned reading, religion, and possibly writing and arithmetic. Girls were also taught needlework and domestic skills. Girls tended to miss school more often than boys; they were kept home on occasion to mind younger children or to help with housework, especially on washday.

More important than schooling was work, a prominent feature of working-class childhoods. Before 1860, children might start work as young as the age of five or seven. In agricultural work, boys would tend sheep, and later plow, while girls helped women with dairying and vegetable gardening. Boys were trained in workshops of ten or fewer workers, doing various manufacturing trades; they were often beaten by their masters. Girls were more likely to go into female trades such as dress or lacemaking, or into domestic service. Boys remained at home until they married; girls who were not servants did too, but girls in service had to live in the homes in which they worked. Most children disliked long hours at work and cruelty from employers, but liked the fact that they contributed to the family economy. But while girls and boys both worked hard, girls' work often took the form of unpaid household labor, while boys were sent out to earn wages.

For middle- and upper-class children, the differences between boys and girls were starker. Boys were often physically punished, but girls were not. Inside the house, boys played with mechanical and military toys, such as toy soldiers; girls drew, played the piano, or sang. Outside, girls would tend flower gardens, while boys played sports, thought to build character.[5] Middle-class parents paid for boys to attend school between the ages of seven and sixteen or even older. Some went to day schools; others, to boarding schools. The mid-nineteenth century saw a proliferation of "public" (fee-paying) schools for middle-class boys. These were modeled after elite boys' schools but often stressed practical, business-oriented subjects, including maths and the natural sciences, along with sports and camaraderie. These schools helped to create a more uniform middle class, which for the first time spoke with a relatively uniform accent. In addition to, and almost more important than, their education, boys made contacts of which they could avail themselves when the time came to enter the military or a profession. Middle-class girls' education was much shorter, less formal, and less academic. The most affluent middle-class girls would be educated at home by a governess, but most would be sent to a day school. Their schooling covered similar subjects to upper-class girls' schooling, and was of a similarly varying quality. Subjects included English literature, mathematics, geography, history, and modern languages. Ideally, they would also learn music, art, and dancing. Quality varied widely; some teachers were well-educated and serious, others were neither.

In the upper class, the differences between education for boys and for girls were greatest. Upper-class childhoods were quite long, with upper-class children usually dependent on their parents well into their twenties. Children were surrounded by and in part raised by servants; they might see their parents for only a few hours a day, and were often devoted to their nannies.

Schooling was highly gendered and helped to inculcate children into the gender roles for which they were destined as adults. Boys received significant formal schooling outside of, and often away from, home, while girls were schooled informally, in the home. Boys from the gentry and aristocracy were sent to boarding schools such as Eton, Harrow, or Winchester, and then on to Oxford or Cambridge, to prepare for their futures as local or national leaders. Their educations stressed the classics; they spent three quarters of their time learning classical Latin and Greek, which went on to serve as a crucial marker of class and status. Boarding schools were thought—especially by reforming headmaster Thomas Arnold (1795–1842), head of Rugby School—to develop discipline, character, and self-control, both through the mental discipline of the curriculum and through the social discipline of younger boys by older ones. Shared experiences of and nostalgia for boarding school culture, and shared references to classical literature, were crucial to social standing (though academic excellence was not). Aristocratic men shunned middle-class masculine ideals in favor of a more physical, unrestrained, pleasure-seeking masculinity that remained popular in their own class and among the masses, but often clashed with rising norms of middle-class male

Figure 8.1 Circa 1912: a horse-drawn campaign van driven by the suffragettes, advertising the newssheet "Votes for Women."

Photo by Hulton Archive/Getty Images.

restraint and sobriety. For elite girls, however, education usually began and ended at home, with a governess. Subjects included curriculum of English literature, mathematics, geography, history, and modern languages. Girls were also expected to learn music, art, and dancing. Education could be thorough, but often consisted of little more than memorizing for a governess passages from *Mangnall's Questions*, on such topics as the royal succession—"By whom was William the Fourth succeeded? By Queen Victoria, who in 1840 married her cousin Prince Albert, of Saxe-Coburg and Gotha, by whom she has a numerous family"—or the principal metals—"Which are the principal Metals? Gold, silver, platinum, quicksilver (or mercury), copper, iron, lead, tin, and aluminium. Of these, gold is the heaviest; tin the lightest; and iron the most useful."[6] Upper-class girls might finish their educations with a year or two of privately-run finishing-style school that emphasized social graces.

Life for adult men and women became even more different. In every class, men had higher status and more power than women. Women were excluded from formal political and economic power. However, they were often able to achieve informal access to the political and economic realms. In the working class, men and women contributed differently to a constant "economy of makeshift" in which a wide range of strategies were all employed so that the family could survive and perhaps even prosper. Men spent their adult lives working hard. Women spent their lives bearing, raising, and educating children and running households. In practice, this meant that most women worked hard too. However, their work was unpaid and was not recognized as work or as economic activity at all; instead, it was classed as domestic activity.

Working-class men worked full-time for wages their entire lives. The upper working-class—sometimes called the "labour aristocracy"—consisted of skilled male artisans and their dependent families. Skilled men made decent wages and commanded respect in their communities. They belonged to Friendly Societies, organizations that combined socializing with savings and insurance schemes. But many other men were less skilled and received lower wages for work that was often seasonal, short-term, or otherwise insecure. All working-class men began working for wages as children, assisting adult workers, then had more taxing jobs in their teens, and finally moved into adult work in their late teens. Their jobs were physically arduous and were often unsteady, either because the work was seasonal or because the industry was vulnerable to economic fluctuations. Once married, men worked full-time in an effort to support their families. However, few were economically secure enough to fully provide for their families (this was called receiving a "breadwinner's wage"; most were happy to receive "a fair day's wage for a fair day's work," which was not the same thing). Like working-class men, working-class women began work as children and gradually moved into adult work. They then stopped their waged work for a few years when they married and had children. Ideally, married women never worked for wages, but in practice most families could not survive on the husband's income alone, and working-class women returned to some kind of work (often part-time). They combined waged work with housework and childrearing, going back and forth in different years or combining them by doing sweated labor, bringing piece-work into the house, taking in lodgers, or going out to work as charwomen or cleaning women. Women were responsible for managing the family budget; good husbands turned their pay over to their wives every Friday. Since working-class men's work was often uncertain, periodic, seasonal, or poorly paid, they were less likely than middle-class men to fashion their identities around their work and the workplace; for them, leisure pursuits including boxing, betting, and drinking were more central to definitions of masculinity. Because men's work was so taxing, and because men were the heads of their households, most families privileged men's diets over women's; men would get more food, and especially more meat, than women and children. In spite of this, their heights suggest that they were inadequately nourished. Women had the scantiest food, because they sometimes went without meat or without meals so that others in their families could eat, and were often in poor health.

Both men's and women's work varied by region. Industrialization played an important role here, dividing the working class into those who lived in the north and worked in manufacturing, and those who lived in the south and worked in agriculture or a service industry. In the industrialized north, women were key workers in textile factories, which were the first factories. They would stop work for a few years when they married, but as soon as their children were no longer very young, they would return to the factories. (Some women never stopped working—in Preston one in four female factory workers was married.) The story was similar in mining areas where, until protective legislation was passed in the 1840s, women and children formed a large part of the workforce: women did full-time waged work all their lives, with the exception of their childbearing years. In part because women's wages were assumed to supplement those of a male head of the household, women were confined to low-paid and auxiliary forms of employment, where they earned at most half of what men earned. The assumption that women's jobs and wages were auxiliary was reinforced by trade unions, which until late in the nineteenth century organized only skilled male workers. Men also worked in textile and other factories and in mines, and unlike women did not stop working when their children were born. Their work was better paid than women's and considered more skilled than women's: men might run the spinning mules, while women were restricted to preparatory or auxiliary tasks related to spinning. In the south, agricultural work was the rule in rural areas. Here too men and women did different jobs—men worked in grain production, women in dairying, vegetable cultivation, and auxiliary tasks such as weeding and hoeing. Men's agricultural work (like the industrial work up north) was physically demanding, but was also relatively unskilled and seasonal, which made it difficult for families to achieve any financial security. In London (and a few other cities, such as York), service work was the rule. Skilled men worked in the building trades or for the railways; less fortunate men worked as unskilled laborers, such as the dockers who trudged from ship to ship hoping to be hired for a day's work unloading ships. Women were most likely to be domestic servants; service was the largest field of work for unmarried working-class women, not only in London but in most urban areas and areas without industries.

In the middle class, too, men and women both worked hard, with men's work recognized as work and women's categorized as domestic in nature. To achieve the respectability that was so important to this class, a middle-class man had to work, provide for his family, attend church, and possibly take part in civic affairs. Because middle-class men had to earn enough money to support non-working wives and children, many postponed marriage until a relatively late age (between 30 and 45), and married younger women. Once married, middle-class men worked long hours outside the home at non-manual, salaried work. This was the age of an entrepreneurial, individualistic masculinity organized around a punishing work ethic, in which home and its comforts were a compensating but rarely experienced validation of work.[7] But many middle-class men were devoted, if often absent, fathers. Before the 1860s, middle-class women were expected to marry and to avoid work. In practice, however, many middle-class women worked alongside their husbands or made their husbands' work possible—by bringing an inheritance to the marriage, working behind the counter at the family shop, or doing the work required of a missionary's or schoolmaster's wife. For example, when George Courtauld (who had already borrowed money from his sister to start his silk mill) married Ruth Minton, they lived on her marriage portion, so that they could reinvest all profits into the mill.[8] Married middle-class women ran their households by directing the servants and keeping the housekeeping accounts. Depending on their status within the middle-class, they might have several servants and very little menial work to do, or they might have a single servant alongside whom they worked. Those who had the time and resources were also engaged in highly organized philanthropic ventures at church, schools, charity bazaars, and as visitors to the homes of the poor and to such institutions as workhouses and women's prisons. Women were intensely focused on childrearing, more so as the century progressed and they were encouraged to spend more time raising fewer children.

In the upper class, men did not leave the home to work all day and return at night. Instead, they managed the family's affairs and estate, often alongside their wives. This might give the impression that aristocratic men and women lived equal or equivalent lives, but this was not the case. In the upper class, men were expected to serve politically, at the local or national level depending on their status. They sought to improve and expand their agricultural and other holdings. Aristocratic men often sat in the House of Commons or Lords, and so were busy with politics half the year. Among the gentry, who did not participate in the London season or in national politics, local politics (such as serving as magistrate) were men's responsibility. Aristocratic women managed their staffs and oversaw biannual moves to London and back. Aristocratic and gentry women were also quite philanthropic, caring for the family's tenants and giving them gifts on holidays. Husbands and wives worked together to maintain the family's wealth and status, in part by furthering their children's interests. This could be a complex task as the legal doctrine of primogeniture dictated that estates and titles passed only to the eldest son, which had profound repercussions for younger sons and for daughters. Younger sons were expected to go into professions such as the military or the church; they could inherit money, but not land or titles. Daughters had to find husbands. Most estates were entailed, which meant they could only be inherited by male heirs. Families without sons were often forced to give their estate to a distant cousin rather than their own daughters, who could not legally inherit. This difficulty is central to many well-known novels beloved by Victorians, such as Jane Austen's *Pride and Prejudice*, in which the Bennet family's home is to be inherited by a distant cousin, the unpleasant Mr Collins, rather than by one of the five Bennet daughters. It is also a feature of the television show *Downton Abbey*.

Upper-class men and women brought titles or property to their marriages. While married women could not own property, upper-class women often had their wealth put into separate trusts administered by their fathers or brothers. This kept their wealth distinct from that of their husbands, but just as they could not inherit entailed estates they could not legally "own" any property. The only exceptions were widows and women who never married; both were rare and socially problematic. Once married, upper-class couples devoted themselves to having large families (so as to ensure an heir) and to managing their estates. Extramarital affairs were accepted as long as they were discreet. However, one result of domestic ideology was that over the Victorian period aristocratic couples came to value sexual fidelity, or the appearance of it, more than they had. On the other hand many upper-class men continued to have affairs and to discreetly support their illegitimate children.

1860–1914: Feminism and legal changes

Ideas and laws

While the basic structure of gender in Victorian society remained consistent throughout the entire period between 1820 and 1914, there were some important changes. Some of these were the result of economic and demographic changes; others came about as the result of concerted effort on the part of determined feminists.

The most important changes were legal ones. The 1857 Divorce Act created a civil divorce procedure and a dedicated London court. This meant that some women could finally escape abusive marriages. Civil divorce was immediately popular; women filed 40% of the petitions for divorce and 92% of the judicial separation proceedings, and they were as successful as men in winning their cases. However, while the new procedure offered men and women trapped in unhappy marriages a way out, it also enshrined a sexual double standard by setting different bars for divorce. Men who sued for divorce needed to prove only that their wives had been unfaithful one single time. Women had to prove ongoing adultery and some additional or "aggravating" factor, such as physical cruelty or incest. In 1861, only four years after the Divorce Court was established, a William Pettit Dawes divorced his wife for adultery alone; the same year, when one Elizabeth Lander wanted a divorce, she had to demonstrate that in addition to being unfaithful, her husband had threatened her with a razor and a gun and struck her with an iron rod.[9] Women were not able to sue for divorce on the same terms as men until 1923.

Even more important than the establishment of divorce—a way to end marriage—were the legal changes to marriage itself. In 1854, Caroline Norton turned her attention from custody to marriage laws in her essay on *English Laws for Women in the Nineteenth Century*. Norton was not affiliated with the women's rights movement—she believed in men's natural superiority and sought rights for married women only because some husbands did not protect and care for their wives—but this essay made her a heroine to many women's rights advocates. Though her approach differed from theirs, Norton's life and writing moved many feminists, including Barbara Leigh Smith, who wrote a *Brief Summary . . . Concerning Women* in the same year that Norton wrote on *English Laws for Women*. Smith, in contrast to Norton, saw legal difficulties beyond unhappy marriages. She and her feminist colleagues argued that *coverture* was unjust; even happily married women were adults, and so like other adults had a right to own property that other adults did not control. Inspired by Norton, the Langham Place feminists began a campaign to change the laws regarding married women. A Married Women's Property Committee (MWPC) which pressured Parliament was founded in 1867, the same year that the first organized calls for women's suffrage were issued. The first result of their efforts, the Married Women's Property Act of 1870, improved women's situation only slightly, by allowing married women control of any wages they earned while they were married. It protected working women from drunken husbands, but did little else. A later 1882 Act enabled married women to control several forms of separate property and make contracts and wills; it was more effective at helping more women. During the same period, feminists also worked to repeal the Contagious Diseases Acts, which allowed police in certain port and garrison towns to stop women they believed were prostitutes on the street, subject them to a physical examination, bring them before a magistrate, and forcibly hospitalize them if they found evidence of venereal disease (in spite of the fact that there were no cures available). Social purity feminists saw the Acts as governmental sanctioning of vice that made clear the connections between women's sexual subordination and their political subordination. The campaign was successful, and the Contagious Diseases Acts were repealed in 1886. Feminists also worked for women's suffrage; that campaign, as we saw in Chapter 2, did not bear fruit until after the Great War.

1860–1914: Lifecycle

In many ways the gendered nature of life events and milestones remained the same throughout the entire Victorian period. But there were some things that changed after about 1860. The most important was education and what it offered to boys and girls. In addition the availability of low-paid, white-collar work for young men and women opened up options for safer, cleaner, less physical work that was also higher-status.

A growing problem for the middle-class was that of the woman who did not marry. Middle-class women who could not find husbands—and from 1851 there seemed to be many more of them—faced a serious problem. Though some might care for aging parents or find a place in the household of a generous brother, most needed an income—but unlike upper-class women they could not rely on family help, and unlike working-class women they could not earn wages without losing their respectability. The only exceptions to this rule were work as a governess, teacher, or dressmaker, with the former the most common. This problem became a topic of frequent discussion during the middle of the nineteenth century, and governesses became iconic of impoverished middle-class womanhood. This problem was one that feminists took up in the second half of the century; they argued that as thousands of middle-class women needed to earn a living, training and jobs needed to be provided so that they did not fall into poverty or prostitution.

From the 1850s, feminists sought to establish academically-oriented secondary schools for girls. The first two were North London Collegiate School (in London) and Cheltenham Ladies' College (in Gloucestershire); by the end of the nineteenth century many more had followed. Modeled on boys' public schools, these schools were embraced by many middle-class families (though they were largely avoided by the aristocracy, at least at first). By the start of the twentieth century, many middle- and upper-class girls were sent to day or boarding schools. They gradually abandoned corsets and lacing, which prevented any physical exertion, and began to engage in sports such as field hockey, golf, and netball. This meant that boys and girls in the middle and upper classes were having experiences similar to one another. After 1860, middle- and upper-class men engaged in a lot of outdoor exercise, as enthusiasm for games and sport swept through boys' public schools. While girls never did the same sports boys did, they followed the same model, in which schools promoted athletics as a way of building character (as well as counterbalancing intellectual exertion, which was seen as potentially dangerous to women's reproductive abilities). In addition, there were campaigns for women's higher education, in London, Oxford, Cambridge, and elsewhere. University education for women began in 1848–1849 with the opening of Queens College and Bedford College. The University of London offered degrees to women from 1878, and a decade later had three women's colleges (Bedford, Westfield, and Royal Holloway). The most elite universities, Oxford and Cambridge, were opened to women by determined Langham Place feminists. At Cambridge, Girton and Newnham Colleges opened in the 1870s. Oxford soon followed suit with Lady Margaret Hall and Somerville Hall for women. By 1900, 15% of university students in Britain were women; by 1939 that number had risen to 23%.

Boys' and girls' education changed for the working-class too. While paid and unpaid work remained an important feature of working-class childhoods, Factory Acts and rising real wages meant that hours were going down; in the 1880s and 1890s, most working-class children did not begin working until they were 12 or 14 years old. At the same time, the 1870 Education Act established elementary education for all children. But this new education was not gender-neutral. "Board schools," as they were called, were physically segregated by gender, with separate rooms, playgrounds, and even entrances for girls and boys. Girls and boys were taught differently. For example, in "Experimental Science," introduced at the turn of the century, girls learned about the radiation of heat, so as to understand why cotton clothing was preferable to woolen in summer, while boys learned "why it is necessary, when descending into mines, that the safety-lamp should be surrounded by a gauze of close mesh."[10] Domestic subjects were a large part of working-class girls' school curriculum, and women were encouraged to see housewifery as a profession.

Work options also expanded. Middle-class and upper-class men saw little change in their work lives, but as we saw in Chapter 6, from the 1860s, new employment options became available for some in the working and middle classes in the rapidly expanding white-collar fields of clerking and retail sales work. For those with enough education, the physical comfort and prestige of these jobs made them very attractive even though the pay was no more than many manual forms of work offered. Many men became clerks in government or commercial offices. This could be a career for them, though they found it difficult to advance as the field became more crowded. They enjoyed the privilege of non-manual labor, but were often portrayed as soft, even effeminate. Some young women also began to experience a period of independence before marriage and family.

just like young men. Middle- and working-class young women and men alike moved out of the family home before marriage, into boarding houses, lodgings, or inexpensive flats they shared with roommates. They pursued jobs including clerking (in all-female offices or departments), working in retail sales, or for the most educated becoming elementary school teachers. For men, entry-level clerking was only the start of a career; for women, there was only the entry level. For middle-class women, this might not be a problem; since most employers had marriage bars, and most husbands had employment bars, middle-class women worked until (or instead) of marriage, but did not earn money once wed. For women who needed to earn money after they married, however, this was a problem.

Before the turn of the century most working-class women did manual labor, and for them little changed over the century. One change was the expansion of domestic service. By 1851, domestic service had become the largest single occupation for women; by the 1880s, one third of all women between the ages of 15 and 21 were in service. The 1891 census listed 1,649,000 people working as servants in England, almost all of them women. Servants were required to live in and could only keep their positions until they married. A stint in service was thought to be good preparation for keeping one's own home, and so reinforced the connection between women and domestic labor. At the other end of the social scale, there was also little change for women—aristocratic women continued to be responsible for socializing and for philanthropy, especially to the family's tenants. For example in the years before World War One, Lady Cholmondeley gave flour and ten pounds of beef to every household in the eight villages that surrounded Cholmondeley Castle every Christmas.[11]

Turning to marriage and family, we see some questions of interpretation amongst historians. As was the case in earlier decades, women of all classes were expected to be wives and mothers first and foremost. But historians argue over what men were doing. Some argue that the period of middle-class male domesticity between 1840 and 1870 was followed by one of reaction, in which there was a male "flight from domesticity" into men's clubs and empire that lasted from 1870 until the start of World War One. But other historians doubt whether there ever was a real flight from domesticity, except perhaps in the realms of music hall songs and adventure stories such as those by G.A. Henty, in which courageous young men had adventures abroad. Certainly many middle-class men were devoted, if often absent, fathers. When the Benson family moved into a new home in 1865, father Edmund Benson decorated the walls of the nursery with prints and pictures. He also read to his children in the evenings, took them on walks on Sundays, and invited them to come and talk to him while he shaved in the morning.[12] In contrast, working-class men were not expected to care for their children or their homes, or to be openly affectionate towards their wives and children. Many working-class marriages were marked by physical violence; one study of working-class Victorian marriages is titled *Cruelty and Companionship*. However, in the middle class there is some evidence that some marriages were becoming more egalitarian in some ways.

Notes

1 Nancy F. Cott, "Passionlessness: An Interpretation of Victorian Sexual Ideology, 1790–1850," *Signs* 4.2 (1978): 219–236.
2 Robert Gray, "Factory Legislation and the Gendering of Jobs in the North of England, 1830–1860," *Gender & History* 5.1 (1993): 56–80.
3 Quoted in Philippa Levine, *Victorian Feminism 1850–1900* (London: Hutchinson Education, London, 1987), p. 134.
4 Quoted in Margot C. Finn, "Women, Consumption and Coverture in England, c.1760–1860," *Historical Journal* 39 (1996): 703–722, p. 715.
5 Ginger Frost, *Victorian Childhoods* (Westport, CT: Praeger, 2009).
6 The full title of the book popularly known as *Mangnall's Questions* was *Historical and Miscellaneous Questions for the Use of Young People* by Richmal Mangnall, first published in 1800. These quotes come from pages 153 and 489 of the 1859 edition.
7 John Tosh, "Masculinities in an Industrializing Society: Britain, 1800–1914," *Journal of British Studies*, 44:2 (2005): 330–342, p. 331.
8 S.L. Courtauld, *The Huguenot Family of Courtauld*, 3 Volumes (1957) Volume 2, 13, quoted in Leonore Davidoff and Catherine Hall, *Family Fortunes: Men and Women of the English Middle Class, 1780–1850* (Chicago: University of Chicago Press, 1987), p. 280.
9 Gail L. Savage, "'Intended Only for the Husband': Gender, Class, and the Provision for Divorce in England, 1858–1868," in Kristine Otteson Garrigan (ed.), *Victorian Scandals: Representations of Gender and Class* (Athens: Ohio University Press, 1992), pp. 26, 24, 32.
10 T.A. Spalding, *The Work of the London School Board* (London: P.S. King and Son, 1900), p. 212, quoted in June Purvis, *Hard Lessons: The Lives and Education of Working-Class Women in Nineteenth-Century England* (Minneapolis: University of Minnesota Press, 1989), p. 109.
11 Pamela Horn, *Ladies of the Manner: Wives and Daughters in Country-House Society 1830–1918* (Stroud, UK: Sutton, 1991), pp. 65, 121.
12 John Tosh, "Domesticity and Manliness in the Victorian Middle Class: The Family of Edward White Benson," in John Tosh and Michael Roper (eds), *Manful Assertions: Masculinities in Britain Since 1800* (London: Routledge 1991), pp. 48–49, 61.

Relevant fiction that students might enjoy

Jane Austen, *Pride and Prejudice* (1813)
Charlotte Brontë, *Jane Eyre* (1847)
Emily Brontë, *Wuthering Heights* (1847)
Charles Dickens, *Hard Times* (1854)
Elizabeth Gaskell, *North and South* (1854–1855)
Thomas Hughes, *Tom Brown's Schooldays* (1857)
Mrs Henry Wood, *East Lynne* (1861)

Further reading

Leonore Davidoff and Catherine Hall, *Family Fortunes: Men and Women of the English Middle Class 1780–1850*, 2nd ed. (Oxford: Routledge, 2002).
Lydia Murdoch, *Daily Life of Victorian Women* (London: Greenwood, 2013).
Susie Steinbach, *Women in England 1760–1914: A Social History* (London: Weidenfeld and Nicolson, 2004).
Susie Steinbach, "Women in Great Britain since 1800," in Bonnie G. Smith (ed.), *Encyclopedia of Women in World History*, Volume (Oxford: Oxford University Press, 2007): 395–401.
Susie Steinbach, "Can We Still Use 'Separate Spheres'? British History 25 years after Family Fortunes," *History Compass* 10.11 (November 2012): 826–837.

Online resources

Lesley Hall's Web Pages: www.lesleyahall.net/ and http://lesleyahall.blogspot.co.uk/

The Women's Library: www.lse.ac.uk/library/collections/featuredcollections/womensli brarylse.aspx

Women's History Network: http://womenshistorynetwork.org/

Women's History Sourcebook: http://legacy.fordham.edu/halsall/women/womensbook. asp

Gender History in the Institute of Historical Research Library: www.history.ac.uk/library/ collections/gender-history

9 A "dignified part"
Monarchy

Introduction

Histories of the Victorian era were once routinely written without reference to Victoria, the monarch after whom the period was named. Because Queen Victoria wielded less political power than her predecessors had, political historians focused on parliament rather than monarchy. Study of the monarch herself was relegated to biographers (academic as well as popular), but she was not considered in any larger context. Her popularity with her subjects was acknowledged, but not investigated.

Since the 1980s this has changed, and Queen Victoria is now a well-studied part of Victorian history. Historians of gender set out to investigate the paradox of a female head of a patriarchal state and society. Cultural historians—noting the persistent popularity of the British monarchy and royal family (in spite of the many scandals of the 1990s)—set out to analyze Victoria's insistent presence in Victorian visual and print culture (especially advertising). Political historians recognized that if eighteenth-century monarchs had political power, and twentieth and twenty-first century monarchs did not, then something worth investigating must have occurred during the Victorian period. And so it did: during Victoria's reign, Britain retained its monarchy even as it developed—without bloodshed—into a parliamentary democracy. Historians also take seriously Walter Bagehot's analysis of the monarchy. As we saw in Chapter 2, Bagehot argued that the monarchy was one of the dignified parts of government. As such it was revered by the people, and so established the government as both spectacular and legitimate. The retention of the monarchy is striking in the larger European context: the monarchy was abolished in France's Third Republic in 1870, in Spain's First Republic from 1873 to 1874, in Portugal in 1910, and in Russia in 1917, and in Germany in 1918.

From 1820 until 1837, Britain was ruled by two of Victoria's uncles, George IV and William IV, whose own unpopularity brought the monarchy to its nadir of unpopularity. Victoria's reign lasted for 63 years, seven months and two days, and, until September 9, 2015, was the longest in British history. (On that date, the reign of the current monarch, Queen Elizabeth II, surpassed that of Queen Victoria in length.) We will consider Victoria and her reign in three parts. In the first two decades, Victoria reigned as a wife and mother and worked to portray herself as accessible to her people. In the 1860s, she withdrew from some of the public aspects of her work, and suffered political criticism as a result. From the early 1870s until her death, she was the symbol rather than the ruler of Britain and its empire, personifying it where previous monarchs had led it. Following her death, her son and grandson's early twentieth-century reigns were in many ways a continuation of the style of monarchy that had been established during her long lifetime.

1820–1861: From kings to a queen

George IV ruled from 1810 as Regent on behalf of his mentally and physically incapacitated father, George III, and as extremely unpopular monarch from 1820 (though he was more popular in Scotland than in England or Wales). Though a generous and discerning patron of the arts, his extravagance and womanizing meant that he personified aristocratic corruption, immorality, and excess. In 1819, he gave the order that resulted in the death of 11 political protesters near Manchester in an event that came to be known as "Peterloo." In 1820, in the Queen Caroline Affair, he barred his wife from his coronation; popular political feeling went with Caroline. During his combined regency and reign he managed to alienate both the Whig and the Tory parties, making himself the first modern British monarch who had neither personal influence with, nor official support from, either political party. This weakened his ability to rule, as did his opposition to Catholic Emancipation, which was passed in 1829 by the Prime Minister, the Duke of Wellington, over the king's objections. When he died in 1830, the *Times* declared that "[t]here never was an individual less regretted by his fellow creatures."[1] George IV was succeeded by his brother, William IV, whose rule lasted only seven years, no great surprise given that he was 69 years old when he was crowned. Better liked than his older brother, he gained popular support when he insisted on a modest coronation ceremony. Politically, his brief reign was dominated by the passage of the 1832 Reform Act. Since the king had no legitimate children, his niece Victoria was his heiress apparent from a young age.

Victoria became queen in 1837 when she was only 18. In an often-recounted scene, the princess, still in her nightgown, was informed by the Archbishop of Canterbury and the Lord Chamberlain that (as she recorded in her journal) "my poor Uncle, the King, was no more . . . and consequently . . . I am *Queen*."[2] A public fascination with royal women had already begun with George IV's daughter Princess Charlotte, whose death in childbirth in 1817 transfixed the nation, and with her mother Queen Caroline. Unlike them, however, Victoria was the reigning monarch. The paradox of a woman—who, by nineteenth-century standards, was by definition non-political—as the head of state produced both political anxiety and advantages throughout the reign.

Questions about how to resolve this tension plagued even Victoria herself, as became apparent in the Bedchamber Crisis. In 1839, the leader of the Whig government and Victoria's favorite advisor, Lord Melbourne, lost his majority in the House of Commons and was forced to resign. The queen now had a responsibility to summon a leader of the opposition party and request that he form a new government. As ladies' places in the royal household were political appointments that changed with administrations, that leader would, as a matter of course, ask the Queen to replace the Whig ladies of her royal household with women from Tory families. Victoria called on Tory leader Robert Peel to form a new administration, but to everyone's surprise, refused to reorganize her household, insisting that her ladies were not political appointments but personal friends and that she never discussed politics with them. Peel argued that a monarch had no private life separate from affairs of state, but Victoria maintained that even though she was the sovereign, when at home she was not political. Victoria's refusal to yield on this point had significant political ramifications, as it forced the Whigs and Lord Melbourne back into office for two more years. (Peel did come to office two years later, in 1841; a clear Tory majority in that election left the queen no choice but to appoint him.) In the Bedchamber Crisis, Victoria had a major political impact, but she accomplished it by asserting herself as female and apolitical. For the rest of her reign the queen's court was portrayed in the London daily newspapers as a female, domestic, apolitical space. By extension, the queen had represented not only her court but herself as separate from politics.

Before 1832, Britain had been governed jointly by monarch and Parliament, but the Reform Act gave Parliament the lion's share of governing power (as well as making it responsible to a new, larger electorate). In the Bedchamber Crisis and elsewhere, Queen Victoria worked to maintain a degree of monarchical power within this new political reality by locating herself above politics. She was aided in this by her German cousin, Prince Albert, whom she married soon after taking the throne. (Her gender made the marriage even more politically sensitive than most royal couplings: as a monarch Victoria could not be proposed to, but as a woman she ought not to propose to a man (though she did). One broadsheet worried that "[s]ince the Queen did herself for a husband 'propose,' [t]he ladies will all do the same, I suppose."[3]) Albert held that the proper role of the monarchy was to be impartial. From the early 1840s, Victoria and Albert built on this notion to position themselves as concerned with the interests of the nation, in contrast to the political parties. Rejecting party affiliations or even sympathies, they were above party without being outside politics.

Albert was politically astute and craved a clear role in governance, but as the non-ruling husband of a female monarch, his position remained ill-defined and uncomfortable. Victoria wanted Parliament to declare them co-rulers, as William and Mary had been in the late seventeenth century, but this never happened. Frequently attacked as a foreign interloper, Albert had to be careful in crafting his public persona. He never had an official ruling role—indeed, he gained the title by which we know him, Prince Consort, only in 1857—but he worked closely with the queen. Victoria often received ministers and other politicians with Albert by her side. However, he declined the post of commander-in-chief of the army when the Duke of Wellington retired in 1850, opting to extend his influence in less overtly political ways. He was very involved in promoting scientific, artistic, and industrial endeavors, and was a planner of the Great Exhibition. He was also interested in industrialization and its effects on the skilled working class, and spoke against child labor and in favor of increased education. He was intimately involved in the passage of the Government of India Act of 1858, which transferred direct rule of India from the East India Company to the Crown following the 1857 Rebellion. Historians disagree over whether his role was as minor as that of Victoria's secretary or as major as one half of a "dual monarchy." On his death, Benjamin Disraeli went even farther, privately declaring that "[w]ith Prince Albert we have buried our Sovereign. This German Prince has governed England for twenty-one years with a wisdom and energy such as none of our kings has ever shown."[4]

The 1840s also saw the Victorian revival of the reputation of seventeenth-century republican leader Oliver Cromwell (1599–1658). Cromwell had been the leader of the Parliamentarian rebels during the English Civil War, and had ruled England under the title of Lord Protector for a decade until his death and the restitution of the English monarchy. Denigrated as a power-hungry hypocrite for much of the eighteenth century, in the Victorian era Cromwell became quite popular, largely because Thomas Carlyle edited and published his speeches and letters. No longer a tyrant, in Carlyle's hands Cromwell became a man of principle, whose extreme sincerity, passionate Protestantism (and anti-Catholic and anti-Irish feelings), and blunt, even clumsy style were all signs of character and patriotism. In 1899, a statue of him was erected outside Westminster Palace.

In the 1840s and 1850s, the royal couple and the press both worked hard to present Victoria's marriage as a happy and devoted one (which by all accounts it was), Victoria as a devoted mother (she gave birth to nine children but hated pregnancy and was not a particularly warm parent), and her family in effect as typically middle class (which it certainly was not). Victoria was not the first queen to be represented as a virtuous wife and mother above all—Queen Charlotte (1744–1818), wife of George III, had presented herself as virtuous and maternal and portrayed the royal family as domestic, familial, and familiar—but improving communications and travel and expanding print culture meant far more visibility for Victoria than for previous royal women.

The image of Victoria as typical was, of course, only an image—Victoria reigned over the world's largest empire, lived in castles, was waited on by an enormous retinue of servants, and ate from solid gold plates. But the representation of the queen as someone who was like and familiar with her subjects helped to secure the monarchy as socially and culturally important as it became politically less powerful. The fact that Victoria was a woman made her an ideal monarch during this period of transition: as a wife and mother she was more easily represented as domestic than any man could have been. Sustained representations of the monarchy as middle class, domestic, patriotic, and spectacular helped make the transition to a parliamentary democracy that included a monarchy not only smooth but possible.

This may have been because there were similarities between nineteenth-century conceptions of the monarch's role and of a middle-class wife's role that made a married woman the ideal occupant of the throne. Both were to refrain from ruling or leading but were expected to advise. In *The English Constitution*, in which Bagehot argued that the monarchy was one of the "dignified" parts of government, he held that its proper political rights included the right to be consulted, the right to encourage, and the right to warn. The monarch had a duty to be theatrical and ornamental, because the populace required a spectacular monarchy to behold. The monarch's role, in the eyes of Bagehot and other commentators, would in future be to entertain her people, to advise her ministers, and to refrain from direct action. The Queen, then, was the wife to the Parliament's husband. Such a concept could develop only under a female monarch: a king would have been emasculated by such an argument. Victoria, as mother, wife and widow, and spectacle, was the ideal sovereign to lead her country into an age of stable parliamentary democracy while maintaining the strength of her throne.

Yet we should not assume that Bagehot's vision of the future was an accurate description of contemporary political reality. Like many Victorian wives, Queen Victoria had more power in practice than in theory. The constitutional role of the monarch was contracting as that of the cabinet and parliament expanded. The queen did not have the power to overrule politicians or officials, nor to compel any policy. However, if we look at practice rather than theory, it is clear that royal political power persisted. The Queen still commanded much patronage and retained the power to create peers. A tradition of royal authority combined with Victoria's own strong sense of royal power and interest in politics meant that it was extremely difficult to contradict the queen, and that politicians did not do so if they could avoid it. The cabinet and the Houses of Parliament could not govern without consulting with and often deferring to the Queen. The Queen expected politicians to take her political ideas seriously, and to a large degree they did. She insisted on meeting with ministers, and expected them not simply to "inform" her but to debate with her, to listen to and respect her opinion, and to take her advice. When they were far from her, prime ministers regularly received written word from her, demanding information or issuing pieces of advice that were actually instructions. When she was away from London she demanded that a cabinet minister be with her at all times. Political careers still depended on not making an enemy of the queen. Victoria's anti-Catholic and anti-Irish feelings, which intensified over the course of her reign, mattered, serving as obstacles to reform of the Irish problem throughout her reign. Victoria's sense of royal authority was reinforced by her subjects. Most ordinary people were unclear whether governing power laid with Queen, Parliament, or the House of Commons, and believed that the Queen had political power. This belief became to some extent a self-fulfilling prophecy, at least at the level of popular understandings of and support for the government. Well into her reign, the Queen received hundreds of petitions and letters each year from individuals and small groups requesting her direct intervention or assistance. These may seem to reflect popular ignorance, but they were not so different from the many requests for patronage that the Queen received from members of the political elite every year. Overall, Victoria's powerlessness should not be overstated.

THE ROYAL FAMILY.

DUKE OF CAMBRIDGE   PRINCESS ROYAL   THE LATE PRINCE CONSORT
DUKE OF EDINBURGH   PRINCESS ALICE
PRINCE OF WALES   THE QUEEN.   PRINCESS OF WALES

Figure 9.1 The Royal Family of Queen Victoria, from *The National and Domestic History of England* by William Hickman Smith Aubrey (1858–1916) published London, circa 1890 (litho) by English School (nineteenth century).

Private collection/Ken Welsh/The Bridgeman Art Library.

Above and beyond political power, Victoria was an immensely popular figure. This is not to be taken for granted, given how unpopular the monarchy had become in the 20 years before Victoria took to the throne. Queen Victoria and Prince Albert used extensive public ceremonials to make themselves spectacular and accessible. The spectacular royal ceremonials held after 1880 are well known, but modest yet effective gestures were being staged much earlier. George IV made visits to Dublin in 1821 and Edinburgh in 1822, where he was warmly greeted even just after the Queen Caroline Affair had made him the most hated man in London. From the start of her reign, when the monarchy was relatively unpopular in London, but was well-liked in the provinces, Victoria built on her uncle's visits. The provincial middle classes were growing and asserting themselves in urban political and cultural scenes. Civic authorities would arrange crowd-pleasing spectacles and invite the monarch and her husband to participate. That they accepted these invitations helped to make the monarchy popular. Victoria and Albert made themselves available to their subjects in a varied and unprecedented number of ways. For example, in an 1842 visit to Edinburgh, which the Town Council planned for weeks, the Queen was persuaded to change her itinerary and to publicly proceed through the city, dressed in tartan and surrounded by an honor guard. While this would not have been the Queen's preference, the *Scotsman* newspaper pointed out that public display "attaches to her high station," and fawned that "the desire of a sovereign to hold communion with all classes of her people . . . is an indication of a love of justice, and of . . . beautiful maternal affection." A tour of the Midlands the following year was described approvingly by the *News of the World* as "visits to the people—all the working people as well as" Sir Robert Peel and the Dukes of Devonshire and Rutland with whom the Queen was staying. A visit to Ireland in 1849 was so carefully stage-managed that it seemed a ceremonial success in spite of both the Famine and the Queen's known antipathy to Ireland. There were also foreign visits, such as the one to Paris in 1855, which *Lloyd's Weekly Newspaper* described not as Queen Victoria visiting French ruler Louis Napoleon, but "England who visits France . . . people grasping people."[5] All of these were widely covered in the burgeoning popular press and especially in the many popular weekly newspapers such as *Lloyd's Weekly Newspaper* and the *Illustrated London News*, which helped to create the monarch's popularity even as coverage of the royals boosted their circulation. While the periodical press did publish occasional republican attacks on the monarch and on monarchy, there was far more positive than negative coverage of royal activities.

Another reason for the queen's popularity was her extensive charitable giving. Historian of philanthropy F.K. Prochaska argues that the royal family's generous giving during Victoria's reign was crucial to its transformation into a popular institution.[6] As the constitutional role and political power of the monarchy declined, Victoria and Albert consciously created a royal philanthropic presence that helped them to retain respectability, prestige, and influence. As important as the money they gave to hospitals, prisons, schools, and other institutions was the time and personal appearances that they gave; the charitable and spectacular aspects of monarchy became inextricable. The queen and the prince each chose gender-appropriate philanthropic enthusiasms that reinforced their image as hewing to middle-class standards. Albert was partial to institutions of social improvement and working-class self-help, including adult education schemes and libraries. Victoria preferred the same causes that middle-class women did, those that benefitted women, children, and the poor, and had a particular interest in nursing.

Thanks to the press these displays of royalty were available to the entire nation. Extensive coverage of the queen and her family as domestic, middle class, civic-minded, and generously philanthropic was key in establishing the popular image of the bourgeois monarchy. Indeed, the popular press covered Victoria so extensively that one historian argues not only that Victoria was the "first media monarch" but that the press was dependent on the monarchy as its main subject during its explosive growth during the middle of the century.[7]

1861–1914: Withdrawal as a ruler, emergence as a symbol

The 1860s began a very different phase of Victoria's monarchy, in which the queen withdrew from public life, with significant consequences. The immediate cause was Prince Consort Albert's death in 1861, officially from typhoid fever (though historians think the cause may have been stomach cancer or Crohn's disease). Once again, Victoria's gender created conflict: as a widowed woman, she was expected to withdraw from the world, but as monarch she was expected to carry on. For the next 11 years, though she continued to meet with her ministers, to interest herself in affairs of state, and to be active in philanthropy, Queen Victoria withdrew from the public side of public life. In the short term, her absence from the political arena made possible the rise of republican (or anti-monarchical) feeling, and so seemed to imperil the throne. In the longer term, however, her period of retirement enabled the British monarchy to complete its transition to being into symbolic of, rather than irrelevant to, Britain.

Throughout the 1860s and early 1870s, the queen rarely performed in political ceremonies. For example, though she was expected to open Parliament every year, she refused to do so for several years. When she finally relented, in 1866, the Lord Chancellor read her speech, while she sat on her throne, wearing neither a crown nor robes of state. The queen was mocked as the "widow at Windsor." Some called on her to abdicate in favor of the Prince of Wales, who was now of age. Complaints about the cost of the now-invisible monarchy were sounded. She spent much time in Scotland, a country she loved, but continued to shun Ireland, refusing to establish a royal residence there in spite of political calls for one.

Yet the queen was not invisible: she seems so only if we focus exclusively on the political as the only important function of the monarchy. It would be more correct to say that she went from being visible as a wife and ruler to being visible as a secluded widow. Her absence was a new kind of presence. At the 1866 opening of Parliament she was hardly invisible; rather, she was performing the fact that she was not performing. Indeed, the queen seemed more invisible to politicians, from whom she did withdraw during this period, than she did to her people, to whom she remained available. She kept up her philanthropic works and public appearances. Though she refused to open parliament, in 1871 she brought her children with her to open St. Thomas' Hospital in London. The police who were there to control the crowd failed to recognize Prime Minister Gladstone and kept him standing out of sight as the queen laid the foundation stone. She made frequent dedications of shrines to Albert's memory. Newspapers (those in London, such as the *Times* and the *Morning Chronicle*, and provincial papers too, such as *Jackson's Oxford Journal* and the *Liverpool Mercury*) all reported on her daily schedule in notices entitled "The Court" or "Court Circular." These notices—which appeared every day—would inform readers that the Queen "walked and drove this afternoon" or that she had "taken several rides at Osborne" on her new Highland pony.[8] Papers that included regular pictures of royal occasions, such as the *Illustrated London News*, were also important. Newspapers pictures and articles helped to maintain the image of the Queen as a widow, as they emphasized how sedate and family-oriented her activities were. They did not report on the political work the Queen continued to do every day (this was probably in part the Queen's choice, as details of her activities were sent to the newspapers by her appointed "court newsman").

During this period of widowhood and withdrawal, then, the monarchy became a ceremonial position. Its graceful transition was almost certainly necessary given the passage of the Reform Act of 1867, which gave the vote to millions of working-class men. A forcefully ruling monarch might well have seemed in conflict with an increase in democracy in a way that this decorative monarch did not.

During this time, however, a republican movement arose. Dislike of either monarch or the monarchy was not new in Britain. Nor was republican feeling; most political radicals professed some version of republicanism. Before the late 1860s, however, while there had been moments of intense anti-monarchism, calls for a republic had never been loud. Many opposed monarchy in theory, but they devoted neither resources nor energies to its end. Even Chartism was radical without being republican—overall Chartism reserved its ire for the aristocratic ruling elite, and though republican Chartists existed most Chartists were loyal to the queen even as they agitated for democracy. However, the late 1860s and early 1870s saw the rise of intellectual and populist republicanism. Intellectual republicanism was led by radical and atheist Charles Bradlaugh (1833–1891), who founded the National Republican League. It was a very small movement that never had more than a few thousand members. Many protested the high cost of the monarchy. More widespread was populist republicanism, which was part of a long tradition of populist critiques of government and elites. Popular republicanism was not so much sustained political criticism as a visceral negative reaction to monarchy. It was an expression of popular frustration at the Queen's seclusion (and popular dislike of the Prince of Wales). It was an aspect of hostility to aristocratic rule, which it saw as unrepresentative and despotic, and to aristocratic morals, both political and personal, which were now seen as immoral. Republicanism and anti-monarchism in all their various forms were strongest in the early 1870s. Strikingly, they faded away as soon as Queen Victoria reestablished her public presence and royal ceremonies became common once more (they were not heard of again until World War One). Between 1861 and 1872 Queen Victoria's new relationship to the public, to her people, and to politics helped to intensify the sense that the Queen was less the ruler than the symbol of her people. When she returned to her public duties in 1872, a new emphasis on ceremony and ritual, alongside the Reform Acts, completed this transition.

In 1872, the Queen returned to the public ceremonial performances that made the monarchy spectacular. In late 1871, Albert, Prince of Wales, became gravely ill with typhoid, the disease that was thought to have killed his father, and was expected to die. Upon his recovery, Prime Minister Gladstone arranged a service of thanksgiving at St Paul's Cathedral, which he convinced Queen Victoria to attend. This public celebration marked the end of her seclusion and brought Victoria decisively back into popular favor.

This public appearance was a critical turning point in the Queen's reign. Henceforth, the Queen once again participated in increasingly grand royal rituals. She continued to eschew some explicitly political performances; for example, she very rarely opened Parliament. But until the end of her reign the Queen was the personification of Britain and its empire; she became a powerful symbol. This identification was created, maintained, and identified through several major events: Victoria's coronation as Empress of India in 1877, the celebration of her Golden Jubilee in 1887, and her Diamond Jubilee in 1897. The monarchy came to be defined by these gigantic festive ceremonial occasions, which celebrated Britain's prosperity and stability and the queen as the embodiment of the nation's success. The monarchy became more ceremonial and less political, proof of the nation's prosperity rather than integral to that prosperity.

Empire and the monarchy were used to enhance one another's prestige, and these elaborate imperial ceremonies asserted imperial strength and Britain's global position even as they claimed to simply celebrate it. The passage of a Royal Titles Act in 1876 made Victoria the Empress of India, a new title celebrated in India and Britain in 1877. The festivities were seen as an assertion of Britain's imperial status and global power, and were accordingly praised by pro-imperialists. They were dismissed by some contemporaries as a transparent attempt on the part of Prime Minister Disraeli to flatter the Queen, but the new title emerged out of more than Disraeli's politicking. Victoria had taken a keen interest in India since the 1840s. Indeed, there is evidence that Victoria believed herself to hold the title of Empress of India from 1858.[9] Once Disraeli proposed the 1877 festivities, the new figure of Victoria as Empress was eagerly celebrated throughout Britain and India with an alacrity on the part of populace and media that suggests that more than Disraeli's preferences were at stake. (The Queen's personally warm relationship with the flattering Disraeli, contrasted with her dislike of Gladstone, helped to establish the Conservative Party as royalist.) Not only the prime minister but imperial administrators, journalists, and others, together celebrated Victoria's new status. An imperial *durbah* or public ceremony was held in Delhi, presided over by Viceroy of India, Lord Lytton, who led a three-hour procession riding what was purported to be the largest elephant in India, presented all the major Indian princes with their own coats of arms, and read a telegram from Victoria, whom he described to her Indian subjects as "the Queen, your Empress." (In 1911, George V's coronation as King-Emperor would be celebrated in Delhi exactly where the 1877 pageant had been.) From that day, Victoria signed herself "Victoria R & I" (*regina et imperatrix* [queen and empress]); while it had been intended that she use her new title only in matters Indian, she used it far more widely. No wonder, then, that so many assumed that Victoria was now the Empress of every part of the empire.

The Golden Jubilee continued in the steps of the Thanksgiving service and 1877 festivities by making the Queen part of elaborate public shows of state. For her Golden Jubilee the Queen rode in an open carriage from Buckingham Palace to Westminster Abbey, escorted by Indian cavalry whose presence emphasized Britain's imperial power. She then returned to the palace, where she appeared on a balcony and was cheered by an enormous crowd and watched a fireworks display. In Hyde Park, 30,000 poor children had been gathered to be fed and entertained; each child received an earthenware pot decorated with the queen's portrait. Advertising, souvenirs, memorabilia, and quotidian objects of all sorts celebrated Victoria both as a consumer and as an object to be consumed, both as ordinary, domestic, and middle class, and as head of an enormous empire that was spreading the benefits of British civilization to lesser peoples. "Jubileeana" featured the Queen's face or coat of arms and included portraits, embroidered samplers, rugs, plates, cups, toys, dolls, bracelets, and scent bottles, mostly priced to be affordable for the middle class.[10]

The Diamond Jubilee—a celebration of the length of Queen's reign, which had in late 1896 surpassed that of George III—extended the theme of celebration of the queen as a symbol and personification of nation and empire. At a dinner at Buckingham Palace, the Queen entertained foreign rulers while dining on traditional English roast beef. The prime ministers of every colony and self-governing dominion in the empire were invited to London, as were 25,000 colonial troops, who were housed in tents in Hyde Park, whilst 3 million spectators flooded in to London. The queen travelled through London, preceded by her colonial troops, waving to crowds of people who had waited for hours, even days, to see her as she passed by. When the queen arrived at Paddington railway station to take the royal train to Windsor, she was greeted by three English boys dressed as heralds, and four upper-class Indian boys in native dress.[11] Newspapers and magazines portrayed the Jubilee as proof of Britain's power and prosperity: charts, lists, and figures were provided to prove that Victoria's was a "Record Reign" in accomplishments as well as length. The Diamond Jubilee was the occasion of the first official photographic portrait of the Queen; henceforth photography became another key genre in representations of the monarch. But the official portrait was not remotely the only image of Victoria in 1897: even more so than in 1887, advertisers used the Queen's image to sell hundreds of products from cocoa to tires. There were even more souvenirs available than there had been for the Golden Jubilee, and these—including mugs, cups, medals, and even toast racks, and for celebrations, "Jubiletti, the New Confetti"—were mass-produced and affordable for working-class consumers.

When Victoria died in January 1901 at the age of 81, she was a beloved figure. This was reflected in the uniformly positive depictions of her in both biographies and in anthologies of biographies of admirable women that were so numerous and popular during the Victorian period. In these she was depicted as simultaneously ordinary and spectacular. She was described in one anthology as "always . . . ready to second the plans of sound reform"; her reign was described here as "one of the most beneficently great," and in another as one during which "Mankind progressed in brotherly love[,] Child labor was regulated[,] women were no longer permitted to work in mines; the negro, however savage, was free wherever the British flag waved."[12] Similarly, on her death, the *Times* argued that "to write the life of Queen Victoria is to relate the history of Great Britain during a period of great events . . . and unexampled national prosperity."[13] Victoria was not the ruler of her country, she *was* her country. Her funeral was her final spectacular royal ceremonial, and was the event of much public mourning—more than had been shown at that of William Gladstone three years earlier, for all that he had wielded more political power than the queen he served.

Victoria was succeeded by her son, Edward VII. Because Victoria disliked and distrusted her heir, she gave him no training for or hand in ruling while she was alive; he spent most of his life in frivolous pursuits. His reign, styled the "Edwardian era," is generally remembered as one of peace, and as the last period of stable class hierarchies, imperial celebration, and royal opulence, all of which were to vanish with the start of the Great War. (Though Edward died in 1910 and was succeeded by his son, George V (r. 1910–1936), the "Edwardian" period is generally considered to end only in 1914.) Both Edward VII and George V were more sympathetic than Victoria had been to Ireland, which was an ever-increasing political problem for Britain; George V was very pro-Irish and was believed personally to favor Home Rule. But both monarchs continued Victoria's commitment to royal ceremonials, in their coronations (of Edward VII in 1902 and George V in 1911) and elsewhere.

Notes

1 Quoted in David Cannadine, "The Context, Performance, and Meaning of Ritual: The British Monarchy and the 'Invention of Tradition,' *c.* 1820–1977," in Eric Hobsbawm and Terence Ranger (eds), *The Invention of Tradition* (Cambridge: Cambridge University Press, 1983), p. 109.
2 Quoted in Richard Hough, *Victoria and Albert* (St Martin's Press, New York, 1996), p. 33; italics in original.
3 Quoted in Dorothy Thompson, *Queen Victoria: The Woman, The Monarchy, The People* (Pantheon, New York, 1990), p. 38.
4 G.E. Buckle, *Life of Benjamin Disraeli* (1916), p. 383, quoted in Stanley Weintraub, "Albert [Prince Albert of Saxe-Coburg and Gotha] (1819–1861)," *Oxford Dictionary of National Biography*, available online at: http://www.oxforddnb.com.libproxy.york.ac.uk/view/article/274 (accessed February 23, 2010).
5 Quoted in John Plunkett, "Civic Publicness: The Creation of Queen Victoria's Royal Role 1837–61" in Laurel Brake and Julie F. Codell (eds), *Encounters in the Victorian Press: Editors, Authors, Readers* (Basingstoke: Palgrave Macmillan, 2005), p. 16.

6 F.K. Prochaska, *Royal Bounty: The Making of a Welfare Monarchy* (New Haven, CT: Yale University Press, 1995).
7 John Plunkett, *Queen Victoria: First Media Monarch* (Oxford: Oxford University Press, 2003).
8 "The Court," *Liverpool Mercury*, January 9, 1865; Issue 5286.
9 Miles Taylor, "Queen Victoria and India, 1837–61," *Victorian Studies* 46:2 (2004): 264–274, p. 265.
10 Thomas Richards, "The Image of Victoria in the Year of Jubilee," *Victorian Studies* 31.1 (Autumn 1987): 7–32, pp. 17, 19.
11 Greg King, *Twilight of Splendor: The Court of Queen Victoria During Her Diamond Jubilee* (Hoboken, NJ: Wiley, 2007), pp. 258, 268.
12 Quoted in Alison Booth, *How to Make It as a Woman: Collective Biographical History from Victoria to the Present* (Chicago: University of Chicago Press, 2004), pp. 69, 71.
13 *The Times*, January 23, quoted in Juliet Gardiner, *Queen Victoria* (London: Collins & Brown, 1997), p. 53.

Relevant fiction that students might enjoy

Millicent Garrett Fawcett, *Some Eminent Women of Our Times: Short Biographical Sketches* (1889)
Millicent Garrett Fawcett, *Life of Her Majesty Queen Victoria* (1895)
George Barnett Smith, *Life of Her Majesty Queen Victoria* (1896)
Life of Queen Victoria: A Book for Young People (1897)
Louise Creighton, *Some Famous Women* (1909)

Further reading

Margaret Homans and Adrienne Munich (eds), *Remaking Queen Victoria* (Cambridge: Cambridge University Press, 1997).
Margaret Homans, *Royal Representations: Queen Victoria and British Culture, 1837–1876* (Chicago: University of Chicago Press, 1998).
John Plunkett, *Queen Victoria: First Media Monarch* (Oxford: Oxford University Press, 2003).

Online resources

The Official Website of the British Monarchy—Queen Victoria: an education resource from the Royal Archives: www.royal.gov.uk/The%20Royal%20Collection%20and%20other%20collections/TheRoyalArchives/QueenVictoriaeducationproject/QueenVictoriaeducationproject.aspx
Queen Victoria's Journals: www.queenvictoriasjournals.org/home.do

10 "The court was crowded all day"

The law and the police

Introduction

Open any Victorian newspaper and you would be sure to encounter such head-lines as "Extraordinary Breach of Promise of Marriage Case," "The 'First' Man of the Tichborne Jury," or "*Holmes* vs. *Holmes & Yeats*." The legal system was a pervasive shaper of Victorian society. The creation of the first police forces, changes in criminal law, and the replacement of public hangings with prison sentences put crime and punishment at the forefront of public consciousness. Police became a pervasive presence in urban working-class neighborhoods. The legal system provided Victorians with the gossip, scandals, and *causes célèbres* via high-profile court cases. Debt bound people to one another and meant that many Victorians found themselves in court. Marriage, experienced by most adults, was highly legally regulated. In all these ways legal processes surrounded Victorians, so that, in the words of historian Margot Finn, "familiarity with the law was pervasive, not exceptional, in English society."[1]

Britain's court system was complex and often bewildering. England and Wales shared a legal system, while Scotland and Ireland had similar but not identical legal systems. Criminal and civil law were separate, but most courts heard both types of cases. By the start of the Victorian period, the legal system—unreformed since the medieval era—included several competing and overlap-ping sets of courts that had developed over the centuries and used different bodies of law: common law and equity law, confusingly referred to as law and equity, along with ecclesiastical law. Some courts followed the common law, some equity law, but since courts had overlapping jurisdictions many cases could be tried under either system. There was no system of appeal. Lawyers received very little professional training and were expected to learn on the job by watching. Many cases were tried without lawyers. Trial outcomes often depended on the quality of lawyers', plaintiffs', and defendants' performances (rather than the arguments) given in court, and Victorians were well aware that performances in the courtroom were very like (though not identical to) those in the theater. As historian Rohan McWilliam remarks, "[i]n cultural terms, the distance between the law courts, the political platform and the theatre was not great."[2]

Legal historians emphasize a grand narrative in which a mid-Victorian triumph of contractual individualism—a focus on the responsible individual who entered into contracts with others—was followed by a late Victorian reassertion of more collective values. However, for most people, the rise and fall of contract had little to do with their day-to-day legal experience. Far more important were a perceived rise in crime, the development of police forces, changes in debt law and marriage law, and the decline of jury trials. High-profile cases, as well as more quotidian ones, served as vehicles by which larger political, social, and cultural issues became part of public discussion. Even Victorians who were never involved in legal cases themselves were aware of local and national arrests, trials, verdicts, and convictions. As the Assizes circuit courts made their way around each region of the country, they were greeted with festivities: there would be a special sermon in Church on "Assize Sunday," an Assizes ball, and a generally excited atmosphere. Trials and reports of them were a main way in which people learned about politics; about the foibles of the rich and famous; about male homosexuality (see Chapter 12), marriage and marital breakdown.

Growing paranoia concerning crime and "criminals" 1820–1870: New responses to crime and debt

From the late eighteenth century, middle- and upper-class Victorians became increasingly concerned about crime. This led to the biggest change of the first half-century of our period, the rise of police and prisons. The other big change was the rise of working-class debt. Both significantly changed the lives of working-class people.

High profile cases concerning politics

Between 1820 and 1870 the legal system provided the public with a number of high-profile events. The Queen Caroline Affair centered on a trial of the Queen before the House of Lords for adultery. There was also a high-profile breach of promise case: in 1824, when actress Maria Foote brought a breach of promise suit against former fiancé Joseph Hayne and won £3,000 damages, the case lasted a full day in the Court of King's Bench in London, and the report of the trial dominated the London newspapers the next day and appeared in newspapers around the country within the week. Divorce proceedings also attracted attention. Before 1857, one step in the complex and expensive process of ending a marriage was a trial for "criminal conversation," in which the divorcing husband sued his wife's lover for monetary damages. "Crim con" trials and reports of them were a popular form of scandalous entertainment, including as they did both specific accounts of illicit sex and insight into the lives of the powerful. The sensational Yelverton bigamy trial of 1861, in which minor Irish aristocrat Major Yelverton's marriage was revealed to be bigamous, transfixed the nation even as it educated it about both legal technicalities and the theatrical potential of the courtroom. The case became the inspiration for two novels, *Gentle Blood* (1861) and *A Wife and not a Wife* (1867).

During the early nineteenth century, elites became more and more concerned about crime. At the same time, they came to believe that crime, morality, and socio-economic status were all linked. More and more, crime was seen as something committed by the poor out of immorality. An 1818 select committee's description of "that class of persons who ordinarily commit crime, meaning the poor and indigent" [reveals the assumption that the poor were naturally criminal and the middle class and upper class were naturally law-abiding] Of particular concern to the middle and upper classes were crowds and rioting, violent strangers, juvenile offenders, and professional criminals. And they were convinced that crime was on the rise: in 1844 a writer in *Blackwood's Magazine* argued that "crime in England has increased 700 percent; in Ireland about 800 percent, and in Scotland above 3,500 percent,"[4] a statement that tells us more about Victorian anxieties and faith in statistics than about any actual rise in crime. The fear of working-class crime became a self-fulfilling prophecy: over the Victorian period, definitions of crime (and of debt) shifted to emphasize crimes committed (and debts incurred) by the poor.

Fears about crime were centered on cities; as we saw in Chapter 1, Victorians idealized their ever-shrinking countryside. Victorians were relatively unworried about rural crime, because it did not fit their perception of dangerous, professional criminals who lived in a city. The most common form of rural crime was poaching, and Victorians assumed that poachers were poor men seeking only to feed their families. However, recent work has shown that in mid-century Lancashire, rural poaching was the work of urban gangs, from Liverpool and other industrial towns, and that poached animals were destined for urban markets, not rural dinner tables. Country crime was urban too.

Demonstrations and mass meetings, which were such important political tools for the disenfranchised majority, seemed unruly, dangerous, and threatening to the middle and upper classes, even though Victorian crowds were far more peaceful than Georgian ones. In 1821, pro-Caroline crowds transformed the Queen's funeral procession into an anti-government protest. The debates and votes that led up to the 1832 Reform Act were accompanied by riots all over the country. In the late 1830s, there were a series of agitations protesting the implementation of the New Poor Law, and the violent Rebecca Riots (1839–1843) in Wales. Though historians have called the mid-Victorian decades a period of equipoise, in which working-class radicalism was dormant or absent, agitations continued during the second half of the nineteenth century. In the summer of 1855 over 100,000 people assembled in Hyde Park to protest a bill introduced into Parliament that would have limited shopping on Sundays, the only day of working-class leisure. In Hyde Park, huge crowds gathered in support of Italian independence leader, Giuseppe Garibaldi, in 1862, and in support of Polish revolutionaries in 1863 and 1864. In July 1866, the park's railings and flower beds were demolished during a Reform League protest demanding votes for working-class men. The constant specter of large crowds which, however peaceful in intent, seemed to many observers as if they could turn violent at any moment, meant that police presence at such gatherings became typical.

Trade union gatherings, in particular, were seen as a threat to law and order. A 1799 Combination Act had declared it illegal for workers to join together to demand higher pay or shorter hours from their employers; in other words, it had made all trade union activism, including gatherings and meetings, illegal. Agitation _garroting = mugging_

the illegalization and legalization of stri-kes and unions

by radical Francis Place and others had resulted in repeal in 1824, but an immediate outbreak of strikes led to an 1825 Combination Act that left unions legal but forbade them from any actions other than meeting to bargain over wages and work conditions; strikes were once again illegal. The 1825 Act was also peppered with vague terms such as "obstruct" and "intimidate" that left it unclear whether a trade union was legally a conspiracy and offered police and judges wide latitude to arrest and imprison union members. In spite of this, trade unions grew in size and in organization.

There was a disproportionate amount of attention paid to violent nighttime assaults by strangers in urban areas, called "garroting," similar to what we might call "mugging." There were garroting panics in 1856 and 1862, in part because of extensive press coverage. In the highest-profile case (which appeared in fictiona-lized form in Anthony Trollope's novel _Phineas Finn_), Member of Parliament Hugh Pilkington was attacked and robbed in London at one o'clock in the morning of July 17, 1862 after leaving a late session in the House of Commons. Press reports of garroting increased dramatically, and the public quickly became convinced that there was a serious problem. Garroting panic was so rampant that it became a topic of satire; Punch published several cartoons of men running from their own shadows or from trees that they were convinced were garrotters. One result of the panic was the hasty passage of the 1863 Security from Violence Act, popularly known as the "Garrotters' Act," which legalized whipping for those convicted of violent street robbery and remained law until 1948.[5]

Victorians also worried about juvenile crime; this reflected a demographic shift towards an increasingly younger population, generational tensions, and class tensions. Beginning with the formation of the "Committee for Investigating the Causes of the Alarming Increase of Juvenile Delinquency in the Metropolis" in 1815, Victorians convinced themselves that urban children were trained into gangs by professional thieves (as depicted in _Oliver Twist_). The popular press featured sensational stories of juvenile crime. The legal system began to focus on child offenders. Several new laws, including the Malicious Trespass Act of 1820, the Vagrancy Act of 1824, and the Larceny Act of 1827, either targeted or disproportionately impacted young offenders. The number of children indicted for felony rose. Poor young men, in particular, were targets of the police: one recent study suggests that the majority of people arrested for petty theft (of, for example, silk handkerchiefs in crowds at fairs or marketplaces) were boys and men under 25. In 1861, one out of every 29 males were arrested or summoned, compared with one out of every 120 females, and almost all of them were young and poor. Victorians also recognized that children were different from adults; from the middle of the century children were tried by different standards and incarcerated in child-only reformatories and truant schools.

Another fear was of the professional criminal. Victorians were convinced that there was a separate "criminal class" or even a criminal race, a persistent and ultimately comforting idea that separated the world into criminals on one side, and law-abiding citizens on the other. A wide variety of "hardened" criminals proliferated in fiction and in newspapers, including violent robbers and roving gangs. The nineteenth century's classificatory enthusiasm meant that criminals were increasingly studied and labeled, with one expert claiming that he had identified twelve separate types of professional criminals, from those "trained to it from their infancy" to "idle and dissolute labourers." He assured his readers that if they were to enter a thieves' district, they would immediately notice thieves' "strange physiognomy," explaining that child thieves look "very suspicious and preternaturally sharp," while adult thieves "look seedy and sleepy" and "lounge about." He also claimed that "habitual thieves, male and female, die of consumption, at under or about 35 years of age. Drink, debauchery, irregular hours, the sudden transitions from luxuries to a low prison diet" all led to consumption and an early death.[6] Italian criminologist Cesare Lombroso (1835–1909) insisted that criminal traits were inherited and pioneered the field of criminal physiognomy. One expression of the fear of professional criminals was the passage of the 1869 Habitual Criminals Act, which created a national register of people with a criminal record. (Also much feared were "ticket-of-leave" men, who were out of prison on what we would call parole or probation; a 1864 Penal Servitude Act required that they be kept under police supervision and punished for probation violations.)

[margin note: paranoia incarnate]

All of these fears, combined with developments we have seen in other chapters, such as the expansion of the state and the rise of the middle class and middle-class morality, led to significant changes in the legal practice and culture and the ways that ordinary people experienced the law. In the half-century between 1820 and 1870, while the court system remained confusing, policing became both disciplined and disciplining. Professional police forces developed in urban and rural areas across Britain. Police became a significant factor in the lives of the working class, both because police surveillance of everyday life became a feature of working-class life, especially for those who were young, male, or both, and because most policemen were recruited from the working classes.

Historian V.A.C. Gatrell argues that Victorians, in their quest for order, became accepting of what has called a "policeman-state," in which the state, the law, and the police focused on the detection, prevention, and punishment of crimes committed by poor people against rich people.[7] Another way of putting this is to say that the policeman-state was founded on the Victorian belief that most criminals were poor people, so that that criminality, immorality, and poverty were linked. Policemen walked the streets of poor neighborhoods, not the hallways of banks or manufacturing firms, and so uncovered crimes committed in public by working-class people, not crimes committed in private by their social superiors. While not all historians agree with Gatrell that the disciplinary policeman-state was the main development of the nineteenth century, or that the state was more present in the lives of the working class in the form of police surveillance than via more benevolent initiatives such as sanitation reform, it is clear that the establishment of police forces was a significant development.

The perception that crime was a serious problem led to the formation of professional police forces. Prior to the early nineteenth century Britain had no police forces. Law and order were maintained by a variety of paid and unpaid officers, including local night watchmen, parish constables, and magistrates (London also had "Bow Street Runners" who worked under the magistrates). This system, though amateur and patchwork, was fairly efficient. And even as state-organized police forces developed, other versions persisted, including locally-controlled watches and professional watchmen paid by private businesses (dock, canal, and railway companies all employed their own police to guard their goods and infrastructures). But, overall, policing became more centralized and more state-controlled, and control of police forces shifted from the parish or local level to more centralized control at the county, borough, or national level. Police became a pervasive presence in public spaces, walking the streets and roads of cities, towns, and villages, and public gatherings such as fairs and public executions, targeting the behaviors of the poor and the young.

Police forces began to appear in the 1810s. The 1829 Metropolitan Police Act, championed by Robert Peel (1788–1850), created a centralized, professional force of officers called Bobbies or Peelers (after Peel), who worked full-time, in uniform, for a salary. The London police force was not actually the first in Britain; there were earlier efforts in Ireland and Scotland in the 1810s, and by 1820 many Scottish burghs had already formed police forces. Nor were the Metropolitan Police's structures new; its hierarchal system of supervision, its beat system, and its use of uniforms all came from older parish watches. However, the Metropolitan Police was certainly a major development, and harbinger of more to come. It was also large: the Metropolitan Police numbered 3,000 in 1830, and would number 22,000 in 1914. Over the next few decades policing spread. The Burgh Police (Scotland) Act of 1833 and the Municipal Corporations Act 1835 led to (though they did not require) the establishment of police forces in almost 200 towns. The Dublin Police Force was established in 1836. The Rural Constabulary Act 1839 enabled (but did not require) Justices of the Peace (or JPs) in England and Wales to establish police forces in their rural counties, and by the mid-1850s many rural areas had embraced paid, professionalized policing. By 1851, there were around 13,000 police officers in England and Wales. The 1856 County and Borough Police Act and the 1857 General Police Act (Scotland) required all counties, boroughs, and burghs in England, Scotland, and Wales to have police forces. From 1857, then, every part of Britain had a police force.

The establishment of police forces meant the creation of the new profession of policeman. Police work was hard and poorly paid, and high turnover was a problem. Most officers were working-class men; their job was in tension with the leisure habits of their own class, especially its embrace of drink, gambling, and violent sports. The new forces focused on hierarchy and discipline in an attempt to set officers apart from popular and working-class culture. Some working-class people resisted the police as intrusive; others saw advantages to a policed community. Various Acts reorganized issues of qualifications, pay, and discipline and made policing more uniform. By the end of the nineteenth century, the police had become professional, organized, better-paid, and national. British society had been dramatically transformed into one in which policing was largely accepted by all classes as a basic institution.

The court and prison systems changed more slowly. Legal culture and the world of trials remained chaotic, theatrical, and frequently amateurish into the 1870s. However, there were some changes before 1870. The first was that many more cases, criminal and civil, were brought. This was possible because of an increased reliance on two types of lower courts: magistrate's courts and County Courts (the former longstanding, the latter established in 1846). Both increased in number and heard the bulk of cases, especially those involving small property crimes and small amounts of debt. Cases were tried quickly and without a jury. As criminal trials increased in number, they also became more structured and professional. Before the Victorian period, criminal cases were usually direct confrontations between victims and alleged perpetrators. The latter rarely had counsel, and even if they did, their barristers were not permitted to address the juries. However, following the passage in 1836 of the Prisoners' Counsel Act, anyone tried for a felony had the right to have their defense conducted by counsel. For many defendants, this right was empty without the means to hire a barrister, but the principle was important nonetheless. More and more, criminal trials became adversarial contests between counsels for the prosecution and the defense, rather than face-to-face confrontations between victims and those accused of committing crimes.

There were also changes in punishments. Prior to the Victorian period there were two principal punishments for serious crimes: execution, usually by hanging, and transportation (forced emigration), usually to North America or Australia. In the eighteenth century so many minor crimes were capital—that is, their sentence was death—that the system is often referred to as the "Bloody Code." Those who were executed were usually hanged publicly, and their hangings were spectacles attracting crowds of up to 100,000 people. Because the death penalty loomed so large, and seemed so harsh, many people refused to prosecute people they thought had committed crimes, many juries found defendants innocent whom they knew to be guilty, and many judges issued pardons or commuted sentences. As indeed they had to—by 1820, one observer calculated that actually hanging everyone condemned to death would mean four hangings per day every day of the year (except Sundays), a rate that no one could stomach. This system, in which harsh penalties were often threatened but rarely carried out, made criminal law seem arbitrary to most people; on the one hand, there were many crimes, including small property crimes such as pickpocketing, for which the penalty was death; on the other hand, cases were so rarely tried, and judicial pardons were so frequently granted, that actually being hanged for a crime was exceptional. In the decade and a half before 1820 the number of death sentences handed down tripled, which was surely significant, but at the same time pardon rates doubled.

In the early Victorian period, this system shifted to one of lighter sentences that were more consistently enforced. Treason and murder were maintained as capital crimes, but small offences such as pickpocketing and shoplifting were given new, non-capital punishments, which made victims more willing to prosecute and juries more willing to find guilty. Public hangings became less common and more criticized. The death penalty was reserved for serious crimes, and from 1841 it was effectively reserved for murder. The number of people sentenced to death and the number of hangings actually carried out both dropped about 90% in the first decade of Queen Victoria's reign. The last public hanging was in 1868.

* Transportation (to Australia) remained widely practiced until mid-century. By 1853 over 150,000 people (15% of whom were women) had been transported to Australia, mostly to Van Diemen's Land and to New South Wales, where until the 1830s most white women were convicts. Scottish judges very rarely sentenced convicts to transportation, so very few were Scottish, but fully one quarter were Irish. In the middle of the nineteenth century, public punishments (from whipping to the death penalty), penal transportation to Australia for serious crimes, and capital punishment, all common in the pre-Victorian period, declined or were abolished.

Penitentiaries and prisons developed to replace transportation and hanging with a combination of confinement, hard labor, and probation (via a ticket-of-leave). The most common sentence was for three months of imprisonment in a small local prison. Since crime was the result of moral failure, prison regimes emphasized cleanliness, strict scheduling, surveillance, and religion, with silence and solitary confinement the preferred punishments in large national prisons. However, we cannot generalize too much: prison regimes varied widely by locality, and some were far more humane than others. Penitentiaries and prisons were intended to isolate, reform, and mentally discipline convicts, and used a combination of physical punishments (most commonly lashings) and hard labor to exhaust the body and crush the spirit of the prisoner. Even those convicted of lesser crimes were isolated and forced to do repetitive tasks (such as walking on treadmills) as a form of discipline.

similar to the idea of the book "1984".

One of the most important Victorian ideas about the prison came from utilitarian thinker, legal reformer, and all-around polymath Jeremy Bentham. Bentham noted the inefficacy of penal transportation and capital punishment in deterring crime, and so turned to the notion of the prison. He conceptualized a form of prison he called the "panopticon." The panopticon had a circular design that allowed a small number of prison guards and officials to observe all prisoners at all times, without the prisoners knowing when they were being observed. He believed that this system, in which prisoners had to assume that guards (and more broadly society) could see their every move, would promote social order. No panopticon was ever built (though in the late twentieth century Michel Foucault argued that Bentham's panopticon was a metaphor for a wide range of Victorian and post-Victorian disciplinary regimes in which we are all constantly under surveillance from the state and one another). But the architecture of the Pentonville Prison in London (1842) was influenced by Bentham's panopticon.

Civil law is far less studied by historians than criminal law, but touched the lives of many people. A common way in which people interacted with the legal system was through debt. Credit and debt tied people together in webs of trust, character, and dependency that revealed how theoretical were contemporary legal and liberal-economic theories about the autonomous individual who operated independently in the rational marketplace. Merchants had long extended credit to upper-class and middle-class customers, who kept running accounts with retailers of everything from furniture to groceries and paid their bills only once a year, at Christmas. Enjoying such credit was dependent on maintaining a good reputation. Over the nineteenth century, rising wages and the Victorian retail revolution led more merchants to extend credit to more people, including working-class people. When debts went unpaid, many turned to the legal system for redress. Victorian Britain—like twenty-first century America—had growing numbers of people whose unpaid debts brought them into conflict with their creditors and the legal system. At the same time, trials and punishments for debt, and perceptions of debtors, all changed significantly.

Up through the early Victorian period, prosecuted and incarcerated debtors were generally men of at least some social status, which remained undamaged by their imprisonment. Historical painter Benjamin Robert Haydon, who in the 1820s and 1830s owed several thousand pounds to various creditors, and was imprisoned four times before he died in 1846, always maintained that neither his debts, not imprisonments for them, sullied his character in the slightest. In debtors' prison he met many upper-class men, and he was outraged at "rascally tradesmen" whose use of debt law had imprisoned "men of fortune and family."[8] Debt was seen as a matter of bad luck. Imprisoned debtors were not as criminals or as wrongdoers at all, but rather innocent victims of misfortune. Debtors' prisons were full: imprisoned debtors were the largest single group of inmates. But debtors' prisons were separate from other prisons and were such porous institutions that to our eyes they were hardly deserving of the name. Those in debtors' prison did not do hard labor or suffer under punitive conditions. They had to pay for their own upkeep, and were permitted frequent visitors, who brought them food, books, and other items from outside. Some prisoners even had their families come to live with them in debtors' prison. Others paid a fee to live in the precinct outside the prison, called the "Rules," rather than in the prison itself. Debt was a popular literary topic, and some of the most famous novels read or written by Victorians—including Samuel Richardson's *Pamela* (1740), which was popular and widely read for decades after its publication, Elizabeth Gaskell's *Ruth* (1853), and Charles Dickens' *Bleak House* (1853)—feature debt as a central aspect of life (as well as of plot). Similarly, debtors' prison was a favorite subject of novelistic depiction, with characters in Dickens' *Pickwick Papers* (1837), *David Copperfield* (1850), and *Little Dorrit* (1857) all incarcerated for debt, and characters in William Thackeray's *Vanity Fair* (1848) and Anthony Trollope's *Framley Parsonage* (1861) scrambling to avoid that fate.

Starting in the 1830s and 1840s, however, all of this began to change, to the advantage of the upper and middle classes and to the disadvantage of the working class. Retail credit followed new habits of consumption and spread down the social scale. Widespread credit made nineteenth-century styles of consumption possible. It also produced a new phenomenon: working-class debtors, whom the new County Courts made vulnerable to prosecution. (Interestingly, although married women could not legally incur debt and therefore could not technically appear in debt cases, County Court judges heard them because they recognized that in practice working-class wives were the financial managers of their families.) Financial panics provoked by the expansion of credit trading, mounting into-lerance of the aristocratic tendency to incur large debts with their greengrocers, dressmakers, and the like, the rising cost of caring for the nation's poor, and the rising number of inmates in debtors' prisons all conspired to change perceptions of debt and debtors. As working-class consumer debt rose, debtors were seen more negatively and treated more punitively. Debt was now seen as a personal failing that was indicative of character. More and more, law and society alike labeled debtors profligate and responsible for their own misfortune. At the same time, the 1834 Poor Law (see Chapter 2) had reinforced the notion that financial woes were the fault of the individual, and that while the state might provide a safety net, it would be a minimal and punitive one.

Small debts owed by working-class people were, more and more, an issue that occupied the courts. Working-class debtors were blamed for their own debt, brought before the County Courts, and tried summarily (without a jury). The legal process of debt recovery, originally intended for recovering large amounts from affluent people, was used to demand small amounts from working-class people with consumer debt. Debtors' prisons filled with working-class debtors. Victorians began to reconsider the many privileges that debtors enjoyed in prison and began treating debtors more like other prisoners. Separate debtors' prisons were abolished altogether in the 1860s. New laws favored wealthier debtors: those whose debts were over £50 were no longer vulnerable to imprisonment and could declare bankruptcy (and arrange to pay their creditors only a fraction of what they owed). But working-class people with debts of less than £50 could not declare bankruptcy and were imprisoned. Imprisonment for debt, stripped of its genteel connotations and its customary privileges, no longer appealed to novelists (who by and large turned to divorce proceedings for new plots).[9]

There were other well-known civil actions as well. These included the breach of promise of marriage action, in which plaintiffs—most of whom were working-class and lower middle-class women—whose fiancés had broken their engagements could sue their ex-lovers for their disappointed prospects and their broken hearts. In the early Victorian period breach of promise suits were popular; promises of marriage were taken seriously in court, and the action provided working-class and lower middle-class women with an opportunity to publicly perform their virtue. Before 1870 breach of promise was so popular that most plaintiffs won their cases and were awarded substantial damages for their emotional pain and suffering: in the case of *Jones* vs. *Yeend* (1850), for example, Miss Jones' barrister described her as "injured in reputation, health, spirits and reduced to a state from which she would probably never recover." Winning meant publicly demonstrating that they were not loose women whose suitors had recoiled after learning of their pasts, but virtuous women who had been unjustly deserted by heartless cads; it was not unusual for a woman to claim that she cared nothing for monetary damages but felt "compelled to bring the action to vindicate her character and honour."[10]

Another well-known civil action was for divorce; it was established in 1857 and made divorce more attainable than before.

1870–1914: Detectives, prisons, marriage and divorce

*

In the later Victorian period, scandalous cases continued to delight the public, with divorces a particular favorite. Police forces and prisons continued to develop, trials by jury declined, and there were important changes to marriage law.

High-profile cases continued to fascinate the public. Politician Charles Dilke (1843–1911)'s promising career ended in 1886 when he was named as the co-respondent (that is, the adulterous lover) in the Crawford divorce case, and the political career of popular Irish Home Rule leader Charles Parnell (1846–1891) ended in 1890 when Captain William O'Shea named Parnell in his divorce from his wife Kitty. The most talked about trials of the nineteenth century were those of the Tichborne Claimant, which revolved around issues of imposture and of class privilege and provided the Victorian working class with a flamboyant hero. In 1865, Arthur Orton, an English butcher living in Wagga Wagga, Australia, returned to Britain and claimed to be Sir Roger Tichborne, the heir to a Catholic aristocratic family's estate and title, who had been lost at sea over a decade earlier. Although the Claimant (who weighed about 27 stone, or 378 pounds) looked nothing like Roger Tichborne (who had been slim), was unable to speak French (in which Roger Tichborne had been fluent), and knew no details about the Tichborne family or Roger Tichborne's past, between 1867 and 1886 he had thousands of supporters and he and his story—full of twists, turns, and all manner of melodramatic elements—were everywhere. The heart of the affair was the two very long legal trials in which the Tichborne Claimant appeared, a civil trial in 1871–1872 and a criminal trial in 1873–1874 (he lost both and was sent to prison). There were broadsheets and music hall songs about him, Staffordshire figurines of him, pubs named for him, and a wax sculpture on display at Madame Tussaud's. The Claimant's lawyer, Edward Kenealy (1819–1880), created a Tichborne association, ran a Tichborne newspaper, and at the height of the movement, was even elected to Parliament in 1875 as a Tichborne MP. The question of whether Arthur Orton was Sir Roger Tichborne dominated mass culture and conversation for much of the 1870s.[11] *Mostly paranoia*

Concerns about crime and disorder persisted. Demonstrations and riots were a concern. In the 1870s, there were violent confrontations between the evangelical Salvation Army and urban Irish Catholics all over the country. There were also many employment-related demonstrations. The first Trades Union Congress (TUC) meeting was held in 1868 in Manchester. In 1886, a demonstration in Trafalgar Square protesting unemployment turned violent. During the end of the nineteenth century and the first part of the twentieth century, and especially after 1905, the government became more concerned with industrial disputes and more inclined to pressure employers to recognize unions. Working-class people involved in trade unions and unemployment protests felt themselves to be expressing their

Figure 10.1 Judge Alexander Cockburn presiding over the trial of the Tichborne Claimant, 1873–1874, *Tichborne vs. Lushington.* Butcher Arthur Orton, also known as Thomas Castro, claimed to be Lady Henrietta Tichborne's son Sir Roger Charles. After his conviction for fraud he was tried for perjury in a court case which lasted 188 days. The trials were Victorian sensations.

Photo by Hulton Archive/Getty Images.

legitimate political agency, but many from the employing classes perceived these demonstrations as threats that required police surveillance.

Gangs offered a sense of protection to the younger generation of the time.

Many continued to worry about violent attacks by strangers, professional criminals, and young criminals. Fifteen years after the garroting panic of 1862, a flurry of armed burglaries in London between 1877 and 1886 sparked panic about professional criminals. The never-solved murders of several women in 1888 in London's East End by "Jack the Ripper" stoked existing fears. Regarding juvenile crime, gangs were a particular concern after 1870. Gangs were socially important to many working-class teenagers. Historian Andrew Davies has studied gangs in the working-class sections of two industrial cities, Manchester and Salford. His work indicates that gangs were neighborhood-based, and offered opportunities for young men to demonstrate their masculinity. Fully 90% of those charged in gang-related crimes were teenage boys. But not all gang members were boys; girls were also participants in gang violence, though they were arrested far less frequently and given much lighter sentences when they were arrested.[12]

Police forces continued to grow, as did the presence of police in the lives of working-class people. Police forces grew relative to the population: in 1861 there was one policemen for every 937 people in England and Wales, but by 1891 there was one for every 731 people (and by 1951 there would be one for every 661 people), and in urban areas, the proportion was far greater. From the 1870s, policing became an ever-more respectable working-class profession. While policemen were discouraged from taking part in many aspects of working-class culture, centrally drinking and male-on-male violence, most historians argue that culturally they remained members of the working class. Policing was an attractive job to those seeking respectability. In 1901 men and boys had a one in 24 chance of being arrested or summonsed, and urban working-class men and boys had to expect to have one or more confrontations with the police in their teens and twenties. The cost of policing grew too: the cost to the nation of maintaining its police forces was £1.5 million in 1861 and £6.5 million in 1911.

Another way in which the state increased its surveillance of the working class was via its intrusion into the lives of prostitutes. Prostitutes (who were usually poor and young) were vulnerable to police harassment, particularly in port and garrison towns during the enforcement of the Contagious Diseases Acts between 1864 and 1886 in Britain (and for far longer in parts of the empire). More and more, Victorians had the sense that their actions were being watched by the police, who could arrest them—especially if they were young, working-class, or seemed to pose a threat to authority—on vague charges of "disorderly conduct." (Though the young and the poor were not the only people targeted by the police and the legal system; other targeted groups included men who had sex with men, especially after the passage of the Criminal Amendment Act 1885, which re-inscribed existing penalties for sex between men (see Chapter 12).)

This later period saw a new development in policing, the creation of the detective. Detectives became a well-known part of police forces in the 1870s, with a dedicated Criminal Investigation Department (CID) established in 1878. By the early 1880s, detectives in the London Metropolitan police were arresting 18,000 people every year, and the CID became a large and important part of the Home Office. The detective also proved a rich narrative resource. Detectives first emerged in Britain in the 1870s; the same decade, not coincidentally, saw the rise of the detective novel and of the sensation novel, both of which revolved around secrets, plots, crimes, and broken laws. In these, the detective was usually the hero, or at least a clever and admirable figure, which indicates that Victorians were very comfortable with the idea of police-enforced order and surveillance. Among middle-brow readers, Arthur Conan Doyle's famous detective Sherlock Holmes, who first appeared in a short story in *Beeton's Christmas Annual* in 1887, was popular. Among less educated and less affluent readers, especially working-class boys, detective Sexton Blake, who appeared from 1893 in popular magazines such as *Union Jack* and *The Boys' Friend*, was a hero.

Prisons also continued to develop, with attention now paid to the needs of juvenile prisoners. Policy-makers developed systems that aimed to punish children in age-appropriate ways. From the middle of the century children were tried by different standards and incarcerated in child-only reformatories and truant schools as well as prisons. By the late nineteenth century the "juvenile offender" was a well-established concept in British law and society. The trend towards dealing with young offenders separately was formalized by two 1908 Acts, the Children's Act and the Prevention of Crime Act. These created special juvenile courts and special juvenile prisons called "Borstals," where children would be reformed through a regime of discipline, education, and physical labor.

These youth-specific institutions were important because after 1870 prisons became much harsher in their conditions and punishments. From 1869 until 1895, under Director of Convict Prisons, Edmund Du Cane (1830–1903), prison punishments became increasingly harsher. Du Cane was a proponent of the "silent system," in which prisoners were given spartan living quarters, forbidden from communicating with one another, and made to do hard labor. Such methods were quite cruel, and several prisoner suicides were widely criticized. However, the shift to harsher practices should not be overstated; the changes were gradual and uneven, with many officials resistant. Rates of imprisonment for small crimes began to drop. And there were critics of the growth of prisons: in 1872 MP J.H. Scourfield complained that legislation had grown so much that the best "portray[al of] the advancing civilisation of England might be . . . the representation of a prison."[13] By the end of century many were aware of and opposed to prison cruelty. Jurist A. Wood Renton stated that the prison that relied on cruelty and deprivation was a "manufactory of lunatics and criminals,"[14] and an 1895 Committee Report recommending that the cruelest practices be stopped led to some reforms. However, prisons remained places of strict discipline and cruelty until after World War One.

the confusion of what to do or how to precede with these contradictory jurisdictions

To legal theorists, the most serious problem plaguing the British legal system in the later Victorian period was the overlapping and competing jurisdictions of the common law and equity courts. Judicature Acts, championed by jurists Lords Selborne and Cairns and passed between 1873 and 1875, tried to rationalize the court system by combining the various courts into a single system and creating appeals-level and supreme courts. While these Acts did not accomplish all that their writers had hoped—equity law did not uniformly dominate over common law, as they had intended, and the House of Lords remained the highest court, against their wishes—they did make the court system more logical, and were part of the transformation of a chaotic and amateur system into one more that was more organized and more dominated by professionals.

For most people, though, the more notable development in the second half of the nineteenth century was a steep decline in the proportion of cases heard by juries. The British believed that the system of trial by jury was a defining part of their legal system and a guarantor of liberties. But in practice juries did not guarantee fair trials, especially to the poor. Property requirements meant that jurors (in addition to being male and over the age of 21) were mostly middle-class men who often favored their own class. Well-off defendants could pay a fee to have their cases heard before "special juries" of men even further up the social scale, which could affect both trial and verdict. Jury trials were brief and rushed: most trials, even for felony cases, lasted less than an hour. Defendants were brought before the jury in batches rather than singly, and juries rarely bothered to retire; they simply deliberated briefly in the jury box and then announced their (often seemingly arbitrary) verdicts. Many legal professionals were sharply critical of juries. Judges tried to limit their influence by stressing that juries had to obey judges' directions and could only concern themselves with matters of fact, not of law. Over the Victorian period the proportion of cases tried before a jury declined steeply, from about 90% at mid-century to only 50% by the 1880s (a figure it remained at until World War One). Jury trials remained the rule in cases where people's reputations and characters were at stake (such as libel cases), were still seen as very important in any case involving moral standards and culpability, and were fiercely maintained in the era's more lurid cases. The verdict of one's peers was still seen as a key part of British freedoms. But in 1900 88% of non-violent larcenies were tried without a jury, and the vast majority of cases involving small debts, were tried without a jury.

Also important were a number of shifts regarding marriage law. The breach of promise action, once so popular, came under attack, as the public became suspicious of claims about broken hearts and damages. Success rates and median awards for breach of promise dropped; debate and contempt became more common. The number of divorces rose every decade, well into the twentieth century. Furthermore, from 1878 judicial separations could be granted by local magistrates. Separations were simpler and cheaper than divorce, and absolved spouses of responsibility for one another's debts. By 1900, 10,000 spouses per year—mostly wives—were requesting separation orders.[15] (As we saw in Chapter 8, new laws also allowed married women to own property.) Divorce cases became a popular source of sexual and marital rubbernecking and of scandal. Court audiences and newspaper court report readers learned all sorts of titillating tidbits. In *Birch* vs. *Birch* in 1872, Louisa Birch accused her husband of using "French letters" or condoms—considered appropriate only for sex with prostitutes—during marital "connection."[16] Extensive press coverage of divorces was seen by some commentators as a threat to public morality, especially as literacy increased and non-elite readership grew.

Notes

1 Margot Finn, "Law's Empire: English Legal Cultures At Home and Abroad," *The Historical Journal* 48 (2005): 298.
2 Rohan McWilliam, *The Tichborne Claimant: A Victorian Sensation* (London: Hambledon, 2007), 254.
3 Select Committee on the State of the Police of the Metropolis, 3rd Report, PP 1818, VIII, p. 34, quoted in V.A.C. Gatrell, "Crime, Authority and the Policeman-State," in F.M.L. Thompson (ed.), *The Cambridge Social History of Britain 1750–1950*, Vol. 3 (Cambridge: Cambridge University Press, 1990), p. 251.
4 Quoted in Gatrell, p. 252.
5 R. Sindall, "London Garotting Panics of 1856 and 1862," *Social History* 12.3 (Oct 1987): 351–359, p. 356.
6 W. Holland, "Professional Thieves," *Cornhill Magazine*, vi (1862): 642, 653.
7 Gatrell, pp. 243–310.
8 Margot C. Finn, *The Character of Credit: Personal Debt in English Culture, 1740–1914* (Cambridge, Cambridge University Press, 2003), pp. 67–74.
9 Finn, pp. 151–154.
10 *Morning Chronicle*, March 27, 1850, 7, and *Morning Chronicle*, April 19, 1830, 4.
11 McWilliam.

12 Andrew Davies, "Youth Gangs, Masculinity and Violence in Late Victorian Manchester and Salford," *Journal of Social History* 32.2 (Winter 1998): 349–369.

13 P. Smith, *Disraelian Conservatism and Social Reform* (1967), p. 162, quoted in Gatrell.

14 John Hostettler, *A History of Criminal Justice in England and Wales* (Hook, UK: Waterside Press, 2009), p. 244.

15 Gail L. Savage, "The Operation of the 1857 Divorce Act, 1860–1910 a Research Note," *Journal of Social History* 16.4 (Summer 1983): 104–105.

16 Quoted in A. James Hammerton, *Cruelty and Companionship: Conflict in Nineteenth-Century Married Life* (London: Routledge, 1991), p. 110.

Relevant fiction students might enjoy

Charles Dickens, *Pickwick Papers* (1837)
Charles Dickens, *Oliver Twist* (1838)
William Thackeray, *Vanity Fair* (1848)
Charles Dickens, *Bleak House* (1853)
Charles Dickens, *Little Dorrit* (1855–1857)
Mrs Henry Wood, *East Lynne* (1861)
Anthony Trollope, *Phineas Finn* (1868)
Arthur Morrison, *Tales of Mean Streets* (1894)
Arthur Morrison, *A Child of the Jago* (1896)
Arthur Conan Doyle's Sherlock Holmes stories, including *A Study in Scarlet* (1887), *The Sign of Four* (1890), *The Adventures of Sherlock Holmes* (1892), and *The Return of Sherlock Holmes* (1905)

Further reading

Many works by Clive Emsley, including *Crime and Society in England, 1750–1900* (London: Longman, 1987).

Margot Finn, *The Character of Credit: Personal Debt in English Culture, 1740–1914* (Cambridge: Cambridge University Press, 2003).

V.A.C. Gatrell, "Crime, Authority and the Policeman-State," in F.M.L. Thompson (ed.), *The Cambridge Social History of Britain, 1750–1950, Volume 3, Social Agencies and Institutions*, (Cambridge University Press Online Publication Date 2008, Print Publication 1990), pp. 243–310

Joanne Klein, *Invisible Men: The Secret Lives of Police Constables in Liverpool, Manchester, and Birmingham, 1900–1939* (Liverpool: Liverpool University Press, 2010).

Allyson N. May, *The Bar and the Old Bailey, 1750–1850* (Chapel Hill, NC: University of North Carolina Press, 2003).

Rohan McWilliam, *The Tichborne Claimant* (London: Bloomsbury, 2007).

Various articles by Helen Rogers.

Haia Shpayer-Makov, *The Making of a Policeman: The Social History of a Labour Force in Metropolitan London, 1829–1914* (Farnham: Ashgate 2002).

Online resources

Conviction: stories from a nineteenth-century prison: http://convictionblog.com/

Old Bailey online: The Proceedings of the Old Bailey, 1674–1913: http://www.oldbailey online.org/

Glasgow Police Museum: http://gphs1800.tripod.com/

Metropolitan Police—History: http://content.met.police.uk/Site/history

11 "Good, murderous melodramas"

Arts, entertainment, and print culture

Introduction

In *Oliver Twist* (1838), a friendless orphan falls in with a gang of child pickpockets; he is mothered by a fellow criminal Nancy, who is beaten to death by her lover. In *The Woman in White* (1859), a young woman must save her sister, who has been confined to an asylum under a false identity by her evil husband. In *Adam Bede* (1859), a desperate young woman kills her newborn baby and is to be hanged, but has her sentence commuted to transportation at the last minute thanks to the intervention of the remorseful young aristocrat who seduced her. In *Lady Audley's Secret* (1862), a beautiful and innocent-looking young woman, who claims to be an orphan, marries a wealthy widower; in truth she is already married, has faked her own death, and is determined to remain Lady Audley at any cost, even if it means killing her real husband when he returns from gold-prospecting in Australia. In *Tess of the d'Urbervilles* (1891), a young woman is seduced by a thoughtless young aristocrat; she suffers terribly for the rest of her life, until years later she stabs him, spends a few days of happiness with the man she loves, and is then hanged for her crime. In the early twentieth century, in the Sexton Blake stories, the detective is assisted by a streetwise orphan; fights the Chinese villain Wu Ling; and pursues a criminal who turns out to be his brother.

Victorian artistic, theatrical, and print cultures were rife with conflicts between good and evil. They featured events that were "sensational" and "extraordinary": those words appear again and again in everything from newspaper headlines to advertisements for novels to critical responses to literature and drama. Complex plots revolved around marriage, concealed identities, inheritances, and last-minute reprieves, and often featured debt, entailed estates, detectives, and other features of the Victorian legal system. They also featured violence. Newspaper reporting on violent crimes functioned as both news and entertainment, not just in popular newspapers such as *Lloyd's Weekly Newspaper* but in "quality" papers such as the *Times* as well. Street performances of Punch and Judy puppet shows, which were extremely popular in the early Victorian period, told the humorous story of a husband who beat his wife to death. Murder and public executions by hanging of criminals were of interest to Victorians of all classes; hangings were well-attended and festive occasions, and were accompanied by paraphernalia such as souvenir figurines of murderers being hanged and figures at Madame Tussaud's Chamber of Horrors. "Penny bloods" or "penny dreadfuls"—inexpensive works of serial fiction to whose plots violence was central—were incredibly popular (especially among young men). Tales of horrible murderers who stalked urban and rural areas—including the fictional Spring-heeled Jack and the very real Jack the Ripper—fascinated people of all classes and appeared in middle-class newspapers as well as working-class rumor-mills. Arts and print culture were also full of spectacular and extreme effects, both physical and emotional: plays, novels, and music hall programs alike featured gasp- and tear-inducing moments, snowstorms and shipwrecks, acrobats and magic tricks, elaborate scenery and lighting.

We need only think about how often we judge others by their taste in movies or books to see the importance of cultural products to a society. Moreover arts and literature were often connected to politics, not only when newspapers reported political news, but when the arts set the stage for or even shaped the political. Benjamin Disraeli's trilogy of "Condition of England" novels (*Coningsby* (1844), *Sybil, or The Two Nations* (1845), and *Tancred* (1847)) were both literature and the manifesto of the Young England political movement he led; Thomas Carlyle (1795–1881) was primarily an essayist and historian, but his writings influenced several generations of Victorian writers of both fiction and non-fiction. Furthermore, the roots of many aspects of our own popular entertainment, fiction, and journalism cultures can be found in the Victorian period. British cultural products were particularly important because during the nineteenth century and early twentieth century, Britain was the center of all Anglophone (English-speaking) culture. Its cultural products were consumed in and shaped the cultures of Canada and the United States, and the entire British empire, particularly Australia, New Zealand, southern Africa, and English-speaking India. Conversely many cultural products, in particular American ones, made the trip across the ocean to appear in London, the capital of the English-speaking world. In the 1840s American minstrel shows came to London; at the end of the century Buffalo Bill's Wild West show, which strove to embody all that was quintessentially American, did too. Britain was a destination for culture and British culture, far from being provincial, regional, or even national, was a global culture.

In the consumption of entertainment, respectability was often a theme; many people strove to demonstrate their respectability by pursuing certain forms of entertainment, such as brass bands or elevating lectures, or by eschewing others, such as the alcohol-infused music halls. Working-class people who embraced temperance had to, by definition, reject pub culture, which was often a locus of music and other entertainment, and needed to find or create alternatives. Also important was the movement for "rational recreation" that we saw in Chapter 1; middle-class reformers were intent on luring working-class people away from traditional pastimes to more uplifting ones such as lectures, long walks in the countryside, and certain improving forms of music and theatre.

The Victorian age also had its distinctive forms of architecture and painting. There were several bursts of church building over the period (see Chapter 13); many of these churches still stand, and make the Victorian era present today.

Medieval and gothic styles were popular for churches. Many secular buildings featured wide expanses of glass and steel, especially after the success of the Crystal Palace in 1851. In England, Joseph Paxton, the architect of the Crystal Palace, was a promoter of glass and iron structures; in Scotland, Glaswegian architect Alexander Thomson (aka "Greek" Thomson) was a proponent of large windows of plate glass, especially for commercial buildings such as department stores. Thomson was also well-known for his "Egyptian-Greek" style, for his Gothic and Romanesque buildings, and for several large churches, including Queen's Park Church, which helped to shape and define Glasgow (considered the second city of the empire after London). In the late nineteenth century and early twentieth century, William Morris and others in the Arts and Crafts movement promoted medieval and traditional forms of architecture and interior design that they considered both aesthetically pleasing and anti-industrial.

William Powell Frith (1819–1909) was a prominent portraitist and painter of scenes of contemporary social life; his best-known picture, *Derby Day* (1858), depicting all the classes mixing at the annual horse race, won instant acclaim, and *The Railway Station* (1862) depicts a middle-class family—Frith's own—as the sons leave for boarding school. Fairy paintings enjoyed a vogue; Richard Dadd (1817–1886) was particularly successful in this genre. Animal painters included John Frederick Herring (1795–1865), Richard Ansdell (1815–1885), William Huggins (1820–1884), and Gourlay Steell, (1819–1894). The rebellious badboys of Victorian painting were the self-styled "pre-Raphaelite Brotherhood," a group of artists who began as painters but later expanded into poetry and criticism. Led by William Holman Hunt (1827–1910), John Everett Millais (1829–1896) and Dante Gabriel Rossetti (1828–1882), the pre-Raphaelites sought to revitalize art by challenging overly academic styles. They combined realistic representations with symbolism, and favored eroticized Shakespearean and medieval scenes.

Music was extremely important; the Victorian was a highly musical age. The Victorians were, overall, accomplished musicians; indeed, musical knowledge and technical expertise of the average Briton was far higher than before or since. There was a standard repertoire that spanned class lines, and people of all classes routinely gathered in their own or friends' homes, often on a Sunday evening, to sing and play music. Middle-class families were most likely to make music at home, but lower middle-class and working-class families did too, as much for pleasure as to demonstrate their upward mobility. Learning to play an instrument at home could also lead to job opportunities for lower middle-class and working-class people. Victorian Britain had churches in need of piano and organ players, orchestras and bands in need of players, and students in need of teachers; many people made their living, or part of it, in music performance or teaching. Key musical sites included the pub and church or chapel (for Anglicans and Nonconformists, especially working-class Methodists, respectively). In the north especially, amateur choruses, brass bands, orchestras, and Gilbert & Sullivan societies abounded. Brass bands were a facet of a larger working-class movement for self-improvement. They were part of a cult of respectability, not least because they involved making music without drinking alcohol as was the rule in pubs and music halls. For the upper classes, attendance at the opera was key to maintaining social and cultural status. Until the early 1830s, aristocrats who attended the opera had been more interested in the social scene in the boxes than in anything going on onstage, but from the 1830s opera was seen as high art that required attentive listening. By the end of the century, operatic music was also performed for less elite audiences in music halls, by brass bands, and by touring opera companies.

In this chapter, we will focus on plays, novels, newspapers, and music halls, by which the Victorian era is particularly well-illuminated. These are characterized by a fascinating combination of melodrama, spectacle, and morality. Theatre, print culture, and music hall were mutually interdependent and influential. Theatres and music halls competed for audience members and borrowed one another's techniques, with theatres using music halls' quick pacing and music halls featuring melodramatic scenes that came from both plays and novels (and, at the end of the century, from operas). Theatre borrowed from print culture, with some of the most frequently-produced plays adapted from best-selling novels. Literature was also shaped by theatre: Charles Dickens (1812–1870) worked as a reporter as a young man, was enamored with the theatre all his life, and often gave melodramatic and performative readings on his reading tours. While his various attempts to act, playwright, produce, and direct were never very successful, his work was shaped by key theatrical tropes. His protégé, Wilkie Collins (1824–1889), was more successful at crossing over to theatre, and wrote plays as well as novels. Sensation novels borrowed many of the techniques of melodramatic theater, and were in turn frequently adapted to the stage.

Theatre, novels, and music hall also interacted with real experience in complex ways. In 1840, valet Francois Benjamin Courvoisier murdered his employer, former Member of Parliament Lord William Russell. He claimed that he had been inspired by a novel, William Harrison Ainsworth's *Jack Sheppard* (1839), about a cunning thief, prompting commentators to worry about whether novels were dangerous to the morals of the lower class. Dickens, in his preface to the third edition of *Oliver Twist* in 1841, defended the realistic depiction of criminals in fiction (perhaps self-servingly, as *Oliver Twist* and *Jack Sheppard* were comparable novels). In addition, in *Oliver Twist* Dickens includes a reflection on the similarities between melodramatic plays, lived experience, and (by implication) his own novel:

> It is the custom on the stage: in all good, murderous melodramas: to present the tragic and the comic scenes, in as regular alternation. . . . The hero sinks upon his straw bed, weighed down by fetters and misfortunes; and, in the next scene, his faithful but unconscious squire regales the audience with a comic song. . . . Such changes appear absurd; but they are not so unnatural as they would seem at first sight. The transitions in real life from well-spread boards to death-beds, and from mourning weeds to holiday garments, are not a whit less startling. . . . [but] [t]he actors in the mimic life of the theatre . . . are at once condemned as outrageous and preposterous.[1]

Fiction and theatre were, then, no more outrageous than life itself. But anxieties persisted; in 1890s and the early twentieth century, debates raged over whether the "New Journalism" reflected or caused public demand for less serious journalism, and whether "New Woman" novels reflected existing behaviors, or inspired otherwise docile young women to defy sexual norms.

1820–1870: Melodrama, early music halls, and the rise of the novel

In the earlier Victorian period, theatre, and in particular melodrama, thrived, especially after an 1843 Act abolished the distinction between legitimate and illegitimate theatres. Forerunners of music halls called free-and-easies, singing saloons, or concert rooms flourished and began to develop into large music halls. And print culture—in particular, novels, especially serially-published novels, magazines, and newspapers—grew quickly, aided by Victorian Britain's relatively high literacy rates.

Theatre-going was a favorite pastime (of the upper and working classes, though it was seen as unrespectable by a large portion of the middle class until mid-century. One reason that the most respectable middle-class people avoided the theater was that audiences could be extremely boisterous, talking throughout the performance and even stopping the players). Popular actors—including Charles Kean (1811–1868), well-known for his portrayal of Hamlet, his wife Ellen Tree Kean (1805–1880), for whom Sheridan Knowles wrote several plays, and "O" Smith, (1786–1855), known for ominous characters such as assassins and sorcerers—were celebrities. There was a burst of theatre-building in the 1820s and 1830s, so that by 1830 London had dozens of theatres, and most provincial towns had more than one (Liverpool had six). From the 1820s until the 1860s an evening at the theatre was long and varied: it included a short introductory piece called the "curtain-raiser," a main play called the mainpiece—usually a melodrama or Shakespeare—and one or even two afterpieces (usually farces). The whole affair ended well after midnight, and the cheapest tickets were only a few shillings, with half-price admission for those who arrived after 9:00pm. Upper- and upper middle-class theatergoers, who liked to arrive fashionably late, would miss the curtain-raiser but catch the mainpiece; working-class patrons who worked until well into the evening could arrive after 9:00pm and see the farce (timed to start after half-price entry).

But performances were not confined to public theatres or to professional actors. Throughout the Victorian period, middle-class and upper-class families were fond of private theatricals, including charades and *tableaux vivants*, in which families and friends would stage scenes at home for one another's entertainment. Such scenes are described in many nineteenth-century novels, including *Mansfield Park* (1814) and *Vanity Fair* (1848). Amateur performances for the public were another popular pastime. Charles Dickens was an active enthusiast and promoter of amateur productions (excerpts of his works were favorite choices), which were put on in local theatres or other community spaces, usually to raise money for a charitable

Figure 11.1 "My Missis Thinks She's Trilby" comic song in the craze following the eponymous barefoot heroine of an 1895 melodrama.

© Lordprice Collection/Alamy.

cause. Most published versions of plays were aimed at amateur actors; series such as *Dicks' Standard Plays* and *French's Acting Edition of Plays* indicate how popular amateur theatre was. At the other end of the socio-economic spectrum, "penny gaffs"—short entertainments that could be put on cheaply and performed wherever space permitted—were popular with working-class audiences.

Early Victorian theatre entertained via a combination of artistry, narrative, and spectacle. Its varied offerings included melodrama, Shakespeare, farce, and comedy, as well as pantomime, burlesque, opera, and ballet. It included both "legitimate" and "illegitimate" theatres, urban and suburban theatres, metropolitan and provincial theatres, and a thriving world of amateur performances and private theatricals. Literary historians once dismissed Victorian drama as unworthy of study. With their stock melodramatic characters and outlandish plots, Victorian plays have little to offer when judged as great literature. But if we set aside our own standards to embrace those of the Victorians, and if we think about plays not as texts to be read, but as pieces intended for performance, we are better placed to appreciate Victorian drama. It was not characterized by complex use of language, nuanced characters, or engagement with social issues. Rather, it was emotionally affecting and visually arresting. Dazzling recreations of battles (including live horses onstage), floods, fires, and shipwrecks, were all common. Irish playwright Dion Boucicault's (1820?–1890) play *Pauvrette* (1858) featured an avalanche, and *The Streets of London* (1864) featured a huge fire.

In the early Victorian period, the British theatre had been legally divided for over a century into "legitimate" and "illegitimate" theatre. There were only three legitimate (or patent) theatres: Drury Lane, Covent Garden, and the Haymarket, all in London's West End. Only these were permitted to stage "legitimate" plays with spoken dialogue. All other theatres were considered "illegitimate" or "minor"; they were prohibited from staging standard plays and instead put on various non-verbal performances such as pantomimes and melodramas. Prohibited from performing unadorned dialogue, illegitimate theatre developed a style characterized by physical movement and gesture, music and sound effects, and striking visual effects. While the laws would seem to have created two distinct forms of theatre, by 1820 the distinction between legitimate and illegitimate theatre was dissolving. Illegitimate theatres skirted the letter of the law, for instance by performing Shakespeare with music in the background. At the same time, many features of illegitimate theatre—such as spectacular visuals and melodramatic plots—were so popular with audiences that the patent houses adopted them. The Theatre Regulation Act 1843 abolished the distinction between legitimate and illegitimate theatres and created a free market for theatres. Minor theatres could now put on more serious fare, and began to feature Shakespeare and Italian operas. However, previous blurring of the boundaries between legitimate and illegitimate meant that in many ways the 1843 Act merely recognized an existing landscape in which a variety of venues produced a wide range of spectacularly visual theatrical presentations, from Shakespeare's plays to melodramas to pantomimes to circus acts, all overlapping with, borrowing from, and competing with one another.

The major genres were comedy, farce, and melodrama, with the last by far the most important and most popular genre in Victorian theatre and indeed in Victorian culture; one scholar remarks that melodrama's "presence in Victorian culture is hard to overstate."[2] Technically, the term "melodrama" referred to a drama that was accompanied by music. While today we use the term "melodrama" as a derogatory term that refers to overly, unrealistically, or ridiculously dramatic plots or styles, in the nineteenth century melodrama was a specific genre characterized by stock characters (such as the lascivious villain and the virtuous ingénue), virtue imperiled but ultimately rewarded, complex family histories and secret pasts, and intricate plots that relied on coincidence and recognition scenes. It was ubiquitous in plays, novels, music halls, and even served as a narrative device in court cases and journalism. Some scholars have seen melodrama as a politically conservative art form, but it was multivalent and complex and could be deployed for radical as well as conservative ends; for example, melodrama often critiqued elites by depicting working-class heroines imperiled by aristocratic villains.

Melodrama was so popular that it had sub-genres. Nautical melodramas featured ships, water, and battles on stage. Douglas Jerrold (1803–1857) wrote quite a few of them; in his most famous play, *Black Ey'd Susan* (1829), William, a patriotic and hard-working sailor and a better man than his commanding officer, returns home from the Napoleonic Wars and protects his wife Susan from two predators, his Naval captain and her landlord. Domestic melodramas focused on family and domestic settings. Jerrold's *The Rent Day* (1832) was popular, as was John Buckstone's (1802–1879) *Luke the Labourer* (1827), in which a young man returning home to his village saves the persecuted heroine from the machinations of an evil squire landlord and his villainous assistant. Of course, melodrama was not the only popular theatrical form. London in the 1830s also saw a three-year craze for American actor Thomas D. Rice's show *Jim Crow*, a blackface depiction of a singing, dancing, runaway slave. The show was so popular that imitators were everywhere in London's theaters and streets, the character of Jim Crow became a staple of the satirical press, and the act helped pave the way for a specifically British tradition of minstrelsy and blackface. The buffoonish figure of Jim Crow also provided a way to mock and persecute London's black population.[3]

From the 1860s, a new spate of theatre-building added theatres all over London (while commentators focused on the fashionable West End, two thirds of the theatre seating capacity in London lay outside of it[4]), its outlying districts, and cities all over Britain. A major impetus to 1860s theatre-building was growing competition from music halls, which put pressure on theatre to keep up. (Of course, music halls were not the only threat theatres faced; scientific displays, improving lectures, circuses, and other entertainments also competed.) Some of the newly built theatres were smaller, which allowed for the introduction of a subtler and more intimate style of acting.

Even so melodrama remained the dominant genre, with Boucicault's *The Corsican Brothers* (1852) and *The Colleen Bawn* (1860), set in rural Ireland, both great hits, as was *Faust and Marguerite*, put on at the Princess's Theatre under actor-manager

Charles Kean in 1854. Other popular playwrights were Tom Taylor (1817–1880), who wrote *The Ticket of Leave Man* (1863), T.W. Robertson (1829–1871), who moved from adapting scenes from Dickens and writing music hall songs to writing full-length plays such as the realistic comedy *Society* (1865), and Frank Talfourd (1828–1862), who wrote burlesques such as *The Original Strong-Minded Woman*. Melodramas borrowed from the new sensation novels to morph into sensation dramas, in which elements of gothic and mystery were added to domestic melodrama. An excellent example of a sensation drama is *East Lynne*. The play was even more popular that the best-selling novel by Mrs Henry Wood (1814–1887) on which it was based: the most famous line in *East Lynne*, "Dead! Dead! And never called me mother!" comes from the play, not the original novel. *East Lynne* centered on Lady Isabel Vane, who deserts her husband, children, and home for a heartless seducer (and murderer), and later returns—unrecognizably disfigured from a railway accident—to work as a governess for her own children. Audiences loved the plot, the melodrama, and the spectacle; actresses loved the part of Isabel, which allowed them to essentially play two different characters (though many forewent looking disfigured in favor simply of donning blue-tinted glasses). *East Lynne* was so popular for decades that productions of it were a reliable source of revenue for provincial theatres in search of full houses; three London theaters did versions in 1879 alone, obituaries of Wood noted that play was "almost constantly acted" in either London or the provinces, and one scholar estimates that it played somewhere in Britain or North America every week for 40 years.[5]

Alongside these theatres were music halls, or rather, the forerunners of music halls. The large, ornate music halls that we associate with the Victorian period—or with nostalgia for the Victorian period—did not reach their peak until the 1890s and did not really exist until the 1870s. However they had important progenitors in earlier combinations of music and drinking. In the 1820s, many pubs would allow a group of friends (usually men) to gather in a back room once or twice a week and entertain themselves by singing together—many working-class people were amateur musicians, active in a local choir or orchestra—while they drank. One of the men would act as "chairman," directing the proceedings, but otherwise the night—called a "free and easy"—was informal and participatory. Over the next three decades, pubs welcomed more of these evenings (in part because they boosted sales of alcohol and food), added a piano, and invited local musicians. In addition to groups of friends singing, there might be soloists, or someone performing a comic song in character. These evenings started to be less of a get-together of friends and more an informal program of amateur performances, sometimes called "singing saloons"; historians have found records of singing saloons in the early 1840s in Newcastle, Nottingham, Sheffield, Bristol, and elsewhere. In the north of England, dialect poetry and songs were popular, as were amateur performances and competitions. The feeling remained very informal and participatory—people came and went all evening, and insofar as there was an audience, everyone in it was expected to contribute to the performance. Audiences were working-class, mostly skilled workers and textile factory or mill workers, and included women as well as men. Commentator Angus

B. Reach, writing in the *Morning Chronicle* in the late 1840s about a visit to a singing saloon in Manchester, noted in the audience young single women (mostly in groups), and women with children and babies as well (who were often part of family parties).

Over the 1830s and early 1840s, some of these gatherings gradually became less informal; pubs began hiring professional singers and entertainers from local theatres and providing a small platform from which they would perform. Accomplished amateurs still performed, and listeners still joined in on choruses and popular songs, but there was more of a sense of performers as separate from the audience, and less of an expectation of audience participation. Audiences included middle-class men and working-class people of both sexes. In the decade following the passage of the 1843 Theatres Act things changed even more. Pubs now designated or even built separate "concert rooms" and hired professional singers, comedians, acrobats, and other acts. These rooms—most historians would consider these the earliest things we can call "music halls"—had more formal programs (performers now wore evening dress) and some fancy architectural features such as chandeliers or gas lighting. In terms of both program and patrons, these early music halls competed and overlapped with other forms of entertainment like roadside booths and minor local theatres—and in all of these, eating, smoking, and especially drinking were going on during and in the room with the performances, and audience members still came and went and still talked to one another and to the performers

In the 1850s, the first small purpose-built halls—that is, the first halls that were constructed specifically to serve as music halls—were built. Historians are very interested in the composition of music hall audiences from the 1850s onwards. We once thought that they were the exclusive province of boisterous young working-class men. However, careful research has revealed audiences were actually quite mixed. Newcastle, Nottingham, and Leicester all had purpose-built halls in the 1850s and 1860s. In the 1850s, London's first large purpose-built halls were opened, including the Middlesex in Drury Lane and Wilton's in Whitechapel. Publican Charles Morton (1819–1904) opened the Canterbury music hall in the Lambeth area of London in 1852 and soon moved on to open a music hall in the West End; the Canterbury is often called the first music hall, and Morton the father or inventor of the music hall, but in fact many entrepreneurs, in London and in the provinces, were doing the same things Morton was doing (Morton merely popularized the new halls, and emphasized variety in their programs). Soon London had many large music halls, both in the working-class East End and in the West End. These early halls were not attached to pubs, but they retained pubs' friendly ambience. In 1862, the establishment of a new form of corporation—the limited liability corporation—prompted the development of large syndicates which built chains of halls across the country. In London, these various forms evolved into one another: free-and-easies gave way to singing saloons, which in turn gave way to music halls. In the provinces, however, there was more co-existence, with free-and-easies, singing saloons, and music halls all flourishing alongside each other right into the mid-1890s.

As these entertainments grew—in size, in popularity, in prevalence—the range of acts offered became more diverse. The 1850s music halls had offered a wide variety of entertainments. They offered music and some theatre or dramatic readings; songs that were comic or patriotic were most popular, but there were also ballads and folk songs (especially Irish and Scottish ones), and performances of high or canonical classical pieces as well. Classical music was often very familiar to working-class people, who performed it in local choirs and bands and heard it from street musicians. Programs also featured circus acts, such as jugglers, "freaks," and ventriloquists. There were also spectacular stagings of famous battles, and educational presentations, such as panoramas and dioramas that presented new technologies in entertaining ways. While many historians see these developments as a loss of authentic working-class culture in favor of packaged, mass culture, others emphasize that changes and developments in music halls were not nearly so simple or so negative. Early traditions often persisted as a facet of newer forms, especially in the north of England; mass culture was not necessarily inauthentic or immune from community standards and input.

Print culture encompassed a variety of genres aimed at a variety of audiences. Even before state-provided education, Victorian Britain had a high rate of literacy—the upper and middle classes had achieved full literacy, and by 1840 about two thirds of working-class people had basic literacy—making the potential audience for affordable and appealing reading materials very large. Historian of reading and popular culture Rosalind Crone stresses that early Victorian society had a large number of "semi-literates or readers," and that this potential market led to the expansion of print culture. Along with this expansion and new forms came shifts in popular and critical acceptance of various genres; for example, over the course of the century poetry would become less widely-read, and novels would be embraced as a central literary form.

At the start of the period, poetry was a well-established but increasingly contested literary form (with the novel still something of a generic upstart). The major poets of the Romantic period (c. 1780–1830)—Lord Byron, Sir Walter Scott, and William Wordsworth—were still widely read. Poetry "annuals"— bound volumes containing poems and engravings, often given as holiday gifts—were popular in the 1820s and 1830s. Two popular genres were domestic poetry and working-class poetry. The most famous domestic poet was Felicia Hemans (1790–1835), who though she lived in a tiny village in Wales became tremendously popular across Britain. Her poems, such as "Casabianca" (1829), combine domestic affections with patriotic fervor and were memorized and recited by children well into the twentieth century. Working-class poetry included chants, ballads, broadsides, and religious and political hymns written and read by working-class people. (As the century progressed and literacy, education, and access to literature improved, working-class poetry became less distinct from other forms.) In the middle of the century poetry was closely linked to painting via the pre-Raphaelites; Rossetti's poem *The Blessed Damozel* (1850) describes an ethereal and idealized love between the narrator and a dead woman.

The most important early Victorian poet was Elizabeth Barrett Browning (1806–1861). During the 1830s and 1840s, the unmarried Elizabeth Barrett won increasing praise for her first three collections of poems, most importantly *Poems* (1844), which made her the most famous poet of her day. *Poems* included *Lady Geraldine's Courtship*, which was about an aristocratic woman's love for a poor poet and included praise of the work of a lesser-known poet, Robert Browning. The two began a secret correspondence; in 1846, in defiance of Barrett's father, they married and moved to Italy. Mrs Barrett Browning's most famous later works include *Sonnets From The Portuguese* (1850) and *Aurora Leigh* (1856), an 11,000-line "novel in verse" on the tensions between the identities of woman and artist. She also wrote politically-engaged poetry, such as *Casa Guidi Windows* (1851) and *Poems before Congress* (1860), which were less popular. Her last publication, *Last Poems*, was published posthumously by her husband in 1862.

Another important Victorian poet was Christina Rossetti (1830–94), sister of pre-Raphaelite Dante Gabriel Rossetti. Rossetti was technically accomplished, and many critics admired the complex construction of her poems, but she was also very well-liked by average readers; her 1862 collection *Goblin Market and Other Poems* was extremely popular, and she wrote fairy-tales and poems for children as well. Rossetti was a devout Anglican, and her religious commitment is apparent in many of her poems, which often have melancholy, loss, thwarted love, and death as their themes.

Two other important Victorian poets were Alfred, Lord Tennyson (1809–1892) and Robert Browning (1812–1889), who later in the century became better-known than his wife. Lord Tennyson was both well-respected and commercially successful. His most famous poems include *The Lady of Shalott*, (1833) and *The Princess* (1847). His elegiac poem *In Memoriam*, published in 1850, combined private loss with national anxieties and was a critical and commercial success, selling 5,000 copies in weeks. That same year, he was named poet laureate (succeeding Wordsworth). Following this appointment, he wrote *The Charge of the Light Brigade* (1854), and *Maud, and Other Poems* (1855) both of which were commercially successful. Robert Browning's poems were psychologically complex and often featured troubled speakers. He began publishing poems in 1833, but did not become famous until the middle of the century with the publication of his collections *Men and Women* (1855), and *Dramatis Personae* (1864), and *The Ring and the Book* (1868–1869). Thereafter he was popular and famous; the Browning Society, founded in 1881, is considered by some cultural critics to be the first fan club. In one of Robert Browning's popular poems, *Fra Lippo Lippi*, the speaker defends realism as the highest form of artistic expression, which allows art to instruct and to morally elevate us. Robert Browning's increasing popularity in the latter half of the nineteenth century paralleled the increasing popularity of realism and a rising general preference for novels over poetry.

Turning to the novel, between "Victorian" and "the novel," it is hard to say which defines the other more. The novel first emerged in the eighteenth century— many cite Daniel Defoe's *Robinson Crusoe* (1719) as the first British novel—but reached its fullest expression during the Victorian period. And while we no longer produce pre-1880 Victorian plays, we still read Victorian novels, and see them as among the best products of English-speaking culture. This is not to say that we assess Victorian novels as the Victorians did: Queen Victoria's favorite novelist was not Charles Dickens, or George Eliot (1819–1880), but Mrs Margaret Oliphant (1828–1897). Oliphant, almost entirely forgotten for most of the twentieth century (and rediscovered only in the past 30 years) wrote a wide variety of novels that focused on Scottish provincial and domestic life but included gothic, sensational, and historical novels, and multi-novel sagas. She was extremely popular and widely appreciated for her wit, quiet irony, and strong female characters. At the other extreme and later in our period, the novel *Jude the Obscure* (1895), by Thomas Hardy (1840–1928), is now considered a classic, but reviews written when the book was published were so negative that Hardy, devastated, never wrote another novel (devoting the rest of his career to poetry).

Victorian novels were typically quite long, with large casts of characters and complex but clearly resolved plots. These often revolved around marriage, revealing the institution's centrality to Victorian culture; one history of the Victorian novel could be the history of its marriage plots. More broadly, Victorian novels explored the relationships between the social and the psychological and between the public and private realms. Henry James (1843–1916) complained about what he saw as the "bagginess" of Victorian novels, but they were large canvases on which to work. To Victorians, the novel was, at its best, not just entertainment or a representation of society but a tool for teaching moral lessons. Critic David Masson declared in 1859 that while "the proper business of the Novel" was "the representation of social reality," that the "spirit" of the endeavor should still be "that of the far-surveying and the sublime."[6] Novels ought to make their readers finer people, by developing their sympathetic faculties—George Eliot argued that "[i]f Art does not enlarge men's sympathies, it does nothing morally"—and offering examples of how to live.[7] (This didactic quality was true of Victorian art more generally as well.)

Furthermore, Victorian novels not only reflected contemporary social and political debates but were an aspect of them: novels could challenge and even shape Victorian life. *Oliver Twist* was frequently cited in arguments over the problems of urban slums and juvenile criminality. Queen Victoria—newly crowned and still a teenager when the novel was published—rejected her advisor Lord Melbourne's opinion that she should avoid it and any other novels that depicted "paupers, criminals and other unpleasant subjects." She wrote in her diary that she found Dickens' novel "excessively interesting" and that it taught her about life in London's slums, not far from her palace.[8] Three years later, Victoria and her new husband Albert pursued their interest in depictions of the lives of the poor by reading the Report of Lord Ashley's Mines Commissions and inviting Lord Ashley to the Palace to discuss his work.

Many of the most successful and best-respected Victorian novelists were women; indeed the novel is sometimes criticized as a feminine or even effeminizing genre. Widely-read female novelists included canonical authors Charlotte (1816–1855) and Emily Brontë (1818–1848), George Eliot, and Elizabeth Gaskell

(1810–1865). Gaskell's novels were known for their detailed descriptions of the lives of the poor and for their dynamic female characters, such as Margaret Hale in *North and South* (1854–1855). Oliphant's most popular novel, *Miss Marjoribanks* (1866), focuses on the character of Lucilla Marjoribanks, a young woman who aims to raise the social and cultural tone of her provincial town. Another popular author was Dinah Mulock Craik (1826–1887), author of *John Halifax, Gentleman* (1858). The leading sensation novelists, Mrs Henry Wood and Mary Elizabeth Braddon, were both women who became wealthy from their writing.

In novels, anxieties about gender were evident. As Victorians became more worried about the "surplus women" problem, novels about unmarried women who resisted or were marginalized by the marital ideal became more common. In Charlotte Brontë's *Shirley* (1849), penniless Caroline Helstone shrinks from governessing but wonders what other place she might find in the world; Mrs Gaskell's *Cranford* (1851) revolves around two spinster sisters. Alongside these, novels celebrating masculinity and virility such as Charles Kingsley's *Westward Ho!* (1855) were also popular, especially during the Crimean War (1853–1856). So too were novels set all over empire, and particularly in India after 1857 and in "darkest" Africa (such as Rider Haggard's).

Like the theatre, novels were generally viewed with suspicion by evangelical middle-class Britons. Jane Austen and Sir Walter Scott—both pre-Victorian writers—were the only ones considered acceptable in middle-class circles (and both remained widely read well throughout the century). However, between 1820 and 1850 novels became more affordable, more widely read, and more respectable. From about 1820, the development of machine-made paper and of the rotary steam press made printing much cheaper than it had been and made literature available in a wider range of forms to a larger audience. Novels, while expensive, were available from lending libraries (such as Mudie's) for those who could afford to belong. By 1840, the most popular novels were published in a cheaper serial form: a chapter would appear each month in a monthly magazine that cost only one shilling. (Once completed, serially published novels were then published in the standard three-volume format). Serial publication made novels affordable to a wider range of middle-class readers and so enlarged the novel-reading audience. Serial publication also made novels a social experience, as readers together waited for a new chapter to become available, read it, and made it a topic of conversation. Public dramatic readings of popular novels—Dickens gave readings frequently, with *A Christmas Carol*, the breach of promise of marriage trial from the *Pickwick Papers*, and Nancy's death in *Oliver Twist* especially popular—meant that even the illiterate partook in the culture of novels. Reading aloud was popular in private homes as well.

Popular genres in the 1820s, 1830s, and 1840s included "silver-fork," "Newgate," and Gothic novels. Silver-fork novels portrayed fashionable upper-class life; for example, Edward Bulwer-Lytton's *Pelham, or the Adventures of a Gentleman* (1828) followed the life of dandy and wit Henry Pelham whilst casting a simultaneously fawning and cynical eye on the manners and material culture of the elite. Future Prime Minister, Benjamin Disraeli, wrote several silver-fork and other novels, and used them as sites for developing the political theories which would later guide him as leader of the Conservative Party. Newgate novels glamorized the criminal underworld and criminal-heroes; Ainsworth's *Jack Sheppard* is one of the best-known. Many consider Charles Dickens' second novel, *Oliver Twist* (1838), to be a Newgate novel, and the two appeared in serial form in the same magazine, *Bentley's Miscellany*, in 1840. Sisters Emily, Charlotte, and Anne Brontë wrote Gothic novels such as *Jane Eyre* and *Wuthering Heights* (1847), which both reflected and confronted the limitations that class and gender imposed on lives. The Brontës' works combined realistic settings and coming-of-age tales with mysterious and super-natural happenings, romantic plots, and emotional intensity. Reviewers of *Jane Eyre* were stunned by the main character's refusal to accept society's measure of her as only "a Governess—disconnected, poor, and plain," and found the book powerful and passionate (though some disliked it on those grounds; reviewer Lady Eastlake saw in Jane's insistence on her own worth "the spirit of Chartism," which she considered dangerous, and another reviewer found the book "anti-Christian").[9] Less affluent and less literate readers enjoyed comparable fare. Cheap popular novels were printed by publisher Edward Lloyd (1815–1890) and his ilk, who put out serialized gothic tales, romances, and "penny bloods" that appealed to lower middle-class and working-class readers of all ages and both genders. Penny bloods were published in parts, either in weekly penny periodicals, or alone in one-penny eight-page installments. They narrated the adventures of highwaymen, robbers, pirates, and the like; chapters usually started with an illustration and ended with a cliffhanger (and sometimes in the middle of a sentence).

Major mid-century novels that are still in the canon today include Dickens' *David Copperfield* (1849–1850), *Bleak House* (1852–1853), and *Great Expectations* (1860–1861); *Vanity Fair* (1847–1848), by William Makepeace Thackeray (1811–1863); Mrs Gaskell's *Mary Barton* (1848) and *North and South* (1854–1855), which explored women's roles and the effects of industrialization on society; the Palliser and Barsetshire novels by the prolific Anthony Trollope (1815–1882), which explored the moral choices that inform everyday life; and *Adam Bede* (1859), set in rural England at the turn of the nineteenth century, which though by a then-unknown George Eliot was an immense success, with three printings of the three-volume version and 10,000 copies of the cheaper one-volume version sold in the first year. By the mid-Victorian period, novels were respectable and the dominant literary form; by 1860 they were a central feature of working-class and lower middle-class culture and were common even in most respectable middle-class households. Another manufacturing advance, power-binding, made books cheaper still—by the 1860s the price of a novel could be as low as 1½d. for one serial part or 1s. for one volume—and the rise of the railway journey created a market for cheap reprints of popular novels ("railway novels" being a precursor to today's "airport novels").

In the 1860s, the publishing of popular fiction became a large and profitable business and a big part of popular culture. Penny bloods, now called penny dreadfuls, were now aimed mostly at younger readers. Serially-published stories such as *The Work Girls of London* (1865), *The Boy Detective; or, The Crimes of London*

(1865–1866), and *The Dance of Death; or, the Hangman's Plot* (1865–1866), which incorporated aspects of melodrama, sensation, gothic horror, and escapist romance, and which could be purchased cheaply at newsagents, stationers, sweet-shops, and the like, suggest that clerks, shop assistants, servants, and schoolboys were all spending their pennies on engrossing fiction.

Finally, from about 1860 one of the most important genres in Victorian novels was sensation fiction. Sensation novels emerged from melodrama and the Gothic; they were full of the stock characters, coincidences, and hidden pasts of melodrama and the supernatural creepiness of the gothic, and tended to feature adultery and in particular bigamy. The term "sensation" referred to the fact that readers were made to feel what the characters felt; as Mrs Oliphant put it in a review, "[t]he sensation is distinct and indisputable . . . [every] shock is as sudden, as startling, as unexpected and incomprehensible to us as it is to the hero of the tale. . . . It is a simply physical effect. . . . The effect is pure sensation, neither more nor less."[10] Wilkie Collins' *The Woman in White* is usually considered the first sensation novel (it is sometimes considered the first detective novel as well, and gives us insight into the new figure of the detective, in life and in art). The plot includes a mysterious stranger, a loveless marriage, illegitimacy, an imperiled aristocratic title, switched identities, and false imprisonment in an insane asylum. Serialized in Dickens' magazine *All the Year Round*, *The Woman in White* was a huge success and spawned Woman in White perfumes, bonnets, and waltzes, in addition to huge sales in serial, three-volume, and one-volume editions.[11] Other popular sensation novels included *East Lynne* (1861) by Mrs Henry Wood, and *Lady Audley's Secret* and *Aurora Floyd* (1862), both by Mary Elizabeth Braddon (and both featuring bigamy). *Lady Audley's Secret* went through eight editions in its first three months alone; its total sales outnumbered all other novels of the period, and an adaptation became a staple of Victorian theatre. Sensation fiction even influenced realistic novels; for example, Mrs Oliphant's realistic *Salem Chapel* was rife with hidden pasts and abductions.

Turning to newspapers and magazines, from the 1830s the Victorian period also saw an explosion in magazines and newspapers—what historians call "periodical literature." In the 1810s and 1820s, as part of its attempts to suppress working-class radical politics, the government suppressed the press, in part by imposing taxes on newspapers which came to be called the "taxes on knowledge." Readers of the radical press responded by sharing newspapers in coffeehouses and pubs—historians estimate that in the 1810s and 1820s one copy of a newspaper was read by twenty to thirty people—but the "taxes on knowledge" succeeded in making newspapers and magazines hard for typical working-class Britons to access. This changed in the 1830s, when the 4d. tax on newspapers was reduced to only 1d. (and taxes on advertisements and paper were halved).

The effect was dramatic: the 1830s witnessed a proliferation of periodicals. Popular journals aimed at a broad audience included the *Family Herald* and the *London Journal*, both started in the mid-1840s. In 1846 publisher Edward Lloyd started *The People's Periodical and Family Library*. The first edition featured the murderous barber Sweeney Todd in a story called "String of Pearls," which was so popular that it was republished as a penny novelette and adapted for the melodramatic theater. There were also "class" or "quality" journals, which were aimed at relatively elite readers with specific professional, political, religious, or other interests; these were not new in the Victorian period, but their number and variety was. Various quality journals focused on literature, science, particular trades and hobbies, and at specific groups (such as women or denominational groups; missionary magazines were particularly popular).

Newspapers also expanded rapidly, in variety, in number of titles, and in circulation. The first were affordable Sunday weekly newspapers, based in London and aimed to both inform and entertain a broad audience. They included a wide range of items including serious political reporting, sensational crime reporting, editorial and opinion pieces, royal and celebrity gossip, advertisements, reviews, letters from readers, advice columns, and serial fiction. One of the earliest was the short-lived *Cleave's Weekly Police Gazette* (1834–1836), which mixed "serious" news with entertainment; its pages included political news, reports of sensational crimes and strange occurrences, and popular fiction. The two leading publishers were Edward Lloyd, publisher of *Lloyd's Weekly Newspaper* (f. 1842), and publisher-journalist-novelist G.W.M. Reynolds (1814–1879), founder of *Reynolds's Newspaper* (f. 1850). Another popular paper was the *Illustrated London News*, which by midcentury sold over 100,000 copies a week, making it the best-selling newspaper in Britain. These large, commercial publications sought to appeal to lower middle- and working-class readers, and helped to make newspapers central to British popular culture. There were also politically factional newspapers; the best-known example is Feargus O'Connor's Chartist newspaper *The Northern Star* (1837–1852), which promoted Chartist principles such as universal manhood suffrage.

In 1855 the stamp duty was abolished entirely, and the periodical press grew even more. The 1850s saw the flourishing of provincial newspapers and of affordable daily newspapers, which at 1d. were accessible to the growing lower middle class. One of the best-selling new dailies was the *Sheffield Daily Telegraph*, founded in 1855; another was the London *Daily Telegraph*, which by the 1870s would sell 200,000 copies every day. From the 1860s, these 1d. daily newspapers (which were printed in the morning) were joined by another new genre, 1/2d. daily evening papers. Overall, then, the period from the 1830s to the 1860s saw the rise and flourishing of a more accessible, varied, and robust periodical culture than ever before.

1870–1914: The rise of working-class audiences and readers

In the later Victorian period, arts, print, and entertainment all grew swiftly. There were several key contextual factors here. Rising real wages combined with shorter work hours gave working-class people more money and more time to spend on leisure pursuits. Improvements in transportation made it easier for people go out at night. The Elementary Education Act 1870 raised literacy rates, so that by about 1890 almost everyone in Britain was literate (if not well-educated).

Overall, all of this meant that theatre and music hall attendance increased, as did sales of periodical and other literature. This was the great age of the music halls. In theatre, melodrama and spectacle remained popular, but realistic works on difficult topics appeared as well. In poetry, we see an insistence on "art for art's sake" in the aesthetic and decadent movements. In novels, we see the rise of realist and of popular novels alongside the continued popularity of sensation fiction. And in newspapers and magazines, the emergence of the "new journalism" and the growth of the popular press marked Britain as a nation of newspaper readers.

By the 1870s there were hundreds of music halls across Britain, and they were ever-more numerous and well-attended. The scale of the halls, the eating and drinking, and the variety of the programs, made late Victorian music halls seductive scenes of plenty, pleasure, and excess. Some could seat a few hundred; the Alhambra in the West End seated 3,500. By 1892, music halls were a central feature of Victorian entertainment; one report estimated that there were over one hundred very large music halls in London, and another 160 outside London. In London there was a hierarchy of halls, with the largest and fanciest centrally located in the West End, followed by halls in outlying neighborhoods and suburbs, and then smaller, shabbier halls in the poorest districts. Audiences were made up of mostly working-class and lower-middle class people, but middle-class and even upper-class people might go to the West End halls. In the rest of the country, however, until the turn of the twentieth century, halls were located in the center of town (this was true even for large towns with suburban areas, such as Manchester or Glasgow) and there was little differentiation among them. Outside of London, music halls were music halls. They drew audience members from all neighborhoods and classes.

In 1870, audience members still sat at tables, drinking and smoking (in contrast, theatres had fixed rows of seats and drinking took place only in the bars outside the auditorium). The atmosphere was relaxed and convivial. It was often rowdy: one member of the audience at a music hall in Stockport noted that during songs, "at the end of every verse the audience takes up the chorus with a zest and vigour which speaks volumes—they sing, they roar, they yell, they scream, they . . . bellow again until their voices crack."[12] With wages rising, more young people could afford an evening at the music hall. But music halls were not the exclusive province of rowdy young men. In places like Sheffield or Manchester, where there was work for women (in factories, domestic service, offices, or shops) there were large numbers of young unmarried women in music hall audiences, usually in groups of neighbors or coworkers. But older and married women came as well, sometimes with their children or even their babies. Women with children were less likely to come out for the night than childless women, but signs stating that "children in arms will not be admitted" suggest that they did not stop altogether, and they were not always unwelcome; at the Glasgow Star there was a special area for women with children. One journalist thought that an audience in 1867 was one quarter husbands and wives who had come together. Most people were dressed for a night on the town. And from the late Victorian years into the 1920s, some fashionable middle-class intellectuals made a point of parading the fact that they crossed class lines to enjoy music halls. Overall, though middle-class people were perhaps less likely than others to attend, music hall audiences were diverse in terms of both class and gender.

From the 1890s, music halls became more restrained, more organized, and more standardized, in large part because a small number of syndicates owned an increasing number of halls. In 1906, Moss Empires had nearly 40 halls under centralized management and featuring nationally consistent programs, and perhaps one half of all halls were under some form of syndicate control. By 1914, a mere 16 syndicates controlled 140 halls. The large syndicates reorganized the halls, replacing tables with theatre-style rows of seats and banning drink inside the auditorium. They also tried to impose respectability on performers, by demanding tamer fare, and on audiences (largely via lack of drink). In part as a result of these efforts, the respectable middle-class began to patronize some halls more frequently. (There were other factors at work as well—many middle-class children learned music hall songs from their working-class caregivers, and performers in Christmas pantomimes, which were on the rise from the 1880s and popular with the middle class, were often music hall stars. However, middle-class patrons remained a small segment of the audience, and often sat separately, away from the working-class majority.) Programs were now well-organized and uniform, with performers travelling the country on circuits, offering an ordered sequence of precisely timed acts twice nightly. They continued to develop through the early twentieth-century—in 1912 a music hall, the Hippodrome in London, introduced the first revue.

Actors would appear in character and sing songs interspersed with patter. One of the most popular characters was "Champagne Charlie," a flashily-dressed gent who sang about his constant dancing, gambling, flirting, and drinking. The original Champagne Charlie was George Leybourne (1842–1884), one of the best known music hall performers, who became a star in 1866. Champagne Charlies were a popular feature of programs into the inter-war years. Many music-hall songs evinced an ironic and knowing perspective on life. Some were comic (*My Old Man (Said Follow the Van)*), others romantic (*The Boy I Love is Up in the Gallery*), others sentimental, even maudlin. Many were patriotic and pro-empire, such as G.H. McDermott's (1845?–1901) *The Jingo Song*. Music hall songs were often replete with sexual references and *double entendres* (*What Was There Was Good*) and were intermittently brought before various licensing bodies for censure. One of the most popular music-hall performers, Marie Lloyd (1870–1922), had a very long career, which began with performances at the Eagle in the East End of London in 1885, when she was only 14 years old, and continued into the First World War, when she had a huge hit with the song *A Little of What You Fancy*. Lloyd was famous for her ability to share a wink and a double entendre with her audience, and so was a frequent target of social purity activists and censors. (In 1907, when she was already quite famous, Lloyd participated in a large strike of lesser-known music-hall performers in greater London dubbed the "music hall war"; one night she sent a telegram to the Tivoli music hall declaring that she could not perform because she was sewing her costume.)

Also popular were cross-dressing female performers, most famously Vesta Tilley (1864–1952), who worked in tirelessly music hall from the age of five until she retired in her mid-fifties. Singing such songs as *I'm the Idol of the Girls*, Tilley was incredibly popular, and in the 1890s was the highest-earning woman in Britain. She also did well in the theatre, performing boys' roles in pantomimes. She was even a great hit in American vaudeville, whose audiences usually received British performers coolly, and toured the US six times. Tilley's boyish androgyny, and the contrast between her male looks and her female voice, made her act a simultaneous imitation of and commentary on masculinity. In addition, the sight of a woman "baring" her legs by wearing trousers onstage was sexually titillating for many. In contrast to Lloyd, whose admirers were mainly men, most of Tilley's most ardent fans were young women who seemed drawn to her ambiguous sexuality. In the early twentieth century ragtime music and short "moving pictures" also became features.

Figure 11.2 Stage and Screen, Personalities, picture: circa 1900, Vesta Tilley (1884–1952) British music hall performer, the country's most popular male impersonator.

Photo by Popperfoto/Getty Images.

Historians argue about political meanings and effects of music hall, and many assert that what began as an authentic expression of working-class culture became appropriated by managers and owners to become entirely commercial, imposed from above, and politically conservative. While there is some truth in this, it is an oversimplification. Music hall programs, songs, characters, and audience experiences were all complex, layered, and multivalent. While many lyrics partook of a culture of consolation that had a conservative bent, music hall was not simply conservative or a tool meant to distract and pacify the working class. The figure of the gent or swell, for example, simultaneously envied and mocked the aristocratic man of leisure; different performers and audience members would have responded to a gent onstage in various ways.

When moving pictures first became available, short films were incorporated into music hall programs. Ultimately movies became their own form of entertainment, and from the first decade of the twentieth century the music hall found itself in competition with cinemas, the first of which opened in London in 1906. (The rise of television after World War Two also dealt a severe blow to music halls.) But while music hall began to decline in the years before World War One, this central feature of Late Victorian entertainment remained a part of British culture until at least World War Two.

Theatre flourished alongside music hall. Working-class patrons continued to enjoy melodramatic and spectacular theatrical offerings. Augustus Harris' play, *Pluck: A Story of 50,000* (1882) included a snowstorm, a mob storming a bank, and two railway crashes on stage. Towards the end of the nineteenth century, native-born audiences were joined by immigrants. Theatres in London's East End began featuring plays in Yiddish, such as the melodrama/farce *The Holy Sabbath* and Jacob Gordin's *Mirele Efros* (also known as *The Jewish Queen Lear* (1898)), for large audiences of Jewish immigrants from Eastern Europe. Indeed Jewish theatre was so vibrant that in 1908 the *Pall Mall* magazine ran a long article on "The East-End Jew at His Playhouse" which argued that the Pavilion Theatre in Whitechapel, which had recently become the home of Yiddish theatre in London, was "in some respects the most remarkable place of entertainment in the country."[13] There were other changes as well. Long runs of a single program (once reserved for Christmas pantomimes), which allowed for more elaborate scenery, became common. Programs became shorter, with only one or two pieces and no half-price admission; everyone in the audience came at the start and stayed for the whole performance, but the evening ended earlier. Overall a night at the theatre took on a more restrained and respectable feel. This is part of why more middle-class people bought tickets (a relaxation of strict evangelical culture was another factor here). Better transportation also made it easier for the suburban middle class to come to town for a night at the theatre (and made provincial touring companies possible). In London, the renovated Covent Garden theatre and the new Prince of Wales's theatre in particular attracted the affluent middle class. Middle-class women were an important part of the audience, especially at matinées, which often treated themes of particular interest to women.

From the 1880s there was a new theatrical craze: comic operettas by playwright W.S. Gilbert (1836–1911) and composer Arthur Sullivan (1842–1900). Both had stable but not stellar careers before they came together to form one of the most successful partnerships in theatrical history. Their works—Victorian favorites were *H.M.S. Pinafore*, *The Pirates of Penzance*, *Patience*, and *The Mikado*—satirized everything from liberal theories of education to military discipline to the aesthetic movement. Gilbert's absurd and ironic plots and lyrics combined with Sullivan's complex but accessible compositions to form what was to Victorians an irresistible combination. The operas were wildly popular, especially with the middle class, and became mainstays of both professional and amateur theatre. In addition, much of the music was excerpted and adapted for amateur bands and piano players. The two (who were never close friends) were famous and often caricatured in *Punch* and elsewhere, with a small, cheerful Sullivan next to a tall, severe Gilbert. Both were knighted; obituaries in the *Times* declared that Sullivan was "far above all the other English composers of his day" and that while the works of contemporary realist playwrights Pinero and Shaw had their place, that "none of them had quite the charm of the best things of Gilbert, when those best things were sung to Sullivan's music."[14]

But while Gilbert and Sullivan operettas were favorites, and sensation, melodrama, and spectacle remained mainstays, some middle-class and upper-class theatregoers were drawn to the new realist theatre, plays that offered newly frank and sophisticated critiques of contemporary sexual politics. (Though grim realism was never the only option: witness the popularity of J.M. Barrie's *Peter Pan* (1904), which broke all previous theatrical records.) The arrival of the works of Norwegian playwright Henrik Ibsen (1828–1906) was a major event in British theatre. Two of his plays, *A Doll's House* and *Hedda Gabler*, made a huge splash when they were performed in London in the late 1880s and early 1890s. In *A Doll's House*, the main character Nora comes to realize that her husband, who infantilizes her, loves not Nora but merely the appearance of a perfect bourgeois marriage and wife. At the end of the play, she announces that heretofore she has lived as a mere plaything, a doll of her father, then of her husband, but that now she is leaving her marriage to find out who she is as an individual. She exits, leaving her wedding ring behind. Audiences flocked to this dramatic attack on middle-class hypocrisy, and Ibsen was credited with reviving British theatre. Following in his footsteps, British drama increasingly placed the blamed for the plight of the "fallen woman" not on the individual but on the society that stifled her.

One of the most important authors of this late period was Henry Arthur Jones (1851–1929). His play *The Silver King* (1882) had a typically Victorian melodramatic plot—a young man is tricked into believing he is a murderer, leaves home to make his fortune, and returns home in disguise to establish his innocence—but replaced spectacle with realistic dialogue. Another was Arthur Pinero (1855–1934), whose "problem plays" such as *The Profligate* (1889) and *The Second Mrs Tanqueray* (1893) addressed issues such as sexual fidelity and the sexual double standard. Harley Granville Barker's *The Voysey Inheritance* (1905) and *The Madras House* (1910) were both put on at the Royal Court Theatre, which, managed by Granville Barker and

John Vedrenne, specialized in risky, radical works that were often commercial successes.

Two of the most important late Victorian British playwrights were Irish men who spent their careers in London because it was the international capital of the theatrical world. The plays of Irish writer and socialist George Bernard Shaw (1856–1950) combined the melodramatic figure of the woman with a past with unexpectedly challenging conclusions. Writer and public intellectual Oscar Wilde (1854–1900), who was also Irish, made the biggest splash of all, combining writing with a supremely performative life. In the first half of the 1890s he put onstage, in swift succession, a series of popular and important plays: *Salomé, Lady Windermere's Fan, A Woman of No Importance, The Importance of Being Earnest,* and *An Ideal Husband.* These plays wittily attacked social hypocrisy and celebrated beauty and pleasure. In *The Importance of Being Earnest,* main character Jack Worthing meets proper standards of behavior only by maintaining two separate personae—upstanding county gentleman Jack Worthing, and pleasure-seeking London reprobate Ernest—with predictable confusion ensuing. In *An Ideal Husband,* Lady Chiltern, the wife of a Member of Parliament, learns that her seemingly unimpeachable husband has a compromised past, and that she must become more morally flexible to continue supporting him. Both were playing to large audiences in 1895, and were quickly closed down when Wilde's scandalous trials (see Chapter 12) began.

Wilde's trial took him from celebrity to notoriety, but in general the theatre began to achieve some measure of respectability after 1870. From the 1870s a wide variety of artists were celebrities, and by the end of the century, celebrity actresses were paid to promote mass-produced products and to feature in advertisements (Lillie Langtry (1853–1929) advertised Pears Soap). Popular actors included John Toole (1830–1906), who was known for both farce and domestic melodrama, and Ellen Terry (1847–1928), known for her Shakespearean roles. One of her frequent collaborators was the prominent actor-manager Henry Irving (1838–1905). Irving had been raised in a strict Methodist family that opposed the theatre, but he rebelled. He first arrived on the London stage in 1856, and spent 15 years playing stock roles in Shakespeare plays and popular comedies until his turn as the callow Digby Grant in James Albery's *Two Roses* made him a star. In the 1870s, he was well-known for his portrayals of Richard III and for the dual role of the evil Dubosc and the virtuous Leserques in Charles Reade's *The Lyons Mail.* From 1878, he combined acting with management of the Lyceum Theatre in London. However, his private life was not spotless, and rumors of an affair with Ellen Terry precluded a knighthood in the 1880s. Actors and actresses had always been seen by Victorians as far less than respectable, given that their profession involved behaving falsely (that is, acting) and selling access to their bodies (via performance). After years of campaigning to have theatre recognized on the same plane of respectability and artistry as painting and music, in 1895 Irving was granted a knighthood—the first ever granted to an actor. This was generally taken as a sign that theatre, once synonymous with scandal, was now respectable.

Trends in poetry after 1870 included a fascination with all things medieval, exemplified by Tennyson's *Idylls of the King* (1859–1885) which retold the myth of

King Arthur. In addition aestheticism and decadence emerged as closely-related influential artistic movements. Poetry that emerged from the aesthetic movement, which celebrated beauty in everyday life, and from the decadent movement, which separated the pleasurable from the moral, challenged Victorian reserve with a commitment to excess, and linked literary innovation to marginal sexualities. Aestheticism flourished in the 1870s and 1880s, and focused on beauty and on sensation. The most important aesthetic poet was Algernon Charles Swinburne (1837–1909), author of many important works including the epic poem *Tristram of Lyonesse* (1882). Decadence flourished in the 1890s; its champions included Oscar Wilde, whose poem *The Ballad of Reading Gaol* (1898) was written from and about prison, Arthur Symons (1865–1945), author of the 1893 essay "The Decadent Movement in Literature," and Ernest Dowson (1867–1900), from whose work we get the phrases "days of wine and roses" and "gone with the wind." Another leading figure was the Irish writer William Butler Yeats (1865–1939); he believed that literature and politics were intimately linked, particularly in the case of Ireland. Yeats and many aesthetic and decadent writers knew each other, as members of the Rhymers' Club and contributors to the literary periodical *The Yellow Book*. Important late Victorian female poets included Anglo-Jewish writer Amy Levy (1861–1889) and Michael Field (a pseudonym for co-authors Katharine Harris Bradley (1846–1914) and Edith Emma Cooper (1862–1913)).

In the more robust genre of the novel, the later Victorian period saw the continued popularity of sensation fiction alongside two new trends: the rise of realist novels and the rise of popular novels. Realist novelists attempted to depict life as it actually was rather than as it should be, combining accurate representation with moral education. After the deaths of Thackeray in 1863 and Dickens in 1870, realist George Eliot dominated the literary scene. She argued that "[a]rt is the nearest thing to life . . . a mode of amplifying our experience and extending our contact with our fellow-men beyond the bounds of our personal lot,"[15] and that the task of the novelist was to represent psychological depths truthfully. But the inner lives she portrayed were always firmly linked to a wider social context; one biographer stresses that all her novels illustrate the famous remark from her novel *Felix Holt* that "[t]here is no private life which has not been determined by a wider public life."[16] Her novel *Middlemarch* (1871), set in a small town in the English Midlands during the passage of the Great Reform Act of 1832, is often cited as the apex of British realism (and was recently declared to be "the best British novel of all time" in a *Guardian* newspaper poll of critics from outside the UK[17]). The plot, which references contemporary debates over women's status in marriage, political reform, and the rise of the medical profession, set multiple psyches from various social strata in play with one another. Without descending to idealization of the 1830s or of country life, the novel presents a detailed and multilayered social scene that features pettiness and unkindness as well as generosity and goodness, and encourages us to sympathize with unlikeable as well as with admirable characters. Reviewers enthused about the author's intimate understanding of so many sorts of human lives, male and female, rich and poor, professional and domestic, married and unmarried, happy and unhappy. Henry James wrote that there was "nothing more powerfully real" than the "painful fireside scenes between [the idealistic young doctor] Lydgate and his miserable little wife."[18]

There were other new topics and subgenres as well. These included urban novels (such as George Gissing's *New Grub Street* (1891)), adventure stories, novels of rural nostalgia (by the time Hardy published *Far From the Madding Crowd* in 1874, the rural life it depicted was foreign to most Britons), novels about artists and performers (Oscar Wilde's only novel, *The Picture of Dorian Gray* (1890), was one), and novels with a eugenic bent that promoted notions of racial fitness. Marriage remained both central and increasingly problematized, most notably in the "New Woman" novels that rebelled against Victorian sexual politics. These included Sarah Grand's *The Heavenly Twins* (1893), which attacks the sexual double standard and details the destructive effects men's syphilis had on women and their children, but also calls on middle-class women to choose racially fit mates. Early twentieth-century novelists included Samuel Butler (1835–1902), whose posthumously published novel *The Way of All Flesh* (1903) was seen as one of the first attacks on Victorian society (in particular the Church of England) as immoral, and Arnold Bennett (1867–1931), a prolific writer who was concerned with many contemporary gender issues, including inequalities in marriage. Bennett produced both light, popular fare such as *Anna of the Five Towns* (1902), about a young woman living in the Potteries area of Staffordshire, and more complex novels that extended the genre of realism, including *Whom God hath Joined* (1906), a portrayal of an unhappy marriage. The works of poet and novelist Rudyard Kipling (1865–1936), who was raised in India, were also popular. They included the picaresque *Kim* (1901), which depicted life in India in detail. One of the most important early twentieth-century novelists was E.M. Forster (1879–1970). His early novel *A Room with a View* (1908) depicted middle-class Britons abroad, while *Howards End* (1910) was an observation of cultural clashes within the now-vast middle class.

But although we still read works by Gissing and Forster and New Woman novelists, the late nineteenth and early twentieth centuries saw a flood of popular novels that were more important than any of these—at least if we judge importance by numbers of readers. From the 1880s popular fiction became still more popular. The number of novels published each year rose from about 450 per year in the mid-1880s to 1,600 per year by to the late 1890s. Cheap reprints, sometimes called yellowbacks in reference to their brightly-colored cardboard covers, made novels available to the literate masses. Routledge's "Railway Library" line was published from 1848 until 1899, by which time it offered over 1,200 titles for only one shilling apiece. Titles included *My Official Wife*, *The Diamond Button: Whose Was It?*, and Mary Elizabeth Braddon's bestseller *Lady Audley's Secret*.

Turning to periodical literature, the 1880s saw the emergence of "New Journalism." New Journalism featured content that entertained and attracted readers and focused on violent crime, amusing mishaps, scandals, exposés, and stories that could be pressed into a melodramatic or sensational narrative. It was visually distinctive and appealing, with banner headlines, front pages devoted to news rather than advertisements, and many illustrations. It was participatory, with papers encouraging readers to write in to express their opinions, to ask for advice, to compete in contests. New Journalism created community and helped working-class readers to imagine themselves as a part of the political nation. New Journalism included serious investigative reporting; one of the leading publishers of New Journalism, W.T. Stead, saw himself as a populist reformer and was committed to serious investigative journalism as a way of campaigning for social, legal, and political change. It also featured plenty of entertainment: the penny weekly *Tit-bits*, published by George Newnes, featured very short news pieces and promotions of all kinds such as competitions and prizes; *Answers*, published by Alfred Harmsworth (later Lord Northcliffe) published letters from readers and answers to them; *Comic Cuts* for children and *Forget-Me-Not* and *Home Chat* for women were also accessible and engaging to their audiences. Historian Ian Haywood argues that one of New Journalism's strengths was that it combined popular entertainment with radical politics.[19]

Many commentators disapproved of New Journalism. The term was coined by the famously elitist writer Matthew Arnold, who in an 1887 essay called this new style "feather-brained." Contemporary middle-class commentators and late twentieth-century historians alike characterized New Journalism as the dumbing-down or even the death of serious journalism in Britain, with a commitment to reporting the truth and educating the public replaced by a determination to entertain, a focus on sales figures, and a willingness to pander. More recently, however, historians have taken a second look at the New Journalism, and noted that it was not such a radical break with past practices. Victorian newspapers had been reporting on many of these same topics—violent crimes, especially murder, but also on "extraordinary events" of all kinds—and in melodramatic and sensationalist ways, for decades, since the 1850s abolition of duties and taxes. Moreover these topics and styles were as popular among middle-class as among working-class readers; sensational reporting of violent crime was a central feature not just of the popular weeklies but of the august *Times*. And New Journalism was often good journalism; historian Kate Jackson argues that the *Tit-Bits* actually raised the quality of journalism when it was founded in 1881.[20]

Two of the best examples of the impact of New Journalism come in its reporting of major scandals and crimes. The first was published in the *Pall Mall Gazette* by W.T. Stead. In 1883 Stead took on the editorship of the *Pall Mall Gazette* and revamped the magazine to feature sensational headlines, illustrations, and human interest stories (when Arnold first critiqued New Journalism as feather-brained, he was referring to Stead's *Pall Mall Gazette*). Stead believed himself to be a crusader, a campaigner for moral causes. Sensational exposé and moral campaign came together in July 1885, when Stead published a four-part exposé entitled "The Maiden Tribute of Modern Babylon." In it, he claimed that in the interests of journalism and the pursuit of truth and of legal reform, he had purchased a 13-year-old girl, Eliza Armstrong, from her mother for £5 for the purpose of selling her into white slavery (the term referred to the alleged practice of purchasing young white girls and selling them into lives of sexual slavery—prostitution—on "the continent," that is, mainland Europe). Stead claimed that his purchase revealed the willingness of unfeeling working-class parents to sell their children and of the existence of an enormous and hitherto-unknown white slave trade in the heart of the British Empire. His journalistic standards soon came under scrutiny. Armstrong's mother denied selling her, insisting that she had been given to understand that her daughter was going into domestic service. It was revealed that Stead had—in the interests of authenticity—traumatized the girl with an invasive medical examination and travel to France. Ultimately, Stead served several months in prison for his actions. The series is considered one of the causes of the passage of the 1885 Criminal Amendment Act (in which the age of consent for girls was raised from 13 to 16). "The Maiden Tribute of Modern Babylon" was incredibly popular; the *Pall Mall Gazette* printed 12,000 copies of the July issues, rather than the usual 8,000, and still sold out. The series was instrumental in establishing the possibilities of and standards for New Journalism: it was sensational; it was melodramatic; it was inspired by popular fears, but also helped to maintain or even create those fears; it was more concerned to be fascinating than to be accurate; and it sold papers.

Another signal moment in the history of New Journalism was the coverage of the 1888 "Jack the Ripper" murders. This was a series of murders of women working as prostitutes in the Whitechapel area of the East End of London. First called the "Whitechapel murders," they soon came to be known as the Jack the Ripper murders, after the press's name for the assailant (who was never caught). The murders were first reported and extensively covered in one of the leading new journalism publications, *Lloyd's Weekly Newspaper*, which saw its circulation skyrocket to nearly 900,000 copies per week during its coverage of the Ripper murders. But the murders were also reported in many other New Journalism papers and in more respectable papers such as the *Times*. In many ways the coverage of the Ripper murders in *Lloyd's* and other papers is perfectly emblematic of New Journalism. The coverage was sensational, melodramatic, and titillating about real-life murders. It informed, but it also boosted sales figures dramatically.

From the 1880s, as New Journalism flourished, the weekly Sunday papers saw their circulation figures rise dramatically (cheaper materials, machine-manufactured paper and new printing techniques were a factor here too); they became the best-selling and most widely-circulated reading materials in Britain. *Reynolds's Newspaper* sold more than 300,000 copies per week in the 1880s; by the 1890s *Tit-Bits* sold 500,000 copies per week and *Lloyds Weekly Newspaper* sold more than 600,000 copies per week. All three appealed to a broad, popular audience and featured an appealing variety of content. Their high sales figures reveal a working-class and lower middle-class hunger for education, respectability, and self-improvement, and an interest in the speed, industrialization, and efficiency of modern life. They also reflect the fact that the new papers offered community, fun, and games of chance as well as information and entertainment; in a 1906 report, a newsagent (newspaper vendor) from Salford (outside of Manchester) remarked that when it came to newspapers, "Reading don't matter that much. What does count is the chance of getting something for nothing, £10 notes for tram tickets, gold watches for naming football winners."[21]

Finally, in the 1890s, popular weekly papers were joined by daily papers; some consider this the moment when "popular" journalism became "mass" journalism.

In 1896, Harmsworth began publishing the first ½d. daily, the *Daily Mail*, which focused entirely on short articles about lighter news, entertainment, gossip, and fiction, while maintaining respectability. It aimed at lower middle-class workers such as shop assistants and clerks, including features aimed at female readers. The *Daily Mail* was an immediate success; by 1900 it sold almost 1 million copies every day and had ensured the future of mass-circulation daily newspapers. In 1900, Cyril Pearson (a former employee of George Newnes) founded the similar *Daily Express*. Harmsworth responded in 1903 with the *Daily Mirror*. As the twentieth century started, Britain was a society replete with popular, appealing, and easy-to-digest newspapers.

Notes

1 *Oliver Twist*, Chapter 17; in Oxford World Classics (1999), p. 129.
2 James Eli Adams, *A History of Victorian Literature* (Oxford: Wiley-Blackwell, 2009), p. 49.
3 Tom Scriven, "The Jim Crow Craze in London's Press and Streets, 1836–39," *Journal of Victorian Culture* 19.1 (March 2014): 93–109.
4 Michael R. Booth, *Theatre in the Victorian Age* (Cambridge: Cambridge University Press, 1991), p. 5.
5 Sally Mitchell, "Introduction," Mrs Henry Wood, *East Lynne*, with an introduction by Sally Mitchell (New Brunswick, NJ: Rutgers University Press, 1984), pp. xii–xiv.
6 David Masson, "British Novelists Since Scott," (1859), in Edwin M. Eigner and George J. Worth (eds), *Victorian Criticism of the Novel* (Cambridge: Cambridge University Press, 1985): 158.
7 Hilary Schor, "Fiction," in Herbert F. Tucker (ed.), *A Companion to Victorian Literature and Culture* (Oxford: Blackwell, 1999), p. 336.
8 Alan Hardy, *Queen Victoria Was Amused* (London: John Murray, 1976), p. 26.
9 Elizabeth Rigby, *Quarterly*, 1848, quoted in Adams, p. 117.
10 Margaret Oliphant, "Sensation Novels," *Blackwood's Magazine* xci (May 1862): 565–574, from Norman Page, *Wilkie Collins: The Critical Heritage* (London: Routledge, 1974), pp. 118–119.
11 Adams, p. 200.
12 Quoted in Peter Bailey, *Leisure and Class in Victorian England* (London: Routledge, 1978), pp. 43–44.
13 Anthony L. Ellis, "The East-End Jew at his Playhouse, *Pall Mall* 41 (1908): 173–179.
14 *The Times*, November 23, 1900, p. 7; May 30, 1911, p. 11.
15 George Eliot, *Essays*, edited by Thomas Pinney (New York: Columbia University Press, 1963), pp. 270–271.
16 Rosemary Ashton, "Evans, Marian [George Eliot] (1819–1880)," *Oxford Dictionary of National Biography*, (Oxford: Oxford University Press, 2004).
17 Alison Flood, "The best British novel of all time: have international critics found it?" *Guardian* December 8, 2015, available online at: www.theguardian.com/books/booksblog/2015/dec/08/best-british-novel-of-all-time-international-critics-top-100-middlemarch (accessed December 18, 2015).
18 Ashton.
19 Ian Haywood, *The Revolution in Popular Literature* (Cambridge: Cambridge University Press, 2004), p. 131.
20 Kate Jackson, *George Newnes and the New Journalism in Britain, 1880–1910: Culture and Profit* (Aldershot: Ashgate, 2001), p. 85.

21 J.H. Haslam, *The Press and the People: An Estimate of Reading in Working-class Districts* (Manchester: Manchester City News, 1906), quoted in Victor E. Neuburg, *Popular Literature: A History and Guide* (London: Woburn, 1977), pp. 230–231.

Relevant fiction students might enjoy

George Eliot, *Middlemarch* (1871–1872)
J.B. Priestley, *Lost Empires* (1965)
Sarah Waters, *Tipping the Velvet* (1998)

Further reading

Peter Bailey, "Theatres of Entertainment/Spaces of Modernity: Rethinking the British Popular Stage 1890–1914," *Nineteenth Century Theatre* 26.1 (Summer 1998): 5–24.
Peter Bailey (ed.), *Music Hall: The Business of Pleasure* (Milton Keynes and Philadelphia: Open University Press, 1986).
Various works by Michael Booth on the history of the theatre.
J.S. Bratton (ed.), *Music Hall: Performance and Style* (Milton Keynes and Philadelphia: Open University Press, 1986).
Joseph Bristow (ed.), *The Cambridge Companion to Victorian Poetry* (Cambridge: Cambridge University Press, 2000).
Deirdre David (ed.), *The Cambridge Companion to the Victorian Novel* (Cambridge: Cambridge University Press, 2006).
Dagmar Kift, *The Victorian Music Hall: Culture, Class and Conflict* (Cambridge: Cambridge University Press, 1996).

Online resources

Victoria and Albert Museum—Theatre and Performance: www.vam.ac.uk/page/t/theatre-and-performance/; see especially the section on Music Hall & Variety Theatre at www.vam.ac.uk/page/m/music-hall/
Victorian Women Writers Project: http://webapp1.dlib.indiana.edu/vwwp/welcome.do
The Dickens Project: http://dickens.ucsc.edu/
The Victorian Plays Project: http://victorian.nuigalway.ie/modx/
The Gilbert and Sullivan Archive: http://math.boisestate.edu/gas/index.html
At the Circulating Library: A Database of Victorian Fiction, 1837–1901: www.victorian research.org/atcl/index.php
Victorian poetry, British Library: www.bl.uk/romantics-and-victorians/themes/victorian-poetry
Rossetti Archive: www.rossettiarchive.org/

12 Marriage, free love, and "unnatural crimes"

Sexuality

Introduction

In his 1897 letter-cum-essay *De Profundis*, Oscar Wilde wrote with regret about his sex life:

> The gods had given me almost everything. But I let myself be lured into long spells of senseless and sensual ease . . . I deliberately went to the depths in the search for new sensation. . . . Desire, at the end, was a malady, or a madness, or both. I grew careless of the lives of others. I took pleasure where it pleased me, and passed on. I forgot that every little action of the common day makes or unmakes character, and that therefore what one has done in the secret chamber one has some day to cry aloud on the housetop. . . . I allowed pleasure to dominate me. I ended in horrible disgrace. There is only one thing for me now, absolute humility.

Among other things, Wilde was known as the Victorian most committed to decadence and to excess. Yet here he implies that sex should be indulged in only in moderation, and states that unrestrained pursuit of sexual pleasure ruins one's character. In this—though in little else—Wilde was a typical Victorian.

It is difficult to write the history of Victorian sexuality because today "Victorian" means to most people either an opposition to sexuality, a refusal to discuss it or admit that it exists, or the exact opposite, a pervasive "naughtiness" thinly disguised by false prudery. The stereotype of the repressed Victorian was famously attacked by historian and philosopher Michel Foucault (1926–1984) in the 1970s and 1980s. He and others argued that the Victorian warnings about sex that we had for the better part of the twentieth century interpreted as repression were nothing of the sort. Victorian Britain produced more writing and thought about sexuality than ever before. There were scientific experiments, medical treatises, psychological studies, legal cases, how-to manuals, pornography, and advertisements for quack remedies for venereal diseases. In other words, the problem with the Victorians was not that they never talked about sex, but that they never stopped talking about it. However, more recent historical work has challenged the Foucauldian approach to the history of sexuality, especially its emphasis on the influence of disciplinary discourses and its focus on pronouncements over actual behavior.

Contrary to the impression one might get from reading Foucault, not all Victorians talked about sex. True, endless discussions of sexuality were common among medical and legal experts, the highly educated, and radicals, but most people, certainly most working-class people, never talked about sex. Working-class culture was reticent about all bodily functions; middle-class women prided themselves on their sexual innocence; before the 1890s, most men who loved or had sex with other men knew nothing about theories of "inversion" that sought to explain their desire. Furthermore, the fact that some people talked and wrote a lot about sex and sexuality does not mean that they (let alone others) were actually having a lot of sex. This chapter explores Victorian notions of normal and per-verse sexuality; looks at what people did, whether or not they talked about it; and maps out changes over time in beliefs and practices. Together these can help us understand not only what people did, but perhaps more importantly, what they thought about it.

As with any aspect of history, surviving sources (though they may be uneven or unrepresentative) determine what can be known about Victorian sexuality. It is far easier to research sexual ideas, rules, and prescriptions than it is to research sexual behavior. While prescriptive sources abound, those that describe actual experience are rare. We know very little about heterosexual behavior before the late twentieth century, and we know almost nothing about the marital sexual-ity of the Victorian working class, though bastardy laws and foundling hospitals tell us something about premarital working-class sexual behavior. Demographic historians use censuses and other aggregate data to gain some insight into sexual practices. Some sexually explicit diaries survive, though they are by their nature unrepresentative. Advice manuals can be helpful, as can medical, psychological, and sexological writings. Pornography can offer insight into culturally specific forms of desire. Legal records can be invaluable, especially if transcripts of witness testimony survive. Advertisements for quack medicines that promised to cure venereal disease and impotence and to end pregnancy tell us which problems were considered so secret and shameful that doctors would not address them.

1820–1870: Ideals and realities

Victorian society was marked by a sexual double standard: men's sexual behavior was judged by one standard, and women's by another, with the result that male and female sexuality were defined very differently, and acts and desires considered perfectly normal in men were seen as deviant in women.

Ideal male sexuality was part of a larger masculine ideal of the independent, self-disciplined husband and father who was the sole financial support for his family. Thus male sexuality was first and foremost "uxorious," which means that it was expressed exclusively and entirely with a wife. This was a pronounced contrast with the eighteenth century, during which the bachelor and the rake (a man of dissolute or promiscuous habits) were both admired figures (at least to some). The centrality of marriage to ideal male sexuality would intensify in the later Victorian period. Historian Sean Brady argues that by the 1860s masculinity "*meant a man being married.*"[1] The bachelor, once entirely acceptable and even admirably rakish, became a problematic and ambivalent figure. Men who did not support households were unmanly.

Second, ideal male sexuality was restrained. This may seem to us to contradict the centrality of marriage. However, for the Victorians there was no contradiction, because the essence of marriage was not sex but romantic love. Victorians were extremely sentimental—hence their love of melodrama, which was full of exaggerated and unproblematic declarations of love—and saw love and sex as quite separate. Many people emphasized the spiritual nature of their unions with their spouses, and while today many couples see sex as a way of expressing or furthering their love, Victorian couples saw sex as something that tarnished or diminished the purity of their love for one another. Men were expected to desire sex, but husbands were expected to be able to control their desires; demands for marital sex for purposes other than procreation were ungentlemanly. If a man had to have recreational sex, he was expected to hire a prostitute (this was still considered immoral, but not unnatural), not treat his wife like one. Discreet extra-marital sex was common amongst the aristocracy (although it became less common over the nineteenth century), and aristocratic men could and often did quietly provide for illegitimate children. For example, Royal Naval officer Francis William Lowther (1841–1908) was the illegitimate son of the very wealthy Tory William Lowther, the second earl of Lonsdale; on his father's death in 1872 he inherited £125,000. Frederick FitzClarence, illegitimate son of the future William IV, had a successful military career and was granted an aristocratic title when his father took the throne.

There were two key threats to masculinity: impotence and masturbation. In the early Victorian period, both were linked to "spermatorrhoea." The term was coined in 1836 by a French physician, Claude-Francoise Lallemand, to describe involuntary seminal loss (usually though not always via nocturnal emissions). Spermatorrhoea was believed to be a serious medical condition that caused blushing, crying, breathlessness, melancholy, and sensitivity. Masturbation was a primary cause; impotence, a result (and confusingly, doctors claimed both that masturbation led to impotence and that impotence led to masturbation). Spermatorrhoea was a popular diagnosis between the 1830s and the 1860s, but then became unfashionable and rare.

One of the most famous accusations of impotence in history was against one of the most famous Victorians, writer and critic John Ruskin (1819–1900). His disastrous 1848 marriage to Effie Gray was annulled unconsummated in 1854, allegedly due to his impotence. Impotence was multivalent, considered either proof of effeminacy—men who were "delicate [and] rather feminine in form" were considered especially vulnerable—or the result of excessive intercourse or masturbation ("onanism"). Impotence could be blamed on masturbation, on women, or on society more generally. Wives were blamed for causing impotence either by being insufficiently welcoming, or by being excessively excited or, demanding. Alternately, impotence was seen as a disease of overcivilization. Urban life, non-physical occupations, and the constant strain of modern society, came together to exhaust the nineteenth-century man. Impotent men were often mocked in popular culture, for instance in music hall songs about husbands who could not satisfy their wives. Quack remedies for "lowness of spirits" were advertised, promising "manhood restored."[2]

Male masturbation had long been criticized as a bad habit, but in the Victorian era it became seen as a problem both medical and moral, and susceptible to solutions from authorities on both. The campaign against masturbation is generally seen to have begun in the late eighteenth century following the publication of two tracts, *Onania or the Heinous Sin of Self-Pollution* (which by the mid-eighteenth century was in its twentieth edition) and *Onanism* by French physician Samuel Tissot (which appeared in English in 1766). In the early Victorian period, masturbation was seen as immoral, disgusting, and physically weakening (and, of course, a main cause of spermatorrhoea). Advice about how to avoid masturbation and how to combat its dangerous results came from those claiming medical expertise: doctors, sellers of quack remedies, and from the 1850s phrenologists, who claimed they could know an individual's weaknesses and strengths by reading the bumps of his or her skull. Phrenologist O.S. Fowler's 1856 book, *Amativeness: Or Evils and Remedies of Excessive and Perverted Sexuality*, sold over half a million copies. All of this scientific advice was directed at adult men, who were exhorted to control themselves.

Ideal female sexuality was quite different. Marriage was women's proper destiny, their calling, and their profession. Women who failed to marry were viewed with either pity or contempt if they wanted to marry, with suspicion if they did not, and spinsters were looked on as less than fully adult, since they did not have their own households. However for women, marriage was not pursued because of sex. While husbands restrained themselves in spite of their desires, wives were—ideally— "passionless" beings who had sex to satisfy their husbands and to reproduce. One well-known doctor of the reproductive systems, William Acton, wrote that "the majority of women . . . are not very much troubled with sexual feeling of any kind."[3] That women fell in love and married without any sexual impulses was not experienced as a contradiction, because neither marriage nor love were seen as primarily sexual. On the contrary, sex was a bestial and unworthy expression of love. Victorians believed that women should not, and more importantly did not, experience sexual desire. Some historians have uncovered evidence of Victorian marriages that were sexually active and of individual Victorian women who enjoyed sex, and some now feel that we have overestimated the reach and strength of the doctrine of passionlessness. However, it is true that women who enjoyed sex did so in spite of significant obstacles that included not only the doctrine of passionlessness but fear of pregnancy, pregnancy itself, and fear of sexual violence. Many women internalized the doctrine of passionlessness and believed themselves unbothered by sexual desire. Passionless was associated with respectability—nice women did not experience desire—and contrasted with nonwhites, especially Africans, who were thought to be both uncivilized and highly sexual.

For women, an embrace of the doctrine of passionlessness was on many levels a sensible reaction to the world in which they lived. For working-class women especially, rapid industrialization and urbanization had created a world in which women were easily deserted by premarital sexual partners who had promised to marry them upon pregnancy, and in which unmarried motherhood was a social and economic burden. The age of menarche (the start of menstruation and fertility) was around the age of 12½—though very poor girls might experience a delay due to poor nutrition—so pregnancy was a danger long before marriage was considered appropriate. Female sexuality was also marked by ignorance, which was an aspect of respectability and a point of pride for many women. A late-eighteenth and early-nineteenth century surge in births—to both married and single women—was followed by a reaction, a decline in births that began in 1820 and lasted over a century. Women's determination to limit their births led them to resist sex.

The converse of the wife was the fallen women—one who had once been respectable, but had fallen into sexual vice—and the prostitute. The prostitute was a central figure in the cultural landscape, in which women were divided into virtuous and vicious, innocent and fallen, wife and prostitute. Prostitution exemplified the Victorian sexual double standard. Though widespread, it was considered wrong. Victorians did not assume that whatever is "natural" is "normal"; on the contrary, they considered wrong a wide variety of sexual desires and practices that they recognized as natural. A man's visit to a prostitute was one such practice. Prostitution existed in what historian of sexuality Anna Clark calls "twilight" moments—"those sexual practices and desires that societies prohibit by law or custom but that people pursue anyhow, whether in secret or as an open secret."[4] Prostitution was neither celebrated nor strictly forbidden but, as an open secret, could attract attention.

There is much evidence—from such sources as Parliamentary debates, divorce trials, and the records of hospitals that treated venereal disease—that middle-class and upper-class men often had sex with prostitutes. Because many men married late, and because men were believed to have stronger sexual drives than women, many saw prostitution as a necessary evil, and sex with female prostitutes as an accepted part of male sexuality. Foreign visitors often commented on how visible prostitution was in Britain's major cities. Attempts to quantify were unsuccessful: at mid-century, estimates of the number of prostitutes in London alone varied from 5,000 to 220,000, an outlandish figure which would have been 7% of the metropole's population. However, this mythic number contained in it a grain of truth: as Britain urbanized, larger city populations, more men with access to prostitutes, and more women with economically uncertain lives combined to mean that a larger proportion of the population engaged in prostitution. Furthermore, large numbers of working-class men were uprooted to work on the railway or other aspects of the growing infrastructure; far from home and from prying eyes, they were more likely to engage prostitutes than they were at home. But while men were not, generally, judged for hiring prostitutes, the women they hired were considered irretrievably "fallen" women who had to be either avoided or "rescued."

Between 1820 and 1870, rescue workers spent much time, money, and effort trying to reform prostitutes via harsh regimes in rescue homes followed by offers of work in domestic service.

For any past society in which there was no widely used reliable form of birth control, the population's fertility levels are our best evidence of its sexual activity. Since British family size reached its historical high point in about 1820—at a level of almost six children per married couple—we can infer that reproductive sexuality also reached a high point then. The decline in fertility that followed reveals a decline in reproductive sexuality: after 1820 British men and women had less sex, at least within their marriages. The Victorian decline in sex was achieved principally through what one demographic historian calls a "culture of abstinence": it was culturally acceptable, even desirable, to resist having sex. Victorians valued self-control highly in many aspects of life, including sexual activity. They developed a culture of sexual restraint in which self-control was prized and many married couples routinely went for long periods without having sex. (Delaying the age at which women married could also effectively reduce fertility, but this does not seem to have been a common practice.) The combination of fear of conception and sexual ignorance led to very little sexual pleasure (which in turn made passionlessness easy to embrace). Too much sex was considered physically unhealthy and morally lax.

Sex between men and women was also limited in terms of the acts that were acceptable and widely practiced. Although conception was a fear, anecdotal evidence indicates that Victorians did not, by and large, pursue forms of sex that would not result in conception. They did not practice petting (which we know had been common among the working class in the eighteenth century). Nor did they generally engage in oral or anal sex: neither were typical heterosexual practices in Britain until well into the middle of the twentieth century. So far as we can tell, Victorian heterosexual practice consisted principally of engaging in vaginal intercourse or refraining from it, with the latter more common.[5]

Sex was also dangerous. One danger was the threat of contracting venereal diseases, which were extremely widespread (see Chapter 14) especially in the military (where infection rates hovered around 20%) but in the general population as well (where infection rates were probably about 10%). Gonorrhea and syphilis were the most common sexually transmitted diseases, with syphilis more prevalent and more dangerous. Before the availability of penicillin in the 1940s it was contagious, painful, progressive, and incurable. Venereal diseases were associated with prostitutes, who were thought to be the means of infecting decent society, but in reality venereal diseases were spread to prostitutes as well as from them, from husbands to wives, and other ways. Doctors generally did not treat these shameful ailments, leaving them to quacks who offered a wide variety of cures, principally plasters, injections, and pills that contained mercury (which is poisonous). Other cures included bleeding, emetics, and baths. It was not until after World War One that venereal disease started to be treated as a public health issue rather than an individual's moral failing.

Another danger of sex was pregnancy, which was a far more central part of sexuality than it is today. Indeed it was a far more central part of life; many women spent two or more decades of their lives pregnant or nursing. Women were keenly aware of the risks of pregnancy and childbirth, both of which killed many women and their babies and endangered or exhausted others. Pregnancy was unplanned—contraception was often ineffective and always unrespectable. Pregnancy was tiring, especially for hardworking or undernourished working-class women. For a married couple, a pregnancy was life-changing for both members of the couple, though the man's health and life were not at risk. While aristocratic women usually kept up their social schedules until late in their pregnancies, many working-class women were ashamed of being visibly pregnant. For an unmarried couple, the social and economic brunt of a non-marital pregnancy, which was significant, fell on the woman alone. Middle-class women almost never got pregnant outside of marriage. In the upper class, extramarital affairs were not uncommon; aristocratic men could discreetly acknowledge their illegitimate offspring, but aristocratic women had to hide adulterous pregnancies and give up all contact with their illegitimate children. In the working class, premarital intercourse was common. Working-class culture took an expansive view of marital sex, and was accepting of sex between affianced couples. A courting couple would often have intercourse, aware that it would eventually result in pregnancy, and intending to marry when this occurred. This practice led to high bridal pregnancies (when the intended marriages took place) and high rates of illegitimate birth (when they did not). But while the fathers of these illegitimate children were rarely judged, to be the mother of illegitimate children was a serious stigma for a woman. This stigma was made legal in 1845 when the Bastardy Clause added to the 1834 Poor Law left women unable to claim support from their children's fathers. Small wonder, then, that rural communities tried to compel marriages when women got pregnant, that women sued fickle fiancés for breach of promise of marriage, that the London Foundling Hospital received many times the applications they could accept, and that abortion, desertion, and even infanticide were part of Victorian life.

In addition to "heterosexual" sex there was of course also "homosexual" sex (the words are convenient but anachronistic). In the past two decades there has been a wealth of research on love and desire between men and between women. One of the most important points that scholars emphasize is that same-sex love, desire, and sex can only be understood in the context of the larger society in which they occurred. The Victorian emphasis on marriage, and the assumption that gender difference was natural and fundamental, shaped ideas about same-sex desire.

• One dramatic difference between the Victorian period and our own is that we consider sexual orientation to be an aspect of personal and political identity. But in the Victorian period, the gender of the people an individual was attracted to did not define that individual. Having sex with men did not necessarily make a man a "homosexual"—the term was not in use until the late nineteenth century—either in his own eyes or those of others. What one did sexually could be as meaningful as who one did it with. On the other hand, there was no simple progression from pre-twentieth-century acts to twentieth-century identities.

Discussing sex between Victorian men brings us back to Anna Clark's idea of "twilight": it was recognized but not tolerated, shameful and secret but openly recognized.⁶ Throughout the late eighteenth and nineteenth centuries there was a subculture of "sodomites" or "Mary Annes," which was characterized by cross-dressing and effeminate men, and by such social events as the *bal masque*, a formal costume ball that featured cross-dressed men. But there was also a much larger group of men who had sex with men but did not consider themselves effeminate or "sodomitical." Some men had sex only with other men, others with both men and women. Some men lived in "marriages" with other men; others were married to women, but had sex with men; others remained unmarried. Male "friendship" was a flexible and ambiguous concept that encompassed both sexual and non-sexual relationships. Shame meant that extortion was possible and common. Male prostitution was widespread, and in fact many terms for men who had sex with men, such as "Mary Annes" or "mollies," originally referred specifically to prostitutes.

While sex with a man was effeminizing, men could sometimes preserve their masculinity even when they had sex with men. Throughout the nineteenth century, men pursued a variety of intimate relationships with other men that were defined economically, socially, and sexually through dominance over or equality with one another. Sex between men was one aspect of this. Among working-class people, a man could still be masculine as long as he dominated the man he had sex with, by virtue of either age or penetration during sodomy (anal penetration). Working-class men who had sex with middle- or upper-class men (they were often soldiers and extortionists) could maintain their masculinity if they had sex for financial gain or if they were not penetrated. Similarly, upper-class men cited ancient classical models to claim that sex with another man was not effeminizing as long as one was imposing one's desires rather than submitting to the partner's desires. As with the working class, physical domination of the partner was critical to the maintenance of virility. Upper-class commentators often claimed that working-class men who had sex with men were effeminized by the act; working-class observers of upper-class men made the same accusation.

Sex between men of different classes attracted the most attention during the Victorian period, especially if it took place in a public or semi-public place. Sodomy between men was illegal even if it took place in private between consenting adults. However, family, social, and legal reactions to sex between men varied by class. While sex between men was never accepted, it might be overlooked for years (and then become cause for extortion or arrest). Working-class men whose families needed their wages were not always condemned for having sex with other men, and might maintain their social standing. In the middle and upper classes, the accusation of having sex with another man was a serious affront to a man's character and honor. Yet sex among middle- and upper-class boys, who spent most of their lives before marriage in the same-sex cultures of boarding schools and universities, might be dismissed as youthful experimentation. Sex between upper-class men and between middle-class men was usually kept quite private and was overlooked by the police. Most people assumed that sexual desire for other men was the province of men of low class and low character. Respectability and character, which were so intensely central and valuable to middle-class and upper-class men, were simply not compatible with desire for or sex with men. Respectable men denied such activities, or if caught *in flagrante*, would usually insist that their actions did not reflect their true character.[7]

Sex between men was illegal (and had been since 1533), and so vulnerable to prosecution. As we saw in Chapter 10, the Georgian pattern of rare but dramatic prosecutions and punishments was succeeded by a Victorian pattern of less severe but more consistently and more frequently implemented punishments. In the eighteenth and early nineteenth centuries, prosecutions for sodomy were rare and sensational. While there was popular detestation of "unnatural" relations between men, there was also little government interference, especially if the sex was not cross-class. Arrests, when they did happen, tended to take the form of raids of molly houses, semi-private spaces in which men could meet one another. This pattern changed in the Victorian period. Laws passed in 1827 and 1828 expanded the legal definition of an "infamous crime," identified such crimes as sexual acts between men, and made it easier to prosecute men for attempted sodomy and easier to prove sodomy in court. Raids of molly houses became rare, while arrests of men who were having sex in more public spaces (such as parks) increased.

The police were most likely to disrupt sex between men and make an arrest when the sex happened in a public space between men of different classes. Punishments were uneven—criminal law was still applied flexibly if not haphazardly, and arrests and sentences depended on the individual policeman or magistrate—but overall prosecutions for sex between men rose, with a two-year sentence for attempted sodomy the most common outcome. By 1900, almost 9,000 men in England and Wales had been indicted for sodomy, gross indecency, or other "unnatural misdemeanors." Charges of attempted sodomy were often brought by working-class men against upper-class or middle-class men. While middle-class and upper-class men frequented public spaces such as parks and urinals in search of working-class men to have sex with, the social consequences of same-sex desire were so severe that they often vociferously denied their actions. If accused of attempted sodomy by a partner, they would insist that the accusation was false and slanderous. Indeed, many insisted that false accusations of respectable men, who were simply walking innocently through parks when they were targeted by mercenary working-class men, were a graver social problem than actual sex between men. The legal system actually punished false accusations of "unnatural assault" more harshly than "unnatural assault" itself, and so dissuaded many working-class men from bringing accusations (true or false).

Early Victorian newspapers frequently (if obliquely) reported on arrests and trials of men who had cross-class sex in public or semi-public spaces. Newspaper articles depicted men who engaged in sodomy as secretive, and the term "sodomite" came to not only refer to the sexual act but to imply concealment, secrecy, and imposture. Newspaper reports of "unnatural acts" depicted urban landscapes as rife with secret places in which men furtively did unnamable things to one another. These accounts resonated with the Victorian obsession with imposture and with hidden urban subcultures. Newspapers with upper-class readerships, such as the *Morning Post*, tended to report most fully on false accusations and on the defeat of working-class extortionists who preyed on upper-class men. For example, in 1842 the Churchill and Stringer case was reported in the *Morning Post* for months. William Stringer accosted two men he saw in an "indecent situation" one night in Hyde Park; one ran off, and the other, John Churchill, offered Stringer money for silence. However, when it became clear that Stringer and several associates routinely trawled the park in search of potential extortion victims, the newspapers and public opinion took Churchill's side. One letter to the editor of the *Times* lamented that "a gentleman cannot walk in safety through Hyde-park" unless prepared to deal with this new specimen of highway robber, and another called for the return of hanging as a punishment for anyone who made a false accusation of sex between men.[8] Stringer was transported for life; Churchill was held up as an example of a respectable man who only narrowly escaped false accusations of the worst kind.

We know far less about sex between women than we do about reproductive sexuality or about sex between men. Heterosexuality left multiple historical traces, in part because it dominated social organization, in part because it so often left evidence in the form of children. Most of the evidence we have of sex between men was produced by the fact that it was illegal; in addition thriving urban subcultures left traces for historian to study. Sex between women, however, produced neither children nor trials, and unlike New York, Berlin, and Paris, neither London nor any other British city had a same-sex female subculture. The famous story that Queen Victoria refused to sign legislation that outlawed sex between women because she refused to believe that such a thing was even possible is apocryphal, but it emerges out of a larger cultural truth. Because Victorians equated penile penetration of the vagina with "sex," and because they believed that few women ever experienced sexual desire, Victorians had trouble believing that women had sex with one another, or that anything two women did could properly be termed sex. Where sex between men was subject to hostility and legal repercussions, sex between women went unarticulated, referred to only obliquely or through meaningful silences. However, as with sex between men, many medical and legal officials feared that any public discussion would serve to inform: as late as 1921 an attempt to make lesbian sex illegal was defeated in Parliament out of fear that the passage of any law would teach women about a possibility of which they had been unaware.

Representations of women who desired women focused not on their sexual acts but on gender inversion, that is, on their masculine appearances, intellects, or temperaments. Where understandings of sex between men focused on anal penetration, and particularly on the party who was penetrated, understandings of sex between women focused far more on short hair, deep voices, and the wearing of trousers. Indeed, any reference to a woman's masculine appearance was an implicit accusation of same-sex desire. In the scandalous 1864 Codrington divorce trial, Helen Codrington's close friend, feminist Emily Faithfull, who shared a bedroom with her for three years, was described in gossip as "mannish," and as walking about "London in Male attire" as a way of accusing her of same-sex desire.[9]

Cross-class sex between women does not seem to have been common, and we know almost nothing about working-class women who had sex with one another. In the eighteenth century, stories about working-class women who cross-dressed, seeking either work opportunities or sex with other women, were very popular. In the nineteenth century, however, these vanished. Among working-class women, we have some evidence—for example, in the 1850s and 1860s Sarah Geals lived as William Smith and was married to Caroline Smith for 12 years—but it is scattered.

The sources we do have overwhelmingly concern middle- and upper-class women. The history of love between women in Britain usually starts in the eighteenth century with a famous couple, Lady Eleanor Butler (1739–1829) and Sarah Ponsonby (1755–1832), who lived together in Wales as the "Ladies of Llangollen." Also well-known from the earlier period is Anne Lister (1791–1840), a member of the Yorkshire gentry who left a long, sexually explicit, coded diary. Lister was something of a female rake; such women were, like cross-dressers, far less common in the nineteenth century than they had been in the eighteenth.

In the Victorian era, middle-class and upper-class women who loved and desired women had education and financial resources that could be freeing, but at the same time their class status imposed on them the requirements and restraints of respectability. Inside of these constraints, women who loved and desired women looked to a number of available models—including friendship, marriage, and mother–daughter love—to create different kinds of same-sex relationships. The most common model for intimacy and sexual love between women was the "romantic friendship." In this model, female friends loved one another romantically, were physically close, and may have been sexually intimate. George Eliot had at least two intimate romantic friendships; she addressed her second friend, Sara Hennell, whom she knew in the 1840s, as her "dearly beloved spouse." Like boys, middle-class and upper-class girls spent much of their lives in single-sex settings such as boarding schools, and were expected to form close relationships with fellow teachers and with students there; romantic friendships between teenagers and young women were often socially accepted. These friendships were also acceptable because many Victorians saw loving female friendships as good preparation for marriage. Literary critic Sharon Marcus points out that in many Victorian novels female friendship is an important part of courtship and marriage, because female characters are instrumental in finding husbands for their female friends.[10] While the romantic friendship model could be useful in emphasizing intimacy and equality between two women, and could effectively disguise sexual passion as innocent physical affection, it was also limited. As women aged beyond their twenties, their passionate relationships with other women were more likely to be regarded with social and family disapproval, especially if they were unmarried.

While novelist Charlotte Brontë's passionate friendship with Ellen Nussey raised no eyebrows when they were at school together, as the years went on Brontë worried that her continuing passion for Nussey would meet with disapproval.

Another, related model of female intimacy was the mother–daughter coupling. This model was fairly unthreatening, because it was not obviously erotic and because it implied that the relationship was a temporary stage, and so was sometimes socially accepted. Jane Welsh Carlyle (1801–1866) and novelist Geraldine Jewsbury (1812–1880) had such a relationship, as did George Eliot (1819–1880) and social activist Edith Simcox (1844–1901). Another model was that of a husband and wife; some couples, including Anne Lister and Ann Walker, and Rosa Bonheur (1822–1899) and Nathalie Micas (c.1824–1899), lived together in what they considered to be marriages (though families and society always considered family ties stronger than these same-sex marriages). Painter Rosa Bonheur met Nathalie Micas in 1841, when she was a teenager; their union was blessed by Micas' father, and they lived together as artist and supportive wife for 50 years. In spite of this, Bonheur's siblings felt that they were the proper inheritors of her wealth. A further model was what scholar Martha Vicinus calls queer or triangulated couplings, in which a women was married to a man but in love with a woman.

1870–1914: Scandals and increased freedoms

An important development in sexuality in the later Victorian period was the rise of the social purity movement, which flourished from about 1880 until 1914 and sought to make society more moral by making it more chaste. Activists spanned the political and social realms and included evangelical Christians and feminists. Social purity activists led the campaign to repeal the Contagious Diseases Acts, and argued that the solution to prostitution was not that women avoid "falling," but that men have enough control of themselves that they did not engage prostitutes. (Other reformers, noting the persistent failure of earlier "rescue" efforts, began to analyze prostitution as a structural problem rather than a series of individual failings.)

One of the major scandals of the late nineteenth century—the publication of "The Maiden Tribute of Modern Babylon", by W.T. Stead in 1885—concerned both prostitution and a leading social purity activist. Stead was a complex figure whose passions included sensational journalism and social purity. As we saw in Chapter 11, he claimed to have purchased a 13-year-old girl from her mother for the "white slave trade" to prove how easily it could be done. While Stead's journalistic methods were questionable, the articles were an immediate sensation, and outrage about the fact that young girls were being sold into prostitution for a pittance ran high. In fact, the "Maiden Tribute" scandal distracted Victorians from a far more pervasive reality. It was easy to be outraged about young girls being sold into prostitution abroad, a problem that was exceedingly rare. However, it was more difficult for the middle and upper classes to sympathize with a more typical reality of adult working-class women who cycled in and out of prostitution because of economic exigency.

Social purity activists also opposed male masturbation. Before 1880, masturbation authorities were medical men (both doctors and quacks) reaching out to adult men. However between 1880 and 1914—and especially between 1900 and 1914—social purity activists took on the problem of masturbation. Masturbation was still seen as a simultaneously medical and moral problem, but proclamations now came from a variety of establishment voices beyond the medical. Furthermore, the focus of this advice shifted from adult men to boys and adolescents (and the parents and schoolteachers responsible for them). For example, one popular pamphlet, *The Causes and Prevention of Immorality in Schools* (1883), was not by a doctor but by a schoolmaster Edward Lyttelton (1855–1942); it warned that "[t]he least defilement by hand enormously increases the difficulties of continence in manhood."[11] Another key text was by social purity activist Ellice Hopkins. Her book *The Power of Womanhood: Or, Mothers and Sons* (1899) manages to focus on the dangers of masturbation without ever directly stating the topic, preferring to warn about "vice" or "evil." Hopkins was especially worried about boarding schools—where boys went to sleep without their mothers nearby and where they might learn from other boys. And indeed, most late Victorian experts focused specifically on upper- and middle-class boys and the importance of self-control to these groups in their formative years; working-class boys are almost never mentioned in the vast literature. The idea was that to be able to control others—which upper- and middle-class boys, as leaders of society, would soon have to do—one had to be able to control oneself. Writers warned not so much of dire consequences such as insanity as of more quotidian problems like acne. Boys were encouraged to exercise self-control and renunciation; cold showers, exercise, and plain foods were all thought to help here. And since masturbation was linked to the more general issue of character formation, it was taken up in many venues; even Lord Baden-Powell's *Scouting for Boys* (1908) addressed the issue.

But while social purity was a strong force in sexual politics in the later Victorian period, it was not the only voice. In the several key areas, we see alternative approaches to sexual issues. For example, some sexologists suggested that masturbation was not unnatural; some feminists used this idea to argue that masturbation was a better outlet for male sexual excess than the use of prostitutes. And at the start of the twentieth century, a small number of educated women embraced the notion of women's right to and desire for sex. The notoriously modern and independent "New women" preferred "free love" to the legal protections of marriage and pursued their own sexual satisfaction. "New woman" novelist Cicely Hamilton (1872–1952) not only wrote about such topics but personally approved of both free love and birth control. Some argued that good marriages included sex that both partners enjoyed.

The decline of reproductive sexuality accelerated more quickly after 1870 (and would reach its lowest point in the 1930s). Couples who married in the 1860s had an average of 6.16 children, couples who married in the 1890s had 4.13 children, and couples who married in the 1920s had only 2.31 children. Today in the United Kingdom, complete family size has fallen to only 1.7 children, largely because reliable birth control is easily available and widely used.

The culture of abstinence persisted; in 1885 Dr James Dunn opposed extra-marital affairs principally because they too often involved "excessive venery, especially the oft-repeated coitus in a single night."[12] The emphasis on sexual restraint reached its height at the turn of the twentieth century. Men's ability to control themselves was considered virtuous and admirable. Here ideas about ideal sexuality clearly molded sexual practices: for those couples who did try to limit fertility, men were in control and were expected to either refrain from initiating intercourse or to practice withdrawal; this is in marked contrast to the present, when most birth control practices in the west are controlled by women. After abstinence, the second most widely practiced form of birth control was *coitus interruptus* or withdrawal, though it was probably not used widely until the late nineteenth century. Mechanical forms of birth control were unpopular and widely seen as unrespectable: before 1910 only one in six couples used them. Contraceptive devices and drugs were difficult to develop in an age when very little about women's reproductive cycles, or indeed about reproduction at all, was understood. Ovulation was not observed in women until the twentieth century, and most medical doctors held that women were least fertile at the midpoint between their menstrual periods, which is actually the period of greatest fertility. Condoms were associated with prostitution and with the prevention of venereal disease, so almost no one used them inside of marriage. In addition, any preventive measure implied that a woman was anticipating or even inviting sex, which made women reject them. While a few radicals promoted sponges, pessaries, diaphragms, and spermicidal creams and jellies, they converted very few people. There is evidence that after 1870 some respectable middle-class couples did begin to practice "artificial" forms of birth control; that is, using what we would recognize as birth control so as to engage in intercourse without conceiving. Here, too, men generally took the lead and were in control. However, such practices were unusual, were confined to some portions of the middle class—doctors, for instance, but not priests—were generally practiced by those who considered themselves "advanced" or "radical," and were kept very quiet. More common than strategies to artificially prevent conception were abortifacents, internally taken medicines made by local women or pharmacists to end a pregnancy. Advertisements for pills guaranteed to "bring on" a woman's "interrupted" period—that is, to induce an abortion—abounded. While the involvement of quack medicine indicates a certain degree of secrecy and embarrassment, British culture was relatively accepting of pregnancy termination, in part because most people did not consider a fetus to be a baby.

Pregnancies remained frequent and unplanned, a feature of most marriages and a problem for working-class women who worked long hours and were often under-nourished. Poor pregnant women in 1880s London described themselves as "often weak and low spirited," and "half starved."[13] Delivery was painful and dangerous, and could result in painful perineal tears or uterine prolapse. While death in actual childbirth was not common, death as a direct result of childbirth—usually because of puerperal infection, and usually within a few weeks—was. Because respectable working-class women did not use birth control in their marriages, they did not have any sense of control over their pregnancies. One working-class woman, speaking in the early twentieth century, said of pregnancies and children, "Well, I mean, we never thought of it. They just came and that was it."[14] Until the 1930s, maternal deaths hovered at about five per 1,000 live births. (Hospital births had much higher death rates, but hospitals were expensive and hospital births uncommon before World War One.) Both infant and child mortality were high right through the Victorian period; infant mortality rates actually rose over the century, reaching a peak in 1899 before receding. Infant mortality hovered at about 150 per 1,000 live births (though that is a national figure that hides huge disparities—large cities had much higher rates of infant mortality that stayed high until 1900, while rural areas not only had lower rates but saw those rates decrease from the 1860s).[15] As a point of comparison, today most developed countries have infant mortality rates between 2.3 and 4 per 1,000 live births; the United States has the highest rate of all developed countries, almost 6 per 1,000 live births.[16]

The later nineteenth century saw the rise of urban subcultures of men who loved and had sex with other men. While areas such as Hyde Park were already known as places where men might meet and have sex, London, Manchester and other cities now had a wide range of public places where men could meet one another. These urban sites were invisible to some and visible to others; for example, West End streets were sites of theatre and shopping to some, sites of male same-sex flirtation to others. This new homoerotic geography was marked by class: Piccadilly Circus and Hyde Park were both frequented by working-class male prostitutes, while university settlement houses and the Hellenic galleries of the British Museum were frequented by educated men.

In the 1870s and early 1880s, in continental Europe, the emerging discipline of sexology combined scientific and sociological methods in an attempt to understand human sexuality and gender. Many sexologists focused on classifying and categorizing men who desired men. However, their works were accessible in Britain only to highly educated people who read other European languages. The Labouchere amendment to the Criminal Law Amendment Act (named for journalist and Liberal MP Henry Labouchere) was passed in 1885, which made "gross indecency" a misdemeanor. The Labouchere amendment has been historicized as the turning point at which sex between men became visible and illegal. In fact, as we have seen, sodomy and attempted sodomy were already illegal, and prosecutions common: the Labouchere amendment was part of a process which had begun long before. As with "unnatural crimes," the precise definition of "gross indecency" was never articulated, but in practice the Amendment made it easier to prosecute sex between men without firm evidence of sodomy.

In the late nineteenth century a series of high-profile scandals helped to shape same-sex male desire in the public mind. These scandals reinforced the notion that urban landscapes were rife with cross-class sex between men and associated sex between men with effeminacy and cross-dressing. During the same period, sexology offered new ways to think about same-sex male desire. First was the "Fanny and Stella" scandal. Frederick Park was the son of a judge; Ernest Boulton was the son of a suburban clerk. The two often went out dressed as women,

A RETROSPECT OF THE BOULTON AND PARK CASE.—From Bow Street Station to the Van, April 10th, 1870.

Figure 12.1 Frederick William Park and Ernest Boulton, also known as Fanny and Stella, arrested at the Strand Theatre for incitement to commit an unnatural offence, by going around London at night in women's clothes. They were acquitted at their trial in 1871.

Mary Evans Picture Library.

maintained female personas as "Fanny" (Park) and "Stella" (Boulton), and were well-known in London's fashionable West End. In April 1870, the two were arrested leaving a theatre dressed as women. Over the course of the arrest and trial it was revealed that Fanny and Stella were minor celebrities who had been thrown out of several theatres and arcades for their disruptive flirtations with men, and were fixtures in a larger scene of men who frequented the West End dressed in women's clothing. The scandal intensified when it was revealed that Stella was a paramour of Lord Arthur Clinton, the son of a former cabinet minister, and had even lived with him as his wife.

Newspaper articles make it clear that the crowds that gathered to witness the arraignment in 1870 were titillated and disapproving, but not surprised, to learn of the existence of habitual cross-dressers in central London. Many observers focused on Fanny and Stella's middle-class status, and insisted that while effeminacy and cross-dressing were indications of sodomy among working-class men and male prostitutes, that middle-class and upper-class men could cross-dress occasionally, "for a lark," without having any interest in sex with other men; for them, only habitual cross-dressing indicated a predilection for "unnatural acts." Others drew on older arguments about sodomy and effeminacy to stress that the aristocratic Lord Clinton could associate with the effeminate, cross-dressing Stella, and even commit "unnatural crimes" with him, without being effeminate himself. In the end, Fanny and Stella (and two other men who had been arrested with them) were acquitted of conspiring to commit sodomy. This was probably because the court did not want to explore or reveal that there existed a flourishing subculture in which not only working-class but middle-class and upper-class men were cross-dressing and committing sodomy. The verdict was less an absolution of Fanny and Stella than an insistence that a subculture culture of sodomy did not exist. In spite of the verdict, however, the Fanny and Stella trials associated cross-dressing and effeminacy with sodomy in the public mind.

The second major scandal of the late Victorian period was the Cleveland Street scandal of 1889, in which it transpired that many of the young boys who delivered telegraphs for the Post Office in central London also offered themselves at a male brothel on Cleveland Street whose clients included Lord Euston and Lord Arthur Somerset. Telegraph boys were already known for their side-line in prostitution, so as with Fanny and Stella, while the scandal made the papers, Cleveland Street was more titillation than revelation. As was typical, the police and the law were reluctant to prosecute because it would mean publicizing sodomite subculture, and in this case were especially reluctant to publicize the sodomitical behavior of aristocratic men. Only two men were sentenced: Harry Newlove and G.D. Veck, the young men who recruited boys, both pleaded guilty and served several months hard labor. Their clients were never tried for gross indecency, largely because the affair came so close to the royal family—Somerset was an equerry to the Prince of Wales, who was rumored to be involved himself. This led the Home Office, Chief of Police, Attorney General, and others to cover the affair up as much as possible (which the radical press protested for months). Lord Somerset—against whom there was much evidence—fled England for France, was labeled a sodomite, and lived the rest of his life in ruin and disgrace. Lord Euston, however, remained in London and sued Ernest Parke, a radical newspaper editor who had named Somerset and Euston in print as visitors to the brothel. Even though one boy, John Saul, who described himself in court as a "professional sodomite," testified that Euston had indeed been a visitor to Cleveland Street, Parke was found guilty of libel and sentenced to a year in prison. As had happened before, upper-class men's words were taken over those of male prostitutes, evidence notwithstanding.

Around this time, sexology became more widely available and read in Britain. Until this point, British doctors had been extremely reluctant to even acknowledge the existence of sex between men, but scientific and medical discussions of same-sex desire already common in continental Europe were now more available in Britain. Sexology saw "gender inversion"—effeminacy in men, mannishness in women—as congenital and the cause of same-sex desire. Some sexologists called same-sex desire a perversion; others argued for an intermediate sex. They devised a wide variety of terms for those who experienced same-sex desire, including "inverts," "intermediates," or "urnings." Sexologists included Karl Ulrichs (1825–1895) and Richard von Krafft-Ebing (1840–1902), both of whom argued that same-sex desire was neither immoral nor a conscious choice; rather, it was innate and could not be corrected. British sexologists included John Addington Symonds (1840–1893), whose *A Problem in Greek Ethics* (1883) was the first history in English of same-sex desire between men; Edward Carpenter (1844–1929), who wrote the pamphlet *Homogenic Love, and its Place in a Free Society* (1895) and an influential book on *The Intermediate Sex* (1908); and Havelock Ellis (1859–1939), author of the multi-volume *Studies in the Psychology of Sex* (1899–1928). Overall sexologists promoted the idea that homosexuality—the word had been coined in Germany and was used in Britain from the 1890s—was innate and should not be considered criminal. For upper-class and middle-class men who desired other men, the most important function of sexology was that it allowed them to reconcile their desire for other men with their status as respectable men of character. Sexology was controversial in Britain to start with; the first volume of Ellis's *Studies*, entitled *Sexual Inversion*, was prosecuted as an obscene book. By 1914, however, sexology was more widely read and accepted. It would become a key force in making same-sex desire less unacceptable.

The most famous Victorian same-sex legal trial was the 1895 case of Oscar Wilde (1854–1900). Wilde was a well-known and flamboyant writer, playwright, and aesthete, and (though a husband and a father) was the lover of the much younger Lord Alfred "Bosie" Douglas (1870–1945). When Douglas's father, the Marquess of Queensberry (1844–1900), called Wilde a sodomite, Wilde sued for libel. Wilde had had sex with Bosie and with many young working-class boys, but the accusation was a serious one when leveled against a respectable man, and (as we saw above in the Cleveland Street scandal) Wilde was not the first to sue for libel over a true statement. He lost. Wilde was then prosecuted for gross indecency under the Labouchere amendment, based on evidence amassed during the libel trial of his participation in London's "renter" subculture of working-class male prostitutes and their upper-class clients. During the trials, Wilde famously defended love and sex between men as the "love that dare not speak its name," and this notion of unspeakability emphasizes its twilight status. Wilde was found guilty of gross indecency, was jailed from 1895 to 1898, wrote *De Profundis* (in the form of a letter to Bosie) from prison, and died in Paris in 1900.

While Wilde's trial is usually historicized as a watershed, it exhibits themes that were present throughout the Victorian period: cross-class relationships, urban subcultures, same-sex desire that was simultaneously understood and unnamed. As with the Labouchere amendment, the Wilde trial has often been described as a bigger turning-point than it actually was; it was certainly not the general public's first hint that sex between men existed. Nor was the Wilde trial the first public event to connect effeminacy with same-sex desire between men; as we have seen above, there were links between effeminacy and same-sex desire in Victorian culture long before 1895. That said, the Wilde trial rendered all male intimacy suspicious, and (together with sexology) cemented the association of effeminacy with sex between men. By 1900, the year of Wilde's death, the term "homosexual" was in use in Britain to describe an effeminate man who had sex with men. The standard representation of the modern homosexual had been established.

Excamples of love between women {

There are also examples of love and sex between women in the later Victorian period. One well-studied Victorian marriage, between Edward and Mary Benson, was one of Vicinus' triangulated couplings. Mary Benson was dutifully but un-happily married to her much older, clergyman husband (who would become the Archbishop of Canterbury). Mr Benson eventually accepted the fact that his wife's closest relationships were with women. Indeed, in the late 1880s, it was Edward who invited Mary's friend, Lucy Tait, to live with them; until Mary's death in 1918, Lucy, in the words of Mary's son novelist E.F. Benson (1867–1940), "slept with my mother in the vast Victorian bed where her six children had been born."[17] Some very revolutionary women tried to go beyond existing models. Actress Charlotte Cushman was the leader and center of a community of wealthy British and American women who lived together in Rome during the third quarter of the century. There experimentation was the rule rather than the exception, and many visitors moved in and out of friendships and erotic relationships, and then later settled more permanently—some with female companions, some with husbands.

Notes

1 Sean Brady, *Masculinity and Male Homosexuality in Britain, 1861–1913* (London: Palgrave Macmillan, 2005), p. 1.
2 Angus McLaren, *Impotence: A Cultural History* (Chicago: University of Chicago Press, 2007), p. 128.
3 William Acton, *The Functions and Disorders of the Reproductive Orders in Youth, in Adult Age, and in Advanced Life* (London: John Churchill, 1857).
4 Anna Clark, "Twilight Moments," *Journal of the History of Sexuality* 14.1/2 (January 2005/April 2005): 140–141.
5 Hera Cook, "Demography," in H.G. Cocks and Matt Houlbrook (eds), *Palgrave Advances in the Modern History of Sexuality* (Basingstoke: Palgrave MacMillan, 2005), p. 24.
6 Anna Clark, "Twilight Moments," *Journal of the History of Sexuality* 14.1/2 (January 2005/April 2005): 139–160.
7 Charles Upchurch, *Before Wilde: Sex between Men in Britain's Age of Reform* (Berkeley: University of California Press, 2009), p. 182.
8 Letter to the editor from "A Solicitor," *The Times*, August 17, 1842, p. 3, quoted in Upchurch.
9 Martha Vicinus, *Intimate Friends: Women who Loved Women, 1778–1928* (Chicago: University of Chicago Press, 2004), p. 73.
10 Sharon Marcus, *Between Women: Friendship, Desire, and Marriage in Victorian England* (Princeton: Princeton University Press, 2007).
11 Hon. Edward Lyttelton, *The Causes and Prevention of Immorality in Schools* (London: Social Purity Alliance, printed for private circulation, 1887) p. 15, quoted in Roy Porter and Lesley Hall, *The Facts of Life* (Cambridge, MA: Yale University Press, 1995), p. 151.
12 James H. Dunn, "Impotence in the Male and Its Treatment," *Northwestern Lancet* 5.3 (November 1, 1885): 45.
13 Quoted in Ellen Ross, *Love and Toil: Motherhood in Outcast London 1870–1918* (New York: Oxford University Press, 1993), p. 108.
14 Quoted in Elizabeth Roberts, *A Woman's Place: An Oral History of Working-Class Women, 1890–1940* (Oxford: Wiley-Blackwell, 1984), p. 88.
15 Naomi Williams and Chris Galley, "Urban-rural Differentials in Infant Mortality in Victorian England," *Population Studies* 49:3 (1995): 401–420.

16 Available online at: www.cia.gov/library/publications/the-world-factbook/rankorder/
2091rank.html and www.washingtonpost.com/news/wonk/wp/2014/09/29/our-
infant-mortality-rate-is-a-national-embarrassment/ (accessed December 24, 2015).
17 Quoted in Vicinus, p. 95.

Relevant fiction that students might enjoy

Thomas Hardy, *Tess of the d'Urbervilles* (1891)
Sarah Waters, *Tipping the Velvet* (1998)
Sarah Waters, *Fingersmith* (2002)

Further reading

Anna Clark, "Twilight Moments," *Journal of the History of Sexuality* 14.1/2 (January 2005/
April 2005): 139–160.
H.G. Cocks and Matt Houlbrook (eds), *Palgrave Advances in the Modern History of Sexuality*
(Basingstoke: Palgrave MacMillan, 2005).
Matt Cook, *London and the Culture of Homosexuality, 1885–1914* (Cambridge: Cambridge
University Press, 2003).
Stephen Garton, *Histories of Sexuality: Antiquity to Sexual Revolution* (Oxford: Routledge, 2011).
Seth Koven, *The Match Girl and the Heiress* (Princeton: Princeton University Press, 2015).
Angus McLaren, *Impotence: A Cultural History* (Chicago: University of Chicago Press, 2007).
Charles Upchurch, *Before Wilde: Sex between Men in Britain's Age of Reform* (Berkeley: University
of California Press, 2009).
Martha Vicinus, *Intimate Friends: Women who Loved Women, 1778–1928* (Chicago: University
of Chicago Press, 2004).

Online resources

Lesley Hall, History of Sexuality: www.lesleyahall.net/webdoc3.htm
See also Hall's list of other online resources: www.lesleyahall.net/sexlinks.htm
Bibliography of the history of western sexuality: www.univie.ac.at/sexbib/about.html

13 "Begin and end with the Church whatever you do between-whiles"

Religion

Introduction

The 1851 census asked one new question of each Briton: whether on Census Sunday, March 30, 1851, they had attended church services, and if they had, where. Statistics based on the answers to these questions in the Religious Census of 1851 have been mined for information ever since. To the Victorians, two points jumped out. First, large portions of the population, particularly members of the working class, had not attended church that Sunday. Second, of those who went to services, more the half did so outside the Church of England. To a Christian nation with an established state church, these were surprising and dismaying facts. For many, the census confirmed their conviction that the industrialization, the urbanization, and even the prosperity they were experiencing were causing moral decline. Until recently many historians agreed that modernization either caused or was inevitably accompanied by a decline in religion in which fewer and fewer people believed religious doctrine or observed religious ritual. Scholars call this decline "secularization," and until very recently most historians, relying on the published report of the Religious Census, thought that Victorian Britain was a secularizing society. Some pointed to Enlightenment ideals of rationality and the natural over the supernatural as the cause; others to the decline of the state church, or various aspects of modernization.

But "secularization" may not have occurred as straightforwardly as we have assumed. When our period began in 1820, the vast majority of Britons would have described themselves as Christian. Most people went to church on Sunday and for a variety of annual and life-cycle occasions such as Easter and weddings. The Anglican church dominated the religious landscape. Most of the organizations to which Britons belonged were religiously affiliated. Many of the formal leisure activities they participated in were religiously sponsored. Christian images pervaded public and private spaces. When our period ended in 1914 all of these, except for regular attendance at Sunday services and the preeminence of the Anglican church, were still true. Britain was still a Christian country.

If we move away from Sunday church attendance as our principal measure of religiosity, we can question the secularization thesis. Furthermore, there is no demonstrable link between modernization and secularization. And while statistics suggest that some specific forms of observance that the clergy thought important were declining, neither statistical nor qualitative evidence support the notion that Victorian Britain was becoming a secular nation at all. Descriptions by middle-class observers of declining working-class urban religiosity need to be seen not as objective descriptions but as symptoms of middle-class anxiety, anxiety intensified by the Victorian belief that cities were inherently immoral spaces. As we saw in Chapter 1, many feared that poor urban neighborhoods were "perfect nest[s] of iniquity."[1] If we look beyond Sunday mornings we see religion everywhere in Victorian Britain. Today most historians agree that Britain was a religious country until at least World War One and perhaps until well after World War Two.

This chapter describes how religiosity was expressed and how organized religion shaped public life. The religious landscape included Roman Catholicism and non-Christian religions including the Jewish, Muslim, Sikh, and Hindu faiths, but it was dominated by Protestantism, ranging from the Church of England at one end of the spectrum to various non-Anglican denominations—known as Nonconformist or Dissenting churches—at the other. A nonconformist place of worship was typically referred to as a "chapel," as distinct from an Anglican "church," and many saw British society as divided along "church" (elite) and "chapel" (plebian) lines. Over the course of the nineteenth century the Church of England lost much of its political and bureaucratic power. At the same time many Nonconformist churches grew in number, size, and social and political status. Roman Catholics and Jews gained many civil rights, but continued to face prejudice.

Religion changed in important ways during the Victorian period. The state church was relieved of many of its social and governmental duties, such as the recording of all births, marriages, and deaths, the provision of assistance to the poor, and the provision of education. Britain became a religiously pluralistic—though still predominantly Christian—country, one in which the Church of England competed with other Protestant churches and with the Roman Catholic church for believers and participants. Yet, through all of this, Britain remained a religious society. Christian organizations and assumptions dominated the landscape and most people felt themselves to be believing Christians in some basic way. While a small number of intellectuals experienced what has been termed the "Victorian crisis of faith" (triggered in part by developments in the sciences), for most people in 1914 as in 1820, religion permeated life.

1820–1870: Established and other faiths, reform and resistance

When our period began in 1820 the four countries of the United Kingdom of Great Britain and Ireland had two state churches. The larger was the Church of England, also called the Anglican Church, which was referred to in Wales as the Church of England in Wales and in Ireland as the Church of Ireland. The Anglican church had emerged during the Reformation and possessed both Roman Catholic and Protestant features. Theologians were proud of Anglicanism's status as a *via media* or middle way, a moderate Protestant path between Roman

Catholicism and extreme Protestantism. Catholic features include a hierarchical structure that stretched from parish priests through bishops and archbishops to the monarch, who was the head of the church. Reformation Protestant features include a focus on the scriptures, services conducted in English, and certain Calvinist points of doctrine. Central to Anglican theology were the Book of Common Prayer, a collection of prayers and services, and the Thirty-Nine Articles, a sixteenth-century statement of Anglican doctrine. The Church of Ireland served only a very small portion of Ireland's predominantly Roman Catholic population. This made its status as a state church quite different and a source of debate and tension throughout the Victorian period. The other state church was the Church of Scotland, also referred to as the Kirk. It was Presbyterian, with a more pronounc-edly Calvinist theology and a structure that included councils and had no bishops. In the Disruption of 1843, disagreements over the sovereignty of the established church and whether clergy could be appointed over the objections of a congrega-tion led to a schism, in which many congregations broke away from the Kirk to form the Free Church of Scotland (they would reunite in 1929).

The established Anglican church enjoyed many privileges. Even after the end of the confessional state in 1828 and 1829 (see Chapter 2), it remained the official state religion. Anglican bishops sat in the House of Lords. Until 1828, only Anglican men could vote. The Church administered most poor relief and most schools; the ancient universities of Oxford and Cambridge were Anglican institu-tions. Taxes supported clergy salaries and parish church upkeep. In the Victorian period, the place of the church changed in several ways. First, the church reformed itself through revival of its diocesan structure, organizing parishes into larger dioceses, and through extensive building. Second, the state took over some key bureaucratic services traditionally performed by the church. And third, the rise of various Nonconformist churches and the growth of the Roman Catholic population of Britain reduced the Church of England's influence.

Within the church there was a range of theologies and styles of worship. At one end was evangelicalism, about which more below. At the other was a group of theologians who made up the Oxford Movement, which called for the church to recommit to a more Catholic style of worship. The Oxford Movement, led by theologians John Keble (1792–1866) and John Henry Newman (1801–1890), began in 1833 as a protest against the reduction that year of the power of the Church of Ireland. Members were also known as Tractarians after a series of tracts they published between 1833 and 1841. Tractarians held that Anglicanism lay not between Catholicism and extreme Protestantism, as was traditionally believed, but between Roman Catholicism and all Protestantism—in other words, that it was not a form of Protestantism at all, but a non-Roman form of Catholicism. This emphasis on tradition and on the power of the church appealed to many upper-class and middle-class people and to the Tory party. However, it also made them vulnerable to suspicions that they were simply Roman Catholics in disguise, a suspicion that seemed to be confirmed when their leader, Newman, converted to Roman Catholicism in 1845. (Newman was beatified by Pope Benedict XVI in September 2010, leaving him only one step—canonization—from sainthood.)

But while the formal Oxford Movement ended with Newman's conversion, a "High Church" constituency that emphasized authority, tradition, and ceremonial worship persisted.

Contrary to some negative stereotypes, the Anglican church met the needs of many parishioners, and most priests and bishops were conscientious. However, from the early Victorian era well-publicized abuses inspired demands for change. The lavish wealth of the Archbishops of Canterbury and York, the political power of many bishops, absentee priests who drew salaries from parishes they rarely visited, and the fact that many priests were appointed by local landowners rather than by Church officials angered many, nonconformists in particular. So did a lack of churches: since the late eighteenth century, as the population of Britain had grown in new places, particularly the cities and industrial areas of the North, the church had not responded with new churches. The result was that, by 1820, many Victorians, especially working-class people, did not live anywhere near their official parish church. Where the state church had left a vacuum, various non-conformist faiths had rushed in, establishing congregations in existing buildings or storefronts.

Pressed for calls for reform from both within and without, the church instituted changes. From the 1820s there was a grassroots revival of the church's diocesan structure, which transformed the church from a series of isolated parish churches into a more unified enterprise with a focus on the larger unit of the diocese. From the 1840s, new churches were built to address population shifts, making the mid-Victorian period a golden age of church building and restoration (see Chapter 11). Between 1840 and 1870, the Church of England built and refurbished thousands of churches in England and Wales, many with extensive free seating to make the poor and working class more welcome. (Traditionally, most pews in Anglican churches were rented by local families who could afford them, leaving only benches in the back for the poor.) In Scotland, the state church and the Free Church both built hundreds of new churches as well. To take one example, the Religious Census of 1851 indicated that, since 1821, in Yorkshire alone over 2,000 new churches had been built. Large, impressive churches, often done in a gothic style, domi-nated many town centers. Indeed, churches are one of the main ways in which the Victorian period remains present in Britain today.

The state modified the Church through several major Acts of Parliament. As we saw in Chapter 2, Acts passed in 1828 and 1829 gave nonconformists and Catholics the same political rights as Anglicans, though popular prejudice and the opposition of the Tory party meant widespread protests and criticism regarding Catholic rights. These protests only increased in 1833, when—in recognition of the fact that only about 11% of the Irish population followed the Church of Ireland—the Irish Church Temporalities Act drastically reduced the power and wealth of the Church of Ireland. In 1835, an Ecclesiastical Commission was established to investigate and end abuses such as nepotism, preferment, and sine-cures. Several church rates (taxes that funded local churches) were abolished. In 1836, the Marriage Act allowed non-Anglican clergy to perform legal marriages, and the Births and Deaths Registration Act established a civil procedure for recording births, marriages, and deaths. From mid-century state grants for education were available to Wesleyan Methodist, Catholic, and Jewish schools.

While the Church of England was the official Protestant church of Britain, other Protestant faiths flourished. Older denominations (founded in the seventeenth century) included the Quaker and Unitarian faiths—both small, liberal, and mostly upper middle class—and Baptists. The nineteenth century saw the growth and strength of several newer nonconformist denominations; before 1870 the most important of these was Methodism, which was largely working-class. The largest nonconformist denominations during the early Victorian period were Baptist, Congregational, and Wesleyan, Primitive, and Calvinistic Methodist (the last of which flourished in Wales). In Scotland, there were Presbyterian dissenters before the Disruption, and members of the Free Church afterwards. Wales experienced a huge growth in dissent—in 1800 it had twice as many Anglican as nonconformist houses of worship, but by 1850 it had two and a half times as many nonconformist chapels as Anglican churches. There were theological differences among nonconformists. Quakers emphasized pacifism and the social equality of all worshippers; Unitarians rejected the Christian doctrine of the trinity; Baptists emphasized the importance of adult baptism. But overall the nonconformist faiths tended to eschew ritual and church hierarchy, which they saw as empty and meaningless. Instead they stressed each worshipper's enthusiasm and direct relationship with God, and preaching the Bible. And all nonconformist faiths had in common their fundamentally oppositional nature. In British society, not only was the Church of England closely tied to the landed aristocracy, but the established church was (unsurprisingly, given the term) part of the establishment. It reinforced hierarchical society and values. To be a religious nonconformist was more than a religious stance; it was a fundamentally oppositional, anti-establishment stance. Various Victorian debates over Church rates, tithes, and subsidies revealed deep social divisions between Anglicans and nonconformists and simmering resentment on the part of nonconformists.

Nonconformists argued that there was no necessary connection between the state and the state church, but this was not a popular view among Anglican elites; indeed as we saw in Chapter 2, even in the late nineteenth century Lord Salisbury, as prime minister, found the very concept of a non-Anglican voter a baffling one. The 1828 Repeal of the Test and Corporation Acts made nonconformists eligible to vote, but the state continued to fund the Church of England, by paying its salaries and funding its schools, among other things. This was seen by many nonconformists as fundamentally unjust. Nonconformists protested having to pay church rates (taxes), which funded their local Anglican parish churches.

Most nonconformist chapels, particularly those in poor or working-class urban areas, had very few upper-class members. But chapels attracted middle-class as well as working-class people. Some historians argue that nonconformity, and particularly Methodism, helped to transform Britain by preventing political revolution and by creating a large group of people who sought to prove their worth through hard work. Certainly nonconformity played a role in the rise of the middle class. In the early Victorian period, middle-class nonconformity helped to persuade some portions of the elite that middle-class men were upstanding enough and manly enough to deserve political rights. And from the 1830s, temperance was a central nonconformist movement (though in alcohol-laden Victorian Britain, "temperance" meant not total abstinence but a call to substitute beer for harder liquor).

The largest nonconformist sect in Victorian Britain was Methodism, founded by John Wesley in 1738. There were 87,000 British Methodists in 1801, but 286,000 British Methodists by 1850, many of whom were artisans, skilled working class, or lower middle class. Over time some sects split away from Wesleyan Methodists, including Primitive Methodists (who had broken away from the Wesleyans in 1811 and by 1852 numbered over 100,000) and Bible Christians. For all of these, the individual's experience of salvation and personal relationship with God were the central facets of spirituality. Methodism was very appealing to those who did not feel well-educated enough to follow Anglican's doctrinal debates, or who were not well-dressed enough or well-off enough to occupy the front pews of an Anglican church. It located authority in the congregation rather than the preacher and encouraged itinerant out-of-doors preachers, lay preachers, and enthusiastic styles of prayer and worship that included praying aloud and singing. Group worship might occur in a chapel, but could also take place in a private home or even outdoors in a field. In Wales, over the early Victorian period, nonconformity was growing; many Welsh nonconformists made a point of referring to the Church of England in Wales as the "English" Church to mark it as an outsider's faith. For the Welsh, Calvinistic Methodism, Baptistism, and Congregationalism together formed what was in practice the established Welsh faith. In Scotland, the Free Church was after 1843 the largest alternative to the established Presbyterian church; in addition, the Secession and Relief churches came together as another denomination, the United Presbyterian Church, which was strongest in Edinburgh and Glasgow.

There were also those who were not Protestant at all. In Britain there were three types of Catholics—a small group (less than a quarter of the total number) of old English aristocratic families, a tiny but high-profile group of converts such as John Henry Newman, and a large majority who were post-Famine Irish immigrants (in all three countries Catholics were overwhelmingly urban, working-class, and of Irish origin). The combination posed a problem. The groups were very different socioeconomically, and had different habits of observance, with English aristocrats focused on Mass and confession, converts focused on complex theological points, and Irish immigrants focused on prayers at home, old superstitions, and local shrines. Irish immigrants lived together in tight-knit communities where their language and traditions set them apart from native Catholics, who were often embarrassed by them. Because the majority of British Catholics were Irish immigrants, Catholicism was tightly linked in the popular mind with the Irish: Irish immigration dictated the location of new churches, and "Irish" and "Catholic" were sometimes used interchangeably even by church leaders themselves.

Britain saw itself as a Protestant country—great and free because Protestant, and Protestant because great and free—and there was a lot of anti-Catholic sentiment, including the suspicion that Catholics were not patriots. Indeed, we know from the diaries of Victorian travelers to Catholic Europe that many British people perceived Catholics as lacking in a wide range of important secular qualities that they saw as "Protestant" such as tolerance, cleanliness, and prosperity. Yet, in 1829, Catholic Emancipation gave Catholics many political rights. Then in 1850 the British government allowed Pope Pius IX to reinstate the Roman Catholic hierarchy, including Catholic bishops, in England and Wales. This sparked the last major outburst of anti-Catholic demonstrations in Britain.

The number of non-Christians in Britain was small. The only group of any significant size was the Jewish community. In 1800, there were about 20,000 Jews in England, most of whom lived in London; in 1860, there were 35,000, and there were communities in Manchester and Leeds. Jews were not as fiercely hated as Catholics but certainly experienced discrimination. Many evangelicals argued that Judaism was dominated by oral tradition rather than an individual's relationship with the bible, and that it was therefore bereft of spirituality and of conscience. Many Victorians still believed in blood libels (the idea that Jews used the blood of Christians in religious ceremonies), or believed that Jews were responsible for the death of Jesus Christ. Popular antisemitism was rampant, but even in elite and Liberal circles, less virulent forms of antisemitism were widespread. Liberal politicians often argued that the state had historical and cultural roots of which Jews could never be part. Jews enjoyed more political freedoms in Britain than elsewhere in Europe. They could vote from 1835 and were emancipated in 1858, which allowed the wealthy Jewish banker Lionel Rothschild (1808–1879) to became the first Jewish member of Parliament. However, there was opposition to emancipation: many felt that it was enough that the state had been rendered neither exclusively Anglican nor exclusively Protestant by the Test and Corporations Act and the Catholic Emancipation Act, and that now rendering the state not Christian by allowing Jews to participate in government was going too far. Legal freedoms were granted, but cultural antipathy was more deep-seated.

1870–1914: A more varied religious landscape

The state churches remained important institutions in the late Victorian period. In Scotland the influence of the Kirk on education remained very strong through 1914. After the passage of the 1870 Education Act (passed by a Liberal government), Anglicans no longer dominated primary schooling in England, but the Act funded denominational schools, most of which were Anglican, and this enraged nonconformists. (Both funding and nonconformist outrage persisted after the 1902 Education Act as well.) Nonconformists saw this as proof that they were constantly being discriminated against and treated as second-class citizens. However, Oxford and Cambridge, while they remained Anglican institutions, admitted nonconformist men from the 1850s.

The most dramatic changes to the state churches came in the form of disestablishment. In 1871, Prime Minister William Gladstone's Liberal government disestablished the Church of Ireland as the state church, relieving farmers of a heavy church tithe and the entire population of a minority state church. (Many English nonconformists expected, wrongly, that disestablishment of the Church of England would not be far behind.) This was part of Gladstone's plan to address the "Irish Problem" and was bitterly opposed by many Tories. The Church of England in Wales, the faith of only a minority of the Welsh (who were predominantly nonconformist) was disestablished in 1920. In England and in Scotland the state churches remained established, but they had less wealth and power and their congregants had fewer legal and political privileges than they had in 1820.

Although the Anglican church tended to be characterized as the church of the well-off, and although it lost much of its power and social standing over the course of the nineteenth century, it remained strong. In Wales, the church reached out to parishioners by embracing Welsh culture and traditions. (There were no Welsh-speaking bishops, but there were many Welsh-speaking clergy appointed, especially to parishes where congregants spoke only Welsh.[2]) Most interestingly, the state church was very important in the lives of many working-class Britons, even if they did not attend its Sunday services and even if they were nonconformists. In many areas, working-class Methodists continued to use their local parish church for baptism and marriage long after the passage of the 1836 Acts that provided nonconformist and civil options. For them, the Anglican and Methodist churches served separate and complementary functions. As late as 1914, 70% of British babies received Anglican baptism. The head of one nonconformist family, while having their twins baptized in the parish church in 1862, explained to the vicar that it was always best to "begin and end with the Church whatever you do between-whiles."[3] While this man might never have gone to Anglican Sunday services, the Anglican Church was important to him.

The most important new nonconformist church in the later Victorian period was the Salvation Army, which was largely working-class. Today most Americans know the Salvation Army only by its large thrift shops, but the Salvation Army is a Christian denomination that is best understood as an inner-city form of Methodism. The church was founded in 1865 by former Methodist preacher William Booth and his wife Catherine, who together drew on evangelical and missionary traditions. They started the Army as a domestic evangelical mission in the poverty-stricken East End of London. Salvationists were predominantly working-class and urban. They wore uniforms and thought of their tightly-structured organization as a Christian army. In 1886 the Army had 1,749 congregations and over 4,000 officers in Great Britain, and more abroad. They were well-known for using popular culture to Christian ends, for example by putting Christian words to popular music hall tunes. Unusually, both sexes preached, saved souls, and ran missions. Women who proselytized were known as Hallelujah Lasses; they purposely made spectacles of themselves to attract attention and were a jubilant and disruptive presence in poor urban areas.

Another important inner-city initiative was the Settlement House movement, which flourished in the late nineteenth and early twentieth centuries. Settlement Houses were established by socially activist middle-class and upper-class people in poor urban areas, inner cities and slums and were a form of reform-oriented

Figure 13.1 The Salvation Army (gouache on paper) by Pat (Patrick) Nicolle (1907–1995).

Private Collection/© Look and Learn/The Bridgeman Art Library.

domestic mission. Middle-class and upper-class people (often university students) who believed in breaking down class barriers lived in these houses. Their goals were to experience poverty, get to know and learn from their poor neighbors, and offer various programs for community members. The first university settlement house was Toynbee Hall, founded in Whitechapel in London's East End in 1884 (and named for social reformer Arnold Toynbee (1852–1883)). Many Settlement House workers preached the "social gospel," which Wesleyan minister Samuel Keeble described in 1896 as a gospel "as sacred and as indispensable as the individual Gospel" that was "bent upon saving not only the individual, but also society; upon setting up in the earth the Kingdom of Heaven."[4] Inspired by their Christian faith, they worked to combat social problems such as poverty and alcohol abuse.

Other nonconformist churches continued to be large and important. In 1875, there were 165,000 Primitive Methodists (there would be 220,000 in 1932). In 1906, there were 800,000 Methodists, 290,000 Congregationalists, and 265,000 Baptists in Britain (however, this growth did not keep pace with population growth).

In part because of nonconformity's oppositional stance, nonconformists took an active role in calling for reforms of state and society that is sometimes described the "nonconformist social conscience." The nonconformist social conscience emerged from the social gospel. From about 1870 nonconformists aligned themselves with Gladstone and the Liberal party; they were very politically active and quite effective in demanding government action on a wide range of issues including gambling, housing, and education. (After 1885, many Wesleyan Methodists were Liberal Unionists.) Nonconformist social reformism included the campaign to repeal the Contagious Diseases Acts that we saw in Chapter 8; nonconformists, like feminists, saw the Acts as the state sanctioning of vice. The nonconformist social conscience refused to consider political expediency in the face of morality, insisting, in the words of nonconformist Henry Fowler (1830–1911), the first Methodist to serve in the cabinet (in 1884) and to be elected to the peerage (in 1908), that "what is morally wrong can never be politically right."[5] But even as some nonconformists engaged with the political sphere, others left nonconformity for political reasons. As wealthier middle-class families became more accepted into political and other elite circles, some middle-class men who had been raised nonconformist moved back to the Church of England because it was the church of the social elite into which they wanted entry.

Following the Great Famine and the return of the Catholic hierarchy, the Catholic population grew swiftly in the late Victorian period. In 1851, England and Wales had 750,000 Catholics and Scotland had 172,000; in 1914, England and Wales had 2 million Catholics and Scotland had 244,000 (fully 12% of the Scottish population). However, anti-Catholic prejudice remained broadly spread, deeply felt, and frequently expressed at all social levels. It was akin to racial prejudice today, and its presence in Victorian culture cannot be overstated. It (along with a lack of funds) was one reason that many Catholic churches were small and cheaply maintained buildings on inconspicuous side streets.

In 1870, Britain's Jewish population, while still small, had grown. Still largely concentrated in London, it consisted by 1881 of approximately 60,000 people, led by city and landed men. Prominent English Jews, notably Moses Montefiore (1784–1885) supported the Zionist movement to create a Jewish homeland in

Palestine. (The most famous Jew in British politics, Benjamin Disraeli, was not actually Jewish, his father having converted the family to Anglicanism when Disraeli was a boy. In spite of this, enemies often accused Disraeli of being suspiciously "Eastern" or incapable of true patriotism on account of his Jewish roots.) Jews were admitted to Oxford and Cambridge in 1871. Religiously, English Judaism was dominated by the United Synagogue (f. 1871), a federation to which most synagogues belonged. It promoted moderate levels of observance and an assimilated, British, patriotic tone.

This small, assimilated community was challenged by a wave of immigration. In the decades after 1881 over 120,000 Jews fleeing persecution in Russia immigrated to Britain, so that by 1900 there were 80 synagogues in Britain and by 1914 there were 300,000 Jews in Britain, with communities not only in London, Manchester, and Leeds, but also in Glasgow, Liverpool, Birmingham, Cardiff, and Dublin. Concentrated in the clothing industry, immigrants tended to be politically radical, active in trade unions, and more religiously observant than English Jews. Dissatisfied with United Synagogue practices, they formed their own small congregations. Russian Jewish immigration affected the Anglo-Jewish community in many of the same ways that Irish immigration had affected the Anglo-Catholic community a generation earlier. Like Irish Catholic immigrants, Jewish immigrants lived in distinct communities with styles of religious observance, traditions, and language that set them apart from native English Jews. Immigrant Jews were also often resented by the native unskilled workers with whom they competed for work and housing; claims that Jack the Ripper was Jewish are a symptom of anti-semitism in London's East End, where the murders occurred and where immigrant Jews lived. English Jews sought to help the new immigrants, in part because they were ashamed of them and sought to assimilate them as quickly as possible. They created charities to help immigrants such as the Jewish Board of Guardians (JBG), a relief organization, and the Jewish Association for the Protection of Girls and Women, a rescue organization. Jewish immigration was ended by the Aliens Act of 1905, which claimed to be aimed at keeping criminals and the poor from immigrating but was in fact a move to stem Jewish immigration (the Act was reinforced in 1914 but overturned in 1919).

Late Victorian Britain was also home to small numbers of spiritualists and theosophists. Spiritualists believed that it was possible for the living to communicate with the dead through a person called a medium, an attractive notion in a society in which so many people lost loved ones. Theosophy was a blend of spiritualism, eastern religions, and scientific rhetoric that appealed to those who found western Christianity lacking. Adherents of both tended to be politically radical. Because of the importance of the Indian subcontinent in the British Empire, Britons were aware of Muslims, Sikhs, and Hindus. These groups also had very small communities in Victorian Britain. There were Muslim communities in port towns such as Liverpool, and a wave of Muslim immigration followed the opening of the Suez Canal in 1869; the first British mosques were built in Cardiff in 1860 and in Woking in 1889. The first Sikh temple was built in London in 1900. The first Hindus to come to Britain were visiting scholars and reformers such as Raja

Rammohun Roy, founder of the Brahmo Samaj reform movement, who visited in 1829. In all three of these groups, significant numbers of immigrants arrived in Britain only after the partition of British India in 1947.

In the later Victorian period, Britain also had a very small but high-profile group of nonbelievers or atheists, those who actively rejected religion and denied the existence of God. Nonbelief was linked with leftwing politics, sexual non-conformity, and free thought, and was perceived as extremely radical and even antisocial. The most prominent Victorian atheist was Charles Bradlaugh (1833–1891). Bradlaugh was active in the Reform League (which as we saw in Chapter 2 agitated for the working-class vote) and in 1866 founded the National Secular Society. In 1877, Bradlaugh and his associate, Annie Besant (1847–1933), founded the Freethought Publishing Company as a vehicle through which to publish a birth-control pamphlet, Charles Knowles' *The Fruits of Philosophy*, and were pros-ecuted for obscenity. That Bradlaugh was best-known as a defendant in an obscenity trial regarding contraceptive knowledge, is a good indication of the generally fringe circles with which atheism was associated. When Bradlaugh was elected to Parliament in 1880, he could not sit because he refused to take an oath on the bible. Public opinion was divided between those who saw him as persecuted and those who were outraged that an atheist could even be elected. (In 1888, a right to parliamentary affirmations as a substitute for oaths was established.) Public perceptions of Bradlaugh reveal how pervasive religion was, and how offensive atheism was to most people, even those who were not particularly pious.

Religious life in the Victorian period

To understand Victorians' lived experience of religion, we need to focus on three things: religion in everyday life, gender and religion, and evangelicalism. Regarding everyday life, we have to look beyond Sunday morning and beyond the small group who were intensely religious. As historian of religion Callum Brown stresses, "what made Britain a Christian nation . . . was not the minority with a strong faith, but the majority with some faith."[6] The 1851 Religious Census that caused so much anxiety measured attendance at Sunday services, or to be more precise, measured attendance at a single Sunday service. But even Horace Mann, the civil servant who designed the census, noted that many people attended services irregularly, perhaps twice a month, due to bad weather, the need to care for children or livestock, or lack of easy access to a service. Levels of attendance were also seasonal: in fishing villages men were at sea in summer and attendance was higher in winter, while in resort and spa towns such as Scarborough atten-dance was higher in summer because of visitors. Up until World War One, oral history sources consistently suggest much higher Sunday attendance than the census did, with about half of British families having one adult member who was a frequent attender.

Outside of churches, religion was evident everywhere in Victorian life. Christian ideas, images, and rhetoric pervaded homes, workplaces, and virtually all private and public spaces. Most families possessed and displayed religious artifacts. Every family had a bible, and some better-off families had several. Walls were decorated with crucifixes (in Anglican and Roman Catholic homes) or with pictures of bible scenes (in nonconformist homes). Religious music, from hymns to religious verses set to music-hall tunes, were popular and pervasive. One of the most influential books to be published in the Victorian period was *Hymns Ancient and Modern*. This hymnal emerged out of a conversation between two clergymen on a train journey about the need to standardize the hymns sung in the Church of England; first published in 1861, *Hymns Ancient and Modern* became the canonical hymnal. The text was so revered that when a "new and revised" edition was attempted in 1904, it became the "New Coke" of hymnals, immediately hated as an unnecessary attempt to improve on a classic; the original was republished two years later and remained the standard until 1916. (Evangelical parishes found some lyrics overly "Popish" and preferred *The Hymnal Companion to the Book of Common Prayer*, created by the Bishop of Exeter in 1870.)

Typical reading material consisted of religious tracts, denominational magazines, and "improving" magazines such as *All the Year Round*, *The Strand Magazine*, and *Cassell's Family Magazine Illustrated*, which though secular were evangelical in tone. Alternately there were religious magazines that were secular in presentation: the popular *Boys' Own Paper* was published by the Religious Tract Society. However, it had no explicit references to Christian teachings, but instead strived to provide boys with good, clean adventure stories as an alternative to the violent stories found in penny dreadfuls. Improving magazines were strongly in favor of temperance and constantly ran articles on the destructive effects of drink. Their serialized stories constituted a large portion of the fiction most working- and middle-class Victorians read. They usually carried an evangelical message, often of a lost man saved from drink, gambling, or sexual profligacy by a loving Christian woman.

For many Victorians, then, Sunday services were only one facet of their religious lives, and not necessarily the most important one at that. For example, working-class women were not likely to attend Sunday morning services, because these conflicted with preparations for that other critical ritual: the Sunday dinner, a large, festive, meat-oriented meal eaten at midday. Most Sunday morning services began at 11:00am, the exact time that women needed to start cooking. (In upper- and middle-class households with cooks, women were far more likely to attend Sunday services.) This was particularly true of evangelical nonconformist chapels, which means that those most insistent on linking women with piety also made it most difficult for them to attend the main service of the week. In some families, the father would attend services while the mother cooked (working-class families perceived this as family representation, but enumerators did not). Some nonconformist ministers tried to address the problem by offering Sunday afternoon services for women; in Roman Catholic churches, which offered multiple morning masses, the problem was less acute. But this conundrum, in which the religious leader of the family could not attend Sunday services, probably skewed middle-class observers' perceptions of working-class religiosity.

There were other forms of observance that were far more important to the vast majority of Britons. One was observing Sunday as a day apart, regardless of church attendance. Families would spend the day together, perhaps taking a family walk and certainly enjoying a Sunday dinner. Many families refrained from games or other activities. Adults and children alike wore their Sunday-best clothes (a requirement that girls tended to enjoy and boys to despise). For example, a man named David Mitchell, who as an adult joined the Salvation Army, was born in 1899 to parents who never went to Sunday services. Nevertheless, they raised those children with a strict Sunday observance that included a big Sunday dinner, a family walk on which the father wore his Sunday-best suit, and a no-games-allowed rule.[7]

Another mode of Sunday observance was to make sure that one's children attended Sunday school, which the vast majority of working-class children did regularly. Sending children to Sunday school was a way of raising children as Christians, and of associating the entire family with Christian teachings (it also gave working-class parents one morning a week alone in their small home). For example, Leah Ward was raised in a Nottingham mining village in the 1880s. Though her parents did not attend Sunday services, Leah was sent to Sunday school and was even a member of the local Band of Hope, a children's temperance organization. Reverend W.J. Somerville, the vicar of St. George-the-Martyr parish church in Southwark, London, referred to Sunday school as "religion by deputy," and many parents clearly felt that in sending their children they were expressing their own religiosity. Parents were relatively nonchalant about denominational distinction; as long as the children went to a Sunday school, many were unconcerned about the difference between Anglican and Methodist, or even between Protestant and Catholic. Many Victorians remembered Sunday school stories, hymns, prizes, and teachers fondly and distinctly all their lives.[8]

Also important were many life-cycle services. The "churching" ceremony, a symbolic cleansing of a post-partum woman, had become obsolete amongst the Anglican clergy and was seen as mere superstition by the middle and upper classes, but was still extremely important to most working-class women, who until the mid-twentieth century believed that a post-partum woman was unclean and brought bad luck until she had been churched. Baptisms were considered extremely important—rates were actually on the rise between 1880 and 1914—as were funerals, which amongst the working class were lavish affairs. (Since until the 1890s the death rate for children under five years hovered at about 33%, children's funerals were a separate, very touching, genre unto themselves.) So, too, was a church wedding; indeed, some bigamous couples tried to approximate a church wedding by standing in the back pews and whispering vows to one another during a wedding service, after which they considered themselves married.

Various annual services were popular, too, and were, by mid-century, well-established in Anglican and nonconformist churches alike. "Watch-night" services held at midnight on the last day of the year were extremely well attended (they were more crowded than Christmas Eve services). Attendance was seen as a way of ensuring good luck in the year to come, but was also a form of Christian devotion; people felt it was important to spend the last minutes of the year praying and being spiritually cleansed in church, and there were always several conversions or signings of the temperance pledge right then and there. Sunday School Anniversary Services, which were held in summer, were also crowded, as nearly universal working-class childhood attendance created support and nostalgia. Anniversary Services were also the major fund-raising day for Sunday schools; at one Congregational chapel in Yorkshire in 1902, 78% of the annual fundraising for the Sunday School was accomplished at the Anniversary Service.[9] It might be accompanied by a Flower Festival or Flower Service, at which children decorated the church with flowers. A similar pair of celebrations, the Harvest Festival accompanied by a Fruit Banquet, occurred in autumn. The Reverend Somerville quoted above held that although "to attend the ordinary Sunday Service never seems to enter the mind of the ordinary parishioner," the church was important to them as "the place for baptisms, churchings, weddings and funerals and for attendance on the last night of the year and the harvest festival, on both of which occasions St George's presents a wonderful spectacle being crowded from floor to ceiling."[10]

Religious practice and experience was inflected by gender politics. The Victorian belief that women were naturally the more moral, and therefore the more religious sex, that they were "angels in the house," was most prominently articulated in middle-class evangelicalism, which depicted women as naturally virtuous and encouraged women to cultivate their godliness in domestic ways. If religion was feminine, then it was not, by definition, masculine. Of course, all ministers, priests, bishops and archbishops were men, and God was perceived as male. But spirituality was seen as effeminate, and masculinity was seen as antithetical to religiosity. Religious institutions assumed that men needed to be pulled away from the physical pursuits, gambling, and drinking to which they were naturally inclined. In addition, there were various efforts to create manly versions of Christianity that would allow men to be simultaneously devout and virile. In elite public schools there was a movement for "muscular Christianity," which argued that true Christianity required the same courage, physical strength, and sense of fair play that sports did, and so was acceptably masculine. The Salvation Army sought to combat traditional hard-drinking, gambling, working-class masculinity with an evangelical masculinity in which temperance was an alternative badge of manliness. Organizations such as the Boys' Brigade combined militarized organization with Christianity. Churches even had their own sports teams or boxing rings.

But these efforts did little in the face of the widespread belief that religion was feminine. Women dominated congregations (though they were not generally permitted to lead or to preach): in a series of interviews with priests and ministers conducted in London in 1900, Reverend Springett of St Matthew's, the parish church in Brixton, said that "women, of course, preponderate[d]" in his services, while a Baptist minister from nearby Clapham noted optimistically that a quarter of his congregation was male.[11] This dominance was cultural rather than natural. Women expected to be more religious than men; they might have welcomed church attendance as an opportunity to get out of the house, especially when childcare was offered; and the church often offered women social and leisure opportunities that men found elsewhere. Victorians, however, took women's dominance as evidence of their natural religiosity.

From such perceptions of women's natures sprang responsibilities. Women were expected to provide their children's religious education, including their christening—some working-class fathers did not even attend their children's baptisms—their ability to say their prayers, and their Sunday school attendance. Women were also expected to save the men in their lives—who were seen as vulnerable to temptation—from excess. Women (and particularly mothers) dominated temperance, which was largely a movement of women fighting the evils of men's drinking. Overall, religion was women's responsibility: one vicar reported that any working-class man who opened the door to him was likely to say something along the lines of "Ah, you're from the church; you want to see the missus."[12]

Finally, we cannot understand Victorian religion without thinking about evangelicalism, which swept Britain from the late eighteenth until the mid-nineteenth century and set the tone for religious life and for much of public life generally for the better part of the Victorian period. In the United States today, the term "evangelical" evokes not only a militant and enthusiastic form of Christianity centered on being "born again" through adult baptism, but conservative social and political values; evangelical Christians are often referred to as the Christian Right of the political spectrum. In Victorian Britain, however, evangelicalism was not linked to political conservatism, which was the province of upper-class Anglicans. Evangelicals could be socially conservative, frowning on drinking and even dancing, but many were involved in radical causes such as the campaign to repeal the Contagious Diseases Acts, which involved promoting the civil rights of prostitutes.

Evangelicalism gained popularity as a reaction to what seemed like the spiritual emptiness of high-church Anglicanism. It was not a specific theology, but rather an approach to Christianity. Indeed, Callum Brown suggests that evangelicalism is best understood as a way of life rather than as a theological doctrine.[13] Evangelicals rejected ritual in favor of a direct and personal relationship with God. They emphasized individual salvation, the use of lay leaders and preachers, frequent reading of the Bible (especially the Christian gospel), a proselytizing zeal, and good works as expressions of faith. Evangelical congregations, leaders, worshippers, and principles could be found in all Protestant faiths in the nineteenth century. (Some scholars even suggest that Victorian Roman Catholicism had evangelical overtones, citing the fact that Catholic sisterhoods were more likely to devote themselves to outreach than to isolated contemplation.) Many of the older dissenting religions, including the Baptist church, were invigorated by the evangelical spirit that swept through Britain. Most of the newer religions that were founded during this period—the chief one being Wesleyan Methodism—were products of it. The Methodist church was wholly evangelical. Some Anglicans were evangelical, some were not. The most prominent evangelical Anglican was abolitionist William Wilberforce (1759–1833), who led a group known as the

Clapham Sect. The leading evangelical minister in the Church of Scotland was Thomas Chalmers; unable to reform his church as he envisioned, he went on to found the evangelical Free Church of Scotland (in the Disruption of 1843). By mid-century, evangelicalism dominated nonconformity and was a vibrant part of the established churches, with about two thirds of all churchgoers attending evangelical churches.

Evangelicalism's most important contribution to Victorian society was its assumption that faith should pervade all aspects of life. They accomplished this via Sunday schools for children, tract distribution societies, visiting societies, and the temperance movement. There were evangelically-infused organizations such as the Young Men's Christian Association and Mothers' Meetings, in which local upper-class and middle-class women met with their working-class neighbors to read the Bible, sew, and offer advice. In homes, workplaces and clubs, in schools and in pubs, in local and even national government, evangelical piety was everywhere.

A key facet of evangelicalism was its proselytizing impulse. Christian missions were important to Victorians, who gave generously to missionary organizations such as the Baptist Missionary Society, the Congregationalist London Missionary Society, the Anglican Church Missionary Society, and the Wesleyan Methodist Missionary Society. Hundreds of thousands of pounds were given—and spent—on missionary efforts. Missionaries worked in foreign missions to distant non-Christian countries including Ceylon, Persia, and Morocco, and in domestic missions to the inner city. While few people actually worked as missionaries, missions were omnipresent: children heard and read about them in Sunday school, while adults listened to sermons on them, attended bazaars in support of them, and read about missionary life. Until about 1870, foreign missions were more common and more popular with the public, but after 1870, home missions to such areas as the East End of London were often better-funded by their churches and denominations. While many female missionaries went abroad, domestic missions were generally dominated by middle-class and upper-class men who tried to offer working-class men a sober, nonviolent version of manliness that could serve as an alternative to traditional working-class manliness's stress on drinking and fighting. From the early twentieth century missions focused on providing basic necessities and social services as much as promoting Christian doctrine.

Evangelicalism was one of the main drivers of Victorian philanthropy. One journal commented at mid-century that "there was not a town in the kingdom which did not have its lying-in society, female school, visiting association, nursing institute and many other charitable organizations,"[14] and these were all the more necessary in an age with few publicly-funded safety nets. Philanthropy permeated British society, and especially affected its primary targets, women and children of the working classes. Philanthropy was usually organized around helping the poor by bringing middle-class values of respectability, domesticity, and often evangelical Christianity, to the less fortunate. Philanthropy took the forms of visits (district visiting societies ensured that the homes of the poor received well-meaning visitors armed with Bibles, blankets, and soup; institutional visiting societies went to prisons and workhouses), and the establishment of homes or funds for particular groups (such as fallen women or the blind). While most non-poor people believed that poverty was the fault of the (lazy, perhaps drunken) individual, they worked to alleviate its worst symptoms; in return they expected the poor to adopt their values and to live thriftily.

Notes

1 *Merthyr and Dowlais Times* (May 5, 1893) quoted in Andy Croll, "Street Disorder, Surveillance and Shame: Regulating Behaviour in the Public Spaces of the Late Victorian British Town," *Social History* [London] 24 (1999): 250–268, p. 255.

2 Nigel Yates and Jonathan M. Wooding, "Introduction," in Nigel Yates and Jonathan M. Wooding (eds), *A Guide to the Churches and Chapels of Wales* (Gwasg Prifysgol Cymru/ University of Wales Press, 2011), p. 11.

3 Quoted in Frances Knight, *The Nineteenth-Century Church and English Society* (Cambridge: Cambridge University Press, 1995), p. 26.

4 Samuel Keeble, "Industrial Day-Dreams (London, 1896), quoted in David Thompson, "The Emergence of the Nonconformist Social Gospel" in Keith Robbins (ed.), *Protestant Evangelicalism: Britain, Ireland, Germany, and America c.1750–c.1950* (Oxford: Oxford University Press, 1990), p. 259.

5 Edith Henrietta Fowler, *The Life of Henry Hartley Fowler, First Viscount Wolverhamptom, G.C.S.I.* (London: Hutchinson, 1912), p. 512.

6 Callum G. Brown, *The Death of Christian Britain: Understanding Secularisation, 1800–2000* (London: Routledge, 2001), p. 142.

7 Brown, p. 142.

8 Sarah C. Williams, *Religious Belief and Popular Culture in Southwark, 1880–1939* (Oxford: Oxford University Press, 1999), pp. 126–127, 132–133.

9 S.J.D. Green, *Religion in the Age of Decline: Organisation and Experience in Industrial Yorkshire, 1870–1920* (Cambridge: Cambridge University Press, 1996), p. 335.

10 Quoted in Williams, p. 88.

11 Rosemary O'Day, "Women in Victorian Religion," in David Englander and Rosemary O'Day (eds), *Retrieved Riches: Social Investigation in Britain 1840–1914* (Aldershot: Scolar Press, 1995), p. 340.

12 Quoted in Hugh McLeod, *Religion and Society in England 1850–1914* (London: Palgrave Macmillan, 1996), p. 157.

13 Brown, p. 39.

14 Quoted in Olive Banks, *Faces of Feminism: A Study of Feminism as a Social Movement* (Oxford: Basil Blackwell, 1981), p. 14.

Relevant fiction that students might enjoy

Charles Kingsley, *Westward Ho!* (1855)
Mrs Humphry Ward, *Robert Elsmere* (1888)
Anthony Trollope, *Chronicles of Barsetshire* (1855–1867)
Amy Levy, *Reuben Sachs* (1888)
Dickens, *Oliver Twist* (1838) and *Our Mutual Friend* (1864–1865)

Further reading

Callum G. Brown, *The Death of Christian Britain: Understanding Secularisation, 1800–2000* (London: Routledge, 2001).

Jeffrey Cox, "Worlds of Victorian Religion," in Martin Hewitt (ed.), *The Victorian World* (London: Routledge, 2012), pp. 433–448.

Jeffrey Cox, *Imperial Fault Lines: Christianity and Colonial Power in India, 1818–1940* (Stanford: Stanford University Press, 2002).

S.J.D. Green, *Religion in the Age of Decline: Organisation and Experience in Industrial Yorkshire, 1870–1920* (Cambridge: Cambridge University Press, 1996).

Frances Knight, *The Nineteenth-Century Church and English Society* (Cambridge: Cambridge University Press, 1995).

Hugh McLeod, *Religion and Society in England 1850–1914* (London: Palgrave Macmillan, 1996).

Sue Morgan and Jacqueline deVries (eds), *Women, Gender and Religious Cultures in Britain, 1800–1940* (London: Routledge, 2010).

Rosemary O'Day, "Women in Victorian Religion," in David Englander and Rosemary O'Day (eds), *Retrieved Riches: Social Investigation in Britain 1840–1914* (Aldershot: Scolar Press, 1995).

Mark A. Smith, "Religion," in Sarah C. Williams, *Religious Belief and Popular Culture in Southwark, 1880–1939* (Oxford: Oxford University Press, 1999).

Sarah C. Williams, *Religious Belief and Popular Culture in Southwark, 1880–1939* (Oxford: Oxford University Press, 1999).

Nigel Yates and Jonathan M. Wooding (eds), *A Guide to the Churches and Chapels of Wales* (Cardiff: Gwasg Prifysgol Cymru/University of Wales Press, 2011).

Online resources

See Introduction

14 Vestiges and origins
Science and medicine

Introduction

In 1863, all London was abuzz about "Pepper's Ghost," a new science exhibition in which a human apparently walked through a fully visible ghost. The display used plate glass, screens, and lighting to create the optical illusion of the ghost. (The technique became quite well-known, and was even a plot point in the 2016 New Year's Day special of the popular BBC television show *Sherlock*, "The Abominable Bride."). It was the most famous creation of J.H. Pepper (1821–1900), a showman of science so well-known that he has been styled by one historian "the celebrity chef of Victorian science."[1] The ghost first appeared in a Christmas theatrical performance, and thereafter became the main draw at the Royal Polytechnic Institution, a popular hall to which Londoners and tourists alike flocked to be amazed by the powers of science (after paying the 1 shilling entrance). Pepper's Ghost was a huge sensation that drew thousands of spectators, and gave Pepper the chance to educate by entertaining, astonishing his audiences with the rational powers of science.[2]

A popular scientific demonstration that took the form of spectacular entertainment, Pepper's Ghost crystallizes the place of science in Victorian culture. Fashions in public entertainment and technological advances in mass publishing proved as important as the insights of the men who posited the laws of thermodynamics and the theory of evolution. The revolutionary status of ideas proved as important as the ideas themselves. The period saw major developments in science, in fields ranging from evolutionary biology to the physics of optics and heat; developments in technology, where industrializing Britain was well-poised to make breakthroughs in railway and shipping capabilities, among others; the rise of science as a paid profession, rather than a leisure pursuit; and intense general interest in science, which reached the public in the form of books, magazine articles, and spectacular exhibits of all kinds. It also saw major developments in medicine, the most important of which was that it became more closely related to and based on science. In addition medicine, like science, professionalized, with doctors, nurses, and midwives developing legal qualifications and professional organizations.

Because we think of science as objectively true, rather than culturally specific (the way, say, fashions or literary genres are), historicizing science can be difficult.

However, it would be a mistake to judge the scientific ideas of the past according to contemporary standards. While previous generations of scholars often focused on progress, today historians of science try to investigate the past on its own terms. They take seriously such Victorian practices as phrenology, the science of reading bumps on the skull to assess levels of intelligence and moral fiber; mesmerism, the science of using invisible "magnetic fluids" to enable one person to influence another; and the unseen, omnipresent "luminiferous ether" through which physicists believed all energy and matter moved. Today, these are all considered pseudo-sciences or obsolete ideas, but in the Victorian period deducing intelligence from skull shape seemed as reasonable as tracing the earth's distant past from rock formations, as geologists like Charles Lyell (1797–1875) did. No knowledge exists independent of the society in which it is produced and consumed, and scientific knowledge is no exception.

The standard account of the Victorians holds that science and religion were in conflict, and that sometime during the nineteenth century science won, replacing religion as the highest form of authority. However, this story, part of a larger "secularization" model of history, is highly problematic, not least because neither religion nor science were monolithic. For most Victorians science and religion, far from being in conflict, overlapped and supported one another. For example, "natural theology"—the belief that the complexity of nature demonstrates the existence of God—permeated both expert and popular works. In the *Bridgewater Treatises*, eight scientific essays commissioned by the Royal Society between 1833 and 1836, commitment to science was portrayed as working in concert, not conflict, with a belief in God.

***

Science was of interest to many people across a wide swath of society. Thousands of people joined scientific clubs and institutions, read scientific journals, went to scientific museums, and attended scientific lectures and demonstrations. While there were scientific experts, there was no such thing as a "scientist" until the turn of the twentieth century. In the late eighteenth century, the preferred term had been "natural philosopher." These men (for they were almost always men) were either wealthy or had wealthy patrons. Their interests were very broad, ranging from astronomy to geology to natural history. Their work consisted not only of laboratory experiments but of specimen collections and philosophical reflections, and the main science journal of the day, published by the Royal Society, was called *Philosophical Transactions*. As the status of science and the identity of the people who did scientific research changed over the century, so too did the institutions in which science was taught, researched, and discussed.

In the nineteenth century, the natural philosopher was replaced by the "man of science," who was more specialized than the natural philosopher, but saw his work as having broad applications and implications for society. The typical man of science saw himself as a gentleman, but he probably based this on character rather than birth (especially as the century wore on), and relied less on wealth or patronage than the natural philosopher had. While he was an expert, he was not engaged in full-time salaried employment and did not necessarily do his work in a laboratory or at a university. While today we think of Charles Darwin (1809–1882) as the model of the modern scientist, he is better understood as a man of science; he pursued his researches at his own pace, outside of any institutions, and never held a university post. It was not until the turn of the twentieth century that the man of science was supplanted by the "scientist." Unlike the man of science, the scientist earned his living by his scientific researches; he had a very narrow field of specialization; he worked in a university, government, or industry laboratory, on reproducible results; and he strove for objectivity, refusing to speculate on the larger social or ethical implications of his work. Similarly, by the early twentieth century the doctor was highly trained and officially certified, belonged to professional organizations, and read professional journals. He (or in a very few cases, she) considered medicine a science, and relied on tools such as stethoscopes, laboratory tests, and x-rays to determine a course of treatment.

This chapter begins by looking at what Victorian science and medicine were in 1820, who practiced them, where, and how, with particular emphasis on science as spectacle and communication and on theories of evolution before Darwin. It then turns to the period after 1860 to look at the rise of physics, the growth of public interest in science, the impact of Darwin's theory of evolution, and the rise of both professionalized medicine and effective public health.

1820–1860: Developing infrastructures, radical evolution, early medical practices

Science education, institutions, communication

The early Victorian period was a time of transition for the sciences in Britain. Education and professional societies both changed dramatically, and commercial scientific entertainment emerged. At the start of our period, there was almost no system of formal higher education for science education. There were no science departments at Oxford or Cambridge. The Scottish universities were far better in this regard, as they valued practical skills and provided a wide-ranging education that was better training for industrial and technological work than an Oxbridge degree. Until mid-century, English universities were not only socially exclusive but were dismissive of and distinct from the worlds of industry, science, and medicine. The main society to which natural philosophers belonged was the Royal Society of London for the Improvement of Natural Knowledge, founded in 1660 and better known simply as the Royal Society. But in 1820, the once-exclusive Royal Society was old-fashioned, and by 1830 it had very little cachet. It had hundreds of members, many of whom had been admitted on the basis of social status rather than scientific accomplishment: any educated gentleman who expressed an interest in science could belong, even if he did no collecting, researching, experimenting, or publishing himself. Many members were clergymen who had nothing beyond this to recommend them. Charles Babbage

(1791–1871)—whose calculating engines were the precursors of the modern calculator—criticized the Royal Society's bloat in an 1830 essay entitled *Reflections on the Decline of Science in England*. During the 1830s and 1840s, the Society reformed itself, purging most members of the clergy and restricting membership to active researchers. In addition, more specialized scientific societies were founded, including the Geological Society and the Astronomical Society. Most importantly, in 1831 the British Association for the Advancement of Science (BAAS), which focused on research and on modernizing scientific practice, was founded. The BAAS challenged the social elitism and conservatism of the Royal Society with its meritocratic membership policies and focus on scientific research. Commercial galleries also opened and were also important. The two biggest were the Royal Polytechnic Institution (1836–1881) and the National Gallery of Practical Science, Blending Instruction with Amusement, better known as the Adelaide Gallery (1832–1845).[3] Science museums were built, such as the Museum of Practical Geology (f. 1851). From the 1850s, more professionally-oriented or rigorous programs of science education developed, with geology, botany, and chemistry all becoming formal, degree-seeking subjects.

How scientific knowledge circulated and was exchanged is as important as, even constitutive of, the knowledge itself. Indeed leading historian of science James Secord argues that we should understand science first and foremost as "a form of communicative action."[4] Many of the new institutions that developed served as communicative networks among professionals. In addition, this age of professionalization was also an age of popularization. Science was of interest to many laypeople, and publishers sought writers who (whether or not they were men of science) could communicate new ideas to a lay audience. Science popularization was a huge industry. But what is popularization? The notions of "popular science" and of "popularization" are hotly debated among historians of science, most of whom oppose a definition of "popularization" as a process in which scientific knowledge was produced by experts and then watered down and presented to passive audiences. Lay people were not passive recipients but rather active and demanding consumers of scientific and medical knowledge, who had their own agendas and did their own interpretive work, choosing some ideas and rejecting others as they created their own ideas about the natural world.

One way Victorian science was communicated—and consumed—was as spectacle. As entertainment, scientific exhibitions and demonstrations were competing with artistic, literary, and other displays for audiences' attention and were often very theatrical. Fashions in scientific display changed quickly; in the 1810s, going to the Royal Institution (f. 1799) was all the rage, but by the late 1840s dioramas and panoramas were the thing, quickly replaced by the Great Exhibition in 1851. The Great Exhibition was a defining event in scientific spectacle. It promoted the very latest in science and technology: many electromagnetic motors were on show, with electric telegraphs the most popular electrical exhibits. Charlotte Brontë, describing her visit, said that Great Exhibition was "a wonderful place," a "bazaar" of "[w]hatever human industry has created," including scientific achievements such as "railway engines and boilers."[5] The Great Exhibition sparked a fashion for large international exhibits of the potential of physics. Many of these displays were designed to amaze the public. One of the most popular was called the Venus Kiss: a pretty young woman would be electrified and seated on an insulated stool, and would then invite men from the audience to kiss her. The audience would howl in delight as any takers received an electric shock upon contact.[6] Print culture was another field of science communication; science writing included books, pamphlets, and journal articles in both science and general-interest periodicals. Increasing interest, literacy, and discretionary income, together with decreasing publication production costs, meant that more and more people were consumers of science writing (though like science spectacle, science writing was competing with other genres, including fiction, for readers' attention).[7] Inexpensive reprints of science books were first published in the 1820s; steam printing in the 1840s and power binding in the 1860s made printed matter even more affordable for the growing proportion of the population that was literate.

Figure 14.1 Etching by Thomas Kearnan showing apparatus and visitors in the Adelaide Gallery, Adelaide Street, The Strand, London. The gallery claimed to "Blend Instruction with Amusement" and promoted "the astonishing powers of electricity with the wonders of optical illustration." There were promenade concerts and daily scientific lectures.

Photo by SSPL/Getty Images.

With science unsupported by institutions of higher education before mid-century for most of the period, the distinction between pure and applied sciences was not sharp, and technological breakthroughs remained an aspect of scientific work. Furthermore the process of industrialization was in part based on, and certainly created a demand for, technological advances. Over the course of the nineteenth century, British engineers were able to figure out how to use iron, steel, and steam engines effectively to build cost-effective railways and ships. These two were then used to create networks of transportation and communication, including telegraphs. Developments in all three are nicely illustrated by the career of early Victorian Isambard Kingdom Brunel (1806–1859).

Brunel was trained by his father, an engineer who noticed his son's mechanical aptitude, spent time as an apprentice to a clockmaker in France, and worked as an engineer from the age of 16. He created his first major design, for a suspension bridge over the Clifton Gorge in Bristol, for a competition held by the Bristol Society of Merchant Venturers and judged by engineer Thomas Telford. (That local businessmen sponsored a contest that spurred technological innovation demonstrates the close links between business, industry, and science.) Though the bridge was not completed during his lifetime due to a lack of funding, Brunel established important connections in the Bristol business and entrepreneurial community that led to his appointment in 1833 as the engineer of the Great Western Railway Company, which proposed to build a main line railway from London to Bristol. (See Chapter 4 for more on the development of the railways.) Wanting to build a secure, permanent, and comfortable rail, Brunel decided that the Great Western Railway would be built on broad gauge tracks of seven feet, rather than the narrow gauge tracks of under five feet that were already in use elsewhere, and on longitudinal sleepers rather than on stone blocks or cross-sleepers. These gave the GWR a competitive advantage over rivals, and the railway soon extended all over southwestern England and Wales. While broad gauge tracks never became the industry standard, the GWR was well-engineered and widely admired in its day.

Brunel then proposed that the Great Western Railway Company extend its purview west—much farther west, across the Atlantic Ocean. In the 1830s, most people believed that transatlantic steamships could never be practical or profitable; they took too long—at least three weeks—and needed too much fuel. Defiant, Brunel designed the SS *Great Western*, a large, paddle-wheeled, wooden-hulled ship that in 1838 got to New York in 14 days with fuel to spare. (Soon afterwards, in 1840, the SS *Britannia*, owned by the new Cunard shipping company, crossed in 11 days.) Brunel then went on to design the first large ship made of iron, the SS *Great Britain*; to power it, he had to design a new steam engine as well. Brunel's third ship, the SS *Great Eastern*, could go from Britain to Australia without having to stop for fuel. While the *Great Eastern* was never commercially viable, it was important: the first permanent telegraph cables across the Atlantic, which made telegrams between Britain and the United States and Canada possible, were laid in 1866 by the SS *Great Eastern*.

As these highlights of Brunel's career make clear, technology and science were closely interlinked, and both were shaped but not entirely dictated by commercial considerations. Furthermore both flourished outside of the academy, and both shaped the British and global landscape. Technology was valued by the Victorians; the Great Exhibition was at least as much a celebration of technology and applied science as of pure science. Prince Albert was a leading promoter of both applied science and of the Exhibition, and, as the Victorian period progressed, the British government continued to recognize the potential for profit and imperial governance that steam ships and railways held. The government helped to build and maintain many shipping and railway routes, in Britain but also in and to imperial holdings in South Africa, India, Hong Kong, and elsewhere, and to the Americas and parts of Europe.

Evolution before Darwin

Strangely persistent is the notion that history was forever changed by one book, the *Origin of Species*, published by one genius, Charles Darwin (1809–1882), in one year, 1859. In fact, there were multiple theories of evolution, and their story, as much social and political as scientific, begins in the 1820s, when three radical new sciences—phrenology, mesmerism, and philosophical anatomy—introduced into Britain scientific naturalism, the belief that all aspects of the natural world can be explained without reference to religion, and laid the way for widespread acceptance of evolutionary theory.

Phrenology was the science of deducing an individual's abilities by studying the shape of his or her skull. It held that the brain was divided into externally visible "phrenological organs" that controlled attributes such as intelligence and morality (for example, novelist George Eliot was considered by phrenology's British champion, Scottish writer George Combe (1788–1858), to have large bumps of "concentrativeness" on her head).[8] Phrenology focused on the human body as a physical and observable entity, rather than as the home of an eternal soul. It thereby promoted a scientific naturalist position by connecting humans to the natural world rather than to an unobservable God. While not logically dependent on one another, phrenology and scientific naturalism were linked in the Victorian mind, making phrenology important in the history of science.

Phrenology was developed in Germany in the 1790s by Franz Gall (1758–1828) but championed in Britain by George Combe. His 1828 book, *The Constitution of Man Considered In Relation To External Objects*, promoted both phrenology and scientific naturalism via "the doctrine of natural laws." In *The Constitution of Man*, Combe claimed that phrenology proved that the world was knowable without reference to the unseen, that humans' physical beings were subject to natural law, and that natural law was the only verifiable truth. Phrenology was a powerful tool, a way of understanding human nature that would enable Victorians to address all manner of social and political issues. Along with *The Constitution of Man* it was instrumental in many early Victorians' decision to adopt a scientific naturalist worldview.

Phrenology and *The Constitution of Man* were championed by ambitious young medical men of ambiguous social and marginal professional status. They went on to become popular with a wide range of people of all classes and levels of scientific expertise. Phrenology was familiar to everyone and accepted by many; it was one of the most widespread sciences in Britain, which is remarkable considering that it was practiced by ordinary people rather than anyone who made professional or institutional claims to expertise.[9] *The Constitution of Man* was one of the most influential publications of the century. It was one of the most widely-read books in English: over 100 publishers kept it continuously in print until 1899, by which year it had sold an amazing 350,000 copies, including inexpensive editions that working-class readers snapped up.

Another popular and influential science, also now discredited, was animal magnetism or mesmerism. Developed by a German doctor, Franz Mesmer (1734–1815), mesmerism was popular in Britain in the late 1830s, 1840s and 1850s. Mesmerists believed that all matter, including the human body, contained an invisible magnetic fluid not unlike the ether that energy physicists studied. A mesmerist could influence his subject, using his own magnetic fluid to correct imbalances in theirs. In a mesmeric session, an audience would watch the mesmerist (usually a man) and his subject (usually a woman). Staring into his subject's eyes, the mesmerist would make over her a series of "magnetic passes"— sweeping hand movements in which his hand skimmed but did not touch her body—until she fell into a trance. Once mesmerized, the subject would become a sort of puppet of the mesmerist—she would have no will and no senses of her own, but would instead speak the mesmerist's thoughts, taste the food in his mouth, and so forth. Her senses might also be displaced in her body, so that she could, for instance, read a book with her spine rather than her eyes. The mesmeric subject might also see events occurring far away or in the future. At the end of the session, the mesmerist would once again make magnetic passes over the subject, this time to awaken her.

Mesmerism was many things to many people—medical or psychological therapy, proof of the human mind's limitless potential, and even a form of surgical anesthesia (before it was replaced with ether and then chloroform). While many suspected charlatanism or were put off by the uses of the magnetic passes, which seemed sexual, others were convinced. Mesmerism combined science, medicine, spectacle, and theater in an irresistible blend. It seemed to demonstrate that humans were intimately connected to one another by invisible influences and that the human psyche had untapped potential. In the years before science became definitively located in laboratories, mesmerism's demonstration of the influence one person could have over another was a fascinating and scientific exploration of human abilities.

Like phrenology, mesmerism first appealed to radical young men of science (in the 1840s some combined the two to pursue "phreno-mesmerism.") But it went on to become broadly popular, first in polite circles in London (Charles Dickens was an enthusiast), where it fitted in well with the style of other private entertainments given in aristocratic homes, and later in the provinces, where local mesmeric societies and itinerant mesmeric lecturers flourished. Mesmeric demonstrations were put on in temperance halls, mechanics' institutes, halls of science, and even pubs and inns, which would hire lecturers passing through town as a way of boosting business. One traveling mesmeric lecturer, Swiss Charles Lafontaine (1803–1892), won over audiences by putting his subjects into trances so profound that they were insensible to electric shocks, pins thrust into their flesh, and pistols shot next to their ears. Lecturers spoke to groups of anywhere from a few dozen to a few hundred; their demonstrations would be reported in the paper and often inspired local debates over mesmerism's authenticity.[10] As science changed over the century, mesmerism, which relied on personal contact and testimony, rather than on anything that could be tested or reproduced in the laboratory, was no longer seen as a science, but many continued to praise its therapeutic effects (it had links to later schools of thought, including hypnotism and Freudian analysis) and its home uses.

A third scientific idea, introduced into Britain from France, was a school of anatomical studies called "philosophical anatomy." It argued that all animal species were fundamentally alike, with the same basic structures and the same organs. More sophisticated life forms simply had more complex versions of these structures and organs. From fish to mammal, from monad to man, animal life exhibited a "unity of plan" or "unity of composition." This unity was, philosophical anatomists thought, evident in embryos, which they claimed progressed through earlier, simpler versions of life to more complex ones as they developed, a theory called "recapitulation." Philosophical anatomists disagreed with one another on some points, most notably on evolution. The "functionalism" of Georges Cuvier (1769–1832) held that each species was designed and unchanging, while Etienne Geoffroy Saint-Hilaire (1772–1844) and Jean-Baptiste Lamarck (1744–1829) believed in "transformism" or gradual adaptive changes to species. But their radical ideas meant that humans differed from animals only in their level of structural complexity. It treated humans as physical (rather than spiritual) beings. Victorians, who assumed that social laws were based on natural laws, were quick to see a revolutionary social message in philosophical anatomy.

In the late 1820s, Scottish medical men and men of science studied in Paris and brought philosophical anatomy back to Britain. One important figure in this process was Robert Grant (1793–1874). Born in Edinburgh, he trained in Paris, where he became convinced by Geoffrey's ideas about unity of composition and transformism. Back in Britain, in 1827 he became a professor of zoology at the new London University, and was later given Britain's first chair of comparative anatomy. From these positions he exerted enormous influence (he was one of Charles Darwin's teachers). Other important British philosophical anatomists were Robert Knox (1791–1862), an influential teacher at the College of Surgeons of Edinburgh, and Thomas Wakley, (1795–1862), the founder of the *Lancet*, a weekly medical journal that promoted reform of the medical profession. All three were radicals and, to some degree, outsiders. (Knox was also a promoter of scientific racism; he opposed miscegenation, arguing that blacks and whites were separate species.)

Unity of composition and transmutation were rejected by elitist and conservative groups: Anglicans, Francophobes, Oxford and Cambridge Universities, the Royal Society, and the Royal College of Surgeons. All of these groups and institutions opposed philosophical anatomy with a set of simultaneously scientific and political arguments about a divinely fixed biological and social order. For Anglican Richard Owen (1804–1892), Grant's leading opponent and a member of the Royal College of Surgeons, who became known as "the English Cuvier," transmutation was scientifically, socially, and politically unacceptable, not only because it presented a vision of all life as progressive and competitive, but also because it was championed by radicals who attacked the entire scientific establishment. Owen stressed the place of God's hand in nature and opposed phrenology and theories of evolution.

But from about the 1840s, unity of composition and transmutation were endorsed and taught by a range of radically-inclined men in private medical schools, anatomy schools, and the newer universities in Edinburgh and London. These schools welcomed a scientific theory of life as both progressive and competitive, in part because it resonated with their own commitment to merit and ability over birth. Followers included medical general practitioners, Nonconformists, Francophiles, Benthamites, and political radicals. For example, Grant was a Francophile who, in addition to following Geoffrey's views on transmutation, also opposed the Royal College of Physicians' elitism, and wanted membership to be based solely on merit. For Grant and his followers, comparative anatomy and transmutation were scientifically radical, but they were also part of a larger, socio-political attack on the patronage networks and elite educational and professional communities from which they were excluded because of their class and religion.

The relentless radicalism and anti-elitism of Grant, Wakley, and other philosophical anatomists ensured that evolution was seen as a dangerous and disreputable science throughout the 1830s and early 1840s. The cultural position of evolution began to change with the (anonymous) publication in 1844 of a book called *Vestiges of the Natural History of Creation*. *Vestiges*' re-presentation of evolution as unthreatening made it one of the most important books of the nineteenth century. *Vestiges of the Natural History of Creation* was a grand story of the development of the cosmos, earth, and all life, in what it termed a "universal gestation of nature" in which the entire cosmos were eternally progressing. In its "nebular hypothesis," the universe began as a mist and gradually differentiated into stars and planets. In the same way, the earth's geology began very simply and then became more complex. The pattern was then followed by the earth's plant and animal life. This grand narrative of progress from clouds of gas to the formation of the Earth, animals, and then mankind was an optimistic one that implied that humans would continue to improve in the future. The narrative voice was one of a companionable guide who explored the natural world together with the reader, who deferred to scientific experts, but who also saw nature as a book that was associated with other scientific writings and with the Bible.[11]

Vestiges was not written by a man of science; it was written by journalist and publisher Robert Chambers (1802–1871). Chambers had promoted new scientific ideas before; in 1835, he had published the first cheap edition of the *The Constitution of Man*. But *Vestiges* was not associated with *The Constitution* because unlike many "anonymous" Victorian works, the authorship of which were open secrets, *Vestiges* really was anonymous—while speculation abounded, almost no one knew that Chambers had written it until after his death. This anonymity helped make a wide range of readers open to the book.

As James Secord has demonstrated, *Vestiges* made previously threatening evolutionary accounts of life safe in two ways. First, it subsumed evolution into its much larger scheme of constant natural progress. Second, it made evolution unfrightening by domesticating it. The book was full of images of birth, childhood, and the family. It compared the gestation of nature to the gestation of a baby in its mother's womb. It depicted the development of a new species as nothing "more than a new stage of progress in gestation, an event as simply natural" and no more "startling [than] the silent advance of an ordinary mother from one week to another of her pregnancy."[12] No longer was evolution the province of radicals, atheists, and Frenchmen; here it was simply the way families grew, writ large. This domestic emphasis helped to fend off accusations that the book undermined faith.[13]

Vestiges was a publishing phenomenon. The second edition sold out before 1844 was gone, and all told the book went through 14 editions and sold 40,000 copies in Britain alone, aided by new printing and distribution methods and the new mass market for books. Cheap editions that sold at 2s.6d. were affordable for the lower middle class; working-class readers might find a copy in a pub library or a second-hand bookshop. Moreover, *Vestiges* was a sensation, a topic of discussion and debate, beyond what these figures indicate. Copies were purchased by thousands in a variety of editions, borrowed from circulating libraries, discussed at public scientific meetings and *conversazioni* (social gatherings held by learned societies), and made the subject of lectures and sermons. It was read by upper-class men of science who had their own collections of natural specimens and by aspiring middle-class and working-class readers, by aristocrats and skilled workers, by evangelical Christians and militant freethinkers, by Queen Victoria and Charles Darwin. Thousands were fascinated: devout Methodist Mary Smith, who called it "the wonder and curiosity of the reading world," stayed up nights to read the copy her employer had borrowed from a friend. Many were horrified: Elizabeth Harrison, a shopkeeper's wife in a country village, was going to burn the copy her oldest son left behind when he emigrated to Australia, until her younger son begged her not to.[14] Though many prominent leaders of the Church of England and the Scottish Free Church opposed it, it was widely read by university-educated young men well into the 1850s, and many Oxbridge graduates felt that *Vestiges'* universal gestation of nature could be reconciled with the biblical account of creation in Genesis. Many men of science were critical of the book's theories, especially its nebular hypothesis and its particular evolutionary mechanisms—Chambers was, after all, a journalist, not a man of science. Thomas Huxley's review started with a quote from Macbeth as an attack: "[t]ime was, that when the brains were out, the man would die" (he later apologized).[15] President of the BAAS

John Herschel was offended by the author's anonymity and the book's promiscuous mix of what he considered valid science (such as geology) and invalid quackery (such as phrenology), and spoke out against it.[16] However, many BAAS members endorsed it. One future member, Alfred Russel Wallace (who would become, with Darwin, the co-discover of the evolutionary mechanism of natural selection) was inspired to become a man of science by reading *Vestiges*.

Vestiges' most famous reader was Charles Darwin. As we will see below, in 1844 Darwin had already developed his own theory of evolution; rather than focusing on *Vestiges'* nebular hypothesis and on the larger message of the universal gestation of nature as most readers did, Darwin anxiously read *Vestiges* as a version of his own still-unpublished ideas and found it, to his relief, flawed. As the history of evolutionary theory has become the "Darwin Industry"—a large and well-funded school of scholarship focused relentlessly on Darwin and his writings—Darwin's own interpretation of *Vestiges* as an early, primitive version of *Origin* has become standard. It is difficult to remember that in 1844 *Vestiges* could be no such thing. It was the only work on evolution that most people had ever read. Far from being primitive, it was groundbreaking. And for many, it remained the preferred version of evolution: *Vestiges* outsold *Origin* for many years after the latter was published.

Becoming a science and a profession: Medicine

To our modern eyes, medicine is the most obvious and direct way in which science touches the lives of ordinary people. In the first decades of our period, however, medicine was not particularly scientific, the medical field was overcrowded, and most doctors did not have particularly high social status or standards of living. There was a Royal College of Physicians, which had been founded in 1518. There were three types of medical men—physicians, surgeons, and apothecaries—whose training varied from many years at university to a couple of years of apprenticeship, with physicians the medical elite, and surgeons and apothecaries an overlapping group of general practitioners. An 1815 Apothecaries Act attempted to regulate of medical education and practice but it had little impact. All of these medical men shared patients with and competed for custom with many other practitioners, including midwives, traditional healers, pill and ointment salesmen of all stripes, and nurses. Midwives were working-class women who were usually older and often widows. They had learned their skills by apprenticing rather than any formal education, which meant that the care they provided varied widely, and they offered their services within their communities. Between 1820 and 1860, more men, including doctors, took up midwifery, and male attendants became typical at middle-class and upper-class births. Other local women might make traditional, herb-based medicines. Itinerant salesmen promised cures for venereal disease and other shameful ailments. Nursing was perceived as a form of domestic service, not of medicine; nurses were women who came into private homes to care for the ill, but they were often stereotyped as old, drunk, or both.

Victorian medical practices do not seem very scientific to modern sensibilities. Doctors did not treat patients in offices; sick people of all classes were visited in their homes by their practitioners. Doctors did not usually do physical examinations of their patients; they relied on patients' own reports of their symptoms and on what they could see when they looked at their fully-dressed charges. Similarly, Victorian ideas about health and sickness are foreign to us. Most doctors believed that health relied on keeping the humors (blood, phlegm, and bile) in balance, a theory that dated back to the ancient Greeks. Doctors also subscribed to miasmatic theory, which held that diseases were spread via "miasma," invisible and foul-smelling "bad air." In 1848, the popular *Buchan's Domestic Medicine* listed the most common causes of illness, which included night air, sedentary habits, anger, and sudden changes of temperature. Hospitals were not places for seriously ill people, but charities that cared for the very poor (who might also be sick). Surgeries were very rare and usually fatal. Treatment of almost all illnesses consisted of either rest, tonics, purgatives, courses of bleeding, or some combination of these. For example, in 1848, one doctor treated a child sick with fever, coughing, and diarrhea with two laxatives (milk of magnesia and tincture of rhubarb) and an emetic (ipecac), but decided to refrain from leeches or bloodletting.[17] Doctors also prescribed opiates such as laudanum for pain relief; they were effective but addictive and had side-effects.

Sickness was frightening to most people, and doctors could offer little help. There were many terrifying epidemics and pandemics. The 1830s saw Britain's first cholera epidemic which killed over 50,000, a smallpox epidemic which killed 30,000, and several "fever" epidemics. In the 1840s, fevers continued, along with a typhoid epidemic. There were cholera epidemics in 1848–1849 and in 1853–1854; during the latter, Dr John Snow made his name by deducing that the source of the disease was a single public pump, on Broad Street in the Soho area of London. One of the main causes of death was tuberculosis, known as consumption; authors Emily and Anne Brontë both died of consumption in 1848 and 1849, within six months of each other. Another enormous problem was syphilis, a sexually-transmitted disease which was painful and ultimately fatal. (Gonorrhea was also widespread—doctors believed gonorrhea and syphilis to be two different phases of the same disease—but it was not fatal.) Quacks offered a variety of dangerous remedies: mercury (which is poisonous) was a widely-used treatment. Steel's Aromatic Lozenges promised to "repair the evils brought on by debauchery" (that is, syphilis), but were ineffective, as were all treatments before 1909. Beyond these terrifying diseases, other chronic and acute illnesses, discomfort, and pain were features of life. In the working class, frequent illness was integrated into a culture of stoicism, in which people kept on with their work and daily lives in spite of illness. In the upper and upper middle classes, in contrast, many felt entitled to complain about and be treated for every ache and pain; a culture of invalidism arose, in which some people, predominantly women, spent much of their time and energy trying treatments from various practitioners. Between epidemics, other illnesses, poor sanitation, and poor nutrition, mortality rates were very high. In 1841, 153 babies per thousand died—today in the United States, the rate is about 6 babies per thousand annually—and 21.6 people per thousand died annually.

Given this landscape, it is no surprise that many people of all classes turned to non-medical healers such as hydropaths or homeopaths, whom we might see as quacks. The advice of doctors and quacks was often based on similar understandings of the human body and illness, and treatments had similar success rates. Many alternative healers were quite famous and well-respected. When Dr John St. John Long (1798–1834) died in 1834, grateful patients erected a monument erected over his tomb. In the 1820s and 1830s, James Morison (1770–1840) enjoyed fame and wealth as the promoter of Morison's Vegetable Universal Pills. Morison had a compelling narrative to offer his customers. Morison was a businessman; sick for many years, he consulted dozens of doctors, to no avail, finally came to understand that his troubles stemmed from impurities in his blood, and cured himself with a vegetable remedy. He called his model the Hygeian system and shared his findings by selling Morison's Universal Vegetable Pills from 1825. Morison diversified his efforts, not only manufacturing two kinds of pills, but founding a British College of Health that promoted his system and publishing a *Hygeian Journal* as well as numerous advertisements and pamphlets. His Universal Vegetable Pills made Morison a wealthy man; throughout the 1830s he was making between £25,000 and £35,000 per year, an enormous sum that suggests that consumers were spending as much as £100,000 on his pills annually. And while Morison was unusually famous and wealthy, he was only one of many quacks who flourished throughout the Victorian period.

Between 1820 and 1860, we start to see changes to public health and medical training and professional infrastructure. Probably the largest impact came from state-sponsored initiatives started to improve public health. These began in the 1830s with the new Poor Law, which created medical districts and Poor Law Medical Officers. However, many in the working class were too proud or too frightened to avail themselves of Poor Law medical initiatives such as the smallpox vaccinations that were available for free from 1840 (and were compulsory from 1853, though many opposed compulsory vaccination). The early Victorian leader in public health was Sir Edwin Chadwick (1800–1890), author of the 1842 *Report on the Sanitary Condition of the Labouring Population of Great Britain*. Chadwick's report helped with the passage of a new initiative, the Public Health Acts of 1848, which encouraged the creation of local Boards of Health that would appoint a Medical Officer, provide sewers, and inspect lodging houses and food. The University of London, founded in 1836, offered medical degrees that combined academic instruction and clinical exposure. Doctors sought to become respected as professionals, in part via the founding of professional journals and associations. In 1823 the new radical medical journal the *Lancet* was founded by surgeon and radical democrat, Thomas Wakley. In the 1830s, the Provincial Medical and Surgical Association (PMSA), a forerunner of the British Medical Association, was founded. In 1855, the PMSA became the British Medical Association, and in 1858 the General Medical Council (GMC), which maintained a central registry of doctors, was founded.

In addition, several developments increased medicine's efficacy and the public's respect for medical men. These included widespread adoption of the stethoscope, which by mid-century was the icon of the profession. Also important was the effective use of anesthesia in surgery, which began in the late 1840s and was given the stamp of respectability when Queen Victoria used chloroform when she delivered her eighth child, Prince Leopold, in 1853. In 1847, Hungarian doctor Ignaz Phillip Semmelweis (1818–1865) demonstrated that most cases of the dreaded puerperal fever could be prevented with a simple antiseptic measure— having the practitioner wash his or her hands in a chlorine solution before touching laboring women. However, his methods were adopted only slowly, and many British doctors believed that his findings supported miasmic theory rather than germ theory, and that his method worked because the chlorine solution dispersed harmful miasma.

1860–1914: Evolution becomes respectable, medicine becomes a profession

Science education, institutions, communication

After 1860 science began to be a more respected field, and both technology and medicine became integrated into science and higher education. The sciences were integrated into and supported by major institutions of higher education. The first university laboratory, the Cavendish Laboratory at Cambridge University, was built in 1870, although to get it built, its champion, the Chancellor of the University (William Cavendish, the Seventh Duke of Devonshire) had to pay for its construction himself. From the 1870s, science became an accepted part of the university (and school) curriculum, and university departments, medical schools, and their labs become the institutional home of science. Some fields of knowledge, such as physics, benefited by the move to labs; others, such as mesmerism, suffered. Public interest in science continued: the British Museum's new Natural History wing in the South Kensington area of London opened in 1881.

The sciences also professionalized. One important group here was the "X Club," a group of men of science intent on gaining professional status who, from the 1860s, met monthly for dinner. The process of professionalization was connected to the rise of the term "scientist." As the man of science slowly became someone new, the scientist, science became a profession. The term "scientist" had been coined in the 1830s by Cambridge professor William Whewell (1794–1866), but had not caught on, even among those eager for professional status. Thomas Huxley (1825–1895), the head of the X Club known as "Darwin's bulldog" because he promoted evolutionary theory, rejected the term "scientist" at first; he thought the word so vulgar that he (wrongly) assumed it must have originated in America.[18] But as the nineteenth century became the twentieth, the term did eventually gain traction. And as scientists and laboratories came to dominate science and medicine, collectors, men of science, and museums came to seem antiquarian; collectors, once seen as active researchers, were now simply people who conveyed evidence to scientists, who did research in laboratories. In the twentieth century, the professionalization of science and the creation of the scientist had dramatic effects: in 1911 there were around 5,000 scientists in Britain, but by 1951 there were 49,000, almost ten times as many. Science had become established as a profession and a recognized body of knowledge.

The new status of science was in part due to the rise of physics, in particular the physics of energy; one historian styles the Victorian era the period "when physics became king."[19] In the 1850s and 1860s, various men of science, working together and separately, developed the concept of "energy," a single force behind biological, chemical, electrical, and thermal activity. This new unifying concept allowed them to measure, compare, and theorize about the conservation of various forms of energy. Energy physicists believed that there was an invisible medium, called the "ether," all around us, in which energy was stored and transformed from one form to another. Their work focused on developing laws about how energy worked, and on understanding the nature of the ether.[20] Most of the work done on the physics of energy was done in north Britain, in Glasgow, Edinburgh, and Manchester. Key figures included William Thomson (1824–1907), later Lord Kelvin, after whom the Kelvin absolute scale of temperature is named; James Joule (1818–1889), who derived the relationship between currents, resistance, and heat called Joule's law, and after whom the unit of energy the joule is named; and James Clerk Maxwell (1831–1879), who derived Maxwell's equations and synthesized a series of unrelated observations about electricity and magnetism into electromagnetic theory. They all worked together: after Thomson laid out the laws of thermodynamics, the new science of heat, in his 1851 paper "On the Dynamical Theory of Heat," Maxwell used Thomson's insights to develop his theories of electromagnetism.

Physicists stated clear and compelling laws, and emphasized results that were reproducible in laboratories. As such it became the new gold standard, the premiere science against which other sciences measured themselves. (Darwin worried about whether the "natural selection" he saw as the key mechanism of evolution was a scientific "law" as rigorous as the laws of physics.) There were important social reasons for physics' preeminence. On the one hand, physics appealed to the sons of gentlemen, because of its connections to mathematics (one of the most respected fields of study at Oxbridge), which lent it respectability. On the other hand, the dynamic theory of heat emerged out of very practical concerns that spoke to middle-class men engaged in industry. While many continental scientists saw this connection to trade and industry as degrading—French physicist Pierre Duhem (1861–1916) famously remarked that British physics was the physics of the factory floor—British physicists were not ashamed that their work had practical applications, and after mid-century science and technology became inextricably linked.

Starting in 1900, several provincial universities—called "civic" or "redbrick" universities—were founded to offer access to university education to more students, including local and non-elite students, and to stress scientific research and practical training, often oriented towards local industries. The universities of Birmingham, Liverpool, Leeds, Sheffield, and Bristol were all granted royal charters between 1900 and 1909. By 1914 the redbrick universities taught 20,000 students to

Oxbridge's 7,000 and had changed the complexion of British higher education (though even so in 1914 fewer than 1% of Britons attended universities.) In addition the Imperial College in London, which opened in 1907, offered higher technical education (see Chapter 4). In terms of technological advances, Brunel's *Great Eastern* was finally superseded in the early twentieth century, when the *Lusitania* (1907), the *Titanic* (1912) and the *Imperator* (1913) were built.

Spectacles and publications continued to develop as modes of scientific communication. As we saw at the start of this chapter, J.H. Pepper's ghost show at the Royal Polytechnic was all the rage in 1863. The Royal Polytechnic had other popular spectacles too: a "Diorama Illustrating the Voyage across the Atlantic," a diving bell in which several men could, for a fee, descend into a deep tank of water to impress their female companions, and a hydro-electric machine that produced electric sparks 22 inches long; the *Times* called this demonstration "a triumph of skill and knowledge of which English science may be justly proud."[21] Physics demonstrations and exhibits were among the most popular with the public. Wine merchant and electrical enthusiast John Peter Gassiot (1797–1877) hosted "electrical soirees" for the metropolitan elite. The Adelaide Gallery was famous for its steam gun, which fired off 70 balls in only four seconds several times a day. Lectures, readings, and dramatic stagings were also popular. Huxley's popular 1862 lectures "On Our Knowledge of the Causes of the Phenomena of Organic Nature," which explained Darwin's *Origin* to working-class listeners, were lauded by colleagues such as Lyell as "simply perfect" and became best-sellers when they were published.[22] Public aquariums were fashionable in the early 1870s.[23] For the urban gentry and upper middle class in the later nineteenth century, science was also accessible at *conversaziones* held by groups from the Royal Society down to small local institutions. Attendees, dressed in their finest evening wear, paid an admission fee to spend an evening being educated and entertained by science. For example, in April 1882 at the Free Trade Hall in Manchester, attendees at a *conversazione* walked through exhibits of microscopes and other instruments and listened to a lecture on "The Transit of Venus" that was "illustrated with the oxy-hydrogen lime light."[24] All of these lectures, exhibitions, experiments, and displays demonstrate what an important part of later Victorian culture science was, as education, knowledge, and entertainment.

Science writing was read by a wide swath of interested readers. Because the distinction between professional and popular science was still in flux, the boundary between expert and lay literature was porous. Lay people could read and understand works written by experts for one another, which is no longer true today. Some works that were aimed at lay readers introduced the results of new research and so attracted expert readers as well. Most popular science works were written by prolific writers who were not men of science but who made their living popularizing science. The most successful popularizers were clever writers who paid attention to the styles of writing that sold well in other genres, and whose work was at least as entertaining as it was educational.[25] Many popularizers were Anglican clergymen (who, though they were driven out of scientific societies and institutions, remained a dominant force in popular writing) or women (the most famous was Arabella Buckley (1840–1929), a friend of Alfred Russel Wallace's who gave evolution a spiritualist gloss). Others were showmen of science—J.H. Pepper wrote the *Boy's Playbook of Science* and *Scientific Amusements for Young People*, full of illustrations of steam generators, spectroscopes, telescopes, telegraphs, thermometers, optical lanterns, gas generators, and magneto-electrical machines, and both went through many editions.[26] Other pieces that made science into either a spectacle—such as J.G. Wood's *Man and Beast* (1874)—or an evolutionary epic—like David Page's *The Earth's Crust* and Edward Clodd's *Story of Creation* (1888)—were also very popular. Even as science became a profession in the twentieth century, popular science publishing remained a strong market, with professional scientists eager to write for the public. It was not until after the First World War that laypeople became consumers only, rather than consumers and shapers, of science.

For most people, including most scientists, faith continued to coexist with science into the twentieth century. The members of the X Club opposed any reference to the supernatural or the deity in scientific explanations. But the north British physicists retained their faith; they saw the thermodynamic laws about the innermost workings of the universe that they uncovered as proof of God's existence and benevolence. For example, although Thomson held that dissipated energy was lost energy, he stressed that "no destruction of energy can take place in the material world without an act of power possessed only by the supreme ruler."[27] Most men of science continued to maintain their religious belief through the nineteenth century. But many leading men of science were motivated by religion to explore the natural world. They were able to reconcile their professional pursuits, in which they suggested that the world and humans were physical beings that existed independent of any divine spark, with their belief in God. (On the other hand, the fact that many men of science felt the need to "reconcile" science and faith suggests that there was some sort of conflict that required resolution.) As a result, even at the start of the World War One very few Britons saw religious explanations of the natural world as outmoded and replaced by scientific ones. They were far more likely to fit science and faith together in their world views.

Darwin and evolution

The most famous event in the history of science in the nineteenth century is the publication of Darwin's *On the Origin of Species by Means of Natural Selection, or the Preservation of Favoured Races in the Struggle for Life* (1859); Secord notes that we tend to "attribute to [this] single book an intrinsic power accorded to no other force in history."[28] As we have seen, *Origin* was not the first work that argued for a theory of evolution. This does not mean that Darwin's *Origin* was not important; we need to see its significance in context.

Charles Darwin (1809–1882) was an unimpeachably respectable gentleman from a comfortable, upper-class family. He was a very cautious person who shunned controversy and anything smacking of radicalism. Married to his wealthy cousin, Emma Wedgwood (1808–1896), he never needed to work, and never held a professional position. For him, scientific investigation was a calling, but was not a way of earning a living. As a young man Darwin was directionless. He attended Edinburgh University for a while, and then enrolled at Cambridge, where he spent more time drinking, gambling, and running up bills than studying. In 1831, he was asked to join the crew of the HMS *Beagle* on its trip around the world because the captain wanted a gentleman with scientific interests who could pay his own way on board. The five-year trip inspired Darwin to devote the rest of his life to science. During his travels, Darwin relied on the new work of geologist Charles Lyell to interpret the natural world as one that was dynamic over a long period of time. He puzzled over fossils of extinct mammals and collected species of insects, plants, and birds, many previously unknown to westerners. While looking over his notes regarding the Galápagos Islands on the journey home, he seems to have begun pondering transmutation.

After returning from his voyage, Darwin began to formulate his theory of evolution. The theory relied on the mechanism of "natural selection," in which advantageous inheritable changes to species emerge spontaneously, and are then "selected" over several generations of competition. It is worth noting, however, that the best-known phrase that encapsulates the idea of natural selection—that in nature we see a battle for the "survival of the fittest"—was actually coined by sociologist Herbert Spencer (1820–1903), one of the first social theorists to apply Darwin's ideas to human society. Darwin wrote up his argument in a long essay in 1844, only a few months before *Vestiges* came out, but kept it private; indeed he allowed 15 years to go by before he finally published his theory in 1859 (prompted by the fact that in 1858 Alfred Russel Wallace had independently developed an almost identical theory and sent it to Darwin). Darwin scholars have long debated why Darwin refrained from publishing for so long, but this puzzling decision makes sense in the social and scientific context: Darwin was a member of the establishment whose theory of evolution fitted in better with the ideas of ambitious radical outsiders rather than those endorsed by his own sort. While Darwin believed his theory to be correct, he also knew that it would be embraced and championed in the radical political and social circles in which most evolutionists travelled. Unwilling to be co-opted by such allies, Darwin chose not to publish. He entered the fray only after *Vestiges'* enduring popularity had rendered the idea of evolution less threatening.

In 1859, when Darwin finally made his ideas public, most parts of his evolutionary theory were not new, and the part that was—the mechanism of natural selection—was not well received. Even as late as the 1880s, Alfred Russel Wallace was almost the only man of science who endorsed Darwin's theory of natural selection, which was not widely accepted by scientists until the 1930s.[29] But *Origin* still had an impact: it made evolution scientifically and socially acceptable. Charles Darwin was so eminent, so respectable, and so much part of the social and scientific establishments, that his endorsement of the theory of evolution made the theory itself—for which the public was now ready—respectable. The form and tone of *Origin* also shaped its social and scientific impacts. Clearly written by an expert for his colleagues, it was dense enough that it carried no taint of journalism or provocative potboiler. Yet it was also just accessible enough to be read—or at least purchased and displayed—by a more general public. The effect of the publication of the *Origin of Species* was dramatic. Within a few months, several important and respectable men of science, including geologist Charles Lyell, Thomas Huxley, and even Richard Owen—who had attacked transformism when it was championed by Grant—publicly stated their support for evolution. Within 30 years, 50,000 copies had been sold—a large number, though far lower than the sales figures for *The Constitution of Man* or *Vestiges*. (Of course in the United States today, where fully 40% of the population rejects the theory of evolution, the social connotations of the theory of evolution remain highly charged.[30]) Widespread discussion and debate, along with other presentations of Darwin's ideas such as Huxley's published lectures on them, meant that Darwin's book was well-known.

Darwin maintained that neither his theory nor his book were in any way attacks on religious faith. They did, however reposition humans as simply one species among others, rather than as uniquely privileged in creation. The notion that humans were similar to apes was especially threatening, and satirical cartoons appeared depicting Darwin himself as an ape. In addition, his theory of natural selection, in which changes—the emergence, transformation, and extinction of species—happened constantly and without guidance or inter-ference of any sort, left little for God to do once the world had been created, and opened the door to the notion that God did not exist. Of course, this possibility had been raised earlier in the period, most notably by geology. But Darwin's work added an explanation for the development of species over time that had no need of God. Some experienced this as liberation, others as an attack. Evolutionary theory interested thinkers in many fields and continued to develop in a variety of ways throughout the Victorian period. Literary critic Gillian Beer has analyzed the influence of Darwin's ideas in the novels of George Eliot and Thomas Hardy, both of whom read Darwin's work.[31] George Levine argues that Darwin influenced Victorian literature in a much more pervasive way: Darwinian notions, he holds, became part of the culture and structured novels by Charles Dickens (particularly *Little Dorrit*), Anthony Trollope, and Joseph Conrad, among others.[32]

Also notable is the development of eugenics, the notion that human evolution could be controlled through selective breeding. Eugenic ideas were promoted by Darwin's cousin, man of science Francis Galton (1822–1911), and were influential in the development of the British sociological tradition. They were in evidence during the Second South African War (1899–1902), when the revelations that many of the urban working-class men who flocked to enlist were physically unfit to serve spurred a panic about Britons' racial fitness and an increased interest in eugenics. Once the notion of human racial fitness was taken up by the Nazis in the mid-twentieth century, it lost its intellectual standing in the rest of Europe. Of course, *Origin of Species* cannot be held responsible for eugenics, let alone Nazi racial doctrine. But neither can it be heralded as the book that singlehandedly changed history. Instead, we must recognize it for its key contribution to a complex social and scientific set of debates. *Origin of Species* advanced scientific discourse not by introducing the first theory of evolution, but by making such theories acceptable for respectable men of science to endorse.

Laboratories and germs: Medicine

In the later Victorian period, there were also many developments in medicine. Doctors, nurses, and midwives all got better education, stricter and more centralized certification, and higher social status. Medical knowledge improved, at least from our twentieth-century perspective: germ theory was formulated and (much later) became accepted, antiseptic practices became more common, surgical methods improved. More people were able to access medical care. The overall health of Britain improved: annual death rates per thousand people decreased from 20.5 in 1861 to 16.9 in 1901, and in the third quarter of the nineteenth century life expectancy improved for the first time in centuries.

However, we must note that, for the most part, new medical knowledge did not translate into better health. While medical professionals became more educated and more professionalized, and health improved at the same time, these two were not causally connected. Medicine made what we see as advances—with humor- and miasma-based theories replaced by science-based medicine, and mesmerism replaced by drugs for anesthesia—but the reality is that medical advances did not improve people's health. Mortality declined significantly from the mid-1870s, but this was due to better sanitation and better nutrition, not to improved medicine. Furthermore, the new sanitation measures that improved health were often implemented by people who subscribed to miasma theory and rejected germ theory (Florence Nightingale is a good example). For most people, health remained poor. One third of children died before their fifth birthdays until the 1890s. Maternal mortality rate remained stable, at about five deaths per thousand, into the 1930s. Infant mortality rates actually rose throughout the nineteenth century, peaking in 1899 before they began to decline. There was no treatment for syphilis until 1909. There were no antibiotics until after our period ends. Sickness, pain, and early death remained facts of life, especially for poor and working-class people.

Dangerous epidemics and bad health continued. The 1860s and early 1870s were a particularly unhealthy period, and death rates actually rose slightly. This was right after French scientist Louis Pasteur (1822–1895) had "proved" his theory about invisible organisms called "germs," in the late 1850s, and Joseph Lister had applied this theory and was advocating the use of carbolic acid as an antiseptic from the late 1860s—a good example of the disconnect between medical ideas and actual health. In the early 1860s, there was a typhoid epidemic. In 1866–1867 there was another cholera epidemic, although medical responses to cholera had improved so much after the 1853–1854 epidemic and the work of John Snow and his colleagues that only 14,000 people died in this one. In 1870–1871 Britain suffered its most severe smallpox epidemic of nineteenth century (part of a larger European pandemic). Syphilis remained rampant and untreated, in spite of the

Contagious Diseases Acts, in force between 1864 and 1886 (see Chapter 2), which tried to limit the spread of syphilis by treating prostitutes but not their clients.

But there were changes. Education and certification for doctors, nurses, and midwives changed significantly. Universities now offered education and training for doctors. The General Medical Council controlled entry into the profession through its centralized system of registration. Doctors became loosely divided into two tiers, general practitioners and more elite hospital consultants. By the 1880s they enjoyed a shared professional identity and standards, high social status, and a good standard of living. Their numbers grew, from 14,415 physicians and surgeons in England and Wales in 1861 to 22,698 physicians and surgeons in England and Wales in 1901. In 1886, a Medical Act Amendment Act made medical, surgical, and midwifery qualifications compulsory for all registered medical practitioners.

Women were virtually excluded from medical training and registration. In 1865, feminist Elizabeth Garrett Anderson (1836–1917) became the first British woman registered with the GMC; in 1877, Sophia Jex-Blake (1840–1912) became the second. The two established the London School of Medicine for Women (LSMW) (f. 1874), and from the 1870s several British universities accepted female medical students. Still, in 1900 there were only 200 women registered with the GMC, and, when our period ended in 1914, there were only 1,000; furthermore, in 1914, medical coeducation was rarer in Britain than it was in the United States and western Europe.

Nursing, which had not been seen as a medical endeavor at all, also moved towards being an organized and respected profession, largely due to the celebrity and efforts of Florence Nightingale (1820–1910). Nightingale was committed to miasma theory and to sanitary conditions. Her work led to far more sanitary home and hospital nursing and to rigorous nurse training. The Nightingale Training School, housed at St. Thomas' Hospital in London, was opened in 1860, and later became part of King's College, London. Nurses became seen as caring female medical professionals rather than as elderly drunks who sat by bedsides. Nursing became an attractive profession for upper working-class, lower middle-class, and middle-class women (though it was quite hierarchical and quickly became overcrowded). In 1888, the British Nurses Association was founded; it sought official examination and registration for professional nurses (which would be achieved in 1919 with the Nurses Registration Act).

Like nursing, midwifery became more professionalized, more reliant on formal training, and more appealing to women outside of the working class. From the 1870s, training programs were established in several large cities. In 1881, the Trained Midwives Registration Society (from 1886 the Midwives' Institute) was founded by middle-class and upper-class women who wanted professional status. But in spite of campaigns for formal training and registration, most midwives were working-class women who served their local communities. Middle-class and upper-class women insisted on male attendants, often obstetricians rather than midwives. In 1902, formal registration was made a requirement for practice. The 1902 Midwives Act established the Central Midwives Board, a national regulatory authority for midwifery in England and Wales. Its principles were applied to

Scotland and Ireland in the Midwives (Scotland) Act of 1915, and the Midwives (Ireland) Act of 1918. These Acts resulted in very different types of women entering midwifery. Where before the turn of the century most midwives were older, working-class, often widowed, and usually without formal training, after the Midwives Acts there was a shift to women who were younger, unmarried (but not widowed), from a broader socio-economic spectrum, with formal training in both nursing and midwifery. Some saw these changes as improvements; others, as a weakening of working-class communities and relationships.

All of this meant that medical practitioners were better educated and trained and were certified by centralized bodies. They were more respected than they had been in the earlier Victorian period, and enjoyed professional status and incomes. Of course, this did not mean that alternative healers did not continue to operate. As before, some believed that what they offered was superior to standard medical treatment; many of these had radical political as well as medical beliefs. Other were simply clever salespeople seeking to make a profit (or a fortune) hawking remedies they knew to be valueless. From 1863, Dr Browne's Chlorodine promised to cure indigestion, headaches, nervous conditions, and more; as it was mostly a large dose of laudanum, a form of opium, it did indeed provide pain relief, even if it did not cure disease. There were also many devices that delivered a low-wattage current of electricity which would, it was promised, cure all manner of ailments.

Some changes in dominant medical and scientific ideas would ultimately prove correct and improve people's health. The most important was the gradual acceptance of germ theory rather than miasma theory. This happened very gradually and unevenly, over about a half-century starting in 1860. It was part of a larger shift in which medicine became less based on patients' descriptions of their physical state and what practitioners could observe with the naked eye, and more based on what doctors could perceive using special tools such as stethoscopes and microscopes. By the 1890s, as germ theory became widely accepted, laboratories had become as much a part of medical practice as bedside visits, and medicine became more aligned with science.

There were smaller advances in medical knowledge and practice as well. In the 1870s, deaths from consumption began to decline; in the 1880s, it became well understood that the disease was contagious, and isolation practices helped to continue this decline. The agents that caused four of the century's worst diseases—cholera, diphtheria, consumption, and syphilis—were all identified (the first three in the 1880s, the latter in 1905). In 1889, aspirin was developed, and replaced traditional opiate-based painkillers. From 1894, diphtheria could actually be cured, and from 1909 syphilis could be treated (though not cured) with a new drug called Salvarsan. An important technological breakthrough was the development of x-ray machines in 1895. Hospitals had become places in which seriously ill people were treated (they were also valuable training grounds for medical students). Large cities even had specialist hospitals.

From the mid-1870s until the end of the Victorian period the health of the average Briton improved. This was largely due to the fact that working hours fell by almost 10% between 1870 and 1900, permitting more rest, and real wages rose, permitting people to eat more and better food and to have better living conditions. For example, in Scotland in 1861 the average dwelling was home to 7.6 people; by 1901 that number had fallen to 4.7. Improvement in living conditions led to improvements in health. There were also improvements in the social safety network; for example, a 1906 Act meant that many local authorities provided free school meals to hungry children. But improvements in public health also helped, largely by improving sanitation and preventing the spread of infection. The 1866 Sanitary Act compelled local authorities to make their areas clean and safe, and forced them to provide sewers and clean water. The 1867 Metropolitan Poor Act made state provision of medical care for the poor separate from poor relief. Both of these Acts encouraged the founding of isolation hospitals for contagious diseases. The 1872 and 1875 Public Health Acts dramatically improved water supplies and sewer systems, and regulated food safety and some polluting industries. All of these public health initiatives helped to improve lives, and in particular the lives of ordinary people. Most dramatically, the 1911 National Insurance Act gave working Britons a way of insuring against illness and unemployment. Wage-earners, employers, and the state all had to contribute; participants received free medical care and medicine.

In some ways medical care in 1914 resembled medical care in 1820. Formal and organized systems for delivering care were not widely available, were too costly for many, and were in competition with alternative health providers. Doctors could not cure most infectious diseases and often offered dangerous cures. Patients were often blamed for their illnesses—prostitutes for their syphilis, the poor for their cholera. But in other ways, medical care in 1914 resembled medical care in 2016. Medical care aligned itself with science, care providers were trained and certified but faced competition from various forms of alternative medicine, and laboratories, tools, and hospitals were all central.

Notes

1 J.A. Secord, "Quick and Magical Shaper of Science," *Science* 297.5587 (September 6, 2002), 1,648.
2 Bernard Lightman, *Victorian Popularizers of Science: Designing Nature for New Audiences* (Chicago: University of Chicago Press, 2007), pp. 167–168.
3 Aileen Fyfe and Bernard Lightman, "Science in the Marketplace: An Introduction," in Aileen Fyfe and Bernard Lightman (eds), *Science in the Marketplace: Nineteenth-Century Sites and Experiences* (Chicago: University of Chicago Press, 2007), p. 6.
4 James Secord, "Knowledge in Transit," *Isis* 95.4 (2004): 663.
5 Elizabeth Gaskell, *The Life of Charlotte Bronte*, 2 Volumes (London: Smith, Elder and Co., 1857), 1: 633n., quoted in Laura J. Snyder, Review of Aileen Fyfe, and Bernard V. Lightman (eds), *Science in the Marketplace: Nineteenth-Century Sites and Experiences*. H-Albion, H-Net Reviews. February, 2009.
6 Iwan Rhys Morus, *When Physics Became King* (Chicago: University of Chicago Press, 2005), pp. 105–120.
7 Ralph O'Connor, "Reflections on Popular Science in Britain: Genres, Categories, and Historians," *Isis* 100.2 (2009): 333–345, p. 338.
8 Quoted in Rosemary Ashton, 'Evans, Marian [George Eliot] (1819–1880)', *Oxford Dictionary of National Biography*, (Oxford: Oxford University Press, 2004); online edition, accessed November 29, 2010.

9 John van Whye, "The Diffusion of Phrenology Through Public Lecturing," in Fyfe and Lightman, p. 60.
10 Alison Winter, *Mesmerized: Powers of Mind in Victorian Britain* (Chicago: University of Chicago Press, 1998), pp. 112–114.
11 James A. Secord, *Victorian Sensation: The Extraordinary Publication, Reception, and Secret Authorship of* Vestiges of the Natural History of Creation (Chicago: University of Chicago Press, 2001), pp. 97–104.
12 *Vestiges*, p. 223, quoted in Secord, p. 108.
13 Secord, pp. 101–102.
14 Secord, pp. 1–15.
15 Secord, pp. 504.
16 Secord, pp. 406–409.
17 Mary Wilson Carpenter, *Health, Medicine, and Society in Victorian England* (Santa Barbara, CA: Praeger, 2010), p. 13.
18 Paul White, *Thomas Huxley Making the "Man of Science"* (Cambridge: Cambridge University Press, 2002), p. 1.
19 Morus.
20 Iwan Rhys Morus and Peter J. Bowler, *Making Modern Science: A Historical Survey* (Chicago: University of Chicago Press, 2005), p. 93.
21 Iwan Rhys Morus, *Frankenstein's Children: Electricity, Exhibition, and Experiment in Early-Nineteenth-Century London* (Princeton: Princeton University Press, 1998), pp. 75–83; "The Great Induction Coil at the Polytechnic Institution," *Times* (April 7, 1869): 4, quoted in Iwan Rhys Morus, "'More the Aspect of Magic than Anything Natural': The Philosophy of Demonstration," in Fyfe and Lightman, p. 336.
22 Lightman, pp. 353–354.
23 Fyfe and Lightman, p. 11.
24 Samuel J.J. Alberti, "Conversaziones and the Experience of Science in Victorian England," *Journal of Victorian Culture* 8.2 (2003): 208–230, p. 208.
25 Lightman, p. 35.
26 Secord, p. 1,649.
27 C. Smith and M. N. Wise, *Energy and Empire: A Biographical Study of Lord Kelvin* (1989), 329, quoted in Crosbie Smith, "Thomson, William, Baron Kelvin (1824–1907)," *Oxford Dictionary of National Biography* (Oxford: Oxford University Press, 2004); available online at: www.oxforddnb.com/view/article/36507 (accessed December 25, 2015).
28 Secord, p. 516.
29 Morus and Bowler, p. 154.
30 Available online at: www.gallup.com/poll/170822/believe-creationist-view-human-origins.aspx (accessed November 23, 2015).
31 Gillian Beer, *Darwin's Plots: Evolutionary Narrative in Darwin, George Eliot and Nineteenth-Century Fiction* (Cambridge: Cambridge University Press, 2000).
32 George Levine, *Darwin and the Novelists: Patterns of Science in Victorian Fiction* (Cambridge, MA: Harvard University Press, 1988).

Relevant fiction that students might enjoy

Mary Shelley, *Frankenstein or, The Modern Prometheus* (1818)
Charles Dickens, *Little Dorrit* (1855–1857)
Edward Bulwer-Lytton, *The Coming Race* (1871)
George Eliot, *Middlemarch* (1871–1872)
George du Maurier, *Trilby* (1894)
Edith Wharton, *The House of Mirth* (1905)

Further reading

Lucinda McCray Beier, *For Their Own Good: The Transformation of English Working-Class Health Culture, 1880–1970* (Ohio: Ohio State University Press, 2008).

Anne Borsay and Billie Hunter (eds), *Nursing and Midwifery in Britain Since 1700* (London: Palgrave MacMillan, 2012).

Peter J. Bowler, *Science for All: The Popularization of Science in Early Twentieth-Century Britain* (Chicago: University of Chicago Press, 2009).

Mary Wilson Carpenter, *Health, Medicine, and Society in Victorian England* (Santa Barbara, CA: Praeger, 2010).

Aileen Fyfe and Bernard Lightman (eds), *Science in the Marketplace: Nineteenth-Century Sites and Experiences* (Chicago: University of Chicago Press, 2007).

Steven Johnson, *The Ghost Map: The Story of London's Most Terrifying Epidemic – and How it Changed Science, Cities and the Modern World* (New York: Riverhead, 2006).

Bernard Lightman, *Victorian Popularizers of Science: Designing Nature for New Audiences* (Chicago: University of Chicago Press, 2007).

Iwan Rhys Morus, *When Physics Became King* (Chicago: University of Chicago Press, 2005).

Iwan Rhys Morus and Peter J. Bowler, *Making Modern Science: A Historical Survey* (Chicago: University of Chicago Press, 2005).

James Secord, *Victorian Sensation: The Extraordinary Publication, Reception, and Secret Authorship of Vestiges of the Natural History of Creation* (Chicago: University of Chicago Press, 2001).

Alison Winter, *Mesmerized: Powers of Mind in Victorian Britain* (Chicago: University of Chicago Press, 1998).

Online resources

Wellcome Library: http://wellcomelibrary.org/

British Journal for the History of Science, Digital Archive, 1962–2000: http://journals. cambridge.org/action/displaySpecialPage?pageId=1400

Internet History of Science Sourcebook: http://legacy.fordham.edu/Halsall/science/ sciencesbook.asp

The British Society for the History of Science: www.bshs.org.uk/

The British Library History of Science Blog: http://britishlibrary.typepad.co.uk/oral historyofscience/

Oxford Brookes University Primary Sources for History of Medicine: www.brookes.ac.uk/ library/histmed/primarysourceshistmed.html

Index

Entries in *italics* denote references to figures.

ABC café 120
Aberystwyth 161
abolitionists 46, 78, 275
Aboriginals (Australian) 73–4
abortion and abortifacients 246, 253
activist women 27
Act of Union 43
Acton, William xxii, 243
actors 16, 214–15, 229, 233
Adam Bede xxii, 211, 225
Adelaide Gallery (National Gallery of
    Practical Science Blending Instruction
    with Amusement) xviii, 282, *283*, 295
administrative reforms 38, 88
adultery 41, 135, 176, 196
adventure stories 71, 179, 235, 272
advertisements, advertising: actors in 233;
    and gender 118; Queen Victoria in 182,
    192; and sexuality 241; and shopping
    culture 107–8, 112–13
aesthetic movement 30, 228, 232, 234
Afghan Wars xix, xxv, 73, 80
Africa 54, 70, 79–80, 212, 224, 285
agriculture 84–5, 87, 89–91, 99, 103;
    employment in xxii, xxviii, 55, 90, 130,
    174
Ainsworth, William Harrison xix, 214,
    225
Ajnala 76
Albert, Prince of Saxe-Coburg Gotha:
    death of xxiii, 189; and Great
    Exhibition 94; marriage to Victoria xix,
    184; and the poor 223; public image of
    188–9; role in governance 184–5; and
    science and technology 285; shrines to
    190
Albert, Prince of Wales 189–91, 256

alcohol xxiv, 5, 53, 84, 140, 148–50,
    159–60, 212–13, 269; *see also* beer
All the Year Round 226, 272
Ally Sloper's Half-Holiday 139
amateur choruses 213
Amateur Football Association 158
amateurism 157, 159
amateur theater 215, 217, 232
American letters 69
anal sex 245, 247, 249
Anderson, Elizabeth Garrett xxiii, 300
androgyny 230
anesthesia 286, 293
the Angel in the House 274
Anglican church *see* Church of England
Anglo-Burmese Wars xvii, xxi, xxvi, 73
Anglo-Russian Entente 60
animal magnetism *see* mesmerism
Ansdell, Richard 213
Answers 236
anti-Catholicism 43, 185–6, 265–6, 269
Anti Corn Law League (ACLL) xix, 48, 50,
    135; ACLL bazaars xix–xx, 48, 110
anti-Irish feeling 78, 185–6
anti-monarchism 61, 189–90
anti-Semitism 266, 270
antiseptics xx, 293, 299
apartheid 81
Apothecaries Act 290
aquariums 295
Archbishops of Canterbury and York 183,
    258, 262–3, 274
architecture 12, 94, 101, 202, 213
area studies 67
aristocracy *see* upper class
Armstrong, Eliza 236–7
army 76, 80–1, 184, 267

Arnold, Matthew 236
Arnold, Thomas 171
art galleries 16
The Art of Housekeeping 30
Arts and Crafts movement 213
aspirin xxvi, 301
Asquith, Herbert 61
Assizes circuit courts 196
Aston Lower Grounds 19
Astronomical Society 282
atheism xxv, 190, 271, 289
athletics 150
Aurora Floyd 226
Aurora Leigh 222
Austen, Jane 6, 83, 175, 180, 224
Australia: gold rush 211; market for
    imperial goods 71; transportation to xxi,
    74, 202

BAAS (British Association for the
    Advancement of Science) xviii, 282,
    289–90
Babbage, Charles xviii, 281–2
bachelor 241
back-to-back houses 23
Baden-Powell, Lord 252
Bagehot, Walter 36, 182, 186
Bailey, Peter 28
Bainbridge's 113
Balfour, Arthur 59
The Ballad of Reading Gaol 234
ballet 120, 137, 217
bal masque 247
Band of Hope 273
Bank Charter Act xx, 89
Bank Holidays Act xxiv, 160
banking and finance: bankers and banking
    profession 89, 91, 129, 134; banking
    system xvii, 89–90, 96; branches 96,
    101; joint-stock 96
Bank of England xvii, xx, 89
bankruptcy 96, 99, 204
baptisms 4, 264, 267, 273–5
Baptist Missionary Society (BMS) 69, 276
Baptists 264, 269, 274–5
Barrett Browning, Elizabeth 222
Barrie, J.M. 232: *Peter Pan* 232
barristers *see* lawyers
Barrow 31
bastardy laws 241, 246; *see also* illegitimacy
Bath 44, 110
bathing (swimming) 156, 161
Baudelaire, Charles 16
Bayswater 114

Bayswater Chronicle 116
bazaars: charity 110, 175; commercial 110;
    and department stores 114; in Liverpool
    xvii; in Newcastle xviii; and shopping
    110; supporting missionaries 276;
    and urbanization 16; working-class
    patronage of 119
Beagle *see* HMS *Beagle*; *Voyage of the Beagle*
bear-baiting 149
Bedchamber Crisis xix, 183–4
Bedford College 178
bedrooms 12, 24, 30–1
beer xvii, 5, 12, 116, 149, 159–60; *see also*
    alcohol
Beer, Gillian 298
Beer Act 1830 xviii, 150
beershops 12, 147, 149–50
Beeton's Christmas Annual 207
Belgium 94
Belich, James 68, 79
Belle Vue Gardens 20
Benedict XVI, Pope 262
Bengal Army 76
Bennett, Arnold 105, 235
Benson family 258
Bentham, Jeremy 46, 202, 288
Benthamites 288
Bentinck, William 75
Berlin 54, 99, 249
Besant, Annie xxv, 271
Besant, Walter 26
Betting Houses Act xxi, 152
Bible 4, 132, 264–6, 271–2, 275–6, 288
Bible Christians 265
Bible scenes 272
bicycles 107, 119
bigamy 196, 226, 273
biographies 70, 129
biology 279, 288, 294
Birch v. *Birch* 209
Birmingham: city center 25; and empire
    71; music concerts in 25; parks in 19;
    parliamentary representation of 43;
    population of xvii–xviii, 14, 89, 94;
    suburbs of 20; University of 294;
    urban renewal in 26
Birmingham Daily Gazette 26
Birmingham Daily Post 13
Birmingham Journal 71
Birmingham Political Union 43
birth control *see* contraception
birth rate 4, 94
Births and Deaths Registration Act xix,
    263–4

Black Ey'd Susan 218
blackface 218
Blackpool xxiii, 118, 140, 160, 162
Blackstone, William 169
Blackwood's Magazine 197
Blake, Sexton 207, 211
Blake, William 87
blast furnaces 91
Bleak House xxi, 203, 210, 225
The Blessed Damozel 221
blood libels 266
blood sports 147
Bloody Code 201
Bloomsbury group 1
boarding 23
Boards of Health 292
Bogle, Paul 77
Bonaparte, Napoleon 3
Bond Street (London) 112
Bonheur, Rosa 251
Bon Marché 114, 116
bookmakers 152
Book of Common Prayer 262, 272
books: availability of 7, 41, 107, 119, 225; at bazaars 110; in prisons 203; religious 272; scientific 279, 283, 286; as status marker 112
Booth, Charles xxvi, 5, 26, 138
Booth, William and Catherine 267
borough constituencies 51
borstals 208
"Bosie" *see* Douglas, Lord Alfred
Boucicault, Dion 217–19; *The Colleen Bawn* xxii, 218; *The Corsican Brothers* 218; *Faust and Marguerite* 218
Boulton, Ernest ("Stella") 254–6, *255*
Bournemouth 160–1
bowling 153, 160
Bow Street Runners 200
boxing 147, 151–3, 159, 173, 274
Boys' Brigade 274
Boy Scouts 81
The Boys' Friend 207
Boy's Own Paper 70–1, 272
Boy's Playbook of Science 296
Braddon, Mrs. (Mary Elizabeth) xxiii, 224, 226, 235
Brady, Sean 242
Brahmo Samaj movement 70, 271
brands, branding 107–8, 113
brass bands 40, 212–14
breach of promise of marriage 195–6, 204, 209, 224, 246
breadwinner's wage 48, 168, 173

breastfeeding *see* nursing
Brewer, John 88
brewing 150
Bridgewater Treatises 280
Brief Summary... Concerning Women xxi, 176
Briggs, Asa 1
Brighton 121, 155–6
Bristol, University of 294
Bristol Society of Merchant Venturers 284
Britain, in United Kingdom 2
British Association for the Promotion of Temperance xviii, 149
British Medical Association xxii, 292
British Nurses Association xxvi, 300
Broadwood and Sons 6
Brontë family xx, 83, 180, 223–5, 251, 282, 291
Brown, Callum 271, 275
Browning, Robert 222
browsing 107–9, 114, 120
Brunel, Isambard Kingdom xix, xxii, 284–5
Buchan's Domestic Medicine 291
Buckley, Arabella 296
Buffalo Bill's Wild West Show 212
buildings, tall 101
Bulwer-Lytton, Edward 113, 224
Burdett-Coutts, Angela 128, 136
bureaucracies: of empire 69; expansion of 9; middle-class employment in 134; of political parties 40, 52; of social welfare 27
Burgh Police (Scotland) Act 200
burlesque 217, 219
Burlington Arcade 112
Burslem Park 25, 29
Butler, Lady Eleanor 250
Butler, Samuel 235
bye-law houses 26
Byron, Lord (George Gordon) 221

C. & J. Clark Shoes 108–9
cabinet 58, 137, 255
caffeine 148
Cairns, Lord 208
Calcutta 81
calico cotton cloth 70
Calvinism 262, 264–5
Calvinistic Methodism 264
Camberwell 21, 29
Cambridge rules 151, 157
Cambridge University 53, 137, 262, 270, 293
Canada xxiv, 71, 73, 75, 78, 212

canals 97
Cannadine, David 129, 142
Canning, Lord 77
Can You Forgive Her? xxiii
Cape of Good Hope 71
Captain Swing riots 44
card games 152–3
Cardiff 111, 117, 270
Caribbean 70–1, 73–4
Carlyle, Jane Welsh 251
Carlyle, Thomas xix, 92–3, 104, 185, 212
Caroline, Queen 41–2, 132, 135, 183, 197;
  see also Queen Caroline Affair
Carpenter, Edward xxvi, xxviii, 59, 257
"Casabianca" xviii, 221
Casa Guidi Windows 222
cash sales 107–8, 114
Cassell's Family Magazine Illustrated 272
casual employment 29–30, 98, 130
Catholic Association xvii, 42–3
Catholicism: and church attendance 272;
  in Church of England 261–2; and class
  system 126; in England and Wales xxi,
  xxix, 269; evangelicalism in 275; in
  Ireland 2; Newman's conversion to xx;
  reinstatement of hierarchy xxi, 266; and
  Salvation Army 205; social status of
  261; socioeconomic diversity among
  265; voting rights denied for 37
Catholic schools 264
*The Causes and Prevention of Immorality in
  Schools* xxvi, 252
causes célèbres 195
Cavan 89
Cavendish, William (Duke of Devonshire)
  128, 293
Cavendish Laboratory, Cambridge
  University xxiv, 293
Cawnpore (now Kanpur) 76, *77*
Census 18, 89, 241; 1851 census 94, 260,
  271; 1891 census 31, 179
Central Midwives Board xxvii, 301
Central Poor Law Commission 46
Chadwick, Edwin / Chadwick Committee
  Report xix, 18, 85, 92, 292
chain stores 118–19
Chambers, Robert 288–90
"Champagne Charlie" xxiii, 229
chapels: music in 213; use of term 261; in
  Wales xxi, 264
chaperones 111
character 166, 171
The Charge of the Light Brigade 222
Charing Cross Railway Station *98*

Charing Cross Road (London) 110, 112
charity: refusing to accept 132; *see also*
  philanthropy
Charlotte, Princess 183
Charlottenburg, Royal Technical College
  of 99–100
Chartism xviii, xx, 44, 47–9, 92, 133, 190,
  225, 227
char-women 173
Cheltenham Ladies' College 177
Cheshire 32, 85–6, 90
childbirth 95, 183, 246, 253
child criminals 198–9, 207–8, 211, 223
child labor xviii, 46, 92–3, 95, 102,
  168–71, 185
childrearing 166–7, 173, 175
children: bedrooms for 21; biracial 70;
  games of 20; gender differences between
  171; illegitimate 136, 176, 242, 246
Children's Act 1908 xxviii, 207
China 70, 75
Chlorodine 301
chocolate 70, 100
cholera xviii, xx–xxiii, xxv, 16, 18, 291,
  299, 301–2
Cholmondeley, Lady 179
christening 275; *see also* baptism
Christianity: in India 69; middle-class
  evangelical 133; and social work 27
Christmas 97, 117, 207, 224, 273, 279
church attendance 260, 271, 274
church building 212–13, 263
churches: lack of 263; music in 213
Churchill and Stringer case xix, 249
"churching" ceremony 273–4
Church Missionary Gleaner 70
Church Missionary Society 276
Church of England: abuses in 263;
  baptism into xxix, 267; and class system
  126, 269; Conservative attitudes to
  39–40, 58; Ecclesiastical Commission
  xviii; and education 266; evangelicalism
  in 275–6; novels attacking 235; and
  science 289, 295–6; and scientific
  debates 288; as state religion 37, 260–2,
  264; Whig-Liberal attitudes to 39
Church of England in Wales xxi, 2, 261,
  265, 267
Church of Ireland xviii, xxiv–xxv, 2, 53,
  261–3, 266–7
Church of Scotland xx, 262, 266, 276
church rates 263–4
cigarettes 146; *see also* tobacco
cinemas xxvii, 231

circus acts 217, 221
circuses 20, 218
cities: anxiety about 92, 261; bodily
    metaphors for 16, 19; migration to 16;
    populations of xxviii, 14; as public
    places 13; understanding of 14
city centers: after dark 12; development
    of 25; immigrants and casual laborers
    in 30; office districts in 13; and slums
    17–18, 26; stores in xxvii; women in
    27–8
civic identity 25
civil law 202, 204
civil service 9, 53, 69, 134, 141, 271
Civil War, Ireland 62
Civil War, United States xxiii, 51, 62, 97
class conflict 49, 125–6, 147
classes 6, 123–37; distinctions between 27,
    120–1, 123–8, *127*; equal treatment
    of 88; and gambling 142, 152; and
    masculinity 167; mobility between 138;
    proximity between 26, 156, 268; and
    shopping 111; *see also* middle class; upper
    class; working class
classical learning 100
classical literatures 171
classical music 25, 135
classification 249
cleanliness 4, 30, 92, 266
Cleave's Weekly Police Gazette 227
clerks, clerking, clerical work 10, 27, 29,
    119, 134, 138, 140–1, 179, 254
Cleveland Street scandal xxvi, 256–7
Clifton Gorge 284
Cliveden 15
clocks 109
Clodd, Edward xxvi, 296
clothing: class distinctions in 8, 27, 120;
    door-to-door sales 109; fashionable 106,
    108, 120; formal 117; male spending
    on 117–18, 142; ready-made 107–8,
    116, 119; Sunday best 31, 111, 131,
    273; working-class consumption of 93,
    100–101, 107, 110
clubs, men's *see* gentlemen's clubs; working
    men's clubs
clutter 30
coal: British consumption of xviii, xx, 91;
    coal industry 101
coal miners xxviii–xxix, 62, 91
Coatbridge 23
Cobbett, William 37
Cobden, Richard 48
Cockburn, Judge Alexander *206*

Codrington divorce 250
coitus interruptus 253
coke 91
Coke, Desmond 117–18
Collard and Collard 9
collectors 293
The Colleen Bawn xxii, 218
College of Surgeons of Edinburgh 287
Collins, Wilkie xxii, 70, 214, 226
Colonial and Indian Exhibition xxvi, 71
colonial armed forces 192
Colonial Office 71, 76, 78
Combe, George xviii, 285
Combination Acts xvii, 197–8
comic songs 214, 221
commercial pleasure gardens 12, 16, 20,
    113, 148
Committee for Investigating the Causes
    of the Alarming Increase of Juvenile
    Delinquency in the Metropolis 198
common law xix, 170, 195, 208
Commonwealth of Nations 82
The Communist Manifesto 92
concentration camps 59, 68, 80
"Condition of England" debate 92,
    104
The Condition of the Working Class in England
    xx, 92
confessional state 42–3, 262
Congregationalism 265, 269, 274, 276
Congress of Berlin xxv, 54, 79
Coningsby 50, 212
Conrad, Joseph 83, 298
conservatism, popular 42, 53–4, 128, 132,
    275, 282
Conservative (Tory) Party: constitutional
    ideas of 39–40; and Liberal Unionists
    xxviii; middle class in 141; and the
    monarchy 191; and Oxford Movement
    262; and People's Budget 61; and
    Reform Acts 50–1; and Robert Peel 47;
    splits in xxvii, 38; as Unionist 49
consolation, culture of 231
constitution: balance between institutions
    in 36; Conservative attitudes to 39–40;
    'dignified and efficient' parts of 36, 182,
    186; Whig-Liberal attitudes to 39
constitutional crisis 35, 61
*The Constitution of Man Considered in Relation
    to External Objects* xviii, 285–6, 289, 298
consumer society 86, 106–8
consumption (economic): and class
    distinctions 121; democratization of
    109, 120; discretionary 106–7, 111

consumption (tuberculosis) xxv, 199, 291, 301

Contagious Diseases Acts xxiii, xxvi, 28, 207, 300; movement to repeal 60, 176–7, 251, 269, 275

Contemporary Review 13

contraception (birth control) xxviii, 45, 131, 245–6, 252–4, 271

contracts 37, 196

conversaziones 289, 295

converts 265

Co-op stores 110–11, 118–19

copper 91, 97, 108

Corn Laws 38, 48, 90

Cornwall 69, 86, 155, 162; *see also* Truro

coronations 25, 41, 183, 191, 193

Corporation Street (Birmingham) 112

Corrupt and Illegal Practices Act xxv, 55

corruption, electoral 45

corsets, tight-lacing 178

cottages 14–15, 20, 24, 132, 136

"cottaging" 12, 20, 248–9, 254

cottar houses 15

cotton: in British industry xviii, 86–7, 90; "Cottonopolis" 90; exports to India xxi–xxii

cotton famine 97, 102

cotton textiles xxviii, 85, 90, 102, 108

cotton workers 62, 97

counter-jumpers 27, 120; *see also* "gents"; "knut"; "mashers"; "swells"

countryside xxvii, 14–15, 55, 87, 94, 98, 137, 139, 212; holidays in the xxvii, 14–15; idealization of 24, 197; Reform Acts and 55; and urbanization 14

County and Borough Police Act 1856 xxii, 200

County Courts xx, 201, 203–4; Court of King's/Queen's Bench 196; small-claims courts 169

Courtauld, George 174

Court Circular 190

court system 195, 208

Courvoisier, François Benjamin xix, 214

Covent Garden 48, 110, 217, 231

Craik, Dinah Mulock 224

Cranford xxi, 224

Crawford divorce case 205

credit: consumer *see* retail credit; working-class access to 9

Cremorne 20

cricket xxv, 147, 150, 157

crime: capital 202; in city centers 12; in fiction 207, 211, 214; infamous 248;

juvenile 198, 223; perceptions of 195–7, 205; professional 198–9; punishments for 201–2; unnatural xxvii, 240, 248–9, 254–6; violent 198

criminal class 198

criminal conversation (crim con) 196

Criminal Investigation Department (CID) 207

Criminal Law Amendment Act 1885 xxv, 207, 237, 254

crinolines 27

crisis of faith 5, 261

Crockford's 153

Cromwell, Oliver 185

crop rotation 90

Crosland, T.W.H. 106, 114, 120

cross-dressing 230, 247, 250, 254–6, *255*

crowds 80, 110, 117

crucifixes 272

Crystal Palace 5, 95, 213

cultural history 1–2, 182

cultural products 212

Cumberland 102

Cunard shipping company 284

curtain-raiser 215

Cushman, Charlotte 258

Custody of Children Act xix, 170

Cuvier, Georges 287

cycling 20, 59

Cyprus 79

Daily Express 238

Daily Mail 238

Daily Mirror 238

Dale Street (Liverpool) 110

Dalhousie, Lord 75

dame schools 131

"dark, satanic mills" 46, 87

darts 149, 152

Darwin, Charles xix, xxii; death of xxv; and Eyre controversy 78; as man of science 281; teachers of 287; and theory of evolution 4–5, 285, 289–90, 294, 296–8

Darwin Industry 290

David Copperfield xx, 83, 203, 225

Davison, Emily Wilding xxviii

death penalty 201–2; *see also* executions; hangings

debates, public 19–20

debt: in fiction 203, 211; in working-class neighborhoods 31, 203–4

debt law 118, 195–6, 202–4, 209

debtors' prisons 203–4

decadent movement 228, 234, 240
deference 3, 5, 52
Delhi 191–2
demonstrations: anti-Catholic 266; in
    Hyde Park xxii–xxiii, 51; suffragist 60;
    in Trafalgar Square xxvi, 24, 197
department stores: and early closing 119;
    emergence of 92, 111–14; largest
    116–17; lighting of 113; replacing
    bazaars 110; and urbanization 16;
    and women's mobility 27–8
dependent colonies 73
depression *see* economic depression
De Profundis xxvii, 240, 257
Derby 86
Derby Day 213
deserving and undeserving poor 4, 132
detectives and detective novels 207,
    207–11, 226
diaphragms 253
diaries 241, 250, 266
The Diary of a Nobody 9, 29, 97, 122, 143
dice games 152
Dickens, Charles: and amateur theater
    215, 217; Darwin's influence on 298;
    death of xxiv, 234; and debt 203; and
    Eyre controversy 78; on life and art
    214–15; magazine of 226; and marriage
    law 170; and mesmerism 286; novels of
    xix, xxi, xxiii; readings by 224
Dicks' Standard Plays 217
Dilke, Charles 205
dining rooms 21–2, 31, 116
"Diorama Illustrating the Voyage across
    the Atlantic" 295
diphtheria xxv–xxvi, 301
discipline, personal 5
disestablishment 53, 267
disorderly conduct 207
Disraeli, Benjamin: as Conservative leader
    49, 53, 58; on Gladstone 50;
    governments of xxiv, 53–4; Jewishness
    of 270; novels of xx, 18, 93, 212, 224–5;
    on Prince Albert 185; and Reform Acts
    50–1; and Victoria 191
Disruption of Church of Scotland xx, 262,
    264, 276
dissent 261, 264, 275
division of labor 91; sexual 168
divorce: law of 169–70, 176, 196, 204–5,
    209, 244; scandals 54
Divorce Act 176
Divorce Court xxii, 176
dock workers xxviii, 59, 62, 174

doctors / medical profession: and
    homosexuality 256; and science 281,
    290–3, 299–301; in service sector 91, 99;
    social status of 134, 234; and venereal
    disease 241, 245; and women 22, 253
dog racing 152–3
A Doll's House 232
domestic ideology 21, 23, 133, 166, 168,
    175; *see also* separate spheres
domesticity: and education 135; men
    and 25, 167, 179; middle-class 47, 49,
    133–41; rhetoric of 21; upper class 22,
    136, 286; working-class 48–9, 128
domestic service or servants: in middle-
    class houses 12, 22; numbers of xix,
    xxiv, 98; sleeping quarters 21; spending
    on 103; women as 98, 103, 174, 179
Dominion status 78, 81–2, 192
donkey rides 161
double entendres 229
Douglas, Lord Alfred ("Bosie") 257
Dowson, Ernest 234
Doyle, Arthur Conan 207
drama 217, 232–3
drapers 109, 114
drawing room *see* parlor
Drury Lane (London) 217, 220
Du Cane, Edmund 208
Duhem, Pierre 294
Dukes of Devonshire 128, 142, 188, 293
Dumfries and Galloway 85
Dundee 30, 70, 96
Dunham Massey 15
Dunn, James 253
durbah 191
Durham 85–6, 102

Ealing 20
Early Closing Association 119
earthenware pots 109, 192
The Earth's Crust 296
East End (London) 26, 206, 231, 237, 267
Easter 62
East India Company (EIC) 70, 75–6, 185
East Lynne xxiii, 180, 210, 219, 226
Ecclesiastical Commission xviii, 263
ecclesiastical law 195
economic depression 88, 94, 99–100,
    102–3
economic growth 87–94
economic prosperity 48, 88, 90, 94–9,
    191–3, 260, 266
economic regions 85–6
economic stagnation 99

Eden, Emily 7
Edgbaston 20
Edinburgh: population of 14; University
    of 287, 297
education: and class 125–6, 128, 134–5,
    138–9, 141; Disraeli's reforms to 54;
    expansion of 9; higher 99–100, 178,
    293–5 *see also* universities; popular 41;
    religious 275; technical 99, 102, 295;
    women's access to 81, 178
Education Act 1870 xxiv, 53, 131, 138,
    170, 178, 227, 266
Education Act 1902 xxvii, 59
educational sector 99–100
Edwardian period 103, 193
Edward VII xxvii–xxviii, 61, 189, 193
effeminacy 30, 178, 242, 247, 254–7, 274
Egypt, colonization of 79
elections: rituals of 40; uncontested 55
electoral candidates, expenses of 55
electorate, enlargement of 1, 4, 35, 52;
    see also franchise; women's suffrage
electricity xxviii, 102, 113, 283, 294–5, 301
elevators 101
Eliot, George xxii, xxiv, 223, 225, 234, 251
Ellis, Havelock 257
emigration xxi, 15–16, 48–9, 69–70, 74,
    78–9, 89, 289; *see also* transportation
Eminent Victorians 1
Emma 6
empire: contraction of 82; expansion of
    65–6, 79; impact on Britain 69–70;
    information about 70–1; Liberal and
    Conservative views on 39–40, 53, 58;
    and non-white populations 70; popular
    support for 54, 165; ramshackle or
    rampaging 71–2; shift to Asia-Pacific
    72–5; study of 66–9
Engels, Friedrich xx, 92
England: Conservative base in 40;
    Parliamentary representation of 36;
    privileging of 3; in United Kingdom 2
The English Constitution 36, 186
*English Laws for Women in the Nineteenth
    Century* xxi, 176
engraving 77, 127, 221
Enlightenment ideals 40, 260
*Enquiry into the Sanitary Conditions of the
    Laboring Population of Great Britain* 92; *see
    also* Chadwick, Edwin
entailed states 175
entertainment: politics as 53; spending on
    103
environment 13, 18

epidemics 291, 299–300
equipoise, age of 49, 94, 197
equity law 169, 195, 208
Essex 85
established churches xxiv, 2, 37, 260,
    262–3, 276
estates, open to public recreation 15
ether, luminiferous 280, 294
ether (anesthetic) 286
Eton school 137, 151, 166, 171
eugenics 235, 298
Euston, Lord 256
evangelical Christianity: in Church of
    England 262; in different denominations
    275–6; and domestic ideology 274;
    Gladstone and 49; and Judaism 266;
    in middle class 135, 142, 148, 276; in
    ruling elite 38; use of term 275
evolution, theories of 279, 281, 288–90,
    293, 296–9
executions 200, 211; *see also* hangings
Exeter Change 110
extortion 247, 249
extramarital sex 136, 175, 242, 246, 253
extraordinary events 236
Eyre, Edward John xxiii, 71, 77–8

Fabian Society xxv, 59
factories: child labor in xviii, 46; and
    empire 71; inspection of 27; location of
    13, 84–5, 87, 130; regulation of 50, 54,
    87; and steam power 91; in textile
    industry xix, 90
Factory Acts xviii, xx–xxiv, 46, 95, 97, 130,
    169, 178
factory schools 131
Faithfull, Emily 250
Falkland Islands 73
fallen women 232, 244, 277
Family Herald 226
famine, in Ireland *see* Great Famine
"Fanny and Stella" scandal xxiv, 254–6
farce 215, 217–18, 231, 233
Far From the Madding Crowd 235
farms, size of 14; *see also* agriculture
farm servants 15, 24
fashion 70, 101, 107–8, 118–20
Fashoda crisis 58
Faucher, Leon 17
Faust and Marguerite 218
Fawcett, Henry 52
Fawcett, Millicent Garrett 194
Felix Holt 63, 234
female sexuality 243–4

feminists: and girls' schools xx, 141, 177–8; Langham Place 176; middle-class 129; and sexuality 252; and women's suffrage 52, 55, 60

Fenians *see* Irish Republican Brotherhood (IRB)

Ferguson, Niall 68, 72

Fermanagh 89

fertility 244–5, 253

fever epidemics 291

Field, Michael 234

field hockey 178

financial panics 204

fiscal-military state 87–8

fiscal policy 103

fish 103, 271, 287

fish and chips 146

fishery xxviii, 103

fixed prices 107–8, 114

flâneurs and *flâneuses* 16–17

Flower Festival or Service 274

flowers 119, 274

folk music 32, 221

food: imports of xxix; luxury 117, 140; preparation 99, 139; prices 26, 99, 109, 119

food riots 44–5

football: employers supporting 55; and identity 146; as leisure pursuit xxv–xxvi, 99, 147; in parks 20, 153; in popular conservatism 54; in schools xxvii; as spectator sport 101, 140, 157–8; variations of 151

Football Association (FA) xxiii, 151, 157

Football League 158

Foote, Maria 196

foreign policy 54, 58

Forster, E.M. 83, 235

Foucault, Michel 12, 202, 240–1

foundling hospitals 241, 246

Fowler, Henry 269

Fowler, O.S. 243

Fra Lippo Lippi 222

France: British alliance with 60; department stores in 114; and philosophical anatomy 288; Victoria's visit to 188; and World War One 62

franchise 35–7, 41, 43–5, 48, 50–2

freaks 161, 221

free-and-easies 148, 215, 219–20

Free Church of Scotland xx, 262–5, 276, 289

free love 240, 252

Freethought Publishing Company 271

free trade: disadvantages of 100; and economic growth 93; and People's Budget 61; political debate on 39–40, 48; state associated with 88

Free Trade Hall (Manchester) 25, 295

French Revolution 43–4

French's Acting Edition of Plays 217

Friendly Societies 133, 155, 173

Frith, William Powell 213

The Fruits of Philosophy xxv, 271

furniture 24

Gaelic Athletic Association (GAA) 56

Gaelic football 157

Galápagos Islands 297

Gall, Franz 285

galleries, commercial 282

Galton, Francis 298

gambling: and alcohol 149; as form of leisure 5, 99, 140, 148, 152–3, 160

Gandhi, Mohandas 70

gangs 198, 206, 211

Garibaldi, Giuseppe 51, 197

garroting panic xxii–xxiii, 198

Garrotters' Act 198

Gaskell, Mrs. (Elizabeth) xx–xxii, 87, 180, 203, 223–5

Gassiot, John Peter 295

Gatrell, V. A. C. 199, 207

Gender: changes in roles 176–9; and class 126; and education 134–6, 170–2, 177–8; and leisure 147, 153–4; in novels 224; and religion 274; and sexual desire 167–8; and shopping 26–7, 113–18; use of term 165; and work 173–4; *see also* the Angel in the House

gender ideologies 166

gender inversion 249–50, 256; *see also* effeminacy; mannish women

General Medical Council xxii, 292, 300

General Police Act (Scotland) 1857 200

general practitioners 288; *see also* doctors / medical profession

gentlemanly politeness 167

The Gentleman's House 30

gentlemen's clubs 25, 123, 135, 142, 167, 179

"gents" 27, 120, 229, 231

Geoffroy Saint-Hilaire, Étienne 287–8

geology xxi, 280, 282, 288–98

George III xvii, 183

George IV xvii, 41–2, 63, 182–3, 188

George V xxviii, 61, 192–3

Germany: competition with 58, 60, 78;

pianos made in 7, 9; steel production in xxix; and World War One 62
germ theory xxii, xxvi, 299, 301
Gilbert and Sullivan 142, 213, 232
gin xvii, 149–50
Gissing, George xxvi, 235
Gladstone, William Ewart 49–51, 53–4, 56, *57*, 96, 190–1, 193, 269
Glamorgan 85–6
Glasgow: infant mortality in 92; Irish migration to 48; population of 14, 23
Glorious Revolution 38
Golden Jubilee *see* Jubilees; Royal; Golden
gold standard 88, 93
golf 101, 142, 178
gonorrhea 245, 291
Gordon, George William 77–8
gossip 154, 195, 250
Gothic buildings 213
gothic horror 226
Gothic novels 223–4, 263
governesses 6, 134–6, 171–2, 177, 219, 225
government: public trust in 88; spending 88–9, 96, 101
Grainger Market xviii, 110, 114
Grand, Sarah xxvi, 235
Grand Tours 155
Grant, Robert 287–8, 298
Granville Barker, Harley 232–3
Gray Street (Newcastle) 110
Great Exhibition 1851 xxi; as advertisement 113; and British prosperity 84, 94–5; Prince Albert and 184, 285; and public tastes 22–3; technology and science at 282–3, 285; travel to 156
Great Expectations xxiii, 225
Great Famine xx, 48–9, 79, 86, 89, 269
Great Reform Act: and Ireland 45; middle-class reactions to 135; and monarchy 183–4; passing of 44; widening electorate xviii, 43; working-class reactions to 132–3
Great Western Railway 284
Greek language 171
Greenwood, Thomas 25
Grey, Earl 43
Griffith, Arthur 62
gross indecency xxvii, 248, 254, 256–7
Grossmith, George and Weedon 9, 29, 122
gross national product (GNP) 88, 90
Grosvenor House 142

Hackney 29
Haggard, H. Rider 65, 71, 83, 224
Hagley 15
Haldane Army Reforms 81
Hallé, Charles 25
Hallelujah Lasses 267
Hamilton, Cicely 252
Hampstead 20
Hampstead Heath (London) 19, 29
hand-me-downs 130
hangings xix, 195, 201–2, 211, 249
Hardie, Keir 59
hard labor 202–3, 256
Hard Times 170
Hardy, Thomas xxvii, 223, 235, 259, 298
Harmsworth, Alfred (Lord Northcliffe) 236, 238
Harrison, Elizabeth 289
Harrods 113, 116
Harrow school 137, 171
Harvest Festival and Fruit Banquet 274
Hatfield 15
Haussman, Baron Georges-Eugène 24
Haweis, Mrs. 30
hawkers 109
Haydon, Benjamin Robert 203
Haymarket 217
Hayne, Joseph 196
Hazlitt, William 42
headmasters 134, 171
healers, alternative 290, 292, 301–2
health: Victorian ideas about 291; *see also* public health
The Heavenly Twins xxvi, 235
Hellenic galleries at British Museum 254
Hemans, Felicia xviii, 221
Hennell, Sara 250
Henty, G.A. 71, 179
Herring, John Frederick 213
Herschel, John 290
hierarchy 3, 5, 41; political attitudes to 39; racial 5; social 37, 124–5, 128, 193, 264
High Church 263, 275
high streets 12–13, 26
Hill, Octavia 29
Hinduism and Hindus 75–6, 81–2, 261, 270
Hippodrome 229
hire-purchase system 7, 9
HMS *Beagle* xviii, 297
hobbies 117–18

holidays: upper- and middle-class versions
  of 161–2; week-long 14–15; working-
  class access to 137, 139–40, 154–6,
  160–1
Holloway 29
The Holy Sabbath 231
Home Counties 86
homeopaths 292
Home Rule: Home Rule Bills xxvi, xxviii,
  56–8, *57*, 62; Home Rule MPs 54; and
  Liberal split xxvi, 38
homes: aristocratic *see* domesticity, upper
  class; decorating xvii, 6, 22–3, 30–1,
  108, 112, 112–19; leisure in 7–8;
  meanings of 13, 21; segregation of
  space in 30; as workplaces 12–13, 22,
  31–2, 86–7
Homogenic Love, and its Place in a Free Society
  xxvi, 257
homosexuality: as anachronistic concept
  246–7; and class 247–8; criminalization
  of 196, 207, 248–9; in public places *see*
  "cottaging"; and sexology 256–7; use of
  term 257; *see also* women, sex between
homosocial spaces 166
Hopkins, Ellice 252
horse-drawn vehicles xxi, xxix, 102
horse racing 99, 147, 152, 156, 160, 213
hospitals 22, 136, 188, 244, 254, 301–2
hostesses (political and social) 40, 136
household items, major 118
household suffrage 50
House of Commons: centrality of 61;
  equalizing constituencies for 55; Irish
  members of 2, 43; representation in
  36–7; in UK constitution 35–6; upper
  classes in 137, 143
House of Lords: bishops in 262;
  Conservative control of 60; as highest
  court 208; and Home Rule Bills 62; and
  People's Budget 61; political power of
  36, 55, 142–3; Prime Ministers in 58;
  upper classes in 45, 137
houseplace 21
Houses of Parliament 24, 60, 102, 186
housing: and employment 21; middle-class
  22–3; reformers 27; rural 15
*How I Managed My House on Two Hundred
  Pounds a Year* xxiii, 134
Huddersfield 111
Huggins, William 213
humor theory 291, 299
Hunt, William Holman 213
hunting 137, 156

Hutton, Will 124
Huxley, Thomas xxiii, 78, 283, 289, 293,
  295, 298
Hyde Park (London): demonstrations in
  xxiii, 51, 197; Jubilee in 192; public
  debate in 20; sex between men in 249,
  254
hydro-electric machine 295
hydropaths 292
Hygeian system 292
*The Hymnal Companion to the Book of Common
  Prayer* 272
Hymns Ancient and Modern xxiii, 272
Hyndman, H.M. 59

Ibsen, Henrik 232
ice cream parlors 120
An Ideal Husband xxvi, 233
identities, counterfeit 27
Idylls of the King 233–4
illegitimacy 246; *see also* bastardy laws;
  children, illegitimate
Illustrated London News 188, 190, 227
immigrant labor 30, 62
immigrants: British abroad *see* emigration;
  to cities 16; Irish 30, 48, 265, 270;
  Jewish xxv, 266, 270; Muslim 270
Imperator 295
Imperial College (London) xxviii, 99–100,
  295
imperialism *see* empire
The Importance of Being Earnest xxvi, 233
impostors 120, 205, 249
impotence 241–3
improvement, age of 1
income: and class 125, 128; earned and
  unearned 61
income tax xix, 88, 93–4, 96, 101
independence: and gender 166–8; and
  respectability 37, 131
India: Army 76–7; colonization of 75–7;
  cotton exports to xxi–xxii, 97; as
  dependent colony 73; Government of
  India Act xxii, 76, 185; independence
  movement 70, 81–2; market for imperial
  products 71; novels set in 224; sexual
  relationships in 68; Victoria as empress
  of xxv, 71, 191–2
Indian National Congress 81–2
Indian Rebellion xxii, 71, 76–8, 185
industrial decline 100
industrialization: and class system 6; and
  gender 168, 173–4; and leisure 146;
  Prince Albert on 185; and religion 260;

and rural economy 90; and science 279, 284; uneven nature of 86; and Victorian period 1, 3

Industrial Revolution 84–6

infant and child mortality xxvii, 3–4, 92, 254, 273, 291, 299

infanticide 246

inheritance 174–5, 211

In Memoriam 222

intermediates 256

The Intermediate Sex xxviii, 256–7

international trade: and drug foods 148; in iron and steel xxiv, 97, 102; *see also* free trade

invalidism 291

inversion 241, 249, 256; *see also* gender inversion; homosexuality

investments, overseas xxv, 95

Ireland: and class system 126; Conservative views on 40; farming in 90; food riots in 44–5; Gladstone's commitment to 50, 53–4, 56; lack of industrialization in 86; marriage in 131; official map of 16; partition of 62; political unrest in 78, 81; Poor Law in 46; population of xviii–xix, xxi, xxiii–xxviii; post-Victoria monarchs and 193; Queen Victoria and 188–9; rebellion in 42–3; Reform Acts in 52; spectator sport in 157–8; in United Kingdom 2; urbanization in 23–4

Irish Church Temporalities Act xviii, 263

Irish Home Rule Party 53, 59

Irish independence 43, 62

Irish Land Acts xxiv, 53–4

Irish nationalism xxvii, 49, 53–4, 56, 62

Irish Parliamentary Party (IPP) 54

Irish problem / Irish Question 2, 35, 43, 49, 53–4, 62, 186, 267

Irish Republican Brotherhood (IRB) xxii, xxiv, 49, 62, 78

Irish universities 53

iron: British consumption of xxix; British production of xxiv; in Crystal Palace 5, 95

iron industry: in Birmingham 71; decline in 102; employment in xxi; growth of 91, 93

Irving, Henry xxvi, 233

Isandhlwana 80

Italy, unification movement 49, 51, 141, 197

Jack Sheppard xix, 214, 225

Jackson's Oxford Journal 190

Jack the Ripper xxvi, 28, 206, 212, 237, 270

Jamaica xviii, xxiii, 69, 73, 77–8

James, Henry 223, 234–5

Jameson Raid 80

Jane Eyre xx, 83, 180, 225

Jerrold, Douglas 218

Jewish Association for the Protection of Girls and Women 270

Jewish Board of Guardians 270

Jewish Emancipation xxii

Jewish schools 264

Jews: admitted to Oxbridge xxiv; as boxers 152; and class system 126; prejudice against 261, 266

Jewsbury, Geraldine 251

Jex-Blake, Sophia xxv, 300

Jim Crow 218

The Jingo Song 71, 229

John Halifax, Gentleman 224

Jones, Ernest 47

Jones, Henry Arthur 232

Jones vs. *Yeend* 204

Joule, James 294

journals, 'class' or 'quality' 227

Jubilees, Royal 71; Diamond xxvii, 191–2; Golden xxvi–xxvii, 113

Jude the Obscure xxvii, 223

Judicature Acts xxv, 208

juries xxi, xxvii, 169, 195–6, 201, 208–9

Justices of the Peace *see* magistrates

"Juteopolis" 96

jute production xxviii, 62, 96

Kean, Ellen Tree 215

Kearnan, Thomas *283*

Keble, John 262

Keeble, Samuel 269

Kelvin, Lord *see* Thomson, William

Kenealy, Edward 205

Kensington Gardens 29

Kensington High Street 114

Kerr, Robert 30

khaki 118

King's College, London 300

Kingsley, Charles xxii, 78, 224–5

King Solomon's Mines 65, 83

Kipling, Rudyard 83, 235

Kirk *see* Church of Scotland

Kirkgate xxv, 118

kitchens 21–2, 24, 30–1

kleptomania 113

Knightsbridge 71, 112, 114

Knole 15

Knowles, Charles 271
Knowles, Sheridan 215
Knox, Robert 287
"knut" 120
Krafft-Ebing, Richard von 256

labor: manual 9, 133, 138; nonmanual
    178; sweated 60
labor aristocracy 51, 173
laboratories 280–1, 286–7, 293–4, 301
Labouchere, Henry 254
Labouchere amendment 254, 257
Labour Party xxvii, 54, 56, 59–60, 139
Ladies of Llangollen 250
Lady Audley's Secret xxiii, 211, 226, 235
Lady Geraldine's Courtship 222
The Lady of Shalott 222
Lady's Pictorial 117
Lady Windermere's Fan 233
Lafontaine, Charles 287
laissez-faire 39, 46–7, 93, 135, 141
Lallemand, Claude-Francoise 242
Lamarck, Jean-Baptiste 287
Lamb, William, 2nd Viscount Melbourne
    see Melbourne, Lord
The Lancet xvii, 287
landlords, aristocratic 15, 48, 218
land ownership, and voting rights 37, 44
Land War 54
Langham Place feminists 176
Lansdowne House 142
Larceny Act 1827 xvii, 198
Latin America 79
Latin language 136, 171
laudanum 291, 301
law 28, 35, 45, 47, 62, 70, 76, 96, 113,
    165, 168–9, 207, 244, 248–9, 256
lawn-tennis 101
Leeds 19–20, 25, 94, 110–11, 114, 118;
    University of 294
Leicester 101, 105, 220
Leicester Square 24
leisure: church-sponsored 4; and class
    distinctions 162; history of 145–7; at
    home 109; improving forms of 5; and
    masculinity 173; money available for 84,
    99–101; socialist options for 59; and
    standard of living 88; use of term 146
The Leisure Hour 70
leisure vacuum 146–7
letters, from emigrants 69
Levy, Amy 234, 277
Lewis' department store xxv, 114
Leybourne, George xxiii, 229

libel trials 209, 256–7
Liberal Associations 56
liberalism 4, 39, 42
Liberal Party: and extension of franchise
    55, 60; and Irish Question xxvi, 38,
    49, 58–9; and middle class 141; and
    nonconformists 269; origins of 39; and
    People's Budget 60–1; as progressive 47,
    50–1; and South African War 80;
    taxation policies of 103–4; and World
    War One 62; *see also* Whigs
Liberty's 115
Life and Labour of the People in London xxvi
life-cycle services 260, 273
life expectancy 4, 88, 92, 95
limited liability 96, 220
Lister, Anne 250–1
Lister, Joseph 299
literacy 7–9, 119, 131, 139–40, 170, 221,
    227, 283
literature 70, 142, 171, 214, 298
Little Dorrit 203, 210, 298
Liverpool: Irish migration to 48;
    population of xvii, 14, 94; shopping in
    110–11; slums in 18; theaters in 215;
    University of 294
Liverpool Mercury 190
Livingstone, David xxi
Llandudno 155, *161*
Lloyd, Edward 225–7
Lloyd, Marie 229–30
Lloyd George, David 61
Lloyd's Weekly Newspaper 188, 211, 227, 237
Local Government Act xxvi, 56
Lombroso, Cesare 199
London: City of 101, 136; economy of
    85–6, 174; as financial center 78–9, 89,
    101; growth of 24; as imperial city 71;
    Irish migration to 48; music halls in
    220; parks in 29; population of xvii,
    13, 89, 94; reform riots in 44; shopping
    in 110–11, 114; suburbs of 20, 29;
    theaters in 215; University of 178, 292
London *Daily Telegraph* 16, 53, 227
London Journal 226
"London Labour and the London Poor"
    xx, 17
London School of Medicine for Women
    (LSMW) xxv, 300
Long, John St. John 292
lower middle class: and empire 69;
    expansion of 140; holidays 15; housing
    22–3; and shopping 111, 118–20; in
    suburbs 21, 98; upward mobility into 9,

130, 138, 141; women's employment 27;
  see also middle class
Lowther, Francis William 242
Luke the Labourer 218
Lusitania xxviii, 295
Lyceum Theatre 233
Lyell, Charles 280, 295–8
Lyons café 120
Lyttleton, Edward xxvi, 252
Lytton, Lord 191

Madame Tussaud's 205, 212
The Madras House 232
Mafeking, siege of 80
magazines: availability of 7; popular 207;
  religious 70, 227, 272; serializing novels
  224–5; spending on 103
magistrates: in class system 125; and local
  elites 36; and police forces xix, 200;
  upper classes serving as 137
magistrate's courts 201
"magnetic fluids" 280, 286
"The Maiden Tribute of Modern
  Babylon" xxvi, 236–7, 251
maids-of-all-work 98, 132
male friendship 247
male impersonators *230*
male intimacy 257
male sexuality 196, 241–2, 244, 247–9,
  253; *see also* homosexuality
Malicious Trespass Act 1820 xvii, 198
Malthus, Thomas 45–6, 85
Man and Beast xxv, 296
Manchester: infant mortality in 92; middle
  class in 25; music halls of 228; parks in
  xx, 19; parliamentary representation of
  43–4; population of xvii–xviii, xxiv, 14,
  23, 89, 94; shopping in xxv, 114; textile
  industry in 90–1
Mangnall's Questions 172, 180n6
manliness 166–7, 241–2, 274, 276; *see also*
  masculinity
Mann, Horace 271
manners 117, 224
mannish women 250, 256
manufacturing: growth of 96–7, 100–101;
  middle-class basis of 135
maps, mapping 16
"Maps Descriptive of London Poverty" 26
markets (economic) 39, 48, 71, 88, 92–3
markets (shopping) xviii, 12, 108–15
Market Street (Manchester) 110
Marks & Spencer xxv, 118
Marquess of Queensberry 257

marriage: late 25; for middle-class people
  134, 141, 174, 232; in novels 223, 235;
  performed by non-Anglican clergy xix,
  263; proposing 184; and sexuality
  242–3, 245–6; for upper classes 136,
  175; violence in 179; for working-class
  people 130–1
marriage law 169–70, 176, 195–6, 209; see
  also *coverture*
married women 56, 60, 130, 167, 169–70,
  175–7, 204
Married Women's Property Acts xxiv–xxv,
  176–7
Married Women's Property Committee
  (MWPC) xxiv, 176
Marshall & Snelgrove 115
Marx, Karl 92, 125
"Mary Annes" 247
Mary Barton xx, 63, 225
masculinity: changes in ideals of 165; and
  class 171–3; and consumption 118;
  cross-dressing women and 230; and
  religions 274; and sexuality 241–2, 247
  see also male sexuality; and war 81; and
  work 167, 174
"mashers" 27, 120–1
Masson, David 223
mass production 7, 95, 100–101, 118–19,
  233
masturbation xxvi, 150, 167, 242–3, 252
material culture 107
maternal mortality xxvii, 183, 253–4
mathematics 100, 172, 294
Maxwell, James Clerk xxv, 294
McWilliam, Rohan 35, 195
Medical Act Amendment Act xxvi, 300
medicine and medical knowledge 279, 282,
  290, 299, 301
medieval era 92, 124, 213
Melbourne, Lord (William Lamb, 2nd
  Viscount Melbourne) 183–4, 223
melodrama: India as location for 70; and
  Queen Caroline Affair 42; and
  sentimentality 242; in theater 215,
  217–19, 228, 232; and Tichborne case
  205; in writing 170, 226
memsahibs 70
menarche 244
"men of science" 280–1, 286, 289, 294,
  296–8
menstruation 253
merchant fleet 96–7, 102
mercury 172, 245, 291
Mesmer, Franz 285

mesmerism 280, 285–7
metals industries 97
Methodism: and Church of England 267;
    and class 126, 129, 264; evangelicalism
    in 275; and leisure activities 153;
    number of Methodists xviii, xxvii, 269;
    sects of 265; and temperance movement
    133
Metropolitan Police Act 1829 xviii, 200
Metropolitan Poor Act 302
miasma theory xxii, 18, 291, 293, 299, 301
middlebrow literature 142
middle class: aspiring to aristocratic
    lifestyle 100; children of 171; and
    empire 69; and free trade 48; gender
    roles of 168, 174–5; growth of 7, 168;
    history of 128–9; and home decoration
    22–3, 30; and leisure 142, 148; in
    Liberal Party 39; modern use of term
    124; morality of 42; and music hall
    228–9; and novels 224–5; and parks 20,
    29; political power of xxi, xxv, 135, 141;
    public culture of 25, 135; and public
    opinion 41; and religion 269; rural 52;
    and sexuality 248, 253; standard of
    living 95; in the suburbs 20–1, 29; and
    theater 215, 231; voting rights of xviii,
    43–5; work and income of 128, 133–4,
    140
middle-class radicals 133, 139, 141
middle-class values 20, 44, 49, 138, 167,
    189, 199, 276
middle-class women: and domesticity 133;
    housekeeping by 174–5; leisure of 154;
    and paid work 134, 140–1, 174, 179;
    and politics 44; restricting movements
    of 28; and sexuality 241, 246; and
    shopping 26–7, 111–12, 114–15, 142;
    and theater 231; unmarried 177
Middlemarch xxiv, 122, 143, 234–5, 239
midwives 290, 299–301
Midwives Act xxvii, 300–301
military: fitness for service in 58, 298;
    government spending on 38, 88, 101;
    imperial 60, 71, 81; and public schools
    137; reforms to 53; venereal disease in
    245
military toys 171
milk 99
Mill, John Stuart 3, 39, 52, 78
Millais, John Everett 213
Mines (Ashley) Commission Report xix,
    223
Mines Act 169

mining industry 85–6, 91, 93, 132, 138,
    174
minstrel shows 212, 218
Mirele Efros 231
miscegenation 287
missionaries 69, 132, 174, 267, 276
Miss Marjoribanks xxiii, 224
Mitchell, David 273
molly houses 247–8
monarchy: abolition of 41; as bourgeois
    189; Conservatives as party of 53;
    constitutional role of 185–6, 190;
    popularity of 54, 182; in UK
    constitution 36
Monmouth 85–6
The Moonstone 70
Morison, James 292
Morning Chronicle xx, 17, 190, 220
The Morning Post 249
morning rooms 22
Morris, William 59, 213
mortality rates 299; *see also* infant and child
    mortality; maternal mortality
Morton, Charles 220
mothering *see* childrearing
mothers: paid work by 31; unmarried
    244
moving pictures 212, 230–1
Mrs. Beeton's Household Management 70
Mudie's 224
Municipal Corporations Act 1835 200
Murphy, Shirley Foster 30
Museum of Practical Geology xxi, 282
music: areas of 213; classical 25, 221;
    played at home 6–9; in pleasure gardens
    20; and theater 217
music hall (genre): great age of 228; as
    leisure pursuit 99, 139; political
    meanings and effects 231; in popular
    conservatism 54; sensation in 212; stars
    of xxiii
music halls (buildings): and alcohol
    149–50, 212; audiences of 147–8, 220,
    228–9; first opening xx; forerunners of
    215, 219–20; large xxiv; music
    performed in 213–14;
    professionalization of 140; profitability
    of 101; syndicates of 140, 220, 229;
    and theaters 218; and urbanization
    16; variety of entertainment 221
music hall songs 179, 205, 229, 231, 243,
    267, 272
musicians, professional 7, 9
Muslims 76, 261, 270

Napoleon I *see* Bonaparte, Napoleon
Napoleon III (Louis) 188
National Gallery of Practical Science
    Blending Instruction with Amusement
    see Adelaide Gallery
National Insurance Act 302
nationalist movements 54, 81
National Land Company 47
natural law 285
natural philosophy 280–1
natural selection 290–8
natural theology 280
naughtiness 240
nautical melodrama 218
navy 60
nebular hypothesis 288–90
neighborhoods: elite 17; working-class
    30–1, 109, 131–3, 276
neo-mercantilist policies 100
netball 178
Netherlands 94
never-married 117, 175
Newcastle-upon-Tyne: bazaar in xviii,
    110; Co-op stores in 111; music halls in
    220; overcrowding in 18; singing saloons
    in 219
Newgate novels xix, 224–5
New Grub Street xxvi, 235
New Journalism 215, 235–7
Newlove, Harry 256
Newman, John Henry xx, 262–3, 265
Newnes, George 236, 238
New Oxford Street (London) 110, 112
New Poor Law *see* Poor Law
News of the World 188
newspapers: court coverage of 195–6,
    209; daily 184, 237–8; and politics 41;
    proliferation of 226–7; provincial 17;
    purchasing 119; in reading rooms 118;
    taxes on 226; on unnatural assault
    248–9; working-class readership 140
New Woman novels xxvi, 215, 235, 252
New Zealand 70–1, 73–5, 77, 104, 212
Nightingale, Florence 299–300
Nightingale Training School xxiii, 300
night watchmen 200
nonconformist denominations 261–5,
    267–9, 273
nonconformists: barred from voting rights
    37; and education xxii, 266; and
    evangelicalism 276; middle-class 264–5;
    and scientific debates 288; vote granted
    to xvii, 42; in Wales xxi
nonconformist social conscience 269

nonwhite peoples 70, 73, 78, 218, 243
North and South xxii, 87, 180, 224–5
northern dialects 219
Northern Ireland 3, 62
The Northern Star 227
North London Collegiate School 177
Northumberland 85–6
Norton, Caroline xix, xxi, 170, 176
Nottingham 219–20, 273
novels: *flânerie* in 17; pianos in 6–7, 9;
    popularity of 224–5, 235; serialization
    of 224; subgenres of 234–5; in Victorian
    era 222–3
numeracy 140
nurseries 21, 179
nursing (of infants) 246
nursing (profession) 141, 290, 300
Nussey, Ellen 251

O'Brien, Bronterre 47
obscenity trials xxv, 271
*Observations on the Natural Claim of a Mother to
    the Custody of her Children* xix, 170
O'Connell, Daniel 43
O'Connor, Fergus 47
O'Gorman, Frank 40
old age pensions xxviii, 60, 104
Old Corruption 37–8, 42, 52–3, 88
Old Sarum 43
Oliphant, Mrs. (Margaret) xxiii, 223–4,
    226
Oliver Twist xix, 198, 210–11, 214, 223,
    225, 277
Onania or the Heinous Sin of Self-Pollution 243
one-up-one-down houses 23
On Liberty 39
On the Dynamical Theory of Heat xxi, 294
opera 106, 136–7, 214, 217
operettas, comic 142, 232
opiates 291
opium 75, 301
Opium Wars xix, xxii, 73, 75
oral sex 245
Orange Free State 80
orchestras 213
The Original Strong-Minded Woman 219
Origin of Species xxii, 285, 290, 295–6,
    298–9
ornaments 107–8, 112, 119
orphan 211
Orton, Arthur *206; see also* Tichborne cases
Orwell, George 83, 123–4
O'Shea, Kitty and William xxvi, 205
Ottoman Empire 79

Our Homes, and How to Make Them Healthy 30
outwork 22, 91
overcrowding xxvi, xxviii, 13, 16, 31
overseas investment xxi
ovulation 253
Owen, Richard 288, 298
Owen, Robert (Owenites, Owenism) 41
Oxbridge universities: as Anglican
    institutions 262; Jews admitted to xxiv,
    270; nonconformists admitted to xxii,
    266; science at 281; upper classes at 137;
    women at 178
Oxford, University of xxii, 53, 137, 262,
    270, 287
Oxford Movement xviii, 262–3
Oxford Street (London) xxiv, 24, 110, 112,
    114
Oxford Street Bazaar 110

packaged tours 161
Paddington railway station 97
Page, David 296
painting 119, 203, 213, 233, 251
Pall Mall Gazette 117, 231, 236–7
Palmerston, Emily 142
Palmerston, Lord (Henry John Temple) 51,
    58
Pamela 203
panics 198, 204
Pankhurst, Emmeline and Christabel 60
panopticon 202
pantomime 217, 229–30
paper, machine-made 7, 224
paramilitary 62
Paris Commune 54
parish churches 262–4, 272–4
Park, Frederick ("Fanny") 254–6, *255*
Parke, Ernest 256
parks: city 12–13, 16, 18–20, 28–9;
    regulation of 153
parks movement xviii
Parliament: class composition of 135, 175;
    remuneration of members 36, 47, 61;
    royal opening of 43, 189–91; studies
    commissioned by 4; in UK constitution
    36
Parliament Act 1911 xxviii, 142
parlors xix, 7, 12, 21–31, 131
Parnell, Charles Stewart xxvi, 54, 56, 205
parties (political): cohesiveness of 35, 38–9,
    52–3; major 38; social wings of 56
party canvassers 55–6
passionlessness 166, 243–5
Past and Present xix, 92

Pasteur, Louis 299
pastoral mode 14
patriotic songs 71, 221, 229
patriotism: in Jewish community 270;
    working-class 5, 54
patronage, royal 186
Pauvrette 217
Pavilion theater 231
pawning, pawnbrokers, pawnshops 31, 132
Pearson, Cyril 238
Peckham 29
peddlers 109, 154
Peel, Robert xix–xx, 43, 47–50, 93–4, 184,
    188, 200
Peel Park 19
peerage, peers 44, 61, 128–9, 135, 137,
    186, 209; *see also* House of Lords
Pelham 224
Penal Servitude Act 199
Penge 20
penitentiaries 202
penny dreadfuls / penny bloods 212, 225,
    272
penny-per-mile 97
People's Budget xxviii, 61, 142
People's Charter 47
The People's Periodical and Family Library
    226–7
Pepper, J. H. 279, 295–6
"Pepper's Ghost" display xxiii, 279
periodical literature 226–7, 235
pessaries 253
Peter Pan 232
petting 245
pews 265
philanthropy: deserving and undeserving
    beneficiaries of 132; and evangelicalism
    276–7; and Poor Law 46; slum visiting
    and 27; of upper classes 136; Victoria
    and Albert's roles in 188–9; Victorian
    commitment to 4; women's role in 140,
    175, 179
Philosophical Transactions 280
Phineas Finn xxiii, 198, 210
photography 70, 192
phrenology xviii, 243, 280, 285–6, 290
physics 279, 283, 294–6
pianos: advertisements for *8*; affordability
    of 30–1, 97, 107, 109; meaning of 1,
    6–10; in pubs 7, 219; social prevalence
    of xvii, xix, xxii, xxviii
Piccadilly Circus (London) 254
pickpocketing, pickpockets 198, 201, 211
Pickwick Papers 203, 210, 224

The Picture of Dorian Gray xxvi, 235
piece work 130, 215
pigeon-racing 153, 160
pig-iron 91, 97
Pilkington, Hugh 198
Pinero, Arthur xxvi, 232
Pius IX, Pope 266
Place, Francis 198
placemen 43
plateware 108
Platt's of Oldham 96
plots (narrative) 204, 217–18, 223, 225,
    232
Pluck: A Story of 50000 231
plumbing, indoor 18, 30
poaching 197
pocket boroughs 43–4; *see also* rotten
    boroughs
Poems before Congress 222
poetry 14, 213, 221, 223, 228, 233–4
poetry annuals 221
police forces: creation of xviii, xxii, 195–6,
    199–200; growth of 206–7
policeman-state 199
Polish revolutionaries 197
polite society 107, 129, 136
political parties *see* parties (political)
political unions 43
politics: local 129, 175; out-of-doors 41;
    petticoat 40; use of term 35
Ponsonby, Sarah 250
Poor Law xviii, 45–6, 85, 93, 132, 197,
    204; Bastardy Clause of xx, 246;
    Guardians 46, 140; Medical Officers
    292
Pooter, Mr. Charles 9, 97, 134
popular culture 69–71, 211–12, 225, 243,
    267
popularizers (of science) 283
popular press 76, 188–9
population (of Britain and Ireland): in
    1700 13; in 1821 xvii; in 1831 xviii; in
    1841 xix; in 1851 xxi; in 1861 xxiii; in
    1871 xxiv; in 1881 xxv; in 1891 xxvi; in
    1901 xxvii; in 1911 xxviii, 24; growth in
    3–4, 85, 94, 99; urban 14–15, 23, 89
pornography 42, 240–1
postal workers 9
postcolonialism 67
Post Office 24, 97, 256
potatoes 48, 89
poverty: Booth's study of in London 5,
    138; decline in 104; in Ireland 90; liberal
    ideas on 39; and religion 269, 277; rural

    15, 24; in Scotland 49; as self-inflicted
    132; urban 18, 27
Poverty: A Study of Town Life xxvii, 5, 138
power-binding xxii, 7, 225
The Power of Womanhood 252
preachers 5, 265, 275
pregnancy 126, 185, 241, 243, 246, 253–4
premarital sex 244, 246
Pre-Raphaelite movement xx, 213, 221
Presbyterianism 262, 264–5
Preston 86–7, 174
Prevention of Crime Act 1908 xxviii, 208
Pride and Prejudice 175, 180
Primitive Methodism 264–5, 269
Primrose League 56
Prince, Mary 70
Prince of Wales theatre 231
print culture 41, 182, 185, 211–12,
    214–15, 221, 235, 283
printing, and sheet music 6, 9; *see also*
    steam printing
Prisoners' Counsel Acts xviii, 201
Prisoners' Temporary Discharge for Ill
    Health Act xxviii
prisons 175, 201–2, 207–8, 226
private theatricals 215, 217
prize-fighting *see* boxing
probation (ticket-of-leave) 199, 202
A Problem in Greek Ethics xxv, 257
Proclamation to India 76
professional associations 134
professions 27, 91, 128–9, 167, 171,
    175, 178, 195, 234, 279, 282, 286–7,
    297
The Profligate xxvi, 232
property ownership: and voting rights 44,
    47, 50–1, 55, 170, 208; by women 45,
    60, 167, 209
proselytizing 275–6
prostitutes: attempted reform of 245, 251;
    clothing of 120; and domestic ideology
    167–8; and empire 69; Gladstone and
    50; male 247, 256–7; and marriage 242,
    244; in parks 20; seasonal work as 130;
    state surveillance of 207; in urban
    spaces 17, 26, 28, 112, 116; and
    venereal disease 302; *see also* white
    slavery
Protestantism 37, 42, 62, 126, 185, 261–2;
    see also nonconformists
provincial elites 22
Provincial Medical and Surgical
    Association (PMSA) xviii, 292
prudery, false 240

public health 4, 16, 18, 26, 28, 50, 54, 281, 292, 302
Public Health Acts xx, xxiv–xxv, 18, 26, 28, 292, 301–2
public life, home as refuge from 21
public opinion 39, 41–2, 45, 78, 249, 271
public order 17
public schools xviii, 100, 136–7, 150–1, 166, 171, 178, 274
public service 9, 24, 37–8, 102
public women 17
pubs: Conservatives as party of 40, 53; decline in numbers 159; as form of leisure 146–8; and gambling 153; half-timbered 32; music in 7, 219–20; as social institution xxi, 5, 133, 149–50, 159–60, 212; and urbanization 16; women visiting 99
Punch 110, 117, 120, 142, 156, 198, 232
Punch and Judy shows 156, *161*, 211
Punjab 76

quack medicines 108, 113, 240–1, 253, 290–2, 301
Quakers 264
Queen (periodical) 13
Queen Caroline Affair xvii, 3, 41–2, 48, 132, 135, 165, 183, 188, 196
Queensbury Rules 152
Queens College 178
Queen's Park Church 213

race: and class 124, 126; and leisure 147; and self-government 78
racial fitness 81, 235, 298
racial hierarchies 5
racism 54, 287
radicalism: in ACLL 48; and aristocracy 41; and corruption 55; decline of 49, 58; and evangelicalism 275; and immigration 270; and income tax 94; in Liberal Party 39, 47; and melodrama 218; and Old Corruption 37; and Queen Charlotte Affair 42; and republicanism 190; scientific 286–9; and sexuality 241, 253, 256; and Tories 40; *see also* middle-class radicals; working-class radicals
ragged schools 131
railway novels 225, 235
Railway Regulation Act xx
railways: commuting by 20, 29, 98; and holiday travel 139, 155–6; to London 24; passenger travel xvii, xxi, xxiv, xxix,

97, 101; peak of 102; and science 279, 284; spread of xxi, 90, 97
The Railway Station 213
railway stations xxix, 12, 90, 97, 102, 213
Raj *see* India, British Raj over
rakes 241, 250
Ramabai, Pandita 70
Ramsbotham, Mary 113
rape 12, 76
rational recreation 5, 28–9, 54, 59, 109, 135, 140, 153, 212
ready-made suits 27
realist novels 228, 234
realist theater 232
real wages xxi, 88, 92–3, 95, 100, 107–8, 118, 148, 160, 227
Rebecca Riots xix, 197
recapitulation (theory of) 287
reception rooms 22
redistribution (of Parliamentary seats) 44, 52, 55
Redistribution Act xxv, 55
redundant women xxi, 74, 140, 224
Reflections on the Decline of Science in England xviii, 282
reform, age of 38, 47
Reform Acts: 1832 *see* Great Reform Act; 1867 xxiv, 1, 9, 50–3, 58–9, 78, 139, 190; 1884 xxv, 9, 54–6, 139; 1918 xv, 37; enlarging electorate 35; for Scotland 51
Reformation 261
reformatories 198, 207
refreshments for shoppers 111–12, 116
Regent's Park 29, 99
Regent Street (London) xvii, 24, 110, 112, 115–16
relevant fiction or works students might enjoy 63, 83, 105, 122, 143, 180, 194, 210, 239, 259, 277, 303
relief (government) 45–6, 262, 265
Relief Church (Scotland) 265
religion: by deputy 273; in everyday life 271–2; in parts of United Kingdom 2; and science 280, 288–9, 296, 298; in Victorian period 4–5
religiosity 260–1, 272–5
religious artifacts 272
religious music xxiii, 272
religious tests for entrance to Oxford and Cambridge Universities xxv, 53
religious tracts 272
The Rent Day 218
rents 51, 54, 61, 99, 102, 125, 142

repeal of the Test and Corporation Acts xvii, 42, 45, 264, 266
Report of the Inter-Departmental Committee on Physical Deterioration 81
Report on the Sanitary Conditions of the Labouring Population of Great Britain xix, 18, 292
Representation of the People Acts *see* Reform Acts
rescue (of prostitutes) 50, 251, 270
respectability: and cleanliness 31; and entertainment 212; and housing 30; and leisure 135, 147–8; and playing music 7, 213–14; and prostitution 28; and Reform Acts 44, 78; and roughness 30, 132; of science 294; sexual 48, 243–4; and shopping 112, 116; and slums 26; and theater 215, 231, 233; for women 28, 116, 133, 139, 150; working-class adoption of 49, 51, 129, 131–2
responsible self-government 75
retail credit 9, 89, 109, 169, 202–3
revues 229
Reynolds, G. W. M. 227
Reynolds's Newspaper 29, 227, 237
Rhymers' Club 234
Ricardo, David 125
Rice, Thomas D. 218
ring-spinning 102
riots 44, 51, 78, 197
Ritz Hotel 101
Robertson, T.W. 219
Robinson-Gallagher school 67–8
Rochdale Pioneers xx, 110–11
Roman Catholicism *see* Catholicism
Romanesque buildings 213
romantic friendship 250
romantic love 242
Rook, Clarence 117
rooms, multi-function 21
Roscommon 44, 89
Rose, Field Marshall Hugh 71
Rossetti, Christina 222
Rossetti, Dante Gabriel 213, 221–2
rotary steam press *see* steam printing
Rothschild, Lionel xxii, 266
rotten boroughs 43–5, 52; *see also* pocket boroughs
rough and respectable *see* respectability, and roughness
Rowntree, Seebohm xxvii, 5, 138
Roy, Rammohun 70, 270–1
royal ceremonials 188, 190
Royal College of Physicians 288, 290

Royal College of Surgeons 288
Royal Court Theatre 232–3
royal family 113, 128, 182, 185, *187*, 188, 256; *see also* monarchy
Royal Institution 282
Royal Mail *see* postal service
Royal Polytechnic Institution xix, 279, 282
Royal Society xviii, 94–5, 280–3, 287–8, 295
Royal Technical College of Charlottenburg 99
Royal Titles Act xxv, 191
rugby: as leisure 150; as spectator sport xxv, 157–9; split between Union and League xxvii, 159
Rugby Football Union xxiv, 158
Rugby School 151, 166, 171
the "Rules" 203
rural areas *see* countryside
rural crime 197
rural life, idealization of 32
rural nostalgia 235
Ruskin, John xxii, 78, 242
Russell, Lord John 51
Russell, Lord William 214
Russia 60, 62, 90, 270

Sadler, Michael 92
Sadler Committee Report xviii, 92
Said, Edward 67
Sala, George 119–20
salaries 125, 134, 167, 174, 200, 262–4, 281
Salem Chapel 226
sales work, salespersons 27, 112, 114, 117–18, 120, 128, 134, 138, 141
Salisbury, Lord 54, 58–9, 264
Salomé 233
Salvarsan 301
Salvation Army xxiii, xxvi, 153, 160, 205, 267, *268*, 273–4
same-sex desire 248–51, 254, 256–7
Sanitary Act xxiii, 18, 302
sati 75
Saul, John 256
scandals 54, 182, 195–6, 205, 233, 250, 254
Scarborough 162
"Scenes in Slumland" xxvii, 26
School Boards 138, 140
school meals 302
schools: boarding 134–7, 171, 177, 213, 247, 250, 252 *see also* public schools; day 171; denominational 264; elementary 9,

53, 59, 103, 131, 138–9, 179, 266;
finishing 135, 172; and gender *see*
gender, and education; "National and
British" 131; secondary 59, 138; state
(elementary) 49, 53, 60, 103, 138, 264;
truant 198, 207
science: and crisis of faith 261;
historicizing 279–80; lectures on 138;
popular interest in 279–80, 282, 295;
professionalization of 293–4; and
religion 280; and technology 285
science education 281–2, 293
science museums 280, 282
science writing 283, 295–6
Scientific Amusements for Young People 296
scientific knowledge 280, 282
scientific naturalism xviii, 285
scientists xxvii–xxviii, 280–1, 293–4, 296–7
Scotch drapers 109–10
Scotland: church building in 263; coal
industry 101; Catholics in 269;
Conservatives in 40; emigration from
79; farming in 90; and industrialization
86; Irish migrants to 30; iron industry in
91, 97; limited liability in 96; literacy in
131; overcrowding in 302; population of
xvii–xix, xxi, xxiii–xxviii, 13; rural 24,
103; self-rule for 54, 56; in United
Kingdom 2; universities in xvii, 138–9,
281
Scots language 2
The Scotsman 188
Scott, Sir Walter 221, 224
Scottish Borders 86
Scottish burghs xviii, 200
Scottish Football Association xxiv, 158
Scottish Gaelic 2, 49
Scottish independence 2
Scottish Labour Party 59
Scottish nationalists 49
Scottish Office 56
Scouting for Boys 252
seamstresses 91
seaside holidays xxvii, 98, 139–40, 142,
155–6, 161–2
the Season 40, 175
The Second Mrs. Tanqueray xxvi, 232
Second Reform Act *see* Reform Acts, 1867
Secord, James 282, 289, 296
Secretary for Scotland 56
secret ballot 41, 47, 50–1, 53
Secret Ballot Act xxiv
secularization 260–1
Security from Violence Act 198

Seeley, Sir John 66
Selborne, Lord 208
Select Committee on Public Walks (SCPW)
xviii, 19
self-control 171, 245, 252
self-help 5, 189
Self-Help 5
self-improvement 5, 135, 213
self-reliance 49
Selfridge's xxviii, 113
The Semi-Detached House 7
semi-detached villas 7, 22
seminary 43
Semmelweis, Ignaz Phillip 293
sensation dramas 219
sensation fiction 207, 211, 214, 219, 224,
226, 228, 234
separate spheres 20, 133, 166–8; *see also*
domestic ideology
separations, marital xxv, xxvii, 209
sepoys 76
services, income spent on xxvii
service sector 86, 91–3, 98–9, 103, 128,
130, 132, 140, 174; *see also* bankers;
clerks; doctors; domestic service or
servants; lawyers; musicians; professions;
sales people; teachers
Settlement House movement 254, 267–9
settler colonies xxi, 15, 73–5, 79; *see also*
Australia; Canada; New Zealand; South
Africa
Seven Dials (London) 42
sewage systems 16, 18, 26, 92
sexology 59, 241, 254, 256–7
sexual danger 28
sexual desire 243, 249; *see also* same-sex
desire
sexual double standard 168, 176, 232, 235,
241, 243–4
sexual fidelity 175–6, 232
sexual impropriety 132
sexuality: ambiguous 230; history of
240–1; illicit 12, 20; marginal 234;
reproductive 245, 249, 252–3; *see also*
female sexuality; homosexuality; male
sexuality
sexual misconduct, aristocratic 52
sexual modesty 167
sexual restraint 5, 245, 253
sexual violence 16, 243
Shaftesbury Avenue (London) 110, 112
Shakespeare 213–17, 233
Shaw, George Bernard 232–3
shawl 70

Sheffield 94, 108, 219, 228; University of 294

Sheffield Daily Telegraph 227

shipbuilding xxi, 93, 96, 101

Shirley xx, 224

shoes: C. and J. Clark xxvii; manufacturing of 108–9

shopping: Christmas 117; in city centers 24; culture of 106–8, 111–12; on high streets 13; as leisure pursuit 99; middle-class women and 26–7

shopping districts 106, 110, 112

shopping streets 16, 26, 109–10, 112, 120; *see also* Charing Cross Road (London); Corporation Street (Birmingham); Dale Street (Liverpool); Grey Street (Newcastle); Market Street (Manchester); New Oxford Street (London); Regent Street (London); Shaftesbury Avenue (London); Southwark

The Sign of Four 71, 210

Sikhs 261, 270

Sikh temples xxvii, 270

Sikh Wars xx, 71, 73

silent system 208

silk 174

silver-fork novels 50, 224

Simcox, Edith 251

singing saloons 215, 219–20

Sinn Féin xxvii, 62

slavery xviii, 40, 46, 70–1, 73–4, 80; *see also* white slavery

"slumland" 26

"slumming" 27

slumps (economic) 95; *see also* economic depression

slums: clearing of 26–7; as distressing 14, 17, 26; in fiction 223; overcrowding in 13, 18; and working-class politics 139

smallpox xix, xxi, xxiv, 292, 299–300

Smiles, Samuel 5

Smith, Barbara Leigh xxi, 176

Smith, J.B. 48

Smith, Mary 289

Smith, "O" 215

Snow, John xxii, 16, 291, 299

snowstorm 212

soap 100, 113, 169, 233

Social Democratic Federation 56, 59

social gospel 269

social history 1, 10, 32, 121, 125, 128, 147

social investigators 27

socialism 41, 49, 54, 56, 59, 233

social purity feminists 177

social purity movement 28, 50, 229, 251–2

social reform 15, 39, 45, 58, 81, 93, 269

social welfare programs 27, 101

Society 219

sociological tradition, British 298

sodomy xvii, xxvii, 247–8, 254–7; *see also* anal sex; homosexuality

Soho Bazaar 110

soldiers 76, 80, 108, 247; toy 71, 171

solicitors *see* lawyers

Somerset, Lord Arthur 256

Somerville, Reverend W.J. 273–4

Sonnets From The Portuguese 222

South Africa: market for imperial products 71; migration to 69; Republic of *see* Transvaal Republic; shipping routes to 285; Union of 81; wars in 54

South African War (Second) xxvii, 58–9, 68, 78, 80–1, 118, 298

South Kensington (London) 24, 281

Southwark Street (London) 110, 273

souvenirs 107, 119, 192

spaces: awareness of 12; central 25; domestic 13, 21, 25, 136; green 15, 19, 29; ideal 20; male 25; masculine 22; public 17, 28, 32, 106, 248, 272; rural 14; street 17; urban 24, 28

Spain 182

spectacle: in municipal parks 20; science as 282–3, 295; and shopping 113

spectator sports 157

Spencer, Herbert 297

spermatorrhoea 242–3

spermicidal creams and jellies 253

spinning 85–6, 91, 174

spinning jenny 85–7, 91

spiritualism, spiritualists 270, 296

Splendid Isolation 58

sponges 253

sports: accessories for 101; Church teams 274; gambling on 152; as leisure 150; in parks 20; professional 156–8; at public schools xviii, 178

Springett, Reverend 274

Spring-heeled Jack 212

SS *Britannia* 284

SS *Great Britain* 284

SS *Great Eastern* xxii, 284, 295

SS *Great Western* xix, 284

Staffordshire 85, 205; *see also* Burslem

stagecoaches 155

stamp duty 226–7

standard of living 88, 92, 95

state churches 42, 260–4; *see also* established churches; individual state churches
stately homes 15
statistics 4, 197, 260
statues 25, 71, 185
Stead, W.T. xxvi, 236–7, 251
steam engine 284
steam power xxiv, xxviii, 86, 91, 96
steam printing xix, 7, 17, 224
steamships 155, 284
steel: British employment in xxi; British production of xxiv, xxvii, xxix, 93, 96–7, 102
Steell, Gourlay 213
Steel's Aromatic Lozenges 291
stethoscope 292–3
St. Giles (London) 42
St. James's Park 29
stock characters 42, 218, 226
Stock Exchange 101
stoicism 291
Story of Creation xxvi, 296
St. Paul's Cathedral 191
St. Peter's Field Manchester *see* Peterloo
Strachey, Lytton 1
The Strand (London) 24, 110, 112, 119, 255, 272, 283
The Strand Magazine 272
Strathnairn, Lord *see* Field Marshall Hugh Rose
street games 153
street lights 17
streets: in bodily metaphor 16; freedom to walk in 17; and public order 13–14; rough and respectable ends of 30; as semi-domestic spaces 31; of slums 26
The Streets of London 217
street sweepers 17
strikes xx, xxvi, xxviii–xxix, 59, 62, 91, 139, 198, 229
Stringer, William 249
St. Thomas' Hospital 190, 300
Student's History of England 71
Studies in the Psychology of Sex 257
Subaltern Studies Group (SSG) 67
suburbs: literature of 9; rise of 13, 20, 29
Suez Canal 79, 270
suffragettes xxviii, 60, 115, *172*
sugar 31, 70, 73–4, 100, 111, 169
Sunday newspapers 227, 237
Sunday observance 273
Sunday schools 131, 170, 272–3, 276; Anniversary Services 274
Sunday services 260, 271–4

Sunday shopping xxii, 197
Sunday walks 179, 272
surgery 291
surveillance 14, 17, 32, 114, 202, 206–7
survival of the fittest 297
Swansea 91
Sweeney Todd 226–7
"swells" 27, 120, 231
swimming *see* bathing
Swinburne, Algernon Charles 234
Sybil, or the Two Nations xx, 50, 93, 212
Symonds, John Addington xxv, 257
Symons, Arthur 234
synagogues 270
syphilis xxviii, 235, 245, 291, 299–302

tableware 108
Tancred 212
Taranaki War *see* Maori Wars
tariff reform xxvii, 38, 47–8, 61, 90
taste 22–3, 95, 117
taxation: Conservative limits on 58; local 96; progressive 38, 61; public consent to 88; *see also* income tax
tax policies 88, 104
Taylor, Tom xxiii, 219
Tayside 85–6
tea 24, 47, 70, 100, 111, 149, 169
teachers: close relationships with pupils 250; elementary school 9, 138–9, 179; music 213; piano 9–10, 98; Sunday school 273; teaching profession 9, 91, 126, 134; women as 141, 177, 179
technology 70, 101, 103, 279, 282–3, 285, 294
telegraph: cables laid xx, xxiii, 284; commercial services xx; operators 98, 103; and railways 97; and science 282, 284
telegraph boys 256
telephone xxv, 102–3; operators 103
Telford, Thomas 284
temperance movement: beginnings of xviii; children's groups 273; and drinking habits 149; evangelicalism in 276; and Liberal Party 53; and manliness 274; and nonconformism 265; size of 5; and working classes 133, 153, 160
temperance pledge 274
tenant farmers 24, 42–3, 53–4, 90, 124
tenements 12–13, 119
tennis *see* lawn-tennis
Tennyson, Alfred, Lord 221–2, 233–4
Terry, Ellen 233

Tess of the d'Urbervilles 211, 259
textile factories, in Britain xix, 86, 90–1
textile industry: cotton famine in xxiii;
    employment in xxi, xxviii; growth in 90,
    97; in Ireland 86; steam power in xxiv
textile machines, in Great Exhibition 95
Thackeray, William Makepeace xx, 203,
    210, 225, 234
theater(s): adaptation of novels 214, 226–7;
    cities as 16; East End 231; influence on
    other art forms 214; late developments
    in 231–2; and law courts 195; legitimate
    and illegitimate 217–18; as leisure
    pursuit 136–7, 139, 148; patronage of
    215; in pleasure gardens 20; provincial
    217
theatre-building 215, 218
Theatre Regulation Act 1843 xix, 217, 220
theosophy 270
thermodynamics 279, 294, 296
Thirty-Nine Articles 262
Thomson, Alexander "Greek" 213
Thomson, William (later Lord Kelvin) xxi,
    294, 296
Tichborne cases xxiv, 205, *206*
ticket-of-leave *see* probation
The Ticket of Leave Man xxiii, 219
Tilley, Vesta *230*
timber 15
The Times 183, 190, 193, 211, 232, 236,
    249, 295
tin 97, 172
tires 192
Tissot, Samuel 243
Titanic xxviii, 295
Tit-bits 236–7
tithes 264, 267
tobacco 5, 117, 140, 148, 159, 228
toilets: outdoor 24; separate rooms for 30;
    shared 18; and shopping 28, 111
Toole, John 233
Tories, use of term 38; *see also* Conservative
    (Tory) Party
town halls 12
towns: population of xvii, 13; port 71, 270
Toynbee Hall xxv, 269
Tractarians 262
tract distribution societies 276
Trades Union Congress (TUC) xxiv, 52,
    205
trade unions: demonstrations by 205–6;
    and gender 174; legal restrictions on
    197–8; membership of xxvi–xxix, 59,
    62, 133; power of 52

traditional institutions 53
Trafalgar Square (London) 24; *see also*
    demonstrations
Trained Midwives Registration Society 300
trams 103
transformism 287, 298
transportation (forced emigration) xxi, 74,
    201–2, 211, 249; *see also* emigration
transportation (travel): and leisure 146; by
    rail xxix; and shopping 112; and women
    27–8
transport workers xxviii, 62
Transvaal Republic 80
"treating" 40
Trentham Gardens 15
trials: changes in 203; civil 205; criminal
    201, 205; by jury *see* juries; of Oscar
    Wilde 30, 233, 257; of Queen Caroline
    42, 196
triangulated couplings 251, 258
Triple Alliance 60
Triple Entente xxviii, 60
Trollope, Anthony: Darwin's influence on
    298; novels of xxii–xxiii, 198, 203, 225;
    on small towns 12; on upper classes 142
Truro 17
trusts 169, 175
tutors 134, 136
twilight moments 244, 247, 257
two-up-two-down houses 23
typhoid fever 16, 189, 191, 291, 299

Uitlanders 80
Ulrichs, Karl 256
Ulster 23, 62, 89
Ulster Volunteers 62
Underhill, Edward xxiii, 71, 77–8
unemployment 89, 95, 99
unemployment insurance 61
uniforms 108
Unionist Protestants 62
Union Jack 207
Unitarianism 264
United Kingdom 2–3; formation of 43;
    urban/rural divide in 24
United Presbyterian Church 265
United States: British cultural products in
    212; emigration to 15, 48, 69, 79; pianos
    made in 7, 9; steel production in xxix;
    visitors from 14
United Synagogue 270
unity of composition 287–8
universal gestation of nature 289–90
universal male suffrage 41, 47, 51

Universal Vegetable Pills 292
universities: Catholic admittance to 43; civic or redbrick 99–100, 294–5; medical education at 288; and middle-class work 134; same-sex cultures of 248; women's access to 141; *see also* Oxbridge universities
university settlement houses xxv
unnatural acts *see* crime, unnatural
upper class: aristocracy and gentry in 129; and empire 69; gender roles in 175–6; homes of 22, 109, 142; income of 135–6; leisure of 137, 148; political opposition to 41–2, 48, 61; political power of 41, 52, 56, 61, 135–7, 142–3; representation in Parliament xxiii; in rural areas 15; seduction of working-class girls 211, 218; sexuality among 242, 247
upper middle-class 21–3, 136
urbanization: in Britain 13–14, 23, 32, 94; and crime 197; and food 99; and leisure 146; and religion 260
urban poverty 5, 18
urban subcultures 249, 254, 257
urnings 256

Vaccination Act xix, xxi, 292
vagrancy 198
Vagrancy Act xvii, 198
Van Diemen's Land 202
Vanity Fair xx, 203, 210, 215, 225
Vauxhall Gardens 20
Veck, G. D. 256
venereal diseases 28, 177, 240–1, 244–6, 253, 290; *see also* gonorrhea; syphilis
Venus kiss 283
Vestiges of the Natural History of Creation xx, 288–90, 297–8
via media 261
Viceroy of India 76–7, 191–2
Victoria, Queen: ascension of xix; and Bedchamber Crisis 183–4; dates of reign 3; death of xxvii, 193; favorite novelist of 223; historical study of 182; as imperial symbol 71; marriage of xix; and merchandise 113, 192–3; opening parliament xxiii, 189; philanthropy of 136; political role of 185–6; public image of 185, 188–9; return to public life xxiv, 190–1; and same-sex acts 249; and science 289; use of anesthesia 293; widowhood of 189–90
Victoria and Albert Museum 95

Victorian England: Portrait of an Age 1
Victoria Park (London), debate in 19–20
Victoria Street (London) 110
villages: model 21; predominance of 14
village schoolteachers 124
violence: physical 167, 179; in popular culture 211–12
virtual representation 37
visiting societies 276
voting rights *see* franchise
Voyage of the Beagle xix
The Voysey Inheritance 232

wages: breadwinner's 48, 130, 173; of men 167; and standard of living 88; *see also* real wages
Wagga Wagga 205
Wakley, Thomas xvii, 287–8
Wales: Church of England in 267 (*see also* Church of England in Wales); Liberal Party in 52; mining in 91; nonconformism in xxi, 264; resort towns in 155, 160–2; in United Kingdom 2; urban and rural spaces in 24
Walker, Ann 251
Walker, Henry 116
Walkowitz, Judith 28
Wallace, Alfred Russel 290, 296–7
Walters, J. Cuming xxvii, 26
Walthamstow 29
Ward, Leah 273
The Warden xxii
Warren, Mrs. Eliza xxiii, 134
Watchnight services 273–4
water, clean 92, 302
Waterloo, battle of 137
The Way of All Flesh 235
weaving 22, 87, 91
Webb, Beatrice and Sidney 59
weddings 4, 260, 273
Wedgwood, Emma 296
Weiner, Martin 100
Wellington, First Duke of (Wellesley, Arthur) 43, 137, 183–4
Welsh language 2, 267
Wesley, John 265
Wesleyan Methodism 264–5, 269, 276
West End (London): and East End 26; music halls in 228; protests in 28; sex between men in 254; shopping in 112, 116; theaters in 218
Westminster Abbey 192
Westminster Palace 185
Westward Ho! xxii, 224, 277

Wexford 89
Whewell, William 293
Whigs 38–9, 42, 45–7, 54, 183–4; *see also* Liberal Party
whipping 202
whisky 149
Whitechapel 220, 231, 237, 269
white-collar work 9, 128, 130, 137–8, 177–8
Whiteley's department store 114, 116, 118
whiteness 70, 75, 126
white slavery 236–7, 251
widows 168, 175, 186, 189–90
Wilberforce, William 275
Wilde, Oscar xxvi–xxvii, 30, 233–5, 240, 257
William and Mary 184
William IV xviii, 43, 182–3, 242
Winchester 171
window-boxes 119
windows (plate glass) xxviii, 17, 113, 115, 213
Windsor 189, 192
wine 116–17, 149, 295
wives, male spaces away from 25
Wodehouse, P.G. 123
The Woman in White xxii, 211, 226
women: and ACLL 48; aristocratic 40, 175, 246; and bazaar shopping 110; blamed for racial deterioration 81; in breach of promise suits 204; class distinctions between 26; in domestic ideology 21, 166–7; domestic work of 30–1; and family health 22; and industrialization 86–7; labor agitation among 59; and leisure 147–8, 153–4; and medical training 300; and music hall 228–30; as novelists 223–4; paid work of 22, 27, 130, 168–9, 173–4, 177–9; political power of 35; and Queen Caroline Affair 42; and religion 274–5; in rural life 15; sex between 249–50, 258; and shopping *see* gender and shopping; in sports culture 157; in urban spaces 27–8; wages of 102, 174; working conditions of 93; *see also* married women; middle-class women; working-class women
women's groups 154
Women's Labour League (WLL) 56
Women's Liberal Associations 56
Women's Social and Political Union (WSPU) xxvii, 60

women's suffrage xxiii–xxiv, xxviii, 37, 44–5, 52, 55–6, 60, 176; *see also* suffragettes
Wood, J.G. xxv, 296
Wood, Mrs. Henry xxiii, 180, 210, 219, 224, 226
Wood Green 29
Woodhouse Moor 19
Wooster, Bertie 123
Wordsworth, William 221
work ethic 166, 174
workhouses 46, 132, 149, 167
workhouse schools 131
working-class conservatism 53, 58, 128
working classes: and alcohol consumption 5, 150, 159–60; children of 170–1; consumption by 103, 107; and crime 197; daily life of 130–1; and empire 69; enfranchisement of 9, 44–5, 47, 49–51, 53, 56, 58; and football 157–8; gender roles and 168, 172–3, 178–9; homes of 9, 21–3, 30–1, 119, 128; illness and 291; impact of urban reforms on 27; income of 128; and leisure xvii, 19, 99, 133, 139–40, 148, 197; in Liberal Party 39; living conditions of 18; middle-class attempts to reform 5, 25, 28, 59, 147, 153, 156, 160, 212; and music 221; in parks 20, 29; physical condition of 81; and police 199–200, 207; politics of 35, 59–60, 132–3, 139; poverty among xxix, 104; regional differences in 132; rural 15; and sexuality 241, 247; and shopping 111–12, 118–19; standard of living xxix, 92, 100, 137; in the suburbs 29, 98
working-class radicals 39, 42, 49, 54, 133, 139, 226
working-class women: and African men 70; and Chartism 48; and church attendance 272; in domestic service 98, 132; and family finance 203–4; and gossip 154; housekeeping of 139; paid work of 22, 103, 130, 179; and prostitution 28, 251; responsibility for family health 81; and sexuality 244, 246; working conditions 88, 92–3
working hours 4, 46, 95, 118, 139, 148, 168–9
working men's clubs 159
working week xxiv, xxvii, 101
"workmen's trains" 29
workshops, small 86, 130
World War One: and alcohol 160; beginning of xxix, 62; and colonial nationalism 81

World War Two 65, 82, 231, 261
wrestling 153
Wuthering Heights xx, 180, 225

X Club 293, 296
xenophobia 5, 54
Xhosa Wars xviii, xx, xxv, 73
x-ray machines 301

Yeats, William Butler 234
The Yellow Book 234
Yelverton, Major 196
Yelverton bigamy trial 196

Yiddish theater 231
York 5, 54, 174, 263
Yorkshire 62, 85, 90, 94, 159, 250, 263, 274; West Riding of 23, 85–6
Young, G.M. 1–2
Young England movement 212
Young Men's Christian Association (YMCA) 276

Zincke, Barham 13
Zionist movement 269–70
Zulu Wars xxv, 54, 80